Rebuilding Zion

Rebuilding Zion

*The Religious Reconstruction
of the South, 1863–1877*

Daniel W. Stowell

New York   Oxford
Oxford University Press
1998

Oxford University Press

Oxford   New York
Athens   Auckland   Bangkok   Bogota   Bombay   Buenos Aires
Calcutta   Cape Town   Dar es Salaam   Delhi   Florence   Hong Kong
Istanbul   Karachi   Kuala Lumpur   Madras   Madrid   Melbourne
Mexico City   Nairobi   Paris   Singapore   Taipei   Tokyo   Toronto   Warsaw

and associated companies in
Berlin   Ibadan

Published by Oxford University Press, Inc.
198 Madison Avenue, New York, New York 10016

Oxford is a registered trademark of Oxford University Press

Library of Congress Cataloging-in-Publication Data
Stowell, Daniel W.
   Rebuilding Zion : the religious reconstruction of the South / Daniel W. Stowell.
      p.   cm.
   Includes bibliographical references and index.
   ISBN 0-19-510194-4
   1. Southern States — Church history — 19th century.
2. United States — History — Civil War, 1861–1865 —
Protestant churches.   3. Reconstruction.   I. Title.
BR535.S76   1997
277.5'081 — dc21   97-10589

9 8 7 6 5 4 3 2 1

Printed in the United States of America
on acid-free paper

For Miriam

Acknowledgments

M any people contributed to the successful completion of this study. I owe my greatest intellectual debts to Bertram Wyatt-Brown, the chairman of my dissertation committee, and Samuel S. Hill, Jr. Each helped me to refine and shape the study through several seminars and the research and writing process. They have sharpened my prose as well as my arguments, and my respect for both of them continues to grow. The other members of my graduate committee, Kermit L. Hall, the late Darrett B. Rutman, and C. John Sommerville, have also contributed to my development as a scholar, and to them I also express my appreciation. My gratitude also goes to two anonymous readers for Oxford University Press, whose charitable suggestions for revision have improved the book in many ways.

Several organizations have contributed generously to help finance my graduate education and this study. During the early years of my doctoral program, the Richard J. Milbauer Fellowship from the Department of History at the University of Florida aided me in completing my coursework. A travel grant from the Southern Baptist Historical Library and Archives in Nashville, Tennessee, allowed me to make use of the collections housed there. Finally, a Charlotte Newcombe Dissertation Year Fellowship from the Woodrow Wilson Foundation supported me in the final stages of research and writing. I wish to express my gratitude to each of these organizations for their assistance in my graduate career.

A generous faculty fellowship from the Pew Program in Religion and American History at Yale University provided me with the resources during the 1995–1996 academic year to transform my dissertation into a book. Without such assistance the revisions would have taken far longer. I especially appreciate the encouragement I received from other fellows and the program directors, Harry Stout and Jon Butler, during a year-end fellows conference.

I was privileged to receive the M. E. Bradford Award for the Best Dissertation in Southern Studies from the St. George Tucker Society; I appreciate the confidence that the Bradford Award committee expressed in my work. I also value the opportunity that I had to share a part of my research with the St. George Tucker Society at its annual meeting.

I was fortunate that the Department of History at the University of Florida had an excellent group of graduate students with whom I could study. My special thanks go to my comrades-in-exams, John Guthrie, Jack Henderson, Dave Tegeder, and Joe Thompson. I also wish to thank Michael Justus for his example and Andy Chancey for his understanding. Three of my fellow students deserve special mention. Stan Deaton has been a close friend since we entered graduate school at the University of Georgia. His enthusiasm for the study of the past continues to reawaken in me the love of history that has drawn me to this profession. Tim Huebner, always optimistic, encouraged me in many ways over the past ten years. Most importantly, he has always listened patiently to my lamentations on a variety of topics. Since I completed the dissertation, Andy Moore has consistently cheered me onward in my intellectual pursuits, especially in the revision of my manuscript. I am proud to have such friends.

On a personal level, I would like to thank my parents, Francis and Eunice Stowell, and my brother, Timothy Stowell, who have always encouraged and supported me even when they did not understand why my "paper" took so long to complete. My parents-in-law, Dave and Eula Keener, also offered encouragement throughout my graduate career.

The most important people in my life, my immediate family, have contributed much to this study by shaping how I view both the present and the past. Samuel and Joseph, both born while this study was a dissertation, and Rachel, born during the revisions of the manuscript, have kept me sane and happy by drawing me away from my research and writing long enough not to miss the important events in their lives. Their tears and laughter, their firsts and fits have made the past six years simultaneously challenging and wonderful. My wife, Miriam, has been a constant source of support throughout graduate school, both financially and emotionally. She has applied her considerable editorial skills to polishing my prose, making it consistent where I am not. To Miriam far more than to anyone else goes the credit for the completion of this study. Her faith in me has kept this study moving forward and can only be partially repaid by my profound gratitude and love and by the dedication of this book to her. I am proud to be her husband.

Contents

Rebuilding Zion

Introduction

*Stonewall Jackson and
the Providence of God*

The righteous perisheth, and no man layeth it to heart: and merciful men are taken away, none considering that the righteous is taken away from the evil to come.

Isaiah 57:1

On the evening of May 2, 1863, General Thomas J. "Stonewall" Jackson, a few of his officers, and several couriers rode beyond Confederate lines to reconnoiter the Federal forces along the Plank Road near Chancellorsville, Virginia. Jackson was planning a night attack in the moonlight to capitalize on the successes of the past few hours, when his men had overrun the surprised right flank of the Army of the Potomac. As Jackson's party rode back toward its own lines over the unfamiliar terrain, men of the Eighteenth North Carolina Regiment mistook the horsemen for Federal cavalry and opened fire. Several members of the party were shot from their horses. One of the officers shouted to the pickets that they were firing on their own men. Believing this shouting to be a Yankee trick, the North Carolinians fired again. In this volley, three bullets struck Jackson, one in the right hand and two more in the left arm.

Jackson's horse, Little Sorrel, bolted into the woods, carrying its wounded rider crashing into the branches; Jackson managed to rein the animal in and return to the road. Two of his officers carefully removed Jackson from his saddle; he muttered, "My own men." In the midst of a Federal artillery bombardment, his men with difficulty transported Jackson to a field hospital, where a surgeon amputated his left arm. Despite the success of Jackson's bold flanking maneuver against superior Union forces, General Robert E. Lee was troubled by the news: "Any victory is dearly bought which deprives us of the services of General Jackson, even for a short time."[1]

The following day, Lee sent a note to Jackson congratulating him on his victory

3

and assuring him that "for the good of the country," he would have chosen to be wounded in Jackson's stead. On May 4, Jackson was moved to the home of Thomas Coleman Chandler at Guiney's Station, ten miles south of Fredericksburg. There he showed signs of recovering from the amputation, but two days later he developed pneumonia. His wife Mary Anna and their infant daughter, Julia, not yet six months old, arrived the next day. He assured his wife that he was "perfectly resigned" to accept God's will. He had seen his daughter only once, some two weeks earlier, before Federal troops had marched toward Chancellorsville. He saw her only once more, on Saturday, May 9. By the next morning, his doctors had little hope for his survival. Mary Anna told him that he must prepare for the worst and asked him if he wanted God to have His will with him. "I prefer it," he replied. "Yes, I prefer it." A few hours later, Jackson told those at his bedside, "I always wanted to die on Sunday." That Sunday afternoon at 3:15, his wish was fulfilled.[2]

The Confederacy mourned Jackson as it had no other loss. General Lee lamented to his wife, "I know not how to replace him; but God's will be done! I trust He will raise up someone in his place." Mary Jones in Georgia wrote to her son, "The death of our pious, brave, and noble General Stonewall Jackson is a great blow to our cause! May God raise up friends and helpers to our bleeding country!"[3] On May 15, Jackson's funeral was held in the Presbyterian church in Lexington, Virginia, where Jackson had been a deacon and the superintendent of a black Sunday school. His pastor, the Reverend W. S. White, began the funeral sermon by reading from the fifteenth chapter of I Corinthians: "O death, where is thy sting? O grave, where is thy victory? . . . But thanks be to God, which giveth us the victory through our Lord Jesus Christ." The coffin was covered with flowers, and the grave too was "heaped with flowers." "Sincerer mourning was never manifested for any one, I do think," Jackson's sister-in-law later wrote in her journal.[4]

Several days later in nearby Lynchburg, the Reverend James B. Ramsey of the First Presbyterian Church delivered a memorial sermon on the death of Jackson. Ramsey spoke for the entire Confederacy when he asked, "God has taken him, and why? . . . why this terrible blow? Why raise up just the instrument we needed, and then remove him when we seemed to need him as much if not more than ever?" He declared to his congregation that although "his loss seems irreparable" to both the church and the country in "this hour of our peril," God could raise up others in Jackson's place. Instead of questioning God's decision to take Jackson from them, southerners should be thankful and hopeful that the Confederacy was blessed with such a "perfect Christian Hero." Who could believe that "God would have given us such a man, and answered in every step his prayers for two eventful years, and blessed him as our defender, if he had not designs of mercy for us, and was not preparing for us a glorious deliverance, and us for it?" Jackson was great because "he honored God with all his heart and life," and his success stemmed from his dependence on God. If southerners followed his example, God would certainly secure their independence. Jackson's death was designed to teach the Confederacy this vital lesson.[5]

The Reverend Robert Lewis Dabney, Presbyterian minister, Confederate chaplain, and Jackson's chief of staff for a time, published a discourse on Jackson's life soon after the general's death. Searching for God's purposes in that death, Dabney asked rhetorically, "Can the solution be, that having tried us, and found us unworthy of such a deliverer, he [God] has hid his favourite in the grave, in the brightness of his hopes, and before his blooming honours received any blight from disaster, from the calamities which our sins are about to bring upon us?" Dabney answered with a resounding "Nay." Instead, he suggested, "may it not be, that God, after enabling him to render all the service which was essential to our deliverance, and showing us in him, the brightest example of the glory of Christianity, has bid him enter into the joy of his Lord, at this juncture, in order to warn us against our incipient idolatry." Dabney exhorted his audience, "while man is mortal, the cause is immortal. Away then, with unmanly discouragements, God lives, though our hero is dead."[6]

Ramsey and Dabney hopefully assured themselves that God intended to emphasize Jackson's Christian and military virtues by taking him in the zenith of his career and to teach the South to trust in no man, but in God alone. Other white southerners were less certain of the providential meaning of the hero's death. For the religious citizens of the Confederacy, Jackson was "the chosen standard bearer of liberty" and "the anointed of God to bring in deliverance for his oppressed Church and Country." God had apparently struck him down in the midst of the struggle for southern independence, an act of Providence that raised serious questions about God's plans for the Confederacy. Even the facts surrounding Jackson's death seemed curiously providential: "The very time and circumstances of his death were all such as to awaken peculiar and melancholy interest, and so force attention to his example, as if God intended that not a single element should be wanting to perfect the influence of that example." He was unquestionably a Christian general, devoted to prayer and the religious welfare of his men; certainly God had not seized his life because of his iniquity. He was at the height of his success; his troops had performed brilliantly in what became known as Lee's masterpiece, the battle of Chancellorsville. He was shot down by his own men, not by those of his enemy. Surely God had some message for the South in this calamity: "Men were everywhere speculating with solemn anxiety upon the meaning of his death." Some feared that God had "taken the good man away from the evil to come"; because of their sins, southerners were unworthy of such a deliverer. For the first time in the war, two months before the disasters at Gettysburg and Vicksburg, southerners paused to consider whether God would grant them ultimate victory.[7]

Most Confederates shared the sentiments of Ramsey and Dabney. They quickly reassured themselves that God was only chastising them for their sins (including the sin of idolizing Jackson) and that they would soon regain divine favor. Two years later, under the stress of a far greater disaster, southern evangelicals would repeat this process, assuring themselves that although they had been defeated on the battlefield, God had not deserted them. Confederate attitudes toward rebuilding the religious life of the South began to coalesce here in the midst of the war. After the initial shock of defeat and through the spring of 1866, southern Christians developed a theological understanding of the war that informed their view of the religious needs of the postwar South. Neither the death of Stonewall Jackson nor the collapse of the Confederacy, they believed, was an indication of God's stern hand of judgment. Instead, these tribulations were signs of a father's hand of chastening. This distinction was central to the Confederate understanding of the war. The mysterious providence of God had a greater purpose for the South; in both events, He was scolding white southerners for their sinfulness, but He was not abandoning them. Armed with this interpretation of their recent past, Confederate Christians were ready to face the challenges of reconstructing their religious lives.

Central to their remarkably resilient worldview was the adamant conviction that God still favored the South and its churches. Slavery as an institution and secession were not sinful, though most admitted that some abuses had existed in the practice of slavery. Since northern denominations were hopelessly political and radical, the southern denominations had a duty to preserve the Gospel untainted. Furthermore, while northerners and freedpeople controlled much of the political and economic life of the South, southern evangelicals had to maintain their churches as bastions of regional identity.

For many reasons, white southerners believed, the freedpeople should remain under the religious authority of their former masters. Emancipation did not release southern evangelicals from their duty to evangelize the black race as part of God's providential plan for their elevation. The freedpeople were too ignorant to proclaim the pure Gospel of Christ or to establish and maintain ecclesiastical organizations. They were vulnerable prey to political "missionaries" from the North, radicals who sought to incite them against their true friends, white southerners. Even more threatening was the possibility that ecclesiastical independence might lead to other forms of independence.

While white religious southerners were pondering the meaning of the war and Confederate defeat, two other groups — white northern Christians and black Christians, north and south — were also reflecting on the conflict. Like southern evangelicals, religious northerners also believed that God had been at work in the great events of their day. They had even seen God's hand in Jackson's death. Although they praised his skill, energy, and sincerity, they regretted that he had chosen to support the wrong cause. Methodist layperson and general O. O. Howard, whose troops Jackson's men had surprised and routed at Chancellorsville, expressed this ambivalent attitude, writing shortly after Jackson's death that he wished God would give the North "more men and more leaders than we now have, who possess the virtues of that man." In an article on the Battle of Chancellorsville written decades after the war, Howard admitted: "even his enemies praise him; but, providentially for us, it was the last battle that he waged against the American Union." Henry Ward Beecher announced Jackson's death in his newspaper, *The Independent,* by declaring, "A brave and honest foe has fallen!"[8]

Pious northerners accepted battlefield reverses as God's chastisements upon them, but they remained confident that their cause was just. The collapse of the Confederacy confirmed their belief that southerners had been rebelling against God. God, in righteous indignation against the sins of secession and slavery, had not merely chastened the South, but had brought His fierce judgment upon it. Because secession from the Union was a sin, northern Christians reasoned, secession from the national church bodies was also sinful. Now that the Union was restored, national denominational structures should also be reconstructed. The condition for readmission to the privileges of citizenship was a loyalty oath; naturally, the restoration of ecclesiastical ties should involve a declaration of loyalty to the church and a confession of the sins of secession and slavery. Furthermore, because southern churches were tainted with treason and slavery, they could no longer effectively minister to southern whites or blacks, so a vast new missionary field was open to northern missionaries. Northern evangelicals would take a pure Gospel to deluded white southerners and to the millions of black men and women living in ignorance and superstition in the South.

Like white evangelicals north and south, the freedpeople also drew providential meaning from the war and its outcome. While they agreed with white northerners that God had judged the South for it sins, the monumental providential fact of the war was their deliverance from bondage. Their freedom also provided black evangelicals the opportunity to establish churches and conduct religious services free from white supervision. While they quickly withdrew from the churches of their masters, the freedpeople also realized that they could not provide church buildings, religious literature, or trained ministers without outside help. They accepted help from their former masters in many cases, while they offered their membership to black and white northern denominations in return for houses of worship and educational opportunities.

Religious reconstruction was the process by which southern and northern, black and white Christians rebuilt the spiritual life of the South in the aftermath of the disruptions wrought by the Civil War. Each group, however, had a different vision of what was necessary and how best to accomplish this process. For white southern Christians, the task was primarily to restore the antebellum status quo in their religious lives. In the immediate aftermath of the war, they made their intentions clear as they tried as much as possible to restore the old order — political, social, and religious — and only grudgingly accepted change. For white northern evangelicals, religious reconstruction meant the evangelization and Christianization of the benighted South and its black and white inhabitants. Flushed with cultural pride in victory, white northern Christians sought to purify the South and break the corrupting grip of slavery and treason on the region's religious life. For African-American Christians, religious reconstruction involved not restoration but creation. Enabled for the first time to give expression to their own religious ideals, they set to work establishing a new and separate religious life for themselves.

The competition among these three visions determined the shape of the religious reconstruction of the South in the decade and a half from 1863 to 1877. Each vision of what constituted spiritual renewal was based on a different understanding of God's purposes in emancipation and the overthrow of the Confederacy. No vision triumphed completely nor suffered complete disappointment. Each contributed in part to the formidable task of rebuilding the religious life of the southern states.

None of these three groups was monolithic; each could be divided into smaller, more homogenous groups along denominational and especially along gender and class lines. Historians of mid-nineteenth-century America have demonstrated that class differences divided northern and southern white societies, and social class also divided the freedpeople.[9] Recent scholarship has also established the importance of gender to the study of the Civil War and Reconstruction period.[10] Nonetheless, while denominational, class, and gender differences distinguished American Christians from one another, racial and sectional differences proved far more divisive during this period. On the principal issues of religious reconstruction, evangelicals did not forge bonds of gender, class, or denomination that transcended the cleavages of race and region.[11]

Despite their deep racial and sectional antipathies, all three groups shared fundamentally similar theological views. American evangelicals in the mid–nineteenth century held firmly to a providential view of history and life. As Lewis O. Saum describes it, "Simply put, that view held that, directly or indirectly, God controlled all things." God, they were confident, would achieve His purposes through the war, both for the nation and for them individually. The task of the faithful was, if possible, to understand His purposes and to aid in their fulfillment or at least not to hinder them. Despite this underlying commonality, however, American Christians disagreed vehemently over what God's purposes in the bloody conflict were. By 1860, white northerners and southerners were, in the words of Samuel S. Hill Jr., "third cousins alienated," culturally close to each other yet belligerent.[12]

Religious reconstruction, like political reconstruction, was not an impersonal historical process. Individuals — women and men, blacks and whites, southerners and northerners — wrote, spoke, acted, and reacted according to their varied perceptions of God's will. Their collective words and actions shaped religious reconstruction, and their decisions had profound, and frequently unforeseen, effects on their own religious lives.

The stories of six individual Christians vividly illustrate the impact of religious reconstruction. Eliza Rhea Anderson Fain lived near Rogersville, in Hawkins County, Tennessee. This area of northern East Tennessee was deeply divided between Confederates and Unionists during the Civil War. Eliza Rhea Anderson was born in 1816, and in 1833 she married Richard Gammon Fain, a recent graduate of the West Point Military Academy. At about the same time, she joined the Blountville Presbyterian Church and remained a committed Presbyterian for the rest of her life. Between 1834 and 1858, Eliza Fain had thirteen children, all but one of whom survived to adulthood. By 1860, the Fains were relatively prosperous. Richard Fain was a merchant, and the couple owned a farm and eight slaves. When Tennessee seceded, Richard and five of their sons joined the Confederate forces. Eliza was left to manage their farm and care for their other children, four of whom were under ten years of age. A devout Christian, she firmly believed that God favored the Confederate cause. A week after Stonewall Jackson died, she wrote in her diary: "This evening week our great our noble our lamented Jackson was taken from us. For him we mourn, but may his death teach us an instructive lesson that God will be honored and if we in any way rob him of the honor and glory due to him alone he will bring us to see the evil of our way." Feeling saddened and chastised, Fain was still confident of southern success and demanded retribution; Jackson's "ashes will mingle with his native soil, but his blood crieth for vengeance on the oppressor."[13]

Lucius H. Holsey was a house slave at the beginning of the Civil War, the property of Richard Malcolm Johnston, a planter and professor at Franklin College in Athens, Georgia. The son of a white master, James Holsey, and his slave, Holsey was born near Columbus, Georgia, in 1842. When his father and master died in 1848, Holsey became the property and body servant of T. L. Wynn of Hancock County, Georgia. When Wynn lay dying in 1857, he asked Holsey to choose his next owner from between two of Wynn's close friends. Holsey chose Johnston and moved to Athens with the newly appointed professor. Although he held the favored status of body servant, the fifteen-year-old Holsey was illiterate. In Athens he developed an "insatiable craving for some knowledge of books." He bought a Bible, a copy of John Milton's *Paradise Lost*, a dictionary, and two Webster spellers, and with the assistance of an old black man and several white children, he taught himself to read. When the war interrupted the operations of Franklin College, Holsey returned to Hancock County with Johnston and his family and other slaves.[14]

Thomas Hooke McCallie was pastor of the Presbyterian Church in Cleveland, Tennessee, when that state left the Union in May of 1861. Born in eastern Tennessee in 1837, McCallie's family moved to Chattanooga when he was four years old. His father was a successful merchant who owned seven slaves; both his parents were devout Presbyterians. At age sixteen, McCallie entered Burritt College on Cumberland Mountain, from which he graduated three years later in the summer of 1856. He had considered a career in law and politics, but after his conversion at a revival in December 1855, he felt called to the ministry. He entered Union Theological Seminary in New York City in the fall of 1856. Most of the students there were members of the new Republican party, who frequently argued with McCallie and the two or three other southern students over the issue of slavery. "Wherever we went in every religious circle where prayer was offered," McCallie later remembered, "there was an outpouring of petition for the oppressed colored people of the South." McCallie graduated in May 1859 and was licensed to preach by the Third Presbytery of New York; he was twenty-two. After preaching briefly in central Tennessee and Mississippi, he returned to Chattanooga when his father died. In January 1860, he became pastor of the Cleveland Presbyterian Church, where he served for the next two years.[15]

John H. Caldwell was pastor of Trinity Methodist Church, the largest Methodist church in Savannah, Georgia, when that state seceded from the Union in January 1861. Caldwell was born in South Carolina in 1820, but his parents brought him to Georgia as an infant. He was converted at age sixteen and licensed as an exhorter in the Methodist Episcopal Church six years later. In 1844, shortly before the sectional division of American Methodism, Caldwell became a member of the Georgia Annual Conference. Over the next sixteen years, he served in nine different churches and missions in Georgia, including two missions to slaves. When he was assigned to the Cuthbert Station in December 1852, Caldwell worked for the foundation of Andrew Female College, which began operation in 1853; he then served as the school's professor of moral and mental science. He rejoined the ranks of the traveling ministry of the Georgia Annual Conference in December 1857. Caldwell never owned more than three or four slaves, partly because his father-in-law, a wealthy Meriwether County planter, believed that "Methodist preachers had no use for negroes" and gave his daughter most of her inheritance in cash. By 1860, Caldwell was a rising minister in the Georgia Conference, firmly committed to the South and southern Methodism.[16]

Henry McNeal Turner was pastor of Union Bethel Church in Baltimore, Maryland, when the Civil War began. Born to free black parents in 1834 in South Carolina, Turner grew up with all of the uncertainties of free blacks in the antebellum South. His father's death forced his mother to bond Turner to a local planter. As a teenager, he learned the trades of blacksmith and carriagemaker from artisans whom he served as a bonded apprentice. He joined the Methodist Episcopal Church, South (MECS), in 1848 but was not certain of his conversion until 1851; in that year, he was licensed as an exhorter. Two years later, Robert Jones Boyd, the white Methodist minister assigned to the Abbeville circuit, granted the young black exhorter a license to preach the Gospel. Between 1853 and 1858, Turner traveled across the Deep South as an itinerant preacher for the MECS. In New Orleans, he learned of the African Methodist Episcopal (AME) Church, a black denomination centered in the North. In the spring of 1858, Turner preached alongside white southern Methodist ministers to black audiences during a revival in Athens, Georgia; one of the most notable converts in this revival was a teenager named Lucius H. Holsey. Late in the summer of 1858, Turner left the South to join the AME denomination at their annual conference in St. Louis. From 1858 to 1863, Turner pastored AME churches in Baltimore and Washington, D.C., before he returned to the South with the Union Army. Although he condemned the cause for which Stonewall Jackson fought, Turner admitted that the southern general's piety contributed to his success on the battlefield. In March 1863, Turner wrote, "if the rebels out-pray us, they may out-fight us, as little as many think of it." For his part he had no intention of letting Confederates excel either in praying or in fighting.[17]

Joanna Patterson Moore was teaching school in Pennsylvania when the Civil War erupted. Born in 1832, one of thirteen children, on a farm in Clarion County, Pennsylvania, Moore saw five of her siblings die during her childhood; three others had died before she was born. After attending school briefly in the 1840s, she began teaching school herself when she was fifteen years old, and for the next decade, taught various schools in Pennsylvania. While teaching near Reedsburg in 1852, she was converted. Convinced that baptism was part of God's command, she asked her Episcopal father and Presbyterian mother for their consent to her baptism. After waiting a year in vain for her parents to change their minds, she was baptized and joined the Baptist Church. In 1858 she moved with her family to Illinois, taught school there for a year, returned to Pennsylvania, and finally in 1861 returned to Belvidere, Illinois, to live near her family. She taught school in the summers and attended school in the fall and winter.[18]

Each of these six Christians, as the following story makes clear, contributed in various ways to the process of religious reconstruction. United by their belief that God was actively at work in the Civil War and its aftermath, these evangelicals struggled to comprehend what His purposes were. Each developed a particular understanding of the providential meaning of emancipation and Appomattox, an interpretation that, in turn, shaped his or her participation in the struggle for the soul of the South between 1863 and 1877.

To contribute effectively to historical study, scholarship should both explore boldly new subject matter and build creatively on the work of others who have examined similar topics before, refining their observations, challenging their imperfections, and acknowledging their contributions. The scholarship of the Civil War and Reconstruction eras is voluminous and especially rich, but too few scholars have examined the religious life of the postwar South. James M. McPherson's excellent overview of the Civil War era, for example, makes almost no mention of religion, either within the armies or on the home fronts. Despite the centrality of the African-American experience to his masterful synthesis of the Reconstruction era, Eric Foner devotes fewer than ten pages to black churches. Although he asserts that the church was "second only to the family as a focal point of black life," he does not make the black church a focus of his interpretation. Furthermore, Foner and other scholars of this period have neglected the religious lives and motivations of white southerners and northerners almost completely.[19]

Although many scholars have neglected the role of religion, original scholarship on the subject has expanded in quantity and sophistication. Drew Gilpin Faust and the authors of *Why the South Lost the Civil War* offer intriguing examinations of the role of southern evangelicalism in both supporting and undermining Confederate nationalism and morale. James H. Moorhead and Phillip Shaw Paludan have likewise offered valuable insights into the actions and beliefs of northern Protestants during the Civil War era. Gardiner H. Shattuck Jr., Drew Gilpin Faust, and Reid Mitchell have developed subtle understandings of the role of religion in the Civil War armies. For the postwar era, Charles Reagan Wilson and Gaines M. Foster have carefully explored white southerners' perceptions of defeat and their contributions to the Lost Cause movement of the late nineteenth and early twentieth centuries.[20]

Denominational historians have reputations, sometimes deserved, as provincial hagiographers. However, serious historians, both within and outside individual denominations, have made valuable contributions to the study of this period. Among the best studies that focus on single white denominations are those by Rufus B. Spain, John Lee Eighmy, Hunter Dickinson Farish, Ralph Morrow, Donald G. Jones, Louis G. Vander Velde, and Ernest Trice Thompson.[21]

As in other areas of southern history, much of the best recent work on religion in the postwar South involves the experiences of African Americans. Clarence E. Walker's study of the AME Church and Stephen Ward Angell's biography of Bishop Henry M. Turner provide compelling portraits of the work of that denomination and its leading southern bishop during the Civil War and religious reconstruction. Katharine L. Dvorak's perceptive analysis of the separation of black and white Methodists in the aftermath of the Civil War is also a valuable corrective to older interpretations. James Melvin Washington's study of black Baptists provides a pathbreaking examination of the largest group of southern black Christians. William E. Montgomery's excellent synthesis of the history of black churches in the last third of the nineteenth century summarizes much previous scholarship and presents a nuanced portrait of these important centers of the African-American community.[22]

Most recently, Reginald F. Hildebrand has examined the range of denominational choices available to Methodist freedpeople in the postwar South. He posits that these denominations represent three responses to the "crisis of emancipation." First, the reaction of the MECS and the Colored Methodist Episcopal (CME) Church was to create a new brand of paternalism. Second, the AME and African Methodist Episcopal Zion (AMEZ) Churches sent missionaries to the South who proclaimed a gospel of freedom to the freedpeople. Third, the Methodist Episcopal Church likewise sent missionaries who proclaimed stern opposition to "caste" and promised racially integrated denominational organizations. Hildebrand argues that the battle among Methodisms was "waged largely over different interpretations of the meaning of freedom." His typology fits neatly within the interpretation presented here, with the exception of the CME Church. Race divided it from the MECS to a greater degree than paternalism united them, and race united the CME with the AME and AMEZ churches more than class or ideology divided them. As Hildebrand points out, even Lucius Holsey, the preeminent champion of the new paternalism, became disillusioned late in the nineteenth century when faced with segregation and the horrors of lynching. As his old competitor, Henry M. Turner, had done years before, Holsey reluctantly became a separatist.[23]

The fine scholarship on religion in the postwar South has generally neglected to examine the process of religious reconstruction broadly. Too often scholars have focused their attention on only one of the three major groups involved and ignored the other two. When they do consider these other groups, historians tend to view them through the eyes of their own subjects, a practice that distorts their understanding of those who had different visions and priorities. Thus, students of southern denominations find northern Christians uncharitable and unreasonable and view the freedpeople as ignorant and helpless; students of black denominations see southerners as unrelievedly hostile to blacks and consider northerners only marginally better in their paternalism; and students of northern denominations view their efforts as a great humanitarian effort to uplift the benighted freedpeople — though they do seem to agree with some of their subjects' southern critics that northern denominations were unreasonable in their demands for contrition over slavery and secession.

Focusing on the Baptists, Methodists, and Presbyterians as representative of southern religion, this study builds on and advances the current scholarship by examining how southern white, northern white, and African-American Christians faced the challenges of rebuilding the South in the aftermath of the Civil War. These three denominations embraced 94 percent of all the churches in the eleven states of the Confederacy. Methodists and Baptists alone accounted for 91 percent of all the churches in Georgia in 1860, and Presbyterians comprised another 5 percent. Likewise, in Tennessee, 91 percent of the congregations were Baptist, Methodist, Presbyterian, or Cumberland Presbyterian.[24]

While the examination of the response to defeat and the formation of plans for religious reconstruction ranges across the entire South, and includes the North as well, the analysis of the process itself focuses intensively on two states, Georgia and Tennessee. Georgia was the most populous state in the Lower South and ranked only behind Virginia and Tennessee in population among the states of the Confederacy. It provided critical support for the Confederate war effort, supplying both men and materiel. Because the state was united in its support of the Confederacy and invaded by Union armies only late in the war, religious reconstruction did not fully commence there until the end of the war. Under the lenient terms of Presidential Reconstruction, the Georgia state government passed the Thirteenth Amendment but circumscribed the freedoms of black Georgians. But with the passage of the Reconstruction Act of 1867, Georgia was placed under military rule until it would ratify the Fourteenth Amendment and a new state constitution guaranteeing manhood suffrage. Republicans gained control of the state government in 1868 and brought military reconstruction in Georgia to an end. After passing the Fifteenth Amendment and reinstating black members expelled from the legislature, Georgia was readmitted to the Union in July 1870. Later in the year, Democrats regained control of the legislature and completed the "redemption" or the reassertion of white southern political control when they elected a Democratic governor in 1871.

Tennessee's experience was very different. Invaded early in the war, with strong Unionist sentiment in its eastern mountains, this Upper South state was a battleground from February 1862. Nashville surrendered to Union forces in that month; Memphis capitulated in June. Much of the state was occupied by Union armies for the remainder of the war. Military authorities and wartime military governor Andrew Johnson began the process of political reconstruction in 1862 and 1863, while newly arrived northern missionaries and blacks taking their first steps toward freedom inaugurated religious reconstruction in Tennessee. Before the end of hostilities in the spring of 1865, Unionist voters abolished slavery in Tennessee and elected former Methodist minister and editor William G. Brownlow as governor. After the legislature ratified the Thirteenth and Fourteenth Amendments, Congress seated Tennessee's representatives in July 1866. Because of its rapid restoration to the Union, Tennessee avoided the imposition of military rule in 1867. Brownlow remained as governor until he resigned in February 1869 to take a seat in the United States Senate. His successor cooperated with conservatives in the state, and they captured the legislature in August 1869, effectively ending reconstruction in Tennessee.

A comparison of how religious reconstruction developed among the three major evangelical denominations in these two states reveals the roles ex-Confederates, northerners, and freedpeople played in this critical period of southern history. A more complete understanding of each group's view of emancipation and Confederate defeat clarifies how religious Americans, both black and white, northern and southern, formed their respective visions for religious reconstruction. Scholars have too often dismissed the attitudes and actions of one or more of these groups as irrational, narrow-minded, or even un-Christian. In doing so, they have failed to appreciate the powerful influence on these evangelicals' lives of their interpretations of God's purposes in human history. Only by accepting each group's unique view of God's providence and the resulting plan of action and by understanding the interaction among these views can historians achieve a better conceptualization of the efforts to rebuild the spiritual life of the South.

1

God's Wrath

*Disruption, Destruction, and Confusion
in Southern Religious Life*

And the sons of strangers shall build up thy walls, and their kings shall minister unto thee: for in my wrath I smote thee, but in my favour have I had mercy on thee.

Isaiah 60:10

The experience of the Civil War shook the foundations of southern religious life between 1863 and 1865. White religious southerners made a strong commitment to the war effort, and the early years of the war were marked by a confidence in the Confederate cause and God's support of it as evidenced by battlefield victories. As the war raged into a third year, however, the antebellum patterns of southern life became more vulnerable to change. Religious southerners generally did not question their beliefs that God wore gray and the Confederacy would succeed, though a few did. Their concerns were much less philosophical and much more practical. Not only had the North declared war on slavery, but northern armies were occupying larger and larger sections of the South. Slaveowners feared that their human property might flee to Federal lines. Many areas of the South struggled with material privations, and numerous daily routines of life were disrupted by the war.

The war also had a profound effect on southerners' religious lives. Many of the extralocal functions of the churches were disrupted during the latter stages of the war; conferences, conventions, and synods could not meet. Religious newspapers and denominational colleges ceased to operate. In battle areas, church buildings were put to less than sacred use as hospitals, barracks, warehouses, and even stables. Ministers left for the armies or took up secular jobs to support themselves and their families. Some religious leaders complained that the war distracted their members from spiritual concerns and fostered certain types of sin, especially extortion. Northern missionaries followed Union armies and began to establish churches wherever they could find people willing to join, especially among the black population tasting freedom for the first time. The freedpeople also began to test their new powers by forming churches of their own or breaking away from antebellum biracial congregations. Long before Appomattox, the war laid waste to the southern religious landscape, and tentative strategies for its regeneration were being formulated and tested.[1]

Most local southern churches would survive in some form. The questions religious southerners faced in 1865 and 1866 concerned the relationship of local churches to their surrounding world. To whom would they minister? What strategies would they use? What changes were necessary to work effectively in the postwar South? With which other local churches would they unite in pursuit of these goals? How would they channel their resources? What particular endeavors deserved support — religious periodicals, evangelical colleges, Sunday schools, foreign missions, domestic missions with the black and Indian populations? Most importantly, what role did God wish these churches to play? These questions confronted southern whites and freedpeople directly, and northern missionaries also wrestled with them. The varied answers these Christians advocated were influenced by the disordered condition of southern religious life in the aftermath of the Civil War.

One important blow to that life during the war was the disruption of the denominations' organizational apparatus. Established over decades and consolidated since the separation from their northern counterparts, the denominational structures and institutions that provided unity and direction for southern Christians were generally not destroyed during the war, but they increasingly ceased operations in its latter years as Union armies occupied more and more of the Confederacy. These interruptions brought their functions virtually to a standstill.

Across the South, various religious meetings could not be held because of inadequate transportation or the presence of enemy forces. The Presbyterian Synod of Memphis, which included western Tennessee and northern Mississippi, was unable to meet in Trenton, Tennessee, in 1862 because the area had fallen far behind the Federal lines. It met at the College Hill church in northern Mississippi instead. Because "the facilities for travel were destroyed, or monopolized by the army, and absence from home, unprotected, was more or less hazardous," the ministers of the synod "by common consent," chose not to meet at Florence, Alabama, in October 1863. The following year, members from two presbyteries of the Synod of Memphis met in Covington, Tennessee. Although they reassembled each day for three days, no delegates from the other three presbyteries arrived, and they were forced to suspend the session for lack of a quorum. The Synod of Texas suffered a similar fate in 1863. The Synod of Nashville in middle and eastern Tennessee did not meet in 1862, 1863, or 1864. Even the smaller presbyteries had difficulty meeting in some areas. Most presbyteries in Mississippi did not meet in 1863 and 1864, and in eastern Tennessee, the Presbytery of Knoxville did not meet after 1863.[2]

The quadrennial General Conference of the Methodist Episcopal Church, South (MECS), scheduled to meet in New Orleans in the spring of 1862, was postponed when United States forces under Flag Officer David Farragut captured the city in April. The General Conference did not convene again until 1866. The Tennessee Annual Conference did not assemble in 1863, and in 1864 only thirteen of nearly two hundred ministers met with Bishop Joshua Soule to conduct its business. Other conferences suffered as well, especially from a lack of episcopal visitation. The Texas Conference for five years and the Arkansas Conference for four years did not see a bishop. Bishop Soule's home in Tennessee was behind Federal lines for much of the war. Even Bishop George F. Pierce in Georgia met with only the Georgia and Florida conferences in 1861. He wrote to his son, "I am cut off from all my Conferences by war and the lack of money."[3]

Southern Baptists also had severe organizational problems. The Baptists of Mississippi held only one annual state convention during the war, while Arkansas Baptists suspended their convention between 1861 and 1867. The Virginia state organization that met in 1863 had only thirty-five present instead of the usual several hundred, and the entire meeting lasted only a few hours instead of days. The Nolachucky Association in Tennessee did not meet at all during the war, and many other associations gathered irregularly. In Georgia the state convention was to assemble in Columbus on April 21, 1865, but General James H. Wilson's Union cavalry captured Columbus in a night assault on April 16 and the meeting was canceled. The meeting of the Southern Baptist Convention itself was postponed from the spring of 1865 until the following year.[4]

Local churches suffered considerable disruption as well. On Sunday, September 6, 1863, the Reverend Thomas H. McCallie, who had accepted the pastorate of the Chattanooga Presbyterian Church in January 1862, preached to a congregation composed of local citizens and Confederate soldiers. On September 9, Union troops entered Chattanooga. Friends had warned McCallie to flee with the retreating Confederates, reminding him that when the Union army had entered Nashville, "the preachers were among the very first persons sent to prison." McCallie insisted, however, that "the Lord had called me to the work in Chattanooga, that I had more right there than the Federal Army and that if the Lord wanted me there, He could take care of me, protect and sustain me." When McCallie entered his church on Sunday, September 13, he saw "hardly a citizen but the house full of blue coats," whom he believed would expect him to "pray for the President of the United States and for the success of the Union Army." McCallie entered the pulpit "with trepidation" to deliver his sermon, "Who Is On The Lord's Side?" Although his audience "pricked up their ears" when they heard the day's topic, "there was no politics in it. It was on purely spiritual terms. There was no politics in the prayer." Although he passed through this "first ordeal" without difficulty, McCallie faced more serious problems as the war progressed. A week later, after the Battle of Chickamauga, the Federal army seized the Presbyterian church for use as a hospital. The congregation did not meet in it again until the war ended. After five months without religious gatherings in the fortified city, McCallie began to hold worship services in his home. In July 1864, the Union provost marshal informed McCallie that he had been charged with treason, found guilty without trial, and sentenced to deportation north; however, after he waited in suspense for a month, Federal authorities allowed him to resume services in his home.[5]

The Candays Creek Baptist Church in southeastern Tennessee held no sessions between July 1863 and June 1864 because "there Arose a Rebelion People in force and Arms Against the Cuntry and Drove the male memers nearley all from ther homes and throwed the Cuntry in such a deranged Condition that we thought it best not to mete for a while." The Presbyterian Church in Monticello, Georgia, did not have a local meeting of the church elders between March and November 1863, because "all the members of the Session are in the service of the country." In 1864 the pastor of the Methodist Church in Port Gibson, Mississippi, reported that "the Church is scattered and wasted to a great extent by the war. . . . Sunday School is still kept up though frequently interrupted by the Yanks capturing teachers and other causes." A Georgia woman wrote in the summer of 1864 as Sherman's army marched through the state: "No church. Our preacher's horse stolen by the Yankees." The clerk of a Presbyterian church in eastern Tennessee wrote in April 1865, "the state of the church being such at this time owing to the fact that so many of the members were gone to the war on either side of the question that it makes it impossible to make out a true statistical report to Presbytery."[6]

Like the administrative meetings, the primary vehicles of denominational communication — the religious newspapers — also perished, suffering from a variety of wartime conditions. Circulation rates plummeted as the movement of armies and the disruption of the mails cut off subscribers. In December 1860, the Baptist *Christian Index* in Macon, Georgia, had 4,900 subscribers. Two years later in this relatively stable area of the Confederacy, only 2,100 copies were published, many of which went to soldiers in the Confederate armies. Inflation and paper shortages also plagued the religious weeklies. The subscription rate for the Presbyterian *Christian Observer* climbed from $2.50 annually in 1861 to $5 in August 1863, when the size of the paper was also cut in half. By May 1864 subscriptions cost $8, and in January 1865 the price rose to $20 per year. All three of the surviving Methodist weeklies had also raised their rates to $20 by the end of 1864. The *Southern Presbyterian* lamented in April 1863, "it is with deep regret that we return to the half sheet." The paper mill that had supplied its paper had been burned, and the editors had been unable to secure any other supply. Publication was suspended altogether for a month in December 1863 and January 1864 because of lack of paper, and the price of paper and printing rose so steeply that in June 1864 the editors wrote that they could not continue to publish a half sheet without an annual outlay of $10,000 beyond the paper's income. Although they had not expected to suspend so soon, it was "a matter of necessity" because they could no longer procure paper. The newspaper resumed publication in October 1864 with a new subscription rate of $10 for six months.[7]

Each of the three denominations published several newspapers throughout the South. Southern Methodists, for example, were publishing ten weekly papers early in 1861, with a combined circulation of over fifty thousand. Only two remained after a year of warfare, the *Southern Christian Advocate* in Charleston, South Carolina, and the *Richmond Christian Advocate* in Richmond, Virginia. The *North Carolina Christian Advocate* ceased publication in May 1861 but revived with a new editor in April 1863 as the *Christian Advocate* in Raleigh, North Carolina. The *Texas Christian Advocate*, published in Galveston, suspended operations in late 1861 but resumed publication in 1864 in Houston because Galveston was under Federal control. The *Southern Christian Advocate* fled from bombarded and blockaded Charleston to Augusta, Georgia, in April 1862. In mid-April 1865 the editor announced that the paper would move to Macon, Georgia, and resume publication in a few weeks. On

June 29 a single issue appeared from Macon explaining that General James H. Wilson's cavalry forces had "reached Macon before the editor did, and he found the place in possession of the United States forces, and the publishing house in ashes"; this issue was designed to test the newspaper's "future fortunes." Although it had had a "considerable amount of Confederate money on hand," since the currency had collapsed, it was "now left without one dollar" except what it had invested in printing paper. Two months elapsed before another issue appeared.[8]

Perhaps even more devastating for southern Methodists was the loss of their publishing house when Federal forces captured Nashville in February 1862. These facilities had produced the *Nashville Christian Advocate*, tracts for Confederate armies, many religious books, and even a pocket Testament, "proudly proclaimed as the first Bible entirely stereotyped in the South." The editor of the *Nashville Christian Advocate*, Holland N. McTyeire, fled Nashville because "the Yankee officials would hardly allow me to edit such a paper as I liked, and I would not edit such a one as they liked. Even provided the *Advocate* could have been got out as formerly, there were no mails to take it off. Nashville would be cut off from the Confederacy where our readers are." For the rest of the war, the United States Government appropriated the physical plant of the Southern Methodist Publishing House for official printing needs and inflicted much damage on the property.[9]

Baptist and Presbyterian periodicals also suffered. The Union occupation of New Orleans ended the career of the Presbyterian *True Witness*. When Federal troops occupied Fayetteville, North Carolina, in March 1865, all the property of the *North Carolina Presbyterian* was destroyed. The fire that consumed much of Columbia, South Carolina, on February 17, 1865, destroyed the plant that printed the *Southern Presbyterian Review*. Another periodical, the *Southern Presbyterian*, which had left that city and moved to Augusta, Georgia, in the summer of 1864, ceased operations in April 1865, shortly before Union troops arrived, and did not resume publication until 1866. Two Presbyterian newspapers in Richmond, the *Central Presbyterian* and the *Christian Observer*, suspended publication after the fall of that city to Federal forces in April 1865. The printing office of the *Central Presbyterian* and the building and records of the Presbyterian Committee of Publication were destroyed in the Richmond fire, but the *Christian Observer's* press was spared. The fire also destroyed the press that published the Baptist *Religious Herald*. Further south, both the *Christian Index* of Macon, Georgia, and the *South-Western Baptist* of Tuskegee, Alabama, ceased publication in April 1865; the *South-Western Baptist* never reappeared. By May 1865 the primary modes of communication for southern churches were inoperable. Few of the denominational newspapers began to publish again before 1866; some never recovered.[10]

Southern evangelicals' missionary efforts also lay in ruins. Since separating from their northern counterparts in the mid-1840s, southern Baptists and Methodists had been conducting their own foreign and home mission programs. The Methodists supported missionaries in China; in 1861, the Baptists also supported missionaries there and in Liberia, Sierra Leone, and Nigeria. In June 1863, the Foreign Mission Board of the Southern Baptist Convention voted to invest all surplus funds in Confederate bonds, a policy that reaped disastrous results. The Board's corresponding secretary, James B. Taylor, traveled to Charleston and Savannah several times during the war to make arrangements with shipping companies for sending money to the missionaries, and the Board urged southern Baptists in Kentucky, Tennessee, Missouri, and Maryland to send their contributions directly to the missionaries through a provisional committee in Baltimore.[11]

The war made life very difficult for southern missionaries in foreign lands. Matthew Yates, a Baptist, had supported himself through real estate transactions and as an interpreter for the foreign community in Shanghai. When Yates left China for Switzerland in 1863 to rejoin his family, who earlier had fled Chinese rebels near Shanghai, another missionary took his position as interpreter. Methodists Young J. Allen and J. W. Lambuth supported themselves in China; Allen worked for the Chinese government as a translator. Baptist R. H. Graves wrote to the Foreign Mission Board from China in June 1864, "Brethren in America, I look for you to sustain me. I have come down into the well. You hold the rope. Do not let me fall." T. A. Reid wrote from Nigeria in the spring of 1864, "I have not received a letter outside of this country for about three years. This has a discouraging effect upon me." In a remarkable display of Christian charity, Dr. Thomas Carlton, the treasurer of the northern Methodist Missionary Society, honored some large drafts for the southern Methodist China mission. This obligation and others left the southern Methodist Foreign Mission Board with $60,000 in debts when the war ended. By the spring of 1865, the Baptist Foreign Mission Board was almost wholly dependent on organizations in Kentucky and Maryland for the support of its missionaries. Though it had a debt of only $10,000, because many of its missionaries had resorted to self-supporting efforts, at the war's end it had only $20,000 in Confederate bonds and notes, which were worthless, to meet its obligations. In December 1865, it began the process of reconstruction with $1.78 in its treasury.[12]

Southern Presbyterians, only recently divided from their northern brethren, had no organized foreign missionary efforts during the war except for the work of fourteen ministers among several tribes in the Indian Territory, an area considered part of the foreign mission field. The war in the West disrupted efforts among the Indians — the Creek Nation Presbytery was scattered in 1863 and 1864 — and most of the Presbyterian missionaries had to support themselves. One made tubs and barrels, while his wife and daughters made clothes; another became a part-time cobbler. Southern Methodists also had missions among the Indians, though the war decimated their Indian membership: it dropped from over 4,100 to approximately seven hundred during the war.

Most of southern Christians' missionary energies were directed toward the Confederate armies, with considerable success. Revivals swept most of the armies in the latter years of the war, and thousands were converted. However, financial devastation, poor communication with foreign missionaries, and their concentration on army missions left the southern denominations ill prepared to resume normal missionary operations in 1865.[13]

Another important disruption in southern religious life was the suspension of nearly all evangelical colleges during the war. Young men across the South left their studies to take up the weapons of war. By July 1861 Howard College in Alabama had lost forty-two of its sixty-two students, two professors, and its president to the Confederate armies. In October 1861 a faculty member at Centenary College in Louisiana closed the college and wrote in the faculty minutes, "Students have all gone to war.

College suspended: and God help the right!" The Conscription Act of 1862 drew out the remaining students; Presbyterian Oglethorpe University in Georgia closed within six weeks, and many other colleges followed: La Grange Synodical College in Tennessee, Erskine College in South Carolina, East Alabama Male College, and Richmond College in Virginia. Some colleges, such as Roanoke College in Virginia and Trinity College in North Carolina, remained open only by offering preparatory classes for younger students. Some female colleges, such as Wesleyan College in Macon, Georgia, remained open throughout the war, but others, such as the Woodland Female College in northwestern Georgia, disintegrated. The Baptist Female College of Southwestern Georgia and Andrew College, both in Cuthbert, were forced to suspend during the war.[14]

More important than the suspension of classes were the permanent losses these colleges suffered. The Civil War decimated an entire generation of southern men. Thirty students from Mercer University in Georgia died in the war. The faculty of Mississippi College, a Baptist school, led almost the entire student body to the Virginia battle front. Of 104 who left, only eight returned. Large numbers of students and faculty from other evangelical colleges died. In addition, the libraries and furnishings of several institutions, such as Stewart College and Cumberland University in Tennessee, fell victim to the vandalism of both armies. The buildings of the Hearn School near Rome, Georgia, "were much injured, and the library and apparatus were destroyed by the soldiery." A regiment of the Iowa Cavalry rode away from Murfreesboro, Tennessee, with the library and scientific materials of Union University.[15]

The difficulty of recovering from these losses was compounded by the decision of most southern denominational colleges to invest their endowments in Confederate bonds and securities. The Presbyterian Theological Seminary at Columbia, South Carolina, had invested $250,000 in Confederate bonds, which were worthless at the end of the war. Oglethorpe University's South Carolina and Alabama professorships, funded by Presbyterians in those states, evaporated when their endowments likewise became worthless.[16] Randolph-Macon College lost $45,000, Richmond College lost $86,000, and Howard College lost over $58,000 when the Confederacy collapsed; these amounts constituted most of each institution's endowment. Two Alabama Methodist colleges, Southern University and the East Alabama Male College, lost endowments of $200,000 and $100,000, respectively. The Southern Baptist Theological Seminary in South Carolina and Union Theological Seminary and Hampton-Sydney College in Virginia also invested heavily in Confederate bonds. Even those institutions that made safer investments suffered in the general financial wreck of the South. Land values plummeted, scholarships were uncollectible, and few students could afford tuition.[17]

In addition to the disruption of their publication, missionary, and educational endeavors, southern denominations also suffered the physical destruction, death, and loss of their ministers and members. The occupation and destruction of church buildings and evangelical colleges in the South by both armies were widespread. The Confederate armies confiscated many evangelical colleges for use as hospitals throughout the war. Centenary College and Mount Lebanon University in Louisiana, Emory and Henry College and Richmond College in Virginia, Oglethorpe University and Emory College in Georgia, and Howard College in Alabama served as Confederate hospitals during part or all of the war. Two female colleges in Cuthbert, Georgia, also served as Confederate hospitals: the Baptist Female College of South-Western Georgia and the Methodists' Andrew College.[18]

Tennessee colleges suffered extreme hardships because the state was a battle-ground during much of the war. Confederates used Stewart College, run by the Nashville Presbyterian Synod, as a hospital early in the war, and Federals used it as a hospital and barracks later. Federal soldiers who occupied the building in early 1862 "broke open the cases of the mineralogical and geological specimens and carried away many of the most valuable specimens, and choice portions of the books belonging to the Washington Irving Society, chairs, tables, curtains, etc., finally stripping even the College chapel of everything in it." Federal soldiers also took control of La Grange Synodical College in December 1863 and used it for a hospital; later they tore down the college building and used the bricks to build huts and chimneys for their tents as part of their winter quarters. Confederates occupied Cumberland University in Lebanon, Tennessee, early in the war until forced out by the arrival of Federal troops, who destroyed the furnishings and scattered the library. After those troops left the area in 1864, a Confederate brigade burned the main building to prevent its use as a Union armory. The colleges of Tennessee were not the only ones to suffer devastation. Sherman's army destroyed the Cherokee Baptist College in northwest Georgia, and soldiers burned the windows, doors, and sashes of the Fletcher Institute in Thomasville, Georgia. When Union forces occupied Marion, Alabama, at the end of the war, Howard College became a Federal hospital.[19]

Both armies also appropriated churches as hospitals and destroyed hundreds of church buildings. After the Union army used Thomas H. McCallie's church in Chattanooga as a hospital for over a year, "it was in a deplorable condition, seats torn out and gone, carpet destroyed, furnace of no value, walls blackened with smoke, choir-stand gone, pulpit destroyed, roof leaking, and the marks of war on it." In Ringgold, Georgia, and Newnan, Georgia, all of the churches became Confederate hospitals. The Old Sweetwater Baptist Church in eastern Tennessee "was occupied and used by the soldiers of one army or the other, Union or Confederate, for hospital and other purposes, so that church meetings could not be held." The Baptist church of Bolivar, Tennessee, was used by the Federal army for a smallpox hospital for about two years, and the First Baptist Church of Memphis became the "Gangrene Hospital" for Federal troops. The Methodist, Baptist, and Presbyterian churches of Franklin, Tennessee, were used by Federal authorities as hospitals. The army occupied the Presbyterian church for about two months, "removing therefrom the pews, pulpit, and other furnishings, which were materially damaged."[20]

Sometimes southern evangelicals did not give up their church buildings until they were compelled to do so. During the winter of 1862–63, Confederate hospitals in Ringgold, Georgia, were told to expect more casualties from the front. According to one of the nurses present, "negotiations were at once opened for the only church in Ringgold not occupied by the sick." Although the people declined to give it up, authorities seized it and took the pews out and piled them in the yard. Straw was placed on the floor, and when the supply of pillows gave out, "head-rests were made by tearing off the backs of the pews and nailing them slantwise from the base-board to the floor." Other southerners questioned the wisdom of taking the churches for secular uses. Kate Cumming, a Confederate nurse in Newnan, insisted, "I do not think there is any necessity for taking them at present, . . . and, without that, I think we should not have taken them." She mused about the consequences of this action: "We act as if churches were built rather for our amusement than the worship of the living God. He has told us he is a jealous God, and will visit every sin against him; not only visit it on us, but on the third and fourth generation. If ignoring his sacred temple will not bring retribution, I think nothing will." A "Daughter of the Church" from Augusta, Georgia, voiced similar sentiments in correspondence with the *Southern Presbyterian*: "Is it right that God's temple should be set to any purpose but His own praise, unless from most absolute necessity? . . . Now our sanctuary is desolated, two weeks since. Those who profess to be clothed with military authority seized it for a hospital." If there were no other place for the sick and wounded soldiers, "most gladly would we give them our churches, but when there are numbers of houses of business, and places of public amusement, that could have been better adapted to the wants of our suffering soldiers, is it right that these officers should set aside the claims of religion and make their authority higher than His who rules the world?"[21]

While southern civilians questioned whether churches should be used as hospitals, Federal troops confiscated and destroyed southern churches in the name of military necessity. The First Baptist Church of Decatur, Alabama, was destroyed to clear the range of guns. Soldiers tore down the Oak Grove Methodist Church in Jackson County, Alabama, so that they could use the materials to build a pontoon bridge across the Tennessee river. The Boiling Fork Baptist Church of Cowan, Tennessee, the Methodist church of Saulsbury, Tennessee, and the Methodist church of Powder Springs, Georgia, were all dismantled to build quarters for Federal troops. All of the churches in Pine Bluff, Arkansas, Knoxville, Tennessee, and Fredericksburg, Virginia, were damaged or destroyed by Federal armies. The Dover Baptist Association in Virginia reported that "the commodious edifice of one of our largest churches is now a heap of ruins." Another church "pierced by the cannon balls of our invaders shows ghastly rents." Across the South several churches were used as warehouses, and the basement of the Central Presbyterian Church in Atlanta became a slaughterhouse for the Union army.[22]

Federal forces destroyed twenty-six Baptist churches in Virginia alone. Between ninety and one hundred Presbyterian churches were seriously damaged or entirely destroyed throughout the South; approximately one half of these were in the Synod of Virginia. In some cases at least, the destruction went beyond any claims of military necessity. In Hardeeville, South Carolina, an Illinois infantry regiment destroyed a "large beautiful church," as one of them remembered; "the pulpit and seats were torn out, then the siding and blinds ripped off. . . . Many axes were at work. . . . it became a pile of rubbish." The Federal army used the Baptist church in Bolivar, Tennessee, as a hospital, "at the end of which time it was accidentally burned." Other "accidental" fires destroyed Methodist churches in Triune, Tennessee, and Oakbowery, Alabama.[23]

While many local congregations lost their houses of worship, even more lost their ministers. Hundreds of ministers entered Confederate service as chaplains and missionaries to the troops, and hundreds more entered as common soldiers. By the fall of 1862, 20 percent of the Methodist ministers in the Tennessee Conference were in military service. The Ninth Arkansas Regiment numbered forty-two ordained ministers among its ranks. At least 209 Methodist and seventy-two Presbyterian ministers served as commissioned chaplains in the Confederate armies. Many more served as temporary missionaries. At least another 141 Methodist preachers served as either Confederate officers or soldiers. Some did not return; of the 138 Georgia Methodist ministers who entered Confederate service, twenty-two died in battle, of wounds, or of disease. A few ministers, such as Georgia Baptist Henry A. Tupper, combined their religious and military offices; Tupper served as captain and chaplain in the Ninth Georgia Regiment. The Alabama Presbyterian minister F. McMurray entered the army "not only from patriotic motives, but especially to be with the members of his church, who had entered the company of which he was made Captain." A New Orleans Methodist announced, "Nearly every minister we know is a member of a military company."[24]

The preachers who remained in their churches often faced severe difficulties in supporting themselves and their families. Although many congregations raised their pastor's salary, the rapid inflation of Confederate currency made ministers' livelihoods precarious. Pastors like Basil Manly Sr. insisted that their churches pay their salaries or do without their services. Manly wrote in his diary, "Feeling as much responsible for the course of the Confederate States as any single man, I am as ready to bear *my part* in the trouble consequent as any man." Accordingly, he informed one of the deacons of the church that he would accept $400 a quarter while the war lasted, "provided that can be paid with some reasonable promptitude and regularity." Otherwise, "if I have to sustain my own expenses in preaching the Gospel, I must be near my home and resources; and strive to give such attention to my own means and business as to provide my support."[25]

Methodist bishops James O. Andrew, Robert Paine, and George F. Pierce had farms of their own, and Bishop John Early had enough resources to support himself and his family through the war, but many preachers were not so fortunate. A Louisiana Methodist confessed that his church sent its pastor, Benjamin F. White, away "without his salary being paid in full." In 1864, another Louisiana Methodist church sent away its minister, Dan Watkins, who had served at Opelousas Station from 1860 to 1863 and had only one arm, "to dig for the support of his needy family. We drove him from his masters work and said to him in effect go dig with your one hand for your wife and little ones." Ministers across the South were forced to find secular employment to support themselves. By 1862 most of the Methodist ministers in Florida had secular jobs "to supplement their support to the point of actual necessity." School teaching was one of the most popular vocations, but some took up farming or other occupations. Thomas W. Caskey, declaring that his congregation could not pay him, went into partnership with a lawyer. A Methodist minister and historian who lived through the period wrote that the preachers were "forced to field and bench and counter to get bread."[26]

The suspension of seminaries, the drafting of ministerial students, and the inability of congregations to support their ministers created a shortage of clergy in southern churches. Even after the war ended, many preachers continued in secular employment to support themselves. Battle had claimed the lives of some southern

TABLE 1-1 Membership Declines in the Major Southern Denominations, 1860–1866

Denomination	1860–61	1865–66	Decline
Southern Baptist Convention	649,518	—	—
Methodist Episcopal Church, South	748,968	498,847	33%
Presbyterian Church in the United States	72,000	66,528	8%[a]

The Southern Baptist Convention is included despite the lack of information on postwar membership for comparisons of size.

[a] The Presbyterian Church in the United States suffered a net loss in members, despite the addition of approximately ten thousand members from its union in 1864 with the United Synod of the South, the southern branch of New School Presbyterianism. Without this infusion of members, the loss would have been over 21 percent.

preachers, and Baptist minister J. L. M. Curry lamented, "few young men have the ministry in view." Many churches remained without pastors or shared the services of a minister with neighboring churches of the same denomination.[27]

Local southern churches, in addition to the temporary or permanent loss of their building or their pastor, or both, also faced losses in membership from a variety of causes. Thousands of evangelical men went to war, and many were killed on the battlefields. A Georgia Methodist pastor complained, "on one Sunday there were forty male teachers in the Sunday-school, the next there were four." Families fled their homes, and their churches, to move away from the advancing armies. While these refugees sometimes swelled the congregations of churches in interior regions, their absence devastated the churches they left behind. Thomas H. McCallie, for example, the pastor of the Presbyterian Church in Chattanooga, lost all but about fifteen of his 150 members during the war. "They had gone South and had been sent North," he later reflected. Some returned, but "Atlanta received a goodly number of our people. One of my deacons and two of my elders settled there." The Presbyterian churches of North Carolina lost over two thousand members during the war, while the MECS lost approximately one-third of its membership across the South between 1861 and 1866. While nearly 130,000 blacks left the southern Methodist fold, their exodus accounted for only half of that denomination's losses as the membership statistics in table 1 1 show.[28]

Even in the relatively stable state of Georgia, invaded only late in the war, a variety of factors combined to produce dramatic decreases in membership, as table 1-2 demonstrates.[29]

The withdrawal of black members from biracial churches had clearly begun by 1866, but it would not be complete until the mid-1870s. Baptist churches in the Georgia Association lost from 25 to 65 percent of their membership when black members withdrew to form their own churches. Over 90 percent of the Baptist Sunbury Association in Georgia were slaves in 1860. When 6,400 of Sunbury's black members withdrew in 1865 and 1866, the association reorganized as the New Sunbury to include more whites. Boasting over 7,000 members before the war, the new association struggled to number more than 1,000 during Reconstruction.[30]

The excitement of war times also "took people's minds off religion," and unlike

TABLE 1-2 Membership Declines in Georgia Denominations, 1860–1866

Denominational organization	1860	1866	Decline
Georgia Baptist Convention	64,611	53,428	18%
Georgia Annual Conference	84,120	66,122	21%
Synod of Georgia	7,246	6,258	14%

the Confederate soldiers who responded to army revivals, southerners at home generally took less interest in religion. Some lost all faith in the churches. A Kentuckian reported that he had known "elders and deacons, as well as private members, to forsake attendance upon divine service, give up even an outward show of holy living, and betake himself to drinking and swearing, all on account of politics." Even as prominent a southern evangelical as John N. Waddel, president of La Grange College, wrestled with his faith during the war. He "prayed as earnestly as I could" for the success of the Confederacy but could not help feeling "that God is against us and my faith is weakened." A contributor to the *Southern Presbyterian* late in 1864 feared that many "have not only lost confidence in man, but also in God. Yes, *lost confidence in God,* — especially in regard to the public affairs of the country." The writer warned, "it is folly, or worse than folly to say that God has no hand in this war. . . . It is discouraging. . . . It leads men to despair and restrain prayer before God." Because of the great contrast between the spiritual revivals in the armies and the lukewarm state of the churches, the *Central Presbyterian* in Richmond even urged the soldiers to pray for those at home.[31]

When the Confederacy collapsed and the war ended, the strain on southerners' faith was intense. Presbyterian Mary Jones of Georgia admitted that her "faith almost fails" and wondered if God had "forgotten to be gracious." Grace Elmore Brown of South Carolina struggled to comprehend the result of the war: "Hard thoughts against my God arise; questions of his justice, of his mercy arise, and refuse to be silenced." "Night and day in every moment of quiet," she labored "to work out the meaning of this horrible fact, to find truth at the bottom of this impenetrable darkness." Tennessee Presbyterian Eliza Rhea Fain wrote in her diary on April 21, 1865: "I cannot bear to see the Christian heart of the South give way. My dear daughter S. whom I love so much as a Christian seems to be at times so prone to doubt and look with a feeling of distrust on the dealings of God with his children." Yet a month later, when Fain herself saw a group of "bluecoats" pasturing their horses in a neighbor's field, she thought, "How strange that a God of truth, of love should permit such a people to overcome us. How strange that a people so lost to every feeling of humanity, truth and justice should be permitted to come and occupy the places of the loved ones of the Christian of the South."[32]

The Presbytery of South Carolina lamented, "the faith of many a Christian is shaken by the mysterious and unlooked-for course of divine Providence." Presbyterian William Safford wrote from Greensboro, Georgia, to his sister in Bolivar, Tennessee: "Bolivar is not the only place where people have been demoralized by the war, such is the state of things all over the country." Transitions to peace were especially difficult in border states like Kentucky, where one church member wrote in September 1865: "For my own part I have almost become a heathen man as I have resolved, not to sit under the ministry of a teacher, that repudiates the commandment requiring allegiance, faith and loyalty to our government." In 1866, Baptist editor Samuel H. Ford reflected on the demoralization after Appomattox: "It is, indeed, a crisis with the churches, and with Christians throughout the South. The scenes of the last four years have tried, severely, our spirits, our temper, and our faith. . . . We felt that might had prevailed, and that right was overwhelmed. 'Where is God?' seemed to be the anxious questioning of each heart. . . . Is there a God? many, many asked, yet [God seemed] deaf to our prayers and heedless of our wrongs."[33]

Methodist Ella Gertrude Clanton Thomas, a member of the planter elite in Augusta, Georgia, owned more than ninety slaves; the Civil War destroyed much of her wealth, and she and her husband were "reduced from a state of affluence to comparative poverty." Until emancipation, she had not realized "how intimately my faith in revelations and my faith in the institution of slavery had been woven together . . . if the *Bible* was right then slavery *must be* — Slavery was done away with and my faith in God's Holy Book was terribly shaken. For a time I doubted God." From May until July 1865, Thomas lived "a sad life." "When I prayed," she wrote in her journal, "my voice appeared to rise no higher than my head. When I opened the Bible the numerous allusions to slavery mocked me." Reluctantly she admitted, "Our cause was lost. Good men had had faith in that cause. Earnest prayers had ascended from honest hearts — Was so much faith to be lost? I was bewildered — I felt all this and could not see God's hand." Many southern evangelicals shared Thomas's bewilderment. Alfred Mann Pierce, a historian of Georgia Methodism, described their plight in the immediate aftermath of the war: "The faith of some, at least for a period, failed outright; on the part of many others, faith grew feeble; on the part of well-nigh all faith had to struggle hard to survive." For most southern Christians like Thomas, faith survived, but the transition was difficult.[34]

The closing years of the Civil War brought not only disruption and destruction but also confusion to southern religious life. New alternatives arose as northern black and white missionaries entered the South determined to gather southerners into their folds. Black Christians in occupied areas, enjoying freedom for the first time, left the churches of their masters and joined white and black northern denominations. Disaffected whites also joined northern denominations, especially in Unionist areas such as southern Appalachia. In several areas, northern missionaries even seized southern church buildings under War Department orders and held services in them. The northern missionary efforts contributed substantially in many areas to the membership declines suffered by southern churches.

The American Baptist Home Mission Society (ABHMS) met in Providence, Rhode Island, in May 1862 to formulate a plan for missions in the South. A committee recommended that the society take "immediate steps to supply with Christian instruction by means of missionaries and teachers, the emancipated slaves . . . and also to inaugurate a system of operations for carrying the Gospel alike to free and bond throughout the whole southern section of our country, so fast and so far as the progress of our arms, and the restoration of order and law shall open the way." Divine Providence was "beckoning us on to the occupancy of a field broader, more important, more promising than has ever yet invited our toils." In 1864 the society supported twenty-five missionaries in eight southern states; by April 1865 it had 120 missionaries and teachers in the South.[35]

In their fall meeting in 1863, the bishops of the Methodist Episcopal Church determined that their church must play a role in the religious reconstruction of the South, and they began to explore opportunities for missionary labor; over the next two years, their annual conferences sent twenty-one ordained ministers into the South as missionaries. Over five hundred northern Methodist preachers served as chaplains with Union armies at some time during the war, and many Methodist laypeople also journeyed south as teachers and missionaries. They went into areas of the South occupied by Federal armies, such as New Orleans and Baton Rouge, Louisiana; Memphis, Nashville, and Murfreesboro, Tennessee; New Bern, North Carolina; and Beaufort and Charleston, South Carolina. In their 1864 episcopal address, the northern bishops proclaimed, "the progress of Federal arms has thrown open to the loyal Churches of the Union large and inviting fields of Christian enterprise and labor." Although wrongfully excluded for nineteen years by the southern Methodist church, the Methodist Episcopal Church would occupy a "prominent position" in the cultivation of the southern fields. "And now that the providence of God has opened her way, she should not be disobedient to her heavenly calling, but should return at the earliest practicable period." The General Conference of 1864 authorized the bishops to establish annual conferences throughout the South, and it organized the Church Extension Society to aid in erecting church buildings. Methodist missionary John P. Newman in New Orleans explained the northern church's mission in the South: "We hold and teach that loyalty is a religious duty, as truly obligatory as prayer itself." The message of loyalty did attract some southern whites such as those who organized the Holston Conference in east Tennessee during the last year of the war. The conference officially became part of the Methodist Episcopal Church on June 1, 1865. In Kentucky several leading ministers had left the southern Methodist church by the end of the war. Such defections of ministers and members broke up the West Virginia and Western conferences of the MECS and divided the Missouri Conference.[36]

Northern Presbyterians also pursued the wartime missionary endeavors in the South. In 1864 the Committee of Home Missions of the northern New School Presbyterian Church declared, "A great field of missionary operations is opening at the South." In 1857 the Union and Kingston presbyteries in eastern Tennessee had withdrawn, with other southern presbyteries, from the New School Presbyterian Church to form the United Synod of the South. After the United Synod voted to unite with the Presbyterian Church in the Confederate States of America (Old School), these two presbyteries determined in September 1864 to leave the United Synod and return to the northern New School Presbyterian Church. The New School Presbyterians had also begun work in Missouri, but a raid by Confederate general Sterling Price toward Kansas City had disrupted their efforts among Unionists there. The Committee of Home Missions insisted, "the work in Missouri and Eastern Tennessee we think may be considered a fair type of what must be done in fourteen of the Southern states. Both the labor and the expense will be very great. Prejudices will yield very slowly." Old School Presbyterians in the North resolved in their 1865 General Assembly to direct their Board of Domestic Missions "to take prompt and effectual measures to restore and build up the Presbyterian congregations in the Southern States of this Union by the appointment and support of prudent and devoted missionaries." This decision to organize loyal presbyteries and synods in the South was taken in response to the "loud call from the Lord Jesus Christ to pass over and help to rebuild that part of the American Zion which has been so sadly laid waste by the rebellion and civil war."[37]

The early successes of northern missionaries among whites in Unionist and border areas such as eastern Tennessee and Missouri proved to be their greatest, but neither they nor southern Christians were certain of that outcome in 1865. Northern evangelicals were confident that these gains were only the first of many; their southern counterparts feared they were right. Southern ministers had more reason to fear the loss of their black membership, as northern missionaries of both races had much greater success among the freedpeople, who were beginning to act out their own interpretation of religious reconstruction.

In 1864 the General Assembly of the Presbyterian Church in the United States of America (PCUSA) (Old School) organized two committees to work among the freedpeople. Northern Methodists initially worked through nondenominational agencies, but in 1866 they formed their own Freedmen's Aid Society. The American Baptist Home Mission Society also worked actively among the freedpeople. Franklin C. Talmage, a historian of Georgia Presbyterianism, insisted that while the southern Presbyterian churches remained open to the freedpeople, they "abandoned the affiliation with the Southern church and formed a connection with the Assembly of the Northern church because of hopes aroused by the Freedmen's Bureau of that church."[38]

Black northern Christians also sent missionaries into the South to gather freedpeople into their denominational folds; the two most active were the African Methodist Episcopal (AME) and the African Methodist Episcopal Zion (AMEZ) churches, who believed the South had been providentially opened to them. "Heaven has graciously opened the way for the spreading of our beloved Zion in that land," wrote one AME minister. The AME Church sent its first two missionaries to the sea islands of South Carolina in May 1863; seventy-five more would follow them into the South by 1870. In December 1863, Bishop Daniel Payne went to Nashville and admitted two black Methodist congregations from the southern Methodist church into the AME Church. In the ten years following the war, the AME Church gained two hundred and fifty thousand members, the vast majority of them in the South. The AMEZ Church established itself in the South by receiving a black congregation in New Bern, North Carolina, early in 1864 and began missionary work in Florida and Louisiana later that year. By the end of the war, the exodus of black members from the biracial southern denominations had barely begun, but perceptive observers, north and south, realized what the wartime departures meant for the future.[39]

Northern denominations solicited and received the aid of the Federal government and the Union armies in their missionary efforts. Throughout the South, church buildings whose ministers had gone to war or fled approaching Federal armies sat vacant. After Union forces captured New Orleans in 1862, at least forty churches, including all five Methodist and all five Presbyterian churches in the city, were without regular services. A chaplain with Federal forces in Nashville wrote to northern Methodist bishop Matthew Simpson that most of the local pastors had deserted their congregations; the church buildings were either empty or occupied by the army. The Methodist Episcopal Church could "regain" the churches "if the matter could be properly presented to the government authorities." Bishop Edward R. Ames hurried to confer with his friend, Secretary of War Edwin M. Stanton. On November 30, 1863, Stanton issued an order instructing generals in the Departments of Missouri, the Tennessee, and the Gulf to "place at the disposal of Bishop Ames all houses of the Methodist Episcopal Church, South, in which a loyal minister, who has been appointed by a loyal Bishop of said Church does not officiate." The generals were also directed to "furnish Bishop Ames and his clerk with transportation and subsistence when it can be done without prejudice to the service and will afford them courtesy, assistance, and protection." On December 9, the War Department issued the same order concerning Methodist churches in the departments of North Carolina, Virginia, and the South, over which the northern bishops Osmon C. Baker and Edmund S. Janes had authority. On December 30, Stanton repeated the order for Kentucky and Tennessee under the direction of Bishop Simpson.[40]

Similar orders for the other northern denominations streamed from the War Department in the first three months of 1864. A January 14 order instructed commanders to turn over Baptist church buildings "in which a loyal minister of said Church does not now officiate" to the ABHMS. On February 15, missionaries of the United Presbyterian Church were given authority to seize Associate Reformed Presbyterian churches in the South. A War Department order of March 10 declared that military commanders were to give missionaries of the Board of Domestic Missions of the Presbyterian Church (Old School) and the Presbyterian Committee of Home Missions (New School) "all the aid, countenance, and support which may be practicable and in your judgment proper in the execution of their important mission." Missionaries from the northern denominations quickly took advantage of these orders. Within the first four months, representatives of the ABHMS seized about thirty buildings.[41]

The northern Methodists engaged in the most extensive campaign of church occupation in the South. Believing that thousands of southern Methodists were eager to rejoin the northern Methodist church, Methodist missionaries and several of the bishops themselves entered the South to seize buildings and organize local, loyal churches. Bishop Ames left for the lower Mississippi valley almost immediately after Stanton issued the order. Within a few weeks he had "appropriated, under the order of the War Department" and supplied a dozen churches formerly belonging to the MECS in Memphis, Little Rock, Pine Bluff, Vicksburg, Jackson, Natchez, Baton Rouge, and several in New Orleans. Bishop Simpson traveled to Nashville in January 1864 to establish loyal Methodism there; he placed Michael J. Cramer in charge of the churches in Nashville and authorized Chaplain Calvin Holman to occupy churches in Chattanooga. Cramer, after appealing over the heads of local officials to his brother-in-law, Ulysses S. Grant, secured both McKendree Chapel and the German Methodist Church in Nashville. Chaplain H. A. Pattison acquired an order from General George H. Thomas granting possession of the

Methodist church in Murfreesboro, Tennessee. Northern Methodist agents also occupied churches in Norfolk and Portsmouth, Virginia; Fernandina, Jacksonville,
and St. Augustine, Florida; and Beaufort and Charleston, South Carolina.[42]

Southern Christians did not quietly accept the occupation of their churches
by northern missionaries. In many areas they protested or attempted to disrupt the
enforcement of the War Department directives. On the local level in Texas, Methodist presiding elder R. W. Kennon wrote in June 1865 to one of his preachers,
O. M. Addison, that the minister assigned to the Galveston church was still away on
a trip to acquire Bibles. "The Federals will take possession of the city in about a
week — there will be Yankee Methodist preachers perhaps with the first expedition,
and if we have no preacher in charge of the church, he [sic] will walk into it." Kennon urged Addison to take charge of the church to prevent such an occupation:
"You had better go down at once. I will furnish you with a certificate of your appointment to that charge." Border state Presbyterians around Louisville, Kentucky,
urged the General Assembly of the PCUSA (Old School) to disavow the War Department's order to save the northern Presbyterian church from "the sin, the reproach, and ruin which this thing is calculated to bring upon her." Also at Louisville, Kentucky, in April 1864, a convention of southern Methodist ministers from
states within Union lines met to protest the order, which they regarded as "unjust,
unnecessary and subversive alike of good order and the rights of a numerous body
of Christians." They appealed to President Abraham Lincoln, who they rightly believed was not pleased with Stanton's order, to "restrain and prevent its enforcement." Lincoln did pressure Stanton to restrict the operation of the order to states in
rebellion, giving border state evangelicals some relief, and by early 1865 Lincoln had
begun the process of restoring the southern churches' property to them. President
Andrew Johnson continued the policy, and by the spring of 1866, with a few notable
exceptions, the properties seized under the War Department orders had been returned to their original owners.[43]

From whatever vantage point southern evangelicals viewed their churches and
denominations in the spring of 1865, they saw disruption, destruction, and confusion, and uncertainty about the religious implications of Confederate defeat was
widespread. Some observers feared that the southern denominations were hopelessly
disorganized. According to one contemporary observer, several members of the southern Methodist church, "losing faith in her future, were coquetting with an Episcopal
Bishop for a union of churches — the M. E. Church South and the Protestant Episcopal South." Others "were proposing to give up and go back to the M. E. Church."[44]
The religious condition of the South spurred all southern evangelicals to contem-
plate God's purposes in the war and His future plans for them.

Where southerners saw devastation, northerners and freedpeople saw opportunity. Northern Christians pondered the providential meanings of the war and the destruction of many southern religious institutions. The *Methodist* in New York City
proclaimed as early as December 1863, "the Methodist Episcopal Church, South, is
shivered to atoms. It is doubtful if its General Conference will ever meet again."[45]
The war and God's judgment upon the South had opened the region to a free and
loyal Gospel proclaimed by northern missionaries; they believed theirs was a vital

role in the spiritual regeneration of the South, and they were determined to pursue that role. Black Christians in the South considered the disruption caused by the war to be their opportunity to shape their own religious lives to a greater degree than ever before.

Between 1863 and 1866, each of these three groups worked out its interpretation of the religious significance of the war. White southern Christians had the most difficulty grappling with the outcome, because they were forced to reconcile the righteousness of their cause with the reality of defeat.

2

God's Chastisement

The Confederate Understanding of the Civil War

For whom the Lord loveth he chasteneth, and scourgeth every son whom he receiveth.

Hebrews 12:6

Religious southerners upheld the Confederacy both in victory and in defeat. Few, if any, groups could surpass Confederate clergymen in their devotion to the southern cause. They preached for it, prayed for it, and interpreted God's purposes in it from the beginning to the end. White religious southerners were certain, even through the bitter spring of 1865, that God favored the Stars and Bars. Then came defeat, sudden and complete. How could such a calamity befall the people and fledgling nation whom God favored and whose cause was righteous? The answer for most white religious southerners was that God was chastening the southern people for greater purposes in the future.

In the fall of 1860 and the spring of 1861, however, southerners had little reason to worry about God's chastening. Abolitionists, Republicans, and northerners in general, southern ministers believed, had much greater cause to fear God's wrath. Southern clergymen supported, and sometimes even led, the movements for secession in the individual southern states. While South Carolina was moving toward secession, with other southern states following closely behind, Louisiana wavered. The state's economic ties to the upper Mississippi valley made secession an especially ominous decision for Louisiana's citizens. New Orleans Presbyterian minister Benjamin Morgan Palmer, a native South Carolinian, seized the chance to address the political crisis in his sermon on November 29, Thanksgiving Day. He insisted that the conflict between the sections was rooted in "morals and religion." God had "providentially committed" to the South the duty "to conserve and perpetuate the institution of domestic slavery as now existing." Northern efforts to interfere with this divine imperative were an offense against God. In short, Palmer proclaimed, "we defend the cause of God and religion." The citizens of "all the Southern States" should "take all the necessary steps looking to separate and independent existence." Closing his sermon with the declaration that "whatsoever be the fortunes of the South, I accept them for my own," Palmer appealed for the divine protection of the South: "May the Lord God cover her head in this her day of battle."[1]

Thousands of copies of Palmer's sermon were published in New Orleans and distributed throughout Louisiana and the South. Several newspapers reprinted the entire text. Thaddeus W. McRae, a Presbyterian minister in Baton Rouge who had Unionist sentiments, marveled at its effect on his own congregation. On the same day that Palmer had delivered it, McRae had preached a sermon that "deprecated the threatened revolution," and several "leading Church members" had congratulated him. The text of Palmer's sermon appeared in Baton Rouge the following morning. "That afternoon I found my own prominent Elders and members on the other side," McRae reflected; Palmer's sermon had "reconciled the majority of Presbyterians in the State to secession."[2]

Palmer, though perhaps one of the more eloquent on the subject, was hardly alone in his sentiments that southerners had a religious duty to protect and uphold slavery, and with it southern society. The Alabama Baptist Convention, meeting at the end of 1860 in Tuskegee, unanimously adopted a resolution offered by Basil Manly Sr. proclaiming that Alabama Baptists felt bound to declare themselves "subject to the call of proper authority in defense of the sovereignty and independence of the state of Alabama, and of her sacred right as a sovereignty to withdraw from this union." In this declaration they were "*heartily, deliberately, unanimously, and solemnly united.*" One observer believed that this declaration, like Palmer's sermon in Louisiana, "did more to precipitate the secession of Alabama from the Union than any other one cause." Throughout the South, thousands of preachers and editors of religious newspapers urged southerners onward toward secession.[3]

Even those who initially doubted the wisdom of secession or opposed it outright became supporters of the Confederacy. Thomas H. McCallie, then in Cleveland, Tennessee, "could not approve of secession. I did not believe in the doctrine." Secession, he believed, "was utterly subversive of the very foundation of government." However, after seven states seceded, he thought that "there was no power in the constitution to bring them back by force, that force was the very essence of tyranny. . . . I was therefore opposed to co-ercion." When Lincoln resorted to coercion, Tennessee left the United States. Despite his "judgment that the whole movement for a separate and independent government here in the South was a blunder and a mistake," McCallie's "sympathies were with the South." "They were my people," he later wrote. "This was my home. I loved my state and the Southern people."[4]

Evidence abounds of southern churches' exhorting their members to support the Confederate cause during the war as well.[5] Publicly, ministers assured southerners that God favored the Confederacy and would ultimately give them the victory. Privately, religion provided individual southerners with the determination to continue in the struggle. From Charleston, South Carolina, Presbyterian Thomas Smyth declared that the fall of Fort Sumter "was a signal gun from the battlements of heaven, announcing from God to every Southern State, 'This cause is mine.'" Shortly after Lincoln issued the Emancipation Proclamation, the *Southern Presbyterian* declared, "if by events a people were ever justified before God, if reason and Scripture are worth anything, then are we today *right*, right before Him and our own hearts, proved right by the terrible wrong and sin surging against us." In March 1863, Bishop George Foster Pierce of the Methodist Episcopal Church, South (MECS), and Benjamin Morgan Palmer of the Presbyterian Church in the Confederate States of America delivered sermons before the Georgia General Assembly. Pierce declared that God "is for us and with us." The fast days that the Confederate Government was willing to proclaim "bring our country . . . into peculiar covenant relations with God, and enlist in our defense, the resources which God alone can command." In Pierce's view there was no "object proposed by our Government . . . [upon] which we may not consistently, piously, scripturally invoke the Divine blessing." The cause of the Confederacy was the cause of God. The reason was simple: "the Southern people . . . have never corrupted the gospel of Christ." Palmer reiterated Pierce's sentiments, declaring "our cause is pre-eminently the cause of God himself, and every blow struck by us is in defense of His supremacy." This paramount fact explained why southern ministers had "borne a distinguished part in this momentous struggle"; their loyalty to God compelled them to strike against the "wicked infidelity" of the North. As for the setbacks of the war, Palmer assured the Georgia legislature that "God is dealing with us, not in judgment, but in discipline." Nine months later, Palmer confidently assured the South Carolina General Assembly that the divine purpose of the Confederacy was to preserve "God's right to rule the world."[6]

Georgia Methodist John H. Caldwell sounded a similar theme from the pulpit in Newnan, Georgia, on April 8, 1864, another national fast day. He insisted that abolitionists were fanatical infidels who declared that "every slave must be made free, and placed on a footing of *equality* with if not *superior* to his master." Abolitionists insisted that "Our sanctuaries of religion must be invaded, and the pastors whom the people love be deposed from their appointed mission, and their places supplied with a puritanical priesthood." They would allow "no freedom of the press, no freedom of speech, no freedom in religion, and, if possible, not even in thought." The present crisis required southerners to perform four duties. First, they must have gratitude to God for His mercy in preserving the Confederacy: "Surely he who looks at the past history of the conflict and views the present situation of things must be persuaded that God is on our side." The second duty was penitence for southern sins; profanity, avarice, extortion, worldly-mindedness, and selfish ambition must be confessed and forsaken. The "cruel tyrant who grinds down the flesh and blood of his slave, refusing to allow him what is 'just and equal'" must admit that "his crimes especially may have provoked that indignation and wrath of God which has been poured out on our guilty land." The third duty was patience; southerners must "be patient, and hope to the end." The fourth duty was to trust in God: "Let us praise Him for all that He has done, and trust Him for the future." The Newnan congregation was so pleased with the sermon that they requested a copy from Caldwell for publication.[7]

The conviction that God was on the side of the South also permeated the Confederate armies. One of the more popular songs among the Army of Northern Virginia was "God Save the South," which included the following verse:

God made the right
Stronger than might.
Millions would trample us
Down in their pride.
Lay *Thou* their legions low,
Roll back the ruthless foe,
Let the proud spoiler know
God's on our side.[8]

Many preachers sent soldiers away to battle with words like those of Methodist Augustus Baldwin Longstreet, the president of South Carolina College: "Gallant sons of a gallant State, away to the battle field, with the Bible in your arms and its precepts in your hearts. If you fall, the shot which sends you from earth, translates you to Heaven."[9]

On a personal level, the "sustaining faith" of Alabama soldier Hiram Talbert Holt encouraged him through many battles with the Thirty-Eighth Alabama Infantry in the Army of Tennessee. Shortly after the war began, he assured his wife that "the God of the just will be with us to shield us from harm & give us victory." After General Braxton Bragg's defeat at Tullahoma, Tennessee, and the fall of Vicksburg in the summer of 1863, Holt despaired of victory. Only his personal faith sustained him as a soldier and as a southerner. In early September, he wrote that while he had suffered much in the past months, "yet I feel even more faith now in the declaration of the inspired writer than ever before. 'That all things work well together for those who serve the Lord.'" Learning of the death of his infant daughter, whom he had never seen, Holt wrote to his wife, "I hope you have borne your loss with Christian fortitude, and that like good old Job, you have exclaimed, 'The Lord giveth & the Lord taketh away, thrice blessed be the name of our Lord.' Also remember whom God loveth he chasteneth." Less than a month later, he fell dead in a skirmish near Dalton, Georgia.[10]

Methodist chaplain Morgan Callaway of Georgia wrote to his wife in 1864: "What a thorough test this war is of faith in Christ." Although it was "a dark hour truly for the Confederacy," Callaway had "unchanged hope in ultimate success." He told his wife, Leila, at home in Cuthbert that if she were able to see the necessity for men in the field, "you would be willing for your own Morgan's life to be sacrificed in the sacred cause." Although his life had been "offered on several bloody fields, God has not yet accepted it." Fellow Georgia Methodist Thomas Conn wrote after the First Battle of Manassas, "knowing the Lord will do right, [I] can face the cannon's mouth, . . . and if it is his will I should die here, can die, like a hero expecting a happy reunion with friends and relatives where there is no war." Callaway survived the war and helped to rebuild the southern Methodist church in Georgia, but Conn was killed in battle.[11]

Southern civilians also relied on their religious faith to help them endure the adversities of war. Sarah M. Manly wrote in early 1862 to her three sons in the army, "I am humbly thankful that I have reason to believe that you have each enlisted under the banner of the cross of Jesus Christ. God knows that my greatest desire is (and has ever been) that you should be, sincere and consistent Christians." Their father, Basil Manly Sr., wrote, "Life itself is not too dear or precious to be offered up in defense of our country and the churches of our God." Neither he nor his wife were willing to withhold their sons from serving their country "in the hour of her need. It is the service of God; and of the cause of humanity and religion."[12]

Many Confederate Christians believed that southerners' sins had aroused God's wrath and that He would punish them by prolonging the war. In July 1863, Basil Manly Jr. wrote to his brother Charles: "I know we have sinned and richly deserve chastisement, and I believe we should have it, and the Yankees may be used as the rod in God's hand; but, for all that, I cannot believe we should be either subjugated or exterminated by them." Methodist Leroy M. Lee addressed the same theme in his sermon to a congregation in Lynchburg, Virginia, on August 21, 1863, a national fast day. Lee insisted that because the Confederate cause was righteous, "failure is impossible, except by default of our own efforts, or by reason of our sins and unworthiness." The chief danger to the Confederacy was "among ourselves. Our reverses are the punishment of our sins." North Carolina Presbyterian minister Calvin H. Wiley wrote in his widely read 1863 book, *Scriptural Views of National Trials*, "God is now chastening the country for its sins in connection with slavery."[13]

The authors of *Why the South Lost the Civil War* have argued that southern religion "served as a trap for Confederate will." Since southerners believed that God controlled events, battlefield victories were a sign of God's favor, which naturally enhanced Confederate morale. "By the same token, however," these authors insist, "if the South began to lose battles, it could only mean that God did not side with the Confederacy, and if God sided with the right, it would mean that the South did not have right on its side and God favored the adversary." While perhaps logical in some sense, this interpretation was not so obvious to southern evangelicals. Nineteenth-century Protestant views of God's providence allowed for more suffering than these authors admit. Although military defeats might indicate God's disfavor with certain aspects of southern society, Confederate Christians did not immediately, if ever, come to the conclusion that it could "only" mean that God favored the North. Chastisements were, for them, a sign of God's nurturing care for the South, not His opposition to it.[14]

When the tide of battle turned against the Confederacy, southern Christians turned for solace and inspiration to biblical examples of God's miraculous deliverance of His chosen people from their enemies. In April 1864 Captain B. F. Eddins, a deacon in the Baptist church at Montgomery, Alabama, was mortally wounded by Union cavalry as they approached the outskirts of the town. Basil Manly Sr. conducted the funeral and chose for his text Judges 6:13: "If the Lord be with us, why then is all this befallen us?" The passage relates the story of Gideon, one of the judges of Israel. When Gideon questioned God's choice of him as a leader of the Israelites, the Lord said to him, "Surely I will be with thee, and thou shalt smite the Midianites as one man." With only three hundred men and the help of God, Gideon miraculously defeated the hosts of the Midianites who, incidentally, were camped on the northern side of the Israelites. The lesson was clear for the embattled Confederates: God's intervention could and would save the Confederacy. He did not need great armies to accomplish His purposes and drive back the invading hosts.[15]

To the very end, religious Confederates were certain that God would deliver the South and uphold its independence. Imprisoned on Johnson's Island in Lake Erie,

Alabamian Daniel R. Hundley wrote in his diary just after the fall of Atlanta: "Jehovah hath spoken the word, and it will stand fast. The South will surely triumph in the end. She is fighting for the correct principles of civil and religious freedom, and panoplied thus in the armor of divine truth and justice, she can never be conquered." The Ebenezer Baptist Association insisted in the fall of 1864 that "while the chastising rod of God has been visited upon us, a wicked people, we still believe we are on the side of truth and justice; and while we humbly bow to an Allwise providence, we humbly trust in God, hoping and believing that success will yet attend our cause." Sounding the same theme, the Reverend H. C. Hornady, the pastor of the First Baptist Church of Atlanta, assured his congregation on December 25, 1864 that the "blackened ruins" amidst which they sat were evidence of the chastening hand of God. Just as an earthly father disciplines his children, "so the Lord by his chastening of us manifests his love to us, and gives us the assurance that we are his children, the dear objects of his love." Despite the destruction, Hornady was confident of God's favor: "My brethren, this is, indeed, one evidence that we are the children of God: that he has not forsaken us. He chastens us as we have been because we are his children, and he loves us as his children. When I survey the ruins by which we are surrounded, I still feel that a father's hand holds the rod while he inflicts on us the stripes." Hornady exhorted his church, "Coming out of the fire purified and chastened, but still not destitute of hope, let us be a faithful, earnest, and devoted people."[16]

Citizens of Coweta County, Georgia, met in the Methodist church in Newnan on January 18, 1865 to reaffirm their commitment to the Confederacy; the large building "failed to accommodate the many who came." They elected a committee of twenty-six of "the most influential, wealthy and intelligent citizens of the county" to draft a set of resolutions; the chairman of the committee was the pastor of the Methodist church, John H. Caldwell. The resolutions denounced the citizens of Savannah who had chosen to cooperate with General William T. Sherman's army. The Newnan citizens proclaimed that "even now in the darkest hour of our struggle, we renew our patriotic covenant and again pledge our fortunes, our lives and our sacred honor to maintain and defend our country's cause, for her to live and die." They resolved that the people of Georgia were "more than ever determined to prosecute the war until their honor is vindicated and their rights acknowledged" and would "entertain no proposition for peace" that did not "secure for us our independence as a nation."[17]

In late February 1865, a writer to the Baptist *Christian Index* warned, "the crying sin of the people of God throughout our beleaguered, devastated, and bleeding country, is their want of faith in God, and our righteous cause." The reason the war had dragged on for four years was simple: "It is our want of faith!" Throughout the war religious Confederates had blamed battlefield reverses on a variety of sins among the southern people, including extortion, moral laxity, miscegenation, intemperance, profanity, desecration of the Sabbath, and abuses of the institution of slavery. Near the end of the war, this Baptist beseeched all southerners to repent of their ultimate sin — their lack of faith in God and in the Confederacy. They must confidently call on the Lord of hosts, and "speedily, we shall be taken out of the fiery furnace . . . [and] established as a separate and independent nation."[18]

In March 1865, Eliza Fain of eastern Tennessee wrote in her diary, "the cause of Southern Freedom seems to be thought by many in a most perilous condition but O my Father thou I trust has implanted within a hope which no adversity can shake. My trust is in thee. I never have felt that the South would be given up by thee and this morning O my blessed Father the hope is deep seated and abiding." A month later, on April 7, she wrote, "I feel I was enabled to pray this morning with stronger faith for the success of our country's cause than I ever felt before and I do feel God has heard me. I feel he will not give us up to our enemies. . . . He is sincere, he is true and I now await with feelings of pleasure the news which shall come to me of the success of our armies from the 5th to the 10 of April 1865." When General Robert E. Lee surrendered the Army of Northern Virginia on April 9, even this calamity did not shake Fain's "confidence in my God as to the position which the South shall occupy among the nations of earth when this struggle shall cease."[19]

The Presbyterian newspapers of the South urged their readers to put away despondency: "Stand fast; quit you like men." Although the Confederacy had suffered serious reverses, other successful causes had struggled through worse circumstances. The editors exhorted their readers to "take good heart in this holy work of defence, to which they are summoned by the unmistakable providence of God." The role of encouragement was the "solemn duty" of the religious papers, because the conflict was devoted to saving for the South "the priceless boon of both civil and religious freedom." In Georgia the *Christian Index* agreed. The editors felt that the crisis "demands that we give words of encouragement and cheer to our people." They were not troubled and felt as strongly as ever that "under God, we will yet gain our independence." They counseled their readers, "despair not, but with eyes fixed on the glorious goal of independence, struggle on unfalteringly, till the shout of triumph goes up all over our land!"[20]

Of course, the shout of triumph that went up across the land was uttered by northern armies, northern citizens, and northern Christians. Crushing the people of the South, defeat deeply perplexed religious Confederates. The editor of the *Christian Index* observed that they had been "taught in every Southern paper, and in almost every Southern pulpit, that the justice of the Southern cause must ensure its success." Now they faced overwhelming defeat. "The South lies prostrate," seventeen-year-old Emma LeConte wrote in her diary in Columbia, South Carolina; "there is no help. . . . who could have believed who has watched this four years' struggle that it could have ended like this! They say *right* always triumphs, but what cause could have been more just than ours? Have we suffered all — have our brave men fought so desperately and died so nobly for *this*?" A month later, when remnants of the southern army had returned to Columbia, LeConte still found it hard to believe the Confederacy was no more: "The army is disbanded now — oh! Merciful God! — the hot tears rush into my eyes and I cannot write."[21]

The Reverend Moses Drury Hoge, Presbyterian pastor in Richmond, wrote to a close friend in May 1865: "The idolized expectation of a separate nationality, of a social life and literature and civilization of our own, together with a gospel guarded against the contamination of New England infidelity, all this has perished, and I feel like a shipwrecked mariner thrown up like a seaweed on a desert shore." He continued, "God's dark providence enwraps me like a pall; I cannot comprehend, but I will not charge him foolishly; I cannot explain, but I will not murmur. . . . I await the development of his providence, and I am thankful that I can implicitly believe that the end will show that all has been ordered in wisdom and love." Hoge, like other southerners, drew comfort from the Old Testament account of Job's righteous suffering. Like Job, he concluded, "Though he slay me, yet will I trust him." In September he was still uncertain of God's purposes in the war: "I have not been very well since the surrender. . . . These inscrutable providences are like the half lines written in the palaces of the Cæsars — what is to come after will explain and complete their meaning."[22]

The Rappahannock Baptist Association gathered just six weeks after Lee's surrender to survey the remnants of their group of churches and begin the work of religious reconstruction. They were certain that "the sore trials through which we have passed and the darkness which now overshadows us are a part of the workings of Providence." Reflecting the common Confederate understanding of the war, they declared, "our severe chastisements . . . are ordained of God, as instruments to work for us a far more exceeding and eternal glory."[23] Like these Virginia Baptists, most religious southerners believed Hebrews 12:6–7 explained God's dealings with them: "For whom the Lord loveth he chasteneth, and scourgeth every son whom he receiveth. If ye endure chastening, God dealeth with you as with sons; for what son is he whom the father chasteneth not?" God loved the South even though he allowed them to be defeated. He had greater things planned for the South that southerners could not then comprehend, according to the scriptural promise, "all things work together for good to them that love God." They had to cling to faith when they lacked understanding.[24] Gone was the confidence and optimism of the 1850s. "God, in the era between Appomattox and Henry Grady," Fred Hobson has rightly observed, "would come to play an increasingly important role in Southern affairs. Southern apologists, many of them Calvinists, could see no reason for their military defeat, save the inscrutable will of a sovereign God."[25] Most remained convinced, however, that God would vindicate the South in some unknown way. This firm belief that the defeat of the Confederacy did not signal God's absolute disapproval shaped most white religious southerners' responses to the issues of religious reconstruction.

The primary duty of southern ministers and editors in 1865 and 1866 was to convince themselves and their congregations that God had not deserted the South: the righteousness of the southern cause, the justice of God, and Confederate defeat could and would be reconciled.[26] Even before the war ended, some ministers were developing a framework within which they could accommodate both the assurance of God's continued favor and the military defeat of the Confederacy. In April 1864 the Baptist minister Thomas S. Dunaway warned a Virginia congregation against believing "an idea which I have heard some advance, when they say that if our cause is just and right it will succeed in any event; and if it fail it is conclusive that our cause is a bad one, and God is displeased with our institutions." Dunaway insisted, "an accurate acquaintance with the ways of Providence as manifested in the Scriptures, will disabuse our minds of this error." Failure did not imply God's final judgment. Rather, it might simply be part of his own "wise purposes" to "withhold success from his most faithful servants."[27] A wide array of southern evangelicals developed this argument in the immediate aftermath of the war to explain why God would permit the defeat of a righteous cause.

Near the end of 1865, a writer in the Baptist *Religious Herald* reflected on the providential meaning of Confederate defeat. Because Confederates had been certain of the righteousness and the eventual triumph of their cause, "the blow that overthrew the Confederacy, shook their faith in the righteous providence of God." Something was obviously awry; "either the Confederate cause was wrong, or Providence does not always favor the right side." The author quickly revealed where the problem lay. "Believing that the Confederate cause was righteous, we need not have our confidence in Divine Providence shaken by its failure." Clearly, right did not invariably triumph over might. "That truth and righteousness will finally triumph, we have no doubt; but it is one of the mysteries of Providence, that in this world, and for a season, they are permitted to be obscured and perverted." In conclusion, "there is nothing in the issues of our late unhappy and ruinous war to change our views as to the rectitude of the Southern struggle for independence." The author examined the southern quest, and found it, on the whole, virtuous. It was their view of God's providence, not their purposes in the war, that Confederate Christians needed to reevaluate.[28]

The General Assembly of the Presbyterian Church in the Confederate States of America, meeting in Augusta, Georgia, in December 1865, assured southern Presbyterians that God had not forsaken them. "Our national sins have aroused God's wrath, and caused Him to visit us with sore national calamities and bereavements." Southern Christians must "cordially acquiesce in the dispensations of his inscrutable Providence" with the firm hope that God would pity His people and deliver them. Georgia Baptist S. G. Hillyer wrote to the *Christian Index*, "let us not falter in our faith, in this time of public and private calamity. Let us accept the chastenings of the Lord with all humility. They are the dealings of a father's hand. His love in the method of its manifestation, may be incomprehensible. But he is too wise to err, and too good to be unkind."[29]

Henry Holcomb Tucker, the editor of the *Christian Index*, admitted that "when the Southern Confederacy fell, thousands of hearts were crushed." To those men and women he offered Christian consolation: "Whether you see the good that is to come of what has happened or not, is immaterial. God will be certain to subserve some grand purpose of mercy by it. The present result is not of man's doings. God is the author of his own providences." While many believed that "Providence had sent upon them an overwhelming calamity," they must not challenge God's will or lose faith in His plans: "The hand of the Lord is then in this thing. It is God who has done it. Will his saints complain? Do they doubt his wisdom? Do they question his goodness?" Instead of questioning God's decision in the conclusion of the war, southern Christians must accommodate themselves to their changed circumstances. If they refused to do so, they were "fighting against his providence, and disobeying the evident inclinations of his will." Tucker insisted that "the facts before us are the materials God has given us with which to operate, and to glorify him." (The conclusion of the Civil War, of course, did not reveal God's will as clearly to everyone as Tucker seemed to indicate. The freedpeople, northern evangelicals, and the southern Christians who worked with them did not interpret the facts before them as the majority of Confederate Christians did.) In conclusion, Tucker wrote, "we may console ourselves with this even in what seems to us to be the darkest providences, that 'all things work together for good to them that love God'; so therefore comfort one another with these words."[30]

Benjamin Morgan Palmer, driven to Columbia, South Carolina, by the war, also believed God would vindicate the southern cause. Even after Lee's surrender, Palmer encouraged his congregation with the hope of future deliverance. Emma LeConte wrote in her journal on April 23, 1865, "Dr. Palmer this morning preached a fine and encouraging sermon. He says we must not despair yet, but even if we should be overthrown — not conquered — the next generation would see the South *free* and independent." Four days earlier, Eliza Fain had privately sounded the same theme in her diary: "Every prayer, every moment, every view I take of our country's cause, every thing I hear in regards to our slaves but serves to impress me more certainly of our final triumph. Whether it is to be independence or not I cannot know but I do believe the honor and character of the South will be maintained before the nations of the earth."[31]

Having convinced themselves in these ways that the Confederate cause was righteous and that God still looked upon them as His people, southern Christians adamantly refused to concede to northern charges that slavery and secession were sins for which God had judged them. They vigorously denied any accusations that the outcome of the war could be attributed to their peculiar institution or to their political course in 1861.[32]

When her husband, Richard, left in mid-May 1865 to take the oath of allegiance in Knoxville, Eliza Fain's soul was "wrung with anguish" at the prospect. The oath bound individuals to support the Constitution of the United States, but Fain felt "it is more important to administer this oath to our enemies than us as they are the ones who have torn to shreds this noble document of patriotic hearts. They are the ones who first violated its sacred compact." She hoped that if God saw fit to reunite the sections, both the North and the South would be "taught by this terrible struggle what is true in relation to slavery." "It has caused the best blood of the South to flow," she continued. "I believe the Bible teaches slavery is right. If this is true every soldier of the Confederate Army who has fallen is a martyr for the truth and no great truth of God's Holy Word has ever been sustained without the seal of the blood of the Christian being affixed."[33]

The General Assembly of the southern Presbyterian church, meeting late in 1865, declared that that church had no commission to propagate or abolish slavery; this matter of policy belonged exclusively to the state. However, "the lawfulness of the relation as a question of social morality, and of scriptural truth" was still a matter of vital importance. The belief that slavery was inherently sinful was "unscriptural and fanatical," and the acceptance of this creed by any church "is a just cause of separation from it." Although southern Presbyterians may have cause to repent "for neglect of duty or actual wrong towards our servants," they did not have "to bow the head in humiliation before men, or admit that the memory of many of our dear kindred is to be covered with shame" because they had held slaves.[34]

In February 1866, a contributor to the Baptist *Religious Herald* challenged an editorial that suggested that the war had been God's method of abolishing slavery.

"Can it be," he asked, "that it was the design of God in the late terrible civil war to overthrow an institution which he himself ordained, established and sanctioned, and which he 'designed' should exist forever?" Such a conclusion was ludicrous. God would not have allowed all of this suffering and bloodshed "that an inferior race might be released from nominal bondage and endowed with a freedom which, to them, is but another name for licentiousness, and which must end in complete extermination, so far as human foresight can judge." The author declared, "I cannot, I will not believe it. . . . It was Satan that ruled the hour."[35]

Presbyterian theologian Robert Lewis Dabney offered a 350-page justification of slavery published in 1867 under the title *A Defence of Virginia, and Through Her, of the South.* To the question "Is not the slavery question dead? Why discuss it longer?" Dabney replied, "Would God it were dead! But in the Church, abolitionism lives, and is more rampant and mischievous than ever, as infidelity." Therefore, the "faithful servants of the Lord Jesus Christ dare not cease to oppose and unmask it." Dabney then proceeded to offer arguments supporting slavery from the Old and New Testaments and from ethics and economics. "A righteous God," he concluded, "for our sins towards Him, has permitted us to be overthrown by our enemies and His." The southern people "suffer silently, disdaining to complain, and only raising to the chastening heavens, the cry, 'How long, O Lord?'" Two years after the war ended, Dabney felt it his Christian duty to uphold the righteousness of slavery and await future vindication by God: "Because we believe that God intends to vindicate His Divine Word, and to make all nations honour it . . . we confidently expect that the world will yet do justice to Southern slaveholders."[36] Likewise, even a full decade after Appomattox, Methodist Thomas O. Summers, editor of the Nashville *Christian Advocate,* attacked the idea that slavery was an inherently sinful institution. As late as 1892, the Southern Baptist Convention articulated a religious defense of the institution through which the black slave "exchanged the degrading idolatry of his native land for the truths of the gospel, and from his cabin home the witchery of Christian melodies banished the voudoism of his fatherland."[37]

Even those southerners who expressed a sense of relief over the end of slavery upheld its righteousness. Looking back on the end of the war nearly forty years later, Presbyterian Thomas H. McCallie, who had owned a few slaves, wrote, "we were glad that in the awful strife slavery had gone out and out forever." However, he remembered the institution as a burden more for white than for black southerners: "Whatever of curse or of blessing to the black race, and blessings unnumbered had come to him through it, yet it had been a burden to master and mistress that we gladly parted with." In his memoirs, written for his children, McCallie extolled his parents, and perhaps himself, as benevolent slaveholders: "the fidelity with which these Christian people dealt with their slaves should be known by their descendants." Neither of his parents believed that "slave-holding was condemned as a sin in the Bible" or that "they were breaking any law of God by being slave-holders."[38]

Southern evangelicals also defended the righteousness of secession, a course they had heartily supported only a few years before. In justifying it, they reasserted their wartime arguments for the constitutional and moral right of states to secede from the Union. The force of arms had determined the fact of the future relationship of the states to the Federal government, but southerners insisted that morally they had acted correctly in 1861. The Christian men of the South, the *Southern Presbyterian* maintained in 1866, "still believe that those views of States' Rights for which they battled so stoutly, and from which the right of secession naturally flows, were the views of the framers of the Constitution." Most still agreed with Presbyterian Thomas Smyth of Charleston who in 1863 claimed that the South had exercised "the divine right of secession."[39]

Thus, neither slavery nor secession had provoked God into forsaking the southern people. Both the peculiar institution and the political separation were righteous before Him, and although God had chastised Confederate Christians, He was only preparing them for greater usefulness in the future. Southern evangelicals brought this understanding to one of the most important issues of religious reconstruction — reunion with their northern counterparts. Northern Christians, meanwhile, had come to very different conclusions about God's providence in the war and had developed their own vision for the religious reconstruction of the South. When the two groups discussed the issue, their divergent visions quickly led to harsh accusations and uncompromising attitudes.

Initially, the southern churches were in such a critical condition that even their leaders displayed some doubts about their future, but Confederate Christians quickly established their interpretation of the war as God's chastening and committed themselves to rebuild their religious institutions. In 1856, one prominent churchman had expressed southern Christians' fear of "Northern domination in our schools and pulpits of the South." A decade later in defeat, southern evangelicals had even more reason for worry and for action. In Sardis, Mississippi, Methodist pastor Robert H. Crozier exhorted his congregation: "If we cannot gain our *political*, let us establish at least our *mental* independence." Christians across the South expressed such sentiments.[40]

The first official signs of life from the southern Methodist church came from Missouri, where, at Palmyra in June 1865, two dozen preachers and a dozen laypeople gathered to discuss their future. They considered the maintenance of a separate and independent ecclesiastical organization "of paramount importance and our imperative duty." For them to go into the Methodist Episcopal Church (MEC) would be "to admit the charge that with the institution of slavery we stand or fall." They acknowledged that different ideas for the religious reconstruction of the South had already been proposed. Referring to the northern Methodists, the report protested, "The only consolidation or reconstruction they would accept would be that we turn over to them our Church property and interests and influence; yield the whole field; confess that we have been wrong; indorse the politics of their Church as a condition of membership; and become political hucksters instead of Gospel ministers." Their congregations demanded with "great unanimity" that the MECS be preserved. The Palmyra Manifesto, coming from a border-state conference, invigorated the southern Methodist church. A month later, Bishop George F. Pierce affirmed in a letter to an Atlanta newspaper, "my deliberate judgment is, that our true policy is to maintain our present organization."[41]

In August 1865 bishops Andrew, Paine, and Pierce of the MECS wrote a pastoral address to southern Methodists, making it clear that they had no intention of reuniting with the MEC. The majority of northern Methodists, they lamented, "have become incurably radical. They teach for doctrine the commandments of men. They preach another gospel. They have incorporated social dogmas and political tests into their church creeds. They have gone on to impose conditions upon discipleship that Christ did not impose." Faithfulness to their "providential mission," the bishops proclaimed, required that southern Methodists "preserve our church in all its vigor and integrity, free from entangling alliances with those whose notions of philanthropy and politics and social economy are liable to give an ever varying complexion to their theology."[42]

The Memphis Conference of the MECS met early in October 1865 to begin the process of reorganization. On the final day of the meeting, the conference resolved, "we are decided in our purpose to maintain intact our present ecclesiastical relations; believing that our membership desire no change; and that any action of this Conference looking to a union with another church would be highly prejudicial to Methodism." The conference also declared, "we heartily approve, and fully endorse the address of our Bishops." Other southern Methodist conferences followed this example as they also expressed their commitment to southern ecclesiastical independence.[43]

The General Assembly of the southern Presbyterians issued a pastoral letter to all of its churches in December 1865. Southern Presbyterians, the letter declared, were forced to organize a separate assembly in 1861, and the reasons for that separation from the Presbyterian Church in the United States of America "not only remain as conclusive as at first, but have been exceedingly strengthened by events of public notoriety, occurring each succeeding year." The General Assembly cautioned all southern Presbyterians to "repel all unworthy attempts of men who may lie in wait to deceive, and to cause you to fall from your own steadfastness." The *Southern Presbyterian* insisted, "there is really no option in the matter." Reunion would imperil the southern Presbyterian church's "purity and safety" and "dishonor the Great Head of the Church."[44]

The ministers of the Georgia Baptist Association pledged their continued support of "the Southern Organizations of our denomination." Any attempt to unite northern and southern Baptists "would be productive of trouble and confusion and not good."[45] In early 1866 the new editor of the *Christian Index* declared that he had received "several ably written articles in opposition to union of organization on the part of Northern and Southern Baptists." Because his readers were "almost unanimous in opposition to this measure," he considered it "needless to discuss it." The following week, he observed that the editor of the *Religious Herald* had declared that ninety-nine of every one hundred southern Baptists favored the maintenance of their own southern organization. Not to be outdone, the editor exclaimed that the figure "nearer the truth" was 999 out of one thousand: "Southern Baptists are so nearly unanimous on this subject, that we think it worse than a waste of time to discuss it." In response to the paper's correspondents who wrote letters on the subject, he insisted, "it will be time enough to combat the proposition for reconstruction, when somebody advocates it. . . . We think that the subject had better be dropped." In sum, "there is not the least prospect of a re-union of Northern and Southern Baptists, for many years to come, if *ever*." Ironically, in subsequent issues, he continued to discuss the reasons why he did not discuss reunion. Evidently he or his readers needed reassurance that no reasonable southern person would advocate reunion.[46]

While rejecting reunion on the terms offered by their counterparts in the North, Confederate Christians affirmed their commitment to rebuild their southern institutions. Destroyed during the war, denominational newspapers and colleges resumed operation only after much effort. Church buildings had to be rebuilt and organizational structures reestablished. Despite the difficulties, southern evangelicals quickly set to work rebuilding their religious lives. Only by reconstructing their "southern Zion" could they hope to maintain a separate religious identity and prepare for the unfolding of God's providential purpose for them.[47]

The religious future of the freedpeople was another vital concern of Confederate Christians. Underlying all southern evangelicals' decisions on this subject was a persistent and profound belief in the inferiority of the black race. Several forces at work in the months following the war determined the future relations between black and white Christians in the South. Some Confederate Christians wanted little to do with the freedpeople, socially or religiously. Infuriated over emancipation, they resented any efforts on behalf of the freedpeople and preferred to leave them to the care of the northerners who had freed them. More southern evangelicals, especially ministers, believed it was their duty to evangelize the freedpeople just as they had evangelized the slaves; North Carolina Baptists termed it "a special duty imposed by the Providence of God on Southern Christians." Texas Baptist F. M. Law insisted that the religious instruction of the freedpeople had to be "taken hold of, conducted and controlled by Southern people."[48] Of course, this effort was in no way intended to implement equality in church relations; the preemancipation structures of religious instruction were to continue between whites and blacks. God's charge to southern Christians to uplift the black race had not ended with emancipation, nor had the attitudes of paternalism died when the slaves became free. This mixture of religious duty coupled with a desire to maintain control over an inferior race motivated most southern evangelicals in 1865.[49]

The Alabama Baptist Convention clearly favored retaining black members in white-controlled churches: "The changed political status of our late slaves does not necessitate any change in their relation to our churches; and while we recognize their right to withdraw from our churches and form organizations of their own, we nevertheless believe that their highest good will be subserved by their maintaining their present relation to those who know them, who love them, and who will labor for the promotion of their welfare."[50] Basil Manly Sr. wrote in late 1865 that the black members of his church had petitioned to be set apart as a separate church, and he doubted the wisdom of such a step: "We think they are not yet prepared for the responsibility of an independent church state. We have told them so, but yet shall let go our hold of them, if after our advice, they desire it."[51]

The Georgia Baptist Association, one of the member associations of the Georgia Baptist Convention, included churches in eastern Georgia between Athens and Augusta. At the end of the war, it had approximately nine thousand members; nearly two-thirds of them were black, including five independent black congregations in Augusta totaling over three thousand members. At the meeting of the association in the fall of 1865, one of the churches sent two queries regarding its black members. After "considerable interchange of opinions" on this vital issue, the association unanimously declared that it was permissible for black members to form churches of their own, but it was not considered "expedient at present in the country." The association also determined that it was scriptural for churches to continue to receive black members.[52]

The Georgia Synod of the southern Presbyterian church, meeting in Augusta in October 1865, feared that its members would believe themselves to be absolved from all obligation to labor for the salvation of black men and women since they were no longer responsible for them as owners. The synod exhorted the churches "not to relax, but rather redouble their exertions for the religious instruction of the colored people." Georgia Presbyterians hoped that when the freedpeople recovered from the "temporary intoxication of suddenly acquiring freedom" they would learn that "after all, their late masters are their best friends and most efficient instructors."[53]

Southern evangelicals insisted that a primary reason for blacks' leaving their churches was that northern missionaries, both black and white, had descended on the South to stir discord among the freedpeople. Confederate Christians had to attribute the exodus either to black ignorance or to outside influences; to do otherwise would shatter the myth of black contentment in slavery and would impugn their own attitudes toward black Christians. The General Assembly of the southern Presbyterians, which met in November 1865, noted a "marked change" in the "religious deportment" of the black population. Instead of crowding the churches for instruction and worship as they formerly had, few of them were to be found in the Presbyterian churches. The General Assembly attributed this calamity to "the insinuations of designing men, who, for sinister purposes, have sought to alienate their affections" from their former ministers, and to a "misapprehension of the feelings we entertain for them as a people." To admit that blacks left the biracial churches on their own initiative and for good reasons would not only undermine southern Presbyterians' confident assumptions of black inferiority and docility, but would also belittle their efforts to evangelize the slaves.[54]

The members of the Georgia Conference of the MECS, also meeting in the fall of 1865, pledged to continue evangelizing the freedpeople under white ministers wherever possible. However, the conference requested the bishop to appoint the black pastors already selected by black congregations because "we are desirous that all our colored members should continue to be members of the M. E. Church, South." Although the conference disclaimed any power to transfer church property used by blacks before and during the war to the freedpeople, it did recommend that trustees of church property permit black congregations to continue to use church buildings even if none of them remained in the southern Methodist fold. By retaining black members within the southern organization or at least within property controlled by white southerners, southern evangelicals hoped to insure the control necessary to maintain a measure of social mastery amid postwar disruptions.[55]

The decisions of most black Baptists, Methodists, and Presbyterians to leave the churches of their masters demolished white plans to maintain antebellum religious relationships. Faced with the fact of black exodus, southern church leaders repeatedly readjusted their stance toward black Christians. Initially, leaders believed that the antebellum patterns of paternalistic biracial churches could continue. Next, they attempted the organization of the freedpeople into separate congregations with white ministers. Later, they accepted the idea that freedpeople might have black ministers under white supervision. Eventually they assisted in the organization of black associations, conferences, and presbyteries. Ultimately, they reluctantly admitted that the freedpeople would have an entirely separate and independent denominational structure. In the five years that it took the MECS to adjust to this reality, it lost all but a few thousand of its over two hundred thousand black members. In 1870 two white bishops of the southern Methodist church superintended the establishment of the Colored Methodist Episcopal Church, into which most of the remaining black members transferred.[56]

Thus Southern Christians, believing that through defeat God was purifying them for a glorious future vindication, zealously began to rebuild the religious life of their southern Zion. Most thought that black people should remain in white churches where they would hear the "pure" gospel and where whites could exercise a measure of control over them, a stance that was modified only gradually in reluctant acceptance of the inexorable black exodus from biracial churches during and immediately after the war. These attitudes, forged between 1863 and 1866, shaped Confederate Christians' actions during religious reconstruction. The competition between their vision and the alternative views held by northern Christians and the freedpeople determined the patterns of religious reconstruction during the next decade.

3

God's Judgment

The Northern Understanding
of the Civil War

For the wrath of God is revealed from heaven against all ungodliness and
unrighteousness of men, who hold the truth in unrighteousness; . . .

But we are sure that the judgment of God is according to truth
against them which commit such things.

And thinkest thou this, O man, that judgest them which do such
things, and doest the same, that thou shalt escape the judgment of God?

Romans 1:18, 2:2–3

L ike their southern counterparts, northern clergy and laity vigorously supported
their section during the Civil War. Like Confederate Christians, the vast majority of the northern religious populace interpreted battlefield victories as evidence of
God's favor and defeats as divine chastisement. As James H. Moorhead has con-
vincingly demonstrated, northern Protestants saw the conflict in millennial terms;
the nation was engaged in an apocalyptic struggle to determine whether it would
fulfill its millennial role in hastening "the day of the Lord."[1] Religious southerners
likewise believed that the Confederacy had been uniquely chosen by God to defend the Bible and Christianity before the nations of the world. There, however, the
similarities ended. The Union cause triumphed, and most northern Christians
confidently assumed that God had given them the victory over the wicked South.
The outcome of the war was God's judgment on the region for the sins of slavery
and secession. A few more modest commentators believed the war was a divine
judgment on the entire nation, but they too thought that God had demonstrated
His displeasure with the causes for which the South had fought. Armed with this
understanding of the spiritual significance of the war, northern ministers addressed

49

the issues of religious reconstruction in ways very different from their southern counterparts.

Phillip Shaw Paludan concluded in his study of northern society during the Civil War that "no force shaped the vision that northerners had of the war more forcefully than religion."[2] No less than southerners, northern Protestants during the war looked to their churches and clergy to help them understand the providential significance of this bloody struggle. How they and their clergy interpreted God's purposes in the war shaped their attitudes toward the issues of religious reconstruction. Although many northern Protestants were initially hesitant about war and called for peace, their reluctance was swept away by the whirlwind of public outrage when the South fired on the flag at Fort Sumter. Once converted, they rallied to the Union cause and demanded a vigorous prosecution of the war.[3]

From the beginning of the war, northern Christians insisted that God had ordained the Federal government; therefore, the South's revolt against the Union was a sin worthy of divine punishment. Members of the Methodist Detroit Annual Conference in 1861 declared that they "saluted the stars and stripes as next in our prayers and affections to the very Cross of the Redeemer." The American Baptist Home Mission Society (ABHMS), meeting in Brooklyn, New York, in May declared, "the doctrine of secession is foreign to our Constitution, revolutionary, suicidal" and the national government "deserves our loyal adhesion and unstinted support in its wise, forbearing, and yet firm maintenance of the national unity and life." With a metaphoric flourish, the Baptist assembly insisted, "what was bought at Bunker Hill, Valley Forge, and Yorktown, was not, with our consent, sold at Montgomery; that we dispute the legality of the bargain, and, in the strength of the Lord God of our fathers, shall hope to contest, through this generation, if need be, the feasibility of the transfer." The equally nationalistic New School Presbyterians, meeting in Syracuse, New York, adopted resolutions expressing their "amazement at the wickedness of such proceedings" as secession and armed rebellion. They also expressed their "undiminished attachment to the great principles of civil and religious freedom on which our national Government is based."[4]

In contrast to the unified Methodists, Baptists, and New School Presbyterians, a deeply troubled and divided General Assembly of the Old School Presbyterians met in Philadelphia in May of 1861. Only half of the presbyteries from the border and southern states were represented, and the two greatest southern Presbyterian leaders, Dr. Benjamin M. Palmer and Dr. James H. Thornwell, were conspicuously absent. On the third day of the meeting, Dr. Gardiner Spring, the aging conservative pastor of the Brick Presbyterian Church in New York City, asked the convention to form a committee to make resolutions of loyalty to the Union. The motion was tabled by a close vote. Undaunted, Spring insisted that the General Assembly take some action, and he offered two resolutions. The first called for a national day of prayer for peace, and the other pronounced it the duty of the ministry and churches "to do all in their power to promote and perpetuate the integrity of these United States, and to strengthen, uphold, and encourage the Federal Government." After five days of debate, the General Assembly passed the Spring Resolutions; in the wake of these resolutions, several southern presbyteries seceded from the General Assembly as soon as they met. On December 4, 1861, ten synods, encompassing forty-five presbyteries with seventy-two thousand members, united to form the Presbyterian Church in the Confederate States of America.[5]

Newspapers across the North published these resolutions by the leading denominations as evidence of the churches' loyalty to the Union. Throughout the war, as Philip Paludan writes, "the churches of the North justified and energized the war effort." Much as churches in the South promoted morale and sanctified the Confederate war effort, northern churches proclaimed the effort to maintain the Union (and later to abolish slavery) a sacred cause. The Reverend W. O. Wyant, a Methodist war-recruit on his way to camp, told a Sunday school service in Greencastle, Indiana, in April 1861, "I have never felt more confident of my acceptance with God, than I do at this moment. The offering that I bring, I am willing to sacrifice on the altar of my country; and should I fall, I will be with Jesus the sooner." Many northern soldiers, like their southern counterparts, gave that sacrifice, each assured that he was dying for the cause of the Lord.[6]

Throughout the struggle, the northern Protestant denominations firmly supported the Federal government. When the Lincoln administration issued the Emancipation Proclamation, thereby making the destruction of slavery a war aim, the churches generally rallied behind the decision, though some believed it should have included all slaves and should have been made earlier. The editor of the *Western Christian Advocate* wrote in 1863: "To emancipate the negro was among the least cherished designs of a loyal people of this country when they reluctantly took up arms against the Southern insurgents. . . . The work of emancipation has gone steadily and rapidly forward." The Philadelphia Baptist Association, meeting in October 1864, declared, "American slavery . . . lies at the basis of the wicked attempt to overthrow the Government, is responsible for the bloodshed and crime of the past three years, and should be held accountable before God and man for every life sacrificed and every drop of blood shed." No lasting peace could be expected "while slavery exists."[7]

Increasingly as the war continued, even those churches that had been silent on the issue of slavery came to condemn it.[8] In 1863 the Old School Presbyterians issued a statement reaffirming their 1818 report, which had said: "We consider the voluntary enslaving of one part of the human race by another . . . utterly inconsistent with the law of God" and "totally irreconcilable with the spirit and principles of the Gospel of Christ." All Christians had the duty "as speedily as possible to efface this blot on our holy religion, and to obtain the complete abolition of slavery throughout Christendom, and if possible, through the world." By May 1864 the conservative Old School General Assembly had become adamant, even in the face of protests from border presbyteries: "The spirit of American slavery . . . has taken arms against law, organized a bloody rebellion against the national authority, made formidable war upon the Federal Union, and in order to found an empire upon the cornerstone of slavery, threatens not only our existence as a people, but the annihilation of the principles of free Christian government." The continuance of negro slavery is "incompatible with the preservation of our own liberty and independence."[9]

Northern churches aided the Union war effort in other ways as well. Two thousand chaplains went south with northern armies, and northern Christians supported a variety of agencies designed to evangelize and comfort the Union soldiers. Ministers spoke at enlistment rallies and offered benedictions over departing troops.[10] Northern ministers and teachers followed Union armies to evangelize and educate the newly freed blacks in the South. These agents of northern denominations began the process of religious reconstruction in the South according to their own understanding of how God was working in human history; in New Orleans, in Tennessee, and in coastal areas of the Carolinas, they began to try to rebuild the religious life of the South on new, very different foundations. Their experiences were important to the formulation of the northern understanding of the Civil War as well as northern plans for religious reconstruction in the postwar South.

One of these early missionary teachers was Joanna Patterson Moore. While studying at Rockford Seminary in Illinois, she attended a "jubilee meeting" on January 1, 1863, the day Lincoln signed the Emancipation Proclamation. Some of the participants shouted for joy, but, Moore later recalled, "to my ears there came with the shout of victory an undertone of sadness, a piteous cry for help." She could not escape the mental image of "bondmen, tied down with cords of ignorance, superstition, and oppression." In February 1863, a man who had traveled in the occupied South visited the seminary and told the young women about his visit to Island No. 10, located in the Mississippi River thirty miles north of Memphis. At a contraband camp there, he told them, 1,100 women and children were living in desperate conditions. "What can a man do to help such a suffering mass of humanity?" the speaker asked. "Nothing," he concluded. "A woman is needed, nothing else will do." Troubled by the suffering of the freedpeople, Moore "asked myself and asked God a thousand questions and only got one answer: 'Go and see and God will go with you.'" Convinced that God would aid and protect her, she determined to go. The Sabbath school of the Baptist church in Belvidere, Illinois, pledged $4 per month, and the government provided her with transportation and soldier's rations. The ABHMS gave her a commission but no salary.[11]

Moore arrived at Island No. 10 in the Mississippi River in November 1863. A Miss Baldwin from Ohio had also arrived on a similar mission, and the two missionaries lived with Baptist minister Benjamin Thomas, who commanded the regiment that guarded the island, and his wife. During their five-month stay on Island No. 10, Moore and Baldwin wrote hundreds of letters to their friends in the North to request clothes for the impoverished freedpeople in the camp during the harsh winter of 1863–64: "Often we found children on the wharf with nothing on them but a part of a soldier's old coat." Herded into the camp from various places, "the women and children were free, but they did not know where to go or what to do." Moore and Baldwin began a Sunday school and took particular joy in reading the Bible "to those who had never heard it before." In April 1864, the entire camp was moved down the Mississippi River to Helena, Arkansas. Moore accompanied the freedpeople and worked with Indiana Quakers in an orphan asylum they had established in Helena until the war's end. While in Helena, Moore also began teaching dozens of African-American soldiers, who were stationed there, to read and write.[12]

As the war drew to a close, northern Christians believed they understood more clearly the workings of God's providence in the ordeal. In early 1863, after Lincoln issued the Emancipation Proclamation, the editors of the *Christian Advocate and Journal* assured their readers that it "required little wisdom to see the moving of His hand" and even "less to see the design to be ultimately accomplished." The New York East Annual Conference of the northern Methodist church declared, "As Christians and as patriots we cannot but recognize, in the events of our Civil War, the guiding hand of a Divine Providence." Presbyterian seminary professor Robert L. Stanton offered in 1864 a 562-page tract on *The Church and the Rebellion* in which he proposed "to set forth what we regard as some among the true purposes of God, now in process of being wrought out, by the stupendous events which are occurring in this nation." Stanton condemned southern writers who had deceived themselves "in attempting to declare, beforehand, what He specifically intends in a given event, or in a series or long course of events." Yet, he insisted, "the honest and devout student, aided by God's word and Spirit, may be able to indicate with some approach to truthfulness, some, at least, of the grand results which the providence of God, as illustrated by daily occurring and consecutive events, is designed to reach." While many southern writers believed that God had providentially committed to them the duty to "conserve and perpetuate" human bondage, Stanton interpreted God's providence as tending to the result of "freedom and elevation to the negro race." Whether the rebellion succeeded or not, Stanton maintained, slavery was doomed. "How can any believer in God's providence, which extends to *all* things, — in whose hand are the hearts of all people, — fail to see in these events the inevitable designs of God? How can he fail to read in them the doom of slavery?"[13]

When the war ended and slavery was abolished throughout the Confederacy, northern Christians felt vindicated that God had favored their cause. They were not completely united on the proper attitude toward the defeated South; some were inclined at first to follow a lenient policy toward their southern brethren. However, the shot fired at Ford's Theatre in Washington, D.C., on April 14, 1865, dramatically changed the attitude of northern Christians. Many who earlier had favored conciliation demanded the imposition of harsh justice on the South for Lincoln's assassination; those who had urged a vigorous policy of political and religious reconstruction became even more committed.[14] A few voices continued to counsel moderation, but they were, for the most part, uninvolved in the activities of the northern denominations in the postwar South. Most northern Protestants believed that southerners were chief among sinners because they promoted slavery and secession, and that they had received their just punishment from God in the war. These radical Christians, as Victor B. Howard labels them, were the ones who became missionaries and teachers, passed resolutions condemning slavery and secession, insisted that northern churches had a duty to aid the freedpeople, and provided the financial support for their denominations' missionary efforts in the South. Formulated toward the end of the conflict, the understanding of the war that gave birth to the northern vision of religious reconstruction was articulated by this large group of northern clergy and laity, whom Chester Dunham described as "opposed to slavery, to secession, to the Confederacy, and to easy terms of reconstruction," either political or religious.[15]

The northern populace and the secular press anxiously anticipated pronouncements from the churches of their attitude toward the defeated South and especially toward southern Christians. The *New York Times* observed in the fall of 1865, "the spirit which the Northern churches will manifest toward the Southern is awaited with great interest for its political as well as its religious bearings." On the churches' actions "depends the early restoration of the cordial reunion of the two sections. . . . No political scheme or policy for sectional concord can prosper unless they too 'follow the things that made for peace.'" In contrast, the *Nation* insisted in the summer of 1866, "religious unity will come after the establishment of moral unity, but not sooner." The editors of the *Nation* wished "less pains were taken by the various religious bodies at the North to bring about ecclesiastical reunion with the South." They believed, perhaps rightly, that "all efforts made by the North just now to heal the breach are only likely to make it wider than ever."[16]

Northern secular observers at the time and historians since have considered the attitude of northern denominations uncharitable or even irrational.[17] However, what they fail to understand is that the posture of the northern churches toward their southern counterparts rested firmly on their conception of the providential results of the war. In an era when church discipline was regularly practiced, northern Christians demanded repentance as a condition for renewed fellowship because they believed the outcome of the war was God's mandate for that repentance. The General Assembly of the Old School Presbyterian Church, meeting in May 1865, declared, "the act of rebellion, to support the institution of slavery, was not only a great sin, but wholly unwarranted." The New York *Independent* in the summer of 1865 concluded, "the apostate church is buried beneath a flood of divine wrath; its hideous dogmas shine on its brow like flaming fiends; the whole world stands aghast at its wickedness and ruin." To a Methodist editor, the South was a "God-smitten region."[18]

In 1866 J. S. Hurlburt captured how many northern Christians understood the outcome of the war in his polemical *History of the Rebellion in Bradley County, East Tennessee.* In a chapter entitled "Pretensions of the Rebels to Divine Favor," he wrote, "the most talented and influential, if not the most pious and godly, among the clergy of the South, never allowed themselves to doubt for a moment that the cause of the rebels was a child of special Providence, and consequently, embodying a reformation or revolution in the affairs of the world, which having God for its author and protector must be triumphant in the end." In the wake of Appomattox, Hurlburt asked the troubling question for southerners: if the Confederacy "was plainly depicted in the Providential signs of the times, if it was unmistakably the voice of God as the rebels pretended, and if His hand was so plainly revealed in its inauguration and in its support, even for years, how is it that the rebellion so signally failed?" Hurlburt mocked, "Did the Almighty forsake his own cherished designs, or was he defeated by the mudsills of the North?" He found it "utterly impossible by any fair course of reasoning to reconcile the fact of the sudden and complete failure of the rebellion with the supposition that God was the instigator of it, or that He ever smiled upon the enterprise, or allowed it to exist and progress with any view to its final success." In a final biblical insult, Hurlburt compared southern ecclesiastical leaders with the Old Testament prophets of Baal; they were "false prophets that the Lord did not send."[19]

Northern religious leaders were confident that many southerners awaited only an opportunity to rejoin their respective national denomination, "the old mother church," as the Methodists especially were fond of calling it. Wicked religious and political leaders had led the southern people astray, but God's thundering judgment in the war had revealed their errors to them. Many other southerners had remained loyal but were simply trapped by their geographical location in the midst of the

Confederacy, a contention supported by the experience of East Tennessee Unionists. Thousands of these Baptists, Methodists, and Presbyterians were eager to have loyal ministers, and only needed to be organized to become once again part of the national denominations. In the midst of the war, the *Christian Times and Illinois Baptist* declared, "if ever a people were deceived, the people of the South, those who compose the rank and file of the Southern army, are so." In 1863, the *Western Christian Advocate* insisted, "the people (Southern) are beginning to see that their real oppressors are the Southern leaders of the rebellion. . . . We have always pitied the ignorant masses of the South. They have been deceived." By 1864 the editors of the same publication believed that the return to the Methodist Episcopal Church (MEC) had begun in the South:

> Already the loyal Methodists of the South are earnestly desirous of returning to the bosom of the Methodist Episcopal Church, where they will be supplied with a loyal ministry. The result will be that the Methodist Episcopal Church will absorb the loyal Methodism of the South, and the Methodist Episcopal Church, South, will die with the rebellion, which she, more than all others, helped to inaugurate. . . . Indeed, the process is already rapidly going on.

The early efforts of the New School Presbyterian church also met with some success in the South: "A people whose loyalty could not be crushed turn fondly to our Church and welcome laborers among them from the North."[20]

By 1865, northern Christians were convinced that southern churches were unfit to minister to the spiritual needs of their members. Their clergy had perverted the gospel message by defending slavery and encouraging rebellion. The New England Conference of the MEC dismissed the Methodist Episcopal Church, South (MECS), as contaminated with sin. Because it had been "so completely leagued with detestable sin," its ministers and leading members were "incapacitated for the work of social, civil, and religious regeneration." They had "fostered the most awful crime against man, society, and God," and they had "nurtured the viper of rebellion in the Church and State." Another commentator contended that the Methodist secession of 1844 and the southern secession of 1861 were both founded on slavery: "The mischief thus begun in the Church has reached its culmination in the state, and now the death of the latter foredooms the former. The Siamese twins must go to one grave." Since the southern Methodist church would continue to be "utterly opposed" to the MEC and the national government, northern Methodists "surely cannot give over to them the spiritual culture of the millions of the regenerated South." A Presbyterian editor in Cincinnati felt certain that "the Christianity of the South has proven itself so far inferior and corrupt as to be unworthy of our confidence, and incompetent to the task of thus elevating, purifying, regenerating the masses of those who have lived under its benumbing power." Northern missionaries had much to do: "A purer faith is to be preached. . . . It is indispensable, even to the civil renovation of the South, that a true Gospel should be implanted there." The Baptist *Christian Secretary* believed that the southern clergy were more devoted to the lost cause of the rebellion than were the politicians: "They went into it on principle . . . that it was their duty, in order to save the divine institution of slavery, and they have not yet given up the argument, although divine Providence has abandoned the institution."[21]

Because of their loyalty to the institution of slavery and general corruption through rebellion, southern denominations were also unable to meet the spiritual needs of the freedpeople. Furthermore, those denominations had been only nominally concerned about black men and women when they were slaves and would remain apathetic. The freedpeople would not accept ministers from the southern denominations, regardless of their attitude. Here were millions of souls suddenly released from physical bondage without spiritual guidance. Here was an enormous mission field thrown open to northern Christians.

With this understanding of God's providential message in the war and the shape of America's religious life, the northern churches set about formulating a plan for the religious reconstruction of the southern states. Developing slowly during the last years of the war, the components of the plan were fully articulated in 1865 and 1866. Because slavery had been at the heart of ecclesiastical as well as political secession, northerners thought that no barriers to the establishment of national institutions now existed. "Slavery, the only ground of the division of the Church, being removed, why should we remain divided?" reasoned Daniel Curry of the New York *Christian Advocate and Journal*.[22] Northern Christians generally favored the reunion of Baptists, Methodists, and Presbyterians to form national denominations. However, they were not prepared simply to forget the war and merge with the southern bodies.

Since the southern clergy were unfit as a body to continue to minister, the best manner of effecting reunion would be through the reception into the northern body of individuals and small groups rather than the organic merger of the northern and southern wings of the respective denominations. Only in this manner could the northern churches be certain that those whom they received were properly penitent over the sins of slavery and secession. Each of the northern denominations required southerners who wished to unite with them to pledge their loyalty to the national government and to the antislavery pronouncements of the denomination. This practice enraged most southerners as an improper political condition for church membership. Northern Christians, however, thought these conditions were necessary to avoid future problems over the twin transgressions of the Confederacy. J. M. Pendleton, a southern Unionist refugee from Tennessee, urged the ABHMS to begin evangelistic endeavors in Kentucky and Tennessee with northern workers. Southern missionaries were unacceptable until they would "repent and do works worthy of repentance." Ministers entering the presbyteries of the Old School Presbyterian church were to be asked whether they aided the rebellion and whether they believed that the "system of negro slavery in the South is a Divine institution." If the candidate held either of these "doctrines," he would not be admitted "without renouncing and forsaking these errors." The *Presbyter* outlined a method for readmitting southern Presbyterians to the Old School church. Ministers who had been leaders of secession "should never be permitted to return to our church as teachers or rulers." Others who had supported the Confederacy "upon proper sense of their sins, and upon proper confessions and promises, might be restored." Finally, those who had always remained loyal to the United States government had "claims to be recognized as still in the church." The General Conference of the MEC in 1864 had revised the Book of Discipline to provide for the admission of southerners "provided they give satisfactory assurances to an Annual or Quarterly Conference of their loyalty to the National

Government and hearty approval of the anti-slavery doctrine of our Church." When the bishops of the northern Methodist church met at Erie, Pennsylvania, in June 1865, they extended an invitation to all members and ministers from any branch of Methodism to unite with them "on the basis of our loyal and antislavery Discipline."[23]

Contempt was the prevailing attitude among northern participants in religious reconstruction — toward the southern churches as institutions and toward their leadership. Since they were fervent supporters of the rebellion to preserve slavery, southern religious leaders were hopelessly corrupt and the institutions they controlled had to be proscribed. Secretary J. S. Backus of the ABHMS denounced the Southern Baptist Convention: "[I]f it is politically and morally wrong to support 'the Southern Confederacy,' how can it be religiously right to support 'the Southern Baptist Convention'?" he asked. "Would not the spirit which seeks now to perpetuate the Southern Baptist Convention, were it in its power, reproduce and sustain the Southern Confederacy?" The Methodist *Western Christian Advocate* insisted that there was a powerful argument for "a deliberate and persistent attempt to disintegrate and absorb" the southern Methodist church: *"the argument of loyalty."* The *Christian Advocate and Journal* believed that the northern church had a duty to enter the South independently of the MECS, which had become "hopelessly debauched with proslaveryism and tainted with treason"; doing so would bring the MEC into conflict with the "spurious local Methodism of the country." Both the church and the state in the South were built on the institution of slavery; "as with the State, so with the Church, the removal of slavery necessitates a disintegration and reconstruction." Daniel Curry, editor of the *Christian Advocate and Journal*, prescribed a "policy of earnest and antagonistic aggression," by which the Methodist Episcopal Church could "disintegrate the rival body, and absorb whatever of it shall be found worth preserving."[24]

If the complete disintegration and absorption of the southern churches proved impossible, northern churches still had work to do in the South among the native Unionist population, Federal soldiers stationed in the South, and the thousands of immigrants from the North who were expected to move south in search of economic opportunities. To all these groups, southern "rebel" churches would be unacceptable. "There are true Union men in all parts of the South," declared the *Western Christian Advocate*, "who can never be gathered into the fold of Southern Methodism, and who are awaiting, with anxious prayers and tears, the advent of the 'old Church.' It is our business to carry the Gospel, the sacraments, and all Church privileges, to these noble patriots and sterling Methodists." The *Christian Advocate and Journal* likewise saw an important field in the South among whites: "There can be no doubt that very many Northern people — many of them soldiers of the Union army, with their families — will become permanent residents of the South. . . . There will also be very many genuine Union men of the South whose abhorrence of the rebellion will lead them to reject the religious services of a set of men by whom they have been so fearfully misled."[25]

As inviting as were the opportunities to minister to southern whites, the potential of millions of converts among the freedpeople was far more appealing. God had brought a field of labor to the very door of zealous northern missionaries. Southern blacks would welcome northern missionaries carrying the true gospel to them for the first time. They had to be educated so that they could read the Bible for themselves and become productive citizens of the reunited nation. As early as 1862, the ABHMS had decided to take "immediate steps to supply with Christian instruction" the freedpeople in the District of Columbia and in other areas controlled by Federal forces and "to inaugurate a system of operations for carrying the Gospel alike to free and bond through the whole southern section of our country, so fast and so far as the progress of our arms, and the restoration of order and law shall open the way." By April 1865, the society had 120 missionaries, teachers, and assistants in the South.[26] Bishop Davis W. Clark of the MEC wrote to his wife from Nashville in early 1866: "it seems that God has committed this work especially to the Church, and calls her to do it *now*. The fields are 'black' for the harvest; but their very amplitude, and the greatness of the harvest, make me stagger as I look at the work to be done." The question of who should reap those fields "black unto harvest" became the occasion of intense denominational competition.[27]

Northern Christians were initially encouraged in their views of religious reconstruction by a small group of southern ministers and laypeople who accepted the northern understanding of God's design in the outcome of the war. Never a large portion of the southern religious population, these "religious scalawags" played a role in the early stages of religious reconstruction far out of proportion to their actual numbers.[28] Generally southern Unionists and uncommitted Confederates, their ranks did include a number of staunch rebels who believed that God had smitten the South because of its sins.[29] Their public affirmations of the northern understanding of the war and their vision of religious reconstruction convinced northern religious leaders that a strict policy toward their southern counterparts would be effective. Many more southerners, they reasoned, would follow these initial converts into the ranks of the northern denominations by admitting that slavery and political and ecclesiastical secession were sins. On the other hand, uneasy southern religious leaders feared that these "traitors" might actually be the vanguard of a more general defection from their disorganized ranks.

The first signs of dissent during the war came from East Tennessee, a stronghold of Unionist political sentiment. In October 1862 the Holston Conference of the MECS met in Athens, Tennessee, under the leadership of Bishop John Early. Twelve preachers were charged with disloyalty to the Confederacy, and their cases occupied much of the meeting's business. Some of the defendents satisfied the conference by making declarations of loyalty to the Confederate government; the conference dismissed two and suspended another for one year. At the next annual meeting in 1863, eleven more ministers were charged with disloyalty, and four were expelled; again in October 1864, the Holston Conference expelled three members from a list of twelve defendants, this time for ecclesiastical rather than political disloyalty. These three men, the convention charged, had met at Knoxville with others for the purpose of joining the Methodist Episcopal Church.[30]

Given this treatment at the hands of their Confederate brethren, Unionist Methodists in eastern Tennessee called for the organization of a rival Holston Conference. In May 1864 several Tennessee Methodists issued a call through the *Knoxville Whig and Rebel Ventilator* for Methodists "who are loyal to the government of the United States" to attend a convention in July. Meeting in the Protestant Episcopal Church in Knoxville, a convention of fifty-five delegates passed resolutions denouncing secession and the southern Methodist church and calling for the establishment of a loyal Holston Conference united with the MEC. Prominent among the leaders of the convention was William G. "Parson" Brownlow, soon to be governor of Tennessee. In a recent visit to the North, Brownlow had met with northern Methodist bishops Matthew Simpson and Davis W. Clark to discuss northern Methodist prospects in Tennessee. The convention estimated that sixty ordained ministers and another sixty-five unordained were ready to reestablish the MEC in East Tennessee.[31]

By June 1865 when Bishop Clark was able to reach East Tennessee to organize the Holston Conference officially, over five thousand Methodists were ready to join the new organization. Bishop Clark met in Athens, Tennessee, with six ministers imported from northern conferences and forty preachers from East Tennessee. With the area divided fairly evenly between Unionists and Confederates, religious reconstruction in eastern Tennessee became a bitter rivalry that sometimes erupted into violence. Preachers were driven from towns by mobs from the opposing church, and litigation over church property continued for years. Northern Methodists distant from the local conflict, however, were greatly encouraged by the rapid acquisition of thousands of members. Surely thousands more across the South wanted to return to the "old mother Church" and only needed to be organized. Thomas H. Pearne, a Methodist missionary in the South, wrote to the *Christian Advocate and Journal* supporting the plan of the General Conference for receiving members. Through this proposal, Pearne argued, forty-seven ministers and 6,500 members from the southern church had already been admitted in Tennessee, Georgia, and North Carolina. When "Methodism again covers all the country, North and South," he wrote, "teaching everywhere a pure, unemasculated Gospel, enforcing alike on all a wholesome discipline, both as to loyalty and liberty, the future unity and integrity of the nation, as well as its early, thorough evangelization, will have a guarantee of incalculable value and strength."[32]

In September 1865 northern Methodists received further encouragement from a group of Kentucky ministers. When the Kentucky Conference of the MECS met for the first time after the end of the war, their Committee on the State of the Church submitted both a majority and a minority report. The majority report favored reunion with the MEC. The conference, however, adopted the minority report, which endorsed the action of the southern Methodist bishops in Columbus, Georgia, who had called for the maintenance of a separate southern organization. Eighteen ministers immediately withdrew from the Kentucky Conference, and the next day fifteen of them were admitted to the MEC on the basis of their declarations against slavery and secession as set forth in the Methodist Discipline. Northern Methodists hailed them as "martyrs for the sake of our glorious Union," who "in the interest of liberty and Union . . . have sacrificed all things."[33]

Several months later, presiding elder Jedidiah Foster followed their lead and transferred to the northern church. In an article in the *Western Christian Advocate* he explained to his fellow southern Methodists why he had made this decision. First and foremost, he reasoned, the cause of separation between the two branches of Methodism was dead. For whatever reason God had permitted the establishment of slavery, he "has certainly taken it away in his wrath." To continue agitating the issue of slavery would be "wicked" and "heedless of the voice of God." Second, because the division of the Methodist church had contributed to the division of the nation, the southern church had a duty to undo "the evil which she has been instrumental in bringing upon the country" by reuniting with the northern church. Third, a reunited church would wield a greater moral influence for the evangelization of the world, unhampered by sectional bickerings. Finally, he could not have held these sentiments in the southern church "without being regarded as a disturber of the peace of the Church." The "leading men of the Southern Church" as well as "all their church papers" were opposed to any talk of returning to the MEC and "laboring not to conciliate, but to exasperate and fill the mind with sectional hate." Again the northern Methodists rejoiced at receiving repentant southern Methodists into their ranks.[34]

John H. Caldwell's actions in central Georgia also encouraged northern Methodists in their plans. The Holston and Kentucky transfers buoyed the spirits of northern Methodists, yet these areas had been noted for Unionist sentiment throughout the war. Georgia, on the other hand, had been deeply involved in both ecclesiastical and political secession and rebellion. The sympathies Caldwell expressed for the work of the Methodist Episcopal Church in Georgia were truly remarkable and vindicated those who argued that many people throughout the South still longed for a reunion with the "mother church" and the national government.

Throughout the war Caldwell had been a vocal supporter of the Confederacy; in December 1862, April 1864, and January 1865 he had publicly proclaimed his belief "in the ultimate success of our cause under the blessing of God."[35] On June 4, 1865, however, he reflected on the defeat of the Confederacy and came to a radically new understanding of the providential meaning of the war. He determined that slavery "more than anything else, caused that war" and its destruction was "one of the great and most beneficent consequences." On the next two Sundays, Caldwell preached two sermons on the abuses of slavery to his congregation in Newnan, Georgia. He insisted that the institution of slavery demanded a corresponding moral responsibility: "The neglect or performance of that obligation determines the moral character of slavery." The practice therefore determined the moral worth of the institution; "judged by this severe test, I fear our institution as we have held it in practice, is wrong." If "our practice had been conformed to the law of God, He would not have suffered the institution to be overthrown." In his second sermon he explored how slavery had corrupted the Methodist church. The war had disclosed to southern Christians one "great paramount fact": "we have sinned, and God has smitten us." Admitting that he had believed that God favored the Confederacy, he concluded that "we were all mistaken." Upon reflection, he had accepted the "only solution of the great providential problem of the war — *God has destroyed slavery because of our sins in connection with it as a system!*"[36]

Caldwell's congregation immediately appealed to the presiding elder to remove him from the Newnan pulpit; when the presiding elder did so, Caldwell appealed to Bishop George Foster Pierce. Because of the irregularity of the mails, Pierce was unable to respond, and Caldwell appealed to Major General George H. Thomas, the Union military commander in charge of Georgia, Alabama, Mississippi, and Tennessee. In a remarkable order issued in September 1865, Thomas reinstated Caldwell to the pulpit of the Newnan church and ordered the military authorities in the area to protect him. In November 1865, after a tour of the northern states during which he met several prominent political, military, and religious leaders, Caldwell went to the meeting of the Georgia Annual Conference. Although his fellow ministers found nothing worthy of censure in his conduct, they did condemn the content of his sermons. On the last day of the conference, Caldwell withdrew from the Georgia Annual Conference and the MECS. Two months later he joined the MEC and began to lay the foundations for the reestablishment of that church in Georgia. Several more southern Methodist ministers soon followed him, and he quickly became the leader of the Methodist religious scalawags in Georgia.[37]

In stark contrast to the reception of Caldwell's sermons in the South, the northern Methodist press hailed him as "a heroic example." The editors of the *Christian Advocate and Journal* believed Caldwell's stand was "a significant indication" of the sentiments of southern Methodists generally: "We cannot doubt that there are many thoughtful ministers of Christ in the South of like mind; let them show like courage. . . . The safety of religion in the South depends to a great extent upon the immediate conduct of its pastors. God's controversy with them is not yet concluded; but he 'waits to be gracious.'" The *Methodist Quarterly Review* rejoiced in the belief that "such bold antislavery truth . . . uttered in Central Georgia" was "part of a revolution which will never go back." The writer hoped that the sermons were "the beginning of a moral revolution of feeling which will result in the full conversion of our Southern brethren to the Gospel of truth and freedom."[38] When a southern-born minister in the heart of the South declared that the practice of slavery had been wrong and that he wanted to return to the MEC, northern Methodists were certain that he was only the first of many who would leave the southern Church. Caldwell's actions confirmed their understanding of the providential meaning of the war as God's judgment upon the South for the sins of slavery and secession, and helped shaped their attitudes toward southern Methodists who did not share Caldwell's convictions.

Old School northern Presbyterians also welcomed southern religious scalawags into their ranks. In North Carolina, for example, eight southern Presbyterian ministers in three separate areas of the state broke with the southern Presbyterian church and organized churches and presbyteries that united with the northern Presbyterian denomination. Like their Methodist counterparts in Georgia, North Carolina's Presbyterian religious scalawags worked mostly among the freedpeople and were ostracized by their former friends. In his study of these religious scalawags, Steven E. Brooks argues: "None of these groups, perhaps would have seriously threatened the Southern Church during 'normal' times, but combined with Yankee rule and Northern clerical invasion, their threat from within the Church itself evoked an intense reaction from their former colleagues." By 1867 these ministers had gathered over eight hundred members into the northern Presbyterian fold.[39]

Thaddeus W. McRae, the Presbyterian minister who had observed the dramatic influence of Benjamin Morgan Palmer's 1860 Thanksgiving sermon on his congregation in Baton Rouge, Louisiana, began organizing the Presbyterian Church in the United States of America (PCUSA) in Texas in 1866. After Louisiana seceded, he had left the state and spent the war years on the coast of Texas and in New Orleans after it was occupied by Federal troops. When the war ended, he returned to Texas to find that he had been discharged from the southern Presbytery of Western Texas; he would be allowed to return if he repented of his "political conduct" in being a Unionist during the war. In early 1866 he became pastor of the First Presbyterian Church in Austin. A majority of the congregation had been Unionists during the war, and soon after McRae arrived they left the southern Presbyterian church and joined the northern Old School Presbyterian church. In 1868, the Austin church, together with churches in Galveston and Georgetown, organized the Presbytery of Austin. The southern papers denounced McRae as "the Beecher of Texas," but his activities encouraged northern Presbyterians to hope that other southerners would follow his lead.[40]

In November 1865, Thomas L. Janeway, secretary of the Board of Domestic Missions, declared that there were many Presbyterians in the South who desired to unite with the old PCUSA. The northern church could not expect to occupy the South all at once, but "in the meanwhile, ministers South, loyal and true through all the storm of passion and of crime, will receive aid. The number of such increases. Every week brings letters from such asking what we can do and in what way the application is to be made." Janeway was committed to helping these ministers; "we do not intend to give up the Southern States." The Board of Domestic Missions reported to the 1866 General Assembly that it had commissioned thirteen loyal men in six southern states: "We have not thought it expedient, in the unsettled condition of things there, to send Northern men. We have found loyal men there, and the number is not so small." Yet the Board admitted that to the extent that southern Presbyterian leaders remained in control, "the South is a sealed land to us."[41]

The New School Presbyterian church also found religious scalawags among the ruins of its southern counterpart, the United Synod of the South. The majority of the New School Presbyterians in the South voted in August 1864 to unite with the Presbyterian Church in the Confederate States of America, the southern Old School organization. In September 1864, representatives of the Union and Kingston presbyteries in East Tennessee rejected union with the southern Old School body and voted instead to rejoin the northern New School General Assembly, which they had left in 1857. Meeting again in April 1865, the members of Union Presbytery declared that the war was not only "a crime against civil government: it is a crime against God, for it is rebellion against his authority." In the fall 1865 meeting, they insisted that "all those who profess [C]hristianity and have aided or abetted in the late rebellion should confess their wrong before the proper church judicatory." The presbytery proceeded to remove from its roll seven ministers "till they give evidence of repentance for complicity in rebellion." Another minister who had supported the Confederacy confessed before the body "that events have convinced him that rebellion was wrong, and that so far [as] he has sympathized with it he has been in the wrong." Accepting this confession, the presbytery recognized him as a member. The New School General Assembly of 1865 reconstructed Holston Presbytery, which — together with the Union and Kingston presbyteries — formed the reconstructed Synod of Tennessee. The General Assembly carefully instructed the three Tennessee presbyteries not to recognize or admit "any minister known to be disloyal to the Government of the United States."[42]

These religious scalawags adopted an interpretation of the Civil War that had much in common with the northern view. The abuses practiced under the institution of slavery, such as disregard for the marriage relationship and the ban on slave literacy, had forced black southerners into sinful relationships and inhibited their religious development. While few believed that slavery as an institution was morally evil, they did argue that the practice of slavery in the South had been wrong and were relieved to see it removed by the hand of God acting through the war. Corollary to this argument was the insistence that the southern Churches were unfit to care for the religious needs of the freedpeople. Whatever their role among southern whites, the northern denominations had a providential responsibility to minister to the newly freed slaves, to whom their southern counterparts were unable and often unwilling to minister.

Religious scalawags also declared secession in both church and state to be sinful, and they generally believed that a small group of leaders had foisted these movements on a reluctant southern public. Consequently, many of their fellow southerners earnestly desired reunion with the northern denominations, so that national churches could be reestablished and carry out their divine mission to evangelize America and the world. To effect this union, they hoped for a simple union of the northern and southern branches of their respective bodies. On this issue they differed with northern leaders, who insisted on individual repentance and the return of small groups to the denominational fold; and as the process of religious reconstruction proceeded, these southern people in northern churches became far less optimistic about any prospects for reunion as the southern denominations stiffened and revived.

When northern Christians pondered the purposes of the Almighty in the years of strife through which they had just passed, the Civil War became a parable through which they might better understand themselves and their role in the providential unfolding of history. The conclusions they reached had profound implications for the process of religious reconstruction in the South. While the whole nation had clearly been chastened and purified in the fiery crucible of civil warfare, God had reserved His harshest judgment for the haughty Southrons who defiantly championed rebellion and human bondage. Many southerners, however, surely had simply been misled into the Confederacy by wealthy slaveholders and religious leaders. By the end of the war, they must have realized their mistake and now anxiously awaited an opportunity to rejoin the national churches that had been barred from the South by the "slave power." The actions and reports of religious scalawags during the closing months of the war and the first months after Appomattox provided ample evidence to northern denominations that many southerners had been cut off from the churches of their choice by the war. Southern denominations were eminently unfit for the task of spiritual revitalization necessary because they were both financially and morally bankrupt. Providence had provided northern evangelicals with an unparalleled opportunity to refashion the spiritual life of the South.

Since slavery, the cause of disunion in church and state, was effectively removed from the nation's life by the Emancipation Proclamation, Federal forces, and the Thirteenth Amendment, northern Christians expected ecclesiastical reunion to follow political reunion. Northern missionaries and southern religious scalawags would preach the pure Gospel in the South; gradually the empty shells of the southern denominations would disintegrate, and the faithful left within them would return to the "national" denominations. Even if the process of absorption took years to complete, many whites in the South — Unionists, northern settlers, European immigrants — would require the services of loyal, national churches because they would never enter a southern, proslavery church. Of course, the freedpeople as well would no longer remain in the churches of their masters, and they needed the resources and the mature spiritual guidance that only northern Christians could provide. When they began their program, however, northern Christians quickly learned that most religious southerners, both black and white, had different ideas about what constituted religious reconstruction.

4

God's Deliverance

The Freedpeople's Understanding of the Civil War

And it shall come to pass, that whosoever shall call on the name of the LORD shall be delivered: for in mount Zion and in Jerusalem shall be deliverance, as the LORD hath said, and in the remnant whom the LORD shall call.

Joel 2:32

Black Christians in Civil War America shared with their white brethren a strong belief in God's providential intervention in human affairs. For northern and southern black evangelicals, the central fact of the war was the deliverance of four million black men, women, and children from the bonds of slavery. The central actor in this drama was God. The results of the war demonstrated His care for His children in bondage and His condemnation of slavery and its beneficiaries. The northern people and northern armies were simply instruments in God's hands to carry out His judgment. As such, however, northerners clearly demonstrated their greater righteousness in comparison to southerners.[1]

Slaves and freedpeople based their vision for the religious reconstruction of the South on this understanding of the theological significance of the war and "their own distinctive appropriation of Christianity," as Katharine L. Dvorak aptly describes it.[2] Greater autonomy in their religious lives was essential to this vision. For some this autonomy meant separate congregations within white-controlled denominations with white or black preachers. For many it meant complete separation from the churches of their masters and the establishment of churches with black pastors and black bishops or other denominational leaders. This process often occurred in spite of the protests of southern white religious leaders, who sincerely doubted the wisdom of independent black religious organizations and just as sincerely lamented their own loss of control over black religious life. The freedpeople accepted northern missionaries for the valuable financial, educational, and organizational help they could offer but insisted that northerners too would not control their religious lives.[3] Determined to form their own identities through their religion, ex-slaves set about reconstructing their religious world as soon as the arrival of Federal troops or the defeat of the Confederacy assured them of their political freedom. Despite their lack of financial resources, most freedpeople left the antebellum biracial churches and formed church organizations of their own to set themselves apart from the religion of their masters. Then began the laborious process of acquiring a meeting place, selecting church officials, establishing denominational connections, and providing for the education of black teachers and preachers. Only then, they believed, could black Christianity in America reach its fullest expression.

The appropriation of evangelical Protestantism by African Americans began in the eighteenth century, but the process accelerated rapidly in the nineteenth century. Many masters, themselves imbued with the spirit of evangelicalism, took their slaves to church with them or allowed them to go. Some who owned many slaves permitted missionaries to preach to their slaves, and some even provided plantation chapels. A few slaves attended semi-independent black churches in the cities and towns of the South, which often had black preachers. Others worshiped secretly in the slave community, led by slave preachers and exhorters from their midst. Whatever the circumstances of their organized worship, many slaves eagerly adopted Christianity and drew from it both comfort and strength. By emphasizing different aspects of the Christian message than their white brethren did and by retaining some elements of African religious systems, slaves developed a new syncretic African-American faith.[4]

Slaves found within Christianity an indictment of the system under which they lived, a validation of their personal worth, and the promise of eventual liberation. Slavery violated God's will because it degraded part of his creation. John Hunter, a fugitive from slavery in Maryland, reported that he had "heard poor ignorant slaves, that did not know A from B, say that they did not believe the Lord ever intended they should be slaves, and that they did not see how it should be so." Francis Henderson drew from the sermons he heard in a Methodist church the conclusion that "God had made all men free and equal, and that I ought not to be a slave." Although Christianity proclaimed that it was the duty of slaves to be obedient to their masters, it also declared that masters had certain obligations toward their slaves, an injunction that slaves quickly appropriated for their benefit.[5]

Slaves were attracted by the message that in God's eyes all men are equal. Even the lowliest in social position are valuable to God, and eventually "the last shall be first, and the first last." Faithful slaves and cruel masters will both receive their just rewards in heaven, even if not on earth. Such doctrines gave slave converts a hope of future vindication and a sense of self-worth in the midst of the dehumanizing institution of slavery. Furthermore, since their African culture lacked a sacred/secular dichotomy, religion permeated the lives of blacks more completely than it did the lives of most whites.

Blacks identified themselves closely with the Old Testament Israelites, who, like them had been enslaved by cruel masters. Although God's children had suffered in bondage for many years, He had intervened and miraculously liberated them.

Moses represented for them deliverance as a people from bondage, while Jesus, who had suffered as they did, would redeem them individually from their personal sufferings by interceding with God. Just as God had delivered the suffering Hebrews from the hands of the Egyptians, so He would deliver His black children from their bondage, although in a manner as inscrutable in His providence as the reasons for their bondage.[6] As the number of free blacks grew and especially as the abolitionist movement gained momentum in the North, W. E. B. DuBois later observed, the "'Coming of the Lord' swept this side of Death, and came to be a thing hoped for in this day." For slaves during the late antebellum period and especially during the war itself, the dream of abolition was an integral part of their religion.[7]

In the biracial churches, slaves found whites listening to them as they spoke of their conversion experiences and enjoyed a greater degree of equality with whites than anywhere else in southern society. Blacks frequently served as elders, deacons, and exhorters; some also ministered as preachers. Slaves especially enjoyed having black ministers preach to them. One ex-slave recalled, "Mostly we had white preachers, but when we had a black preacher, that was heaven." On the eve of the Civil War, at least 350,000 slaves were members of southern Baptist, Methodist, and Presbyterian churches. Hundreds of thousands more participated in southern churches without official membership or worshiped in their own secret gatherings as part of the "invisible institution" of religious life in the slave community.[8]

Joel Williamson argues that during Reconstruction the "most distinctive trait of the black man's religion was its emulation of the white ideal. Yet, there were differences which imparted to the Negro churches a flavor not generally shared by their white neighbors." Peter Kolchin adds, "in most ways the black churches performed very much the same functions that the white ones did, and black religion served the same purposes as did white religion." These interpretations raise the issue of African survivals and the distinctiveness of African-American religion, especially as it emerged after the Civil War. Scholars such as Albert J. Raboteau, Lawrence W. Levine, Sterling Stuckey, and John W. Blassingame have emphasized the persistence of African religious beliefs and practices among southern blacks in the antebellum period and beyond. While some slaves did attend biracial churches, these scholars argue, their primary religious experiences occurred either in a secret "world apart" or cleverly mixed with outward displays of Christianity. In contrast, John B. Boles insists that the "overwhelming majority" of slaves practiced their religion within biracial churches, rather than in the "invisible" religious gatherings of the slave quarters.[9]

William E. Montgomery attempts to resolve this debate by arguing that two kinds of churches evolved among African Americans. The first was formally organized and denominational, while the other was a folk church, "the syncretistic product of a dynamic African-American culture." The strength of the first lay among free blacks in the North and the South; the second consisted of the churches of southern slaves. Emancipation and the bond of race brought the two churches together organizationally after the Civil War with the possibility that the folk churches would be "structurally and doctrinally integrated" into the institutional churches. However, Montgomery argues, differences of class, experience, and culture continued to divide blacks in the postwar South.[10]

Williamson and Kolchin underestimate the differences between black and white churches; they differed in more than just "flavor." Important distinctions existed in preaching and worship styles, views of the social implications of Christianity, the providential meaning of the Civil War, and the proper course for the religious reconstruction of the South. Furthermore, these divergences were more important than the class distinctions within black Christianity that Montgomery highlights. However, the actions of many blacks in the first years of freedom also indicate that their commitment to the institutions and theology of evangelical Protestantism was stronger than many scholars suggest. The organization, ritual, and theology of black churches were in many cases patterned after those of white churches of the same denomination in the area. Newly freed blacks often painstakingly recreated structures and practices parallel to those of their white neighbors, even to the point of denominational bickering. As Boles notes, "perhaps in no other aspect of black cultural life had the values and practices of whites so deeply penetrated as in religious services."[11]

When the southern states seceded and civil warfare erupted, black Christians expectantly awaited their promised deliverance. Having yearned for freedom for their entire lives, slave Christians felt that God had heard their petitions and was coming to their aid and vindication. During the war a slave in Franklin County, Mississippi, went secretly into the woods to pray, but he prayed so loudly that he was discovered and punished. Undaunted, he continued to pray. Decades later, his wife, Candus Richardson, told an interviewer that at one point his master beat him so unmercifully for praying that "his shirt was as red from blood stain 'as if you'd paint it with a brush.'" "I prayed too," she said, "but I always prayed to myself." She proudly declared that it was her husband's prayers and "a whole lot of other slaves' that cause you young folks to be free today." Clayborn Gantling, another ex-slave, reported that he had "heard slaves morning and night pray for deliverance. Some of them would stand up in de fields or bend over cotton and corn and pray out loud for God to help 'em and in time you see, He did." Gantling, like many other slaves, knew the source of their deliverance: "I tell you chile, it was pitiful, but God did not let it last always."[12]

For southern black Christians in 1860, God was real. They knew Him and knew that He cared for them. They also discerned that those who held them in bondage had violated God's will. God would not allow this sin to continue either perpetually or unpunished. Although they were uncertain how or when, black Christians were confident that God would deliver them, and on January 1, 1863, He did. Fundamental to their understanding of the Civil War, as they looked back on it, was the belief that God had divinely intervened in human history to emancipate them. Furthermore, the Civil War itself had been primarily neither a chastisement nor a judgment of the South (though it was certainly the latter), but rather a providential vehicle for the liberation of four million black men, women, and children. The social revolutionary act of emancipation revealed the spiritual significance and purpose of the war. God had heard their prayers; God had been faithful to His children. Henry Blake, a former slave in Alabama, remembered that "aftuh Surrender, Niggers dey sung, dey prayed, dey preached, yassuh." An old slave preacher named Jesse Wallace "'clared dat God loved his folks en sent his angels down tuh set his folks free en yuh shoulder seen de shoutin."[13]

God had also judged white southerners for their sins. Like northern evangelicals, black Christians believed that God had poured out His judgment on the South for the sins of slavery and secession. Savilla Burrell, an ex-slave from South Carolina, related a visit to her old master years after the war: "I went to see him in his last days and I set by him and kept de flies off while dere. I see the lines of sorrow had plowed on dat old face and I 'membered he'd been a captain on hoss back in dat war. It come into my 'membrance de song of Moses: 'de Lord had triumphed glorily and de hoss and his rider have been throwed into de sea.'" The scriptural reference is to Exodus 15:1, which relates the Israelites' celebration of their deliverance from the pursuing Egyptian army that had perished in the Red Sea. Just as the Egyptians had been punished for their enslavement of the Jews, so southerners had been judged for their mistreatment of black slaves.[14]

African Methodist Episcopal (AME) minister Henry McNeal Turner returned to the South with the invading Union Army. Like many other northern blacks, he was disappointed by Lincoln's halting movement toward emancipation as a war aim, but after Lincoln's preliminary emancipation proclamation in September 1862, Turner wholeheartedly supported him and the northern war effort. From his position as pastor of Israel AME Church in Washington, D.C., Turner actively recruited black troops in the summer of 1863, and in November he received a commission as chaplain for the First United States Colored Troops. In this post, he accompanied the regiment into Virginia and North Carolina in 1864 and 1865. Reflecting the common African-American understanding of the war, he told his congregation in August 1863, "God will surely speak peace when His work, which this affliction is designed to produce, is accomplished. . . . Our race that has been afflicted and downtrodden shall then stand still and see the salvation of the Lord."[15]

Bishop Daniel Payne of the AME Church returned to his native state of South Carolina in May 1865. In 1835 the South Carolina legislature had outlawed schools like the one he had conducted for black children in Charleston. A free black, he had fled the state and settled in Philadelphia. There he joined the AME Church and was ordained a bishop in 1852. As he passed through Charleston once again in 1865, Payne reflected on the religious significance of the war. The devastation that surrounded him, "the burned, ruined walls of the Circular and Cumberland Churches," all demonstrated to him "the devastating hand of war, and the hot indignation of that God who, when he stretches out his arm against the oppressor, never draws it back till every fetter is broken and every slave is free." Accompanying Payne was Richard H. Cain, a minister of the AME Church who had been born in Virginia and taken to the North by his parents. As he surveyed the ruins of war-torn Charleston, he declared that the city had become "a monument of God's indignation and an evidence of His righteous judgments."[16]

The North held an important place in blacks' understanding of the providential significance of the war, since they believed that God had chosen northern armies, northern people, and northern Christians as His instruments. A former slave in Arkansas, O. W. Green, recalled: "When the war was over de people jus' shouted for joy. De men and women jus' shouted for joy. 'Twas only because of de prayers of de cullud people, dey was freed, and de Lawd worked through Lincoln." A freedwoman emerging from the water in a baptismal service shouted: "Freed from slavery, freed from sin. Bless God and General Grant." Several South Carolina blacks told missionary Austa M. French of their prayers for the North. One ex-slave told her, "I pray dat God bless you, and gib you success! Massah angry, but mus' pray for de comin' ob de Lord, an' his people." Another said, "I knew God would bless you, an' give victory, I feel it when I pray. . . . I knew God would bless de North."[17]

Thomas L. Johnson recalled that in Richmond, blacks who could read "believed that the eleventh chapter of the Book of Daniel referred directly to the war," and that "we often met together and read this chapter in our own way." Although many were perplexed by verse 5, which told of the great strength of the king of the south, "verses 13–15 would be much dwelt upon," for they spoke of the ultimate triumph of the north:

> For the king of the north shall return, and shall set forth a multitude greater than the former, and shall certainly come after certain years with a great army and with much riches.
> And in those times there shall many stand up against the king of the south: also the robbers of thy people shall exalt themselves to establish the vision; but they shall fall.
> So the king of the north shall come, and cast up a mount, and take the most fenced cities: and the arms of the south shall not withstand, neither his chosen people, neither shall there be any strength to withstand.

As Johnson later reflected, he and others "eagerly grasped at any statements which our anxiety, hope, and prayer concerning liberty led us to search for, and which might indicate the desirable ending of the great War." God would surely bless northern armies against the wicked South, they reasoned.[18] As the war drew to a close, slaves, freedpeople, and free blacks viewed the northern armies as liberating agents of God. Clearly, racist attitudes permeated northern society, and many individual northerners were deeply racist. However, most freedpeople concluded that, given the choice between northern and southern whites, northerners were the more genuinely interested in their political, social, and spiritual interests. The results of the war even seemed to be God's validation of this opinion.[19]

As Johnson's reminiscences suggest, southern blacks struggled to understand the providential meaning of this great conflict. Carter G. Woodson captured only part of the attitude of African-American Christians when he wrote in his *History of the Negro Church*, "God was moving in a mysterious way to perform wonders which in the near future would make all things plain. Stand still, therefore, and see the salvation of the Lord."[20] Although southern black Christians were willing to wait patiently for the Lord's deliverance, they did not stand passively still. Instead, they worked to hasten "the day of the Lord" and began slowly to fashion a new religious life for themselves.

The primary action of many black Christians during the latter half of the war was to leave the biracial churches of antebellum times as an exercise of personal freedom and as an expression of religious independence. For some this action took on a symbolic importance similar to that of leaving their place of bondage. The exodus would not reach its peak until several years after the war, but the vanguard left the churches of their masters in 1863, 1864, and 1865. This movement was most obvious in those areas disrupted by fighting or under the control of Federal forces. In 1864 the Rappahannock Baptist Association in Virginia reported that many of its slave members "have been excommunicated from the churches, and others will be, for joining our enemies, and in some instances entire congregations have been broken up." Soon after Union troops occupied New Orleans in April 1862, blacks in that city began to organize new churches.[21]

Although northern black and white missionaries followed Federal troops into the South to organize churches, they often found black churches or the black members of biracial churches already organized. When Bishop Daniel A. Payne traveled to Nashville, Tennessee, in December 1863, he found a committee waiting for him who represented sixty-three blacks. He immediately organized them into "St. John's Church" and accepted them into the AME Church. When James W. Hood, a missionary of the African Methodist Episcopal Zion (AMEZ) Church, arrived in New Bern, North Carolina, in January 1864, he found four hundred black former members of the Methodist Episcopal Church, South (MECS), ready to join one of the African Methodist congregations. Although a missionary of the Methodist Episcopal Church (MEC) had been ministering to them for a year, they joined the AMEZ Church.[22]

In Savannah and Augusta, Georgia, several black churches with large congregations had existed since before the war. Augusta had six black churches — two Methodist, three Baptist, and one Presbyterian; at least four had black pastors. Throughout the state, there were twenty-eight semi-independent black Baptist churches. N. I. Houston, the pastor of the Third African Baptist Church of Savannah, greeted AME missionary James Lynch when he arrived in the city shortly after Union troops occupied the city in December 1864. Deserted by their regular white pastor from the MECS, the black Methodists of Andrew Chapel in Savannah were being kept together by local black leaders William Bentley, C. L. Bradwell, and William Gaines. When Lynch arrived in the city, he proposed to them that they join the AME Church and made secret arrangements with Bradwell "to take out the church." The proposal was "thoughtfully considered" and "after mature deliberation was accepted." When the Quarterly Conference of the MECS in Savannah met on July 22, 1865, no representative of Andrew Chapel was present, and the minutes noted, "it is said that it has withdrawn from our connections and attached to the African Methodist Church."[23]

Often these black churches were held together or newly organized by slave preachers and exhorters. In the spring of 1865, the Reverend Morris Henderson, a recently freed slave preacher, led the black portion of the congregation out of the First Baptist Church in Memphis to form their own church. Another slave preacher, John Jasper, established the Sixth Mount Zion Church in Richmond. Black Methodist congregations in Norfolk and Portsmouth, Virginia, and a black Baptist congregation at Hilton Head, South Carolina, all had had black pastors before missionaries arrived, and some black pastors had served their churches before the war. White southern evangelicals often looked on black slave preachers with suspicion. Confederate soldier Morgan Callaway wrote to his wife, Leila, in September 1863 about one of their slaves: "I told you in the first letter I wrote you about Lawrence, that he cost me a great deal of money. . . . He is not a very bad negro, but like all negroes who go to the Army he is considerably spoiled. He is a moral negro. I mean he does not curse nor get drunk, but he has no business preaching."[24]

In other areas blacks did not have structured congregations or preachers. Some had simply withdrawn from the churches of their masters and were uncertain how to proceed. Others had left the homes of their masters in search of lost relatives or simply as an exercise of their freedom. The efforts of northern missionaries in Union-occupied areas were vital to the religious organization of these ex-slaves, and all the northern evangelical denominations enjoyed at least some success among the freed-people during the war. The wartime exodus, however, provided only a hint of what was to follow.

A minority of southern black Christians rejected the appeals of northern black and white missionaries and remained within the southern biracial churches. Lucius H. Holsey exemplified this conservative outlook based on strong, paternalistic inter-racial relationships. A favored house slave on a plantation in Hancock County, Georgia, during the war Holsey married in 1862 another young house slave, Harriett A. Turner, who had been owned by Bishop George Foster Pierce of the MECS. Pierce married the young slave couple in his own home and took a strong interest in the young Holsey, whom he tutored in theology immediately after the war. Licensed to preach by Bishop Pierce in February 1867, Holsey continued to minister to the freedpeople in Hancock County.[25]

Holsey's decision to remain in the MECS reflected both genuine gratitude and stubborn pragmatism. He praised southern Methodists for sharing the Gospel with black slaves through their plantation missions and biracial churches. He later wrote of slavery: "I have no complaint against American slavery. It was a blessing in dis-guise to me and to many. It has made the negro race what it could not have been in its native land." Holsey also understood that white southern trustees held the titles to all the church buildings used by black Methodists in the antebellum era. From childhood, Holsey had "always been impressed and so understood . . . that no matter what might take place in the rise or fall of American civilization; and no matter what social or political changes or upheavals might appear, the white man of the South would be on the top." Yet even in these early years as a minister in Hancock County, Holsey looked forward to a separate organization for black Methodists: "There [Sparta, Georgia] I built the first church looking to the organization of our separate and distinct ecclesiasticism."[26]

Unlike Holsey and others who remained in the southern biracial churches, most southern black evangelicals welcomed northern black and white missionaries for the organizational and financial help they could offer. They sometimes made great efforts to connect themselves to the northern denominations. When blacks in northern South Carolina heard that the AMEZ Church was holding a conference in North Carolina, two black leaders walked from Lancaster, South Carolina, to New Bern, North Carolina, a distance of three hundred miles, to learn about it. The following year, Bishop J. J. Clinton organized the South Carolina Conference of the AMEZ Church.

Northern missionaries played an important role in the organization of black reli-gious life in the postwar South, but their role should not be exaggerated. As William E. Montgomery has observed, their "primary contribution to the continued progress of the church was in releasing the great creative energy of southern blacks them-selves." Missionaries often served as catalysts for a change in church relations, but not for the freedpeople's initial desire for separate churches; that desire had roots deep in the antebellum past and was forged in the crucible of war and emancipation.[27]

By 1865 and 1866, then, the freedpeople had developed their own vision of what religious reconstruction should be, based on their interpretation of God's purposes in the war and on their wartime experiences. This vision had five major elements. First, the freedpeople asserted that their former masters could not properly look after their religious interests. The leadership of southern society and southern churches were stained with sin: they had started a fratricidal war to uphold the wicked institution of slavery, and God had judged them severely. Furthermore, southern white ministers often had neither understood nor addressed blacks' spiritual needs. One freedman insisted: "We couldn't tell NO PREACHER NEBER how we suffer all dese long years. He know'd nothin' 'bout we." Even after the war, whites continued to preach to blacks much as they had before. Charles J. Oliver, after preaching a sermon on Lazarus and the rich man to the white congregation, "proceeded to the church of the colored people." It was so late that many had gone home, but to those who remained, Oliver "preached them a little sermon about the *contract*."[28]

Blacks who challenged the antebellum racial barriers after the war met firm resistance. One freedwoman who tried to sit with the whites in a Montgomery, Alabama, church was "very politely told that accommodations were prepared for her in another part of the building, and she moved off quickly and took her place in the gallery." The newspaper that reported the incident ridiculed her: "The old woman was hardly to blame. She knew no better, and probably had been told that she was as good as the whites, and entitled to as many privileges." Implicit in the newspaper's patronizing tone was the widely shared belief that freedpeople were entitled to no more religious privileges than they had as slaves. The white leaders of the Antioch Baptist Church in Savannah allowed blacks to continue to attend, but they had to remain in the gallery as before. If blacks were to enjoy greater religious freedom, they would not find it in the biracial churches of the antebellum period. One black North Carolinian who had joined the northern Presbyterian church told a friend who remained in the southern church, "Come down out of the gallery to the ground floor in your own church."[29]

The second element of the black vision follows directly from the first. Since southern white ministers could no longer care for the spiritual needs of the freedpeople, they needed to establish their own churches where they could govern their own religious lives. Despite advice from their white brethren to the contrary, blacks throughout the South both during and after the war withdrew from biracial churches. When Basil Manly Sr. wrote from Alabama, "We . . . shall let go our hold of them, if after our advice, they desire it," what he apparently did not recognize was that white southern evangelicals could not hold them in the churches if they were determined to leave, as these black members were.[30]

Black ministers representing twenty-six black Baptist churches in South Carolina, Georgia, and Florida met in July 1865 at Hilton Head, South Carolina, to organize the Zion Baptist Association. Other associations quickly followed. The Thomasville Association was formed in 1865 from black Baptist churches in three counties in southern Georgia. The Shiloh Association consisted of churches in east central

Georgia, while the Ebenezer Baptist Association was formed for black churches in northern Georgia. In 1866 in Tuscaloosa, Alabama, freedpeople left the biracial Baptist church and formed the First African Baptist Church of that city. In 1865, black members of the Primitive Baptist churches of the South organized their own denomination, the Colored Primitive Baptists in America, in Columbia, Tennessee.[31]

When a congressional committee asked a black minister in Marietta, Georgia, if blacks preferred their own churches, he told them, "most of them prefer to have them to themselves." In December 1865, the black Methodist congregation in Marietta had "voted the minister out, and he in the pulpit at the time." The Reverend Samuel W. Drayton, a black minister in Augusta, joined the AME Church and took his entire congregation with him. Black Methodists in Macon, Georgia, voted to unite with the AME Church in the summer of 1865.[32]

Also during the summer of 1865, Andrew Brown, a black layman from Dalton, Georgia, met missionary James Lynch in Atlanta, who told him about the AME Church. Later, when the MECS sent a white preacher to the black Methodists in Dalton, Brown told him, "we must look for ourselves." Brown and the rest of the black congregation left the MECS and joined the AME, but they "were in a sad plight, for there was not an ordained [black] minister from Chattanooga to Atlanta."[33]

Some southern white ministers realized their inability to retain black members and helped them withdraw. Methodist preacher David Sullins, appointed to Wytheville, Virginia, by the Holston Conference in 1866, realized that the large black membership of his church was no longer content to remain in the gallery or in the rear seats. He told them about the AMEZ Church: "believing they would do better in that church than in ours, I called their leaders together and explained it to them, and advised them to go into that organization." He invited a minister of the AMEZ Church to Wytheville; "we got the colored folks together, and after a little talk they agreed to go in a body to that church." Sullins took out the church register and transferred all the black members; he concluded, "all were pleased." Few southern ministers were so willing to see their black members depart, although Sullins might be better credited with acceptance of the inevitable. His account demonstrates that these black Methodists had grown restive under the antebellum patterns and "were beginning to assert their independence."[34]

In a few remarkable instances, white ministers actually left the southern denominations to continue to minister to the freedpeople in northern denominations. After North Carolina Presbyterian Samuel C. Alexander was accused of disloyalty to the Confederacy in mid-1864 and his church refused to pay him, he began work among the freedpeople. Another North Carolina Presbyterian, Sidney S. Murkland, organized a separate congregation for black Presbyterians and built a church for them on his farm near the white church; in response the white members drove him from the pulpit. Both Alexander and Murkland later joined the northern Presbyterian church (Old School). As pastor of the Covington and Oxford, Georgia, colored charges for 1866, southern Methodist John W. Yarbrough found that his congregations wanted to transfer to the MEC. Yarbrough was "willing to join that Church and serve them as their pastor." Writing to the superintendent of the Georgia and Alabama Mission District of the northern church, Yarbrough insisted that although he would be "cut off" from many friends and relatives, "I want to do something for the poor colored people and the Church South has not the ability to help us if they had the will. My charge will follow me." A more accurate assessment would be that Yarbrough followed his charge.[35]

Some Baptist churches were quick to encourage black majorities to leave because their congregational form of polity raised the fear of black majority control of local churches. The Coosa River Baptist Association in Alabama advised churches with a few black members to allow them to remain and those with black majorities to seek racial division. In northwestern Alabama, white Baptists encouraged black independence since blacks were in the majority of many local congregations, and "if they saw proper to exercise their rights as members, now being free, they could control those churches and call whom they pleased as pastor."[36]

The decision to leave the biracial churches was sometimes difficult and occasionally even caused dissension within the black community. In Wilmington, North Carolina, 625 black members and seventeen black class leaders voted to leave the Front Street MECS and join the AME Church. Four black class leaders and approximately two hundred black members remained in the congregation with some two hundred white members. General John M. Schofield ordered on March 5, 1865, that the church building would be available to the AME congregation for half of each day and to the southern Methodist congregation for the other half. When one of the AME class leaders was addressing the congregation, he condemned those who had remained in the southern church: "I'se got no faith in no man what won't go wid he own race. Some of dese niggers is reb niggers — dey secessioners. Dey ants to be stayin' in de white folks church. Dey Judases, dey betray dar own color." He then called by name several of the black class leaders who had not left the MECS and concluded, "dey all belong to de secesh crowd." One of those leaders, Tom Smith, was in the crowd and stood up to return the insult: "You de secesh niggers yousef — you secede from de Church of God!"[37]

Black Baptists in Albany, Georgia, suffered from a similar division. Blacks and whites in the Albany Baptist Church worshiped separately, but they belonged to the same local church organization. On October 14, 1866, the leadership appointed a biracial committee to visit the black congregation and "consult with the brethren and examine into their ability to sustain the Gospel and maintain church government." On November 23, the black congregation met in conference; "after some discussion upon the subject of a division or a withdrawal of the colored church from the whites," they "unanimously decided that they remain together at least another year." Seven deacons for the black church would be ordained on the fifth Sunday in December, and the church would retain the Reverend Ralph Watson, a black preacher, as their minister. White church members declared that Watson's "Christian character is above reproach" and that his services were "blessed of the Lord." By February 1867, however, the black Baptists were divided among themselves. Members of the black congregation sent a letter to the white members charging the Reverend David Hines, "a member of our church," with "serious irregularities" including creating a "faction and schism in our church by leading off a portion of our members and establishing a new church." For these and other offenses, they asked that Hines "be suspended from the exercise of his office as an Elder" until he could be tried before the church.[38]

The third part of the freedpeople's plan for religious reconstruction was their determination to have black preachers. Black preachers had been an important part of antebellum black religion and were often the primary ministers to black congregations or the black members of biracial congregations. Eugene Genovese concludes that "slaves heard their own black preachers, if not regularly, then at least frequently enough to make a difference in their lives." Anderson Edwards, a Baptist slave preacher in Texas, preached "what massa told me" publicly, but "on the sly" he told them "iffen they keeps prayin' the Lord will set 'em free." A preacher on a plantation in Mississippi preached on the themes of obedience to masters while whites were present, but when they were not "He come out with straight preachin' from the Bible." Ex-slave James Childress from Tennessee remembered that slave preachers promised that faith in God would deliver them from slavery. Ex-slave Walter Calloway of Alabama reported that whites sometimes sent their minister to the plantation to preach to the slaves, but "dey druther heah Joe," their slave preacher. Although they were usually illiterate, many slave preachers were quite eloquent, and they shared their life experiences with their black congregations, a bond that no white preachers or northern black missionaries shared. In 1863 a white minister observed, "the 'colored brethren' are so much preferred as preachers. When in the pulpit there is a wonderful sympathy between the speaker and his audience. . . . This sympathetic influence seems the result of a . . . peculiar experience."[39]

When freedom came, blacks continued to look to their slave preachers, elders, and exhorters to guide their religious lives. Louise A. Woodbury, an American Missionary Association representative in Norfolk, Virginia, observed that blacks "have been obliged to listen to white ministers provided, or placed over them by their masters, while they have had men among themselves whom they believe were called of God to preach, who were kept silent, by the institution from which they are now freed." To remain under the supervision of white preachers "is too much like old times to meet with their approval. Their long silent preachers want to preach and the people prefer them." An Alabama newspaper complained that the black masses believed the pronouncements of black preachers and preferred them over the whites. Although they might have disagreed over the necessary qualifications, northern black Christians shared with the freedpeople the belief that black preachers were best suited to minister to the ex-slaves. Black Baptist minister Richard De Baptiste of Chicago wrote in 1864: "no persons will prove to be so efficient as laborers among this unfortunate people as pious, intelligent, and properly qualified persons of their own race."[40]

Slave preachers and exhorters were anxious to form autonomous congregations from the plantation missions and the black portions of biracial congregations after the war. One northern Methodist missionary remarked, "Veteran preachers among the late slaves were prompt to offer their welcome services." Monroe Boykin, a member of the Baptist church in Camden, South Carolina, led sixty-six of his fellow freedpeople out of that church and founded the Mount Moriah Baptist Church in 1866. Alexander Bettis, an exhorter in the Baptist church in Edgefield, South Carolina, led seventeen members out of that church and went on to establish dozens more black churches. Nathan Ashby, who had preached to slaves in the basement of the Baptist church in Montgomery, Alabama, founded the new First Baptist Church of Montgomery after the war. White southerners considered these preachers unfit leaders for the freedpeople. A South Carolina Presbyterian missionary complained, "the large negro membership is . . . much scattered, and, I dare say, few can ever be gathered together again. They are, I am told, much carried away and misled by ignorant preachers of their own color."[41]

Although slave preachers and exhorters resented and resisted all efforts on the part of northern black and white missionaries to depose them as leaders of the freedpeople, they eagerly sought out ordination or licensure from denominational representatives. Two northern missionaries ordained Monroe Boykin at his request after he had begun a black Baptist church in Camden, South Carolina. A southern Methodist minister in Virginia wrote AME leaders that blacks in his congregation wanted to join their organization, "but without authority and no one to give it, they can do nothing while others are busy." While organizing a black church in Helenaville, South Carolina, in 1863, AME missionary James Lynch licensed two local preachers and two exhorters; he marveled, "I never saw men appreciate anything so much in my life." Prince Morell of Tuscaloosa, Alabama, made an extraordinary effort to secure his ordination. In November 1865 Morell traveled to Mobile, where he met and was ordained by "persons who went from Mobile to New Orleans for the purpose of being ordained themselves that they might thus be qualified to ordain Prince." They gave him "a certificate that they had ordained him at the call and request" of the Baptist Church in Tuscaloosa. Basil Manly Sr., whose son Charles was pastor in Tuscaloosa, declared that this idea "was wholly and absolutely false." On June 24, 1866, Charles Manly met with the black members of the church and chastised them for the "unscriptural and disorderly way of procuring a sort of quasi ordination for Prince." After Manly left them to discuss the matter, they sent him a note that evening declaring that they wished to withdraw from his church. While most black Christians in the South desired ecclesiastical separation from their former masters, they did not repudiate denominational precepts. Some black preachers, such as Prince Morell, made great efforts to ensure that they were ordained or licensed by legitimate denominational representatives.[42]

The fourth component of the freedpeople's vision of religious reconstruction involved generally welcoming the assistance of northern black and white denominations, provided they did not attempt to exert complete control over the ex-slaves' religious lives. Black southern Christians had had considerable experience with local church life in the antebellum period — some had been preachers, elders, and exhorters — and they had observed, if not always participated in, many of the organizational functions of the local church. In some areas, a committee of black members was appointed to oversee church discipline among the slave members. Although their decisions usually had to be approved by the white congregation, this practice gave black members experience in church government and, as Albert Raboteau maintains, "so laid a foundation upon which freedpeople would rapidly build their own independent churches after emancipation."[43]

There had been, however, clear limits to black participation in antebellum church life. While they had been received into the fellowship and governed by the same church discipline, black members had not had a voice in the selection of pastors or other church leaders. Furthermore, they had had little experience with denominational organization. In this area especially, southern black Christians had to rely on northern black and white missionaries and on southern white ministers for guidance. The extralocal aspects of church polity were quite important in the hierarchical Presbyterian and Methodist churches (considerably less so in Baptist churches). This gap in the slaves' religious experience explains why northern missionaries often found independent black congregations in many areas of the South. Although these freedpeople were certain that they no longer wished to remain in biracial churches, they were not sure how and with whom to connect at the denominational level. Much of the early growth of the AME and AMEZ churches in the South occurred when preexisting local black congregations added their names to the roll of those denominations. In Georgia, for example, the AME Church enrolled strong black churches in Augusta and Savannah in 1865. From these two centers, "it was only a matter of time when the radiating influence should draw in other outstanding bodies of Methodist Christians." Soon, "large and interesting bodies of colored Methodists" in Macon, Columbus, and Atlanta were added to the AME Church.[44]

The fifth and final element in the freedpeople's vision of religious reconstruction was their intense desire for schools to teach their children and colleges to train their preachers and teachers. The main objective of many black Baptist associations was education. They often established a school or joined with other associations in founding schools. Andrew Caldwell, a Methodist religious scalawag, reported from Rome, Georgia, that all the freedpeople there "unite in one thing, and that is a great desire to have their children educated." Here again, northern black evangelicals shared the same vision as Christian freedpeople. Leonard Grimes, pastor of the Twelfth Baptist Church in Boston and president of the black Consolidated American Baptist Missionary Convention, appealed to the American Baptist Home Mission Society for assistance in educating the freedpeople: "I want the young men recently converted, the 125,000 children who are in the schools, to have educated preachers. I want an institution where the promising young men of the colored race may be educated. . . . In the name of my oppressed race, I ask for some definite organization to educate the young men just emancipated."[45]

In this aspect of religious reconstruction, northern missionaries and northern funds were particularly welcome, and they played a vital role in the erection of schoolhouses and churches and the provision of teachers until black teachers could be trained. The Freedmen's Aid Society of the MEC established fifty-nine schools for freedpeople throughout the South in its first year of operation. All three biracial evangelical denominations in the North established colleges in the South to train black teachers and preachers, as did the two African Methodist denominations. This accomplishment formed the northern evangelicals' most enduring legacy from religious reconstruction. The federal government, through the Freedmen's Bureau, also supplied desperately needed funds for schools and teachers.[46]

The vision of religious reconstruction, which included these five elements, was not universal among black Christians. Northern black missionaries, like Henry M. Turner and the missionaries of the AME and AMEZ churches, embraced four of the five elements outlined here; on the issue of the proper role of northern denominations, while they generally accepted the views of the freedpeople, local struggles for control sometimes caused friction. Southern black conservatives, like Lucius H. Holsey and the members of the Colored Methodist Episcopal Church, did not share two of the five elements with the majority of freedpeople: they were less likely to view the white southern churches as corrupt; and they opposed most of the initiatives of northern black and white denominations in the South, being far more likely to look to white southern Christians than to northern missionaries for assistance. Furthermore, black Christians in the postwar era were not a monolithic group; as in the case of their white counterparts, differences of class, section, and gender divided them. On the whole, however, they shared more in common than they did with either northern or southern white Christians.[47]

The black church became the central institution in most black communities, a center of social, economic, educational, political, and, of course, religious activity. From that church came the black community's leaders.[48] From that church sprang the hope that God, who had delivered black people from bondage, would continue to watch over them in freedom. Throughout much of Reconstruction and beyond, black religion functioned as, in the words of E. Franklin Frazier, "a refuge in a hostile white world."[49] Ironically, this role parallels that played by the religion of white southerners in the postwar South: a refuge in a world that for a time was controlled by others.

5

Crossing Jordan

The Black Quest for Religious Autonomy

For ye shall pass over Jordan to go in to possess the land which the LORD your God giveth you, and ye shall possess it, and dwell therein.

Deuteronomy 11:31

Emancipation provided new opportunities and new challenges for all black southerners, but those who were Christians drew special meaning from the event. They had prayed for deliverance, and God had heard their plea. By 1865 they were free to shape their religious lives — or, in the terms of their favorite biblical metaphor, they had been delivered from their Egyptian bondage and the exodus had begun. However, much remained to be done to reach their spiritual promised land. The wilderness and the River Jordan remained to be crossed.[1] Over the next decade, the freedpeople made that voyage with help from a variety of sources. During this period their vision of religious reconstruction, formulated during the war and in the immediate aftermath, took concrete form.

While some black Christians left biracial churches during the war and in 1865, the period from 1866 to 1870 witnessed the largest black withdrawal.[2] As figure 5-1 demonstrates, the three major evangelical denominations in Georgia lost their black members quickly after 1865. By 1870, the Methodist Georgia Annual Conference reported only 1,504 black members out of a membership of 27,371 a decade earlier. In that same year, the constituent associations of the Georgia Baptist Convention counted only 10,354 out of a prewar membership of 27,691.[3] The Presbyterian Synod of Georgia had few, if any, black members by 1870; that church had ceased reporting black membership statistics in 1866 because there were so few. The majority of the Synod of Georgia's 643 black members in 1860 had gone into the northern Presbyterian church or left the Presbyterian fold entirely and joined the Baptists or Methodists. In 1877, only one Baptist association had more than a handful of black

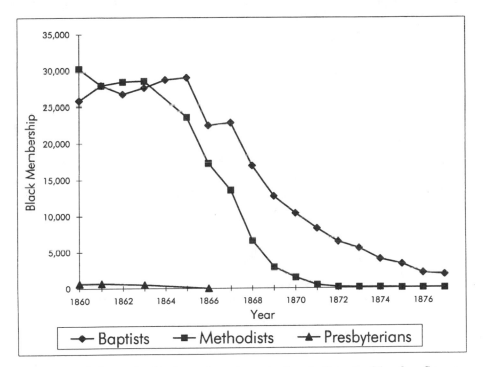

FIGURE 5·1 Black membership in southern denominations in Georgia, 1860–1877. *Sources:* Georgia Baptist Convention, *Minutes*, 1860–1877; Georgia Annual Conference (MECS), *Minutes*, 1860–1866; North Georgia Annual Conference (MECS), *Minutes*, 1867–1877, South Georgia Annual Conference (MECS), *Minutes*, 1867–1877; Synod of Georgia, *Minutes*, 1860 1877.

members, and most of them drifted away in the following years. The autonomy of local congregations and a loose denominational structure helped Baptist churches retain more of their black membership longer, but the trend was clear in their case as well. Refused equality in ecclesiastical bodies and generally treated with indifference, black Baptists slowly withdrew and formed associations of their own.

Southern denominations in Tennessee also suffered a rapid exodus of their black membership (see fig. 5-2). When the Presbyterian Church in the United States (PCUS) stopped reporting statistics on its "colored" members in 1866, most of the 517 blacks who had belonged to Tennessee's biracial Presbyterian churches in 1860 had already departed them. Southern Methodism in Tennessee had lost the majority of its 1860 black membership of 12,267 by the war's end. By 1870 only 320 remained, and in 1877 only seventeen, scattered singly and in pairs in fifteen local churches in the central and eastern parts of the state.[4]

The black withdrawal from white churches sometimes disrupted white ecclesiastical structures. At the beginning of 1865, for example, the Sunbury Association of Baptist churches along the coast of Georgia from Savannah to Darien boasted 7,542 members, of whom 6,857 (91 percent) were black. In July 1865, twenty black

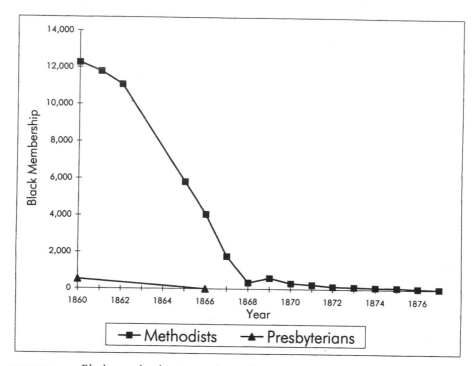

FIGURE 5-2 Black membership in southern denominations in Tennessee, 1860–1877. *Sources: Minutes of the Annual Conferences of the Methodist Episcopal Church, South,* 1860–1877 (Memphis Annual Conference, Tennessee Annual Conference, Holston Annual Conference); General Assembly of the Presbyterian Church in the United States of America (Old School), *Minutes,* 1860; General Assembly of the Presbyterian Church in the Confederate States of America, *Minutes,* 1861–1864; General Assembly of the PCUS, *Minutes,* 1865–1877 (Synod of Memphis, Synod of Nashville).

Baptist churches withdrew from Sunbury and, together with three Florida and three South Carolina churches, formed the all-black Zion Association. With this massive loss of membership, Sunbury dissolved. On November 24, 1866, Baptists from eleven churches in three separate associations — Sunbury, Piedmont, and Union — met in Liberty County to organize the New Sunbury Association. Even with the influx of churches and members from neighboring areas, this New Sunbury Association had only 843 members, of whom 115 (14 percent) were black. By 1875 the New Sunbury Association reported no black members.[5]

The Georgia Association of Baptists, which included the city of Augusta and neighboring counties to the northwest, had a very different experience with its black members. It initially lost 55 percent of its black membership in 1866, when it "granted Letters of Dismission to the following churches, all in full fellowship and good standing, viz: Central African, Ebenezer African, Spirit Creek African, Springfield African, and Thankful African." These five black congregations, all located in Augusta, had enjoyed a semi-independent status in the antebellum period, and quickly departed the association after the war. However, other blacks in the Georgia

Association who attended biracial churches were slow to leave it. While most associations were rapidly losing their black members, the Georgia Association still had 2,172 blacks in 1870 and 2,046 in 1875. In the latter year, the Georgia Association had almost twice as many black members as all of the other associations in the Georgia Baptist Convention combined. The reluctance of some black Baptists to leave the Georgia Association may have been due to its willingness to ordain black ministers in the antebellum period and to white members' support for slave marriages and slave preachers. Many of the blacks who left joined the all-black Ebenezer Association, organized in 1867. Reflecting continued good will, the Ebenezer Association exchanged fraternal messengers with the Georgia Association from 1869 to 1880.[6]

The experience of the Stone Creek Baptist Church during religious reconstruction is also instructive on the larger patterns of racial adjustments in southern evangelicalism. Located in Twiggs County in central Georgia, Stone Creek had over three hundred members in the 1860s, a slight majority of whom were black. Unlike most other black Baptists, the black members of this congregation remained in the biracial church until 1874. The white membership's reaction to the black members' initiatives was crucial to the perpetuation of this arrangement. As early as August 1865, the church minutes for the first time recorded black members' speaking out at church conferences. In 1867 a biracial committee considered the "propriety of the Blacks holding their own conference," but after consideration, "the colored members desired to continue their conference with the whites as heretofore." Responding to the wishes of its black membership, the church also ordained two black deacons. In 1868, the church established separate conferences for blacks and whites, but it continued to appoint biracial committees for some purposes. Beginning in 1870, black members began seeking letters of dismission, and in August 1874 the black conference withdrew "not from ill will but for the better government of ourselves." This newly formed black congregation built their own church a quarter of a mile away and named it Stone Creek as well.[7]

After black Georgia Baptists withdrew from biracial churches, they began to create associations of their own; their primary motive was to support education. Many of the associations founded a school or joined with other associations in establishing schools. After some of these early schools closed, the associations diverted their efforts toward scholarships to the handful of black colleges that had been erected with the aid of northern Christians. Often the black associations drew their membership from biracial associations with similar geographical boundaries. The Zion Association, organized in 1865 along the Georgia coast, as noted, drew heavily from the biracial Sunbury Association. The Walker Association (1868) in east central Georgia absorbed much of the black membership of the Hephzibah Association, while the Southwestern Georgia Association (1870) consisted largely of black members of the Bethel Association. The freedpeople of the Walker Association began the Walker Baptist Institute in Waynesboro in 1881, and the Southwestern Georgia Association operated the Americus Baptist Institute in Americus. In 1870 representatives from several black associations met in Augusta to form the Missionary Baptist Convention of Georgia. By 1877, Georgia had twenty-six black Baptist associations with a combined membership of over ninety-one thousand.[8]

The Georgia Annual Conference of the Methodist Episcopal Church, South

(MECS), also experienced a dramatic loss of members. The black congregation of Andrew Chapel in Savannah left the MECS in the summer of 1865 and joined the African Methodist Episcopal (AME) Church; when the Georgia Annual Conference met in January 1865, it did not appoint a minister for Andrew Chapel, but when the local quarterly conference of the MECS met in November, it voted to request that the Georgia Annual Conference continue to appoint a preacher to Andrew Chapel. Like many other white southern Christians, these Savannah Methodists were confident that the freedpeople would soon return to the fold. In June 1867 the Eatonton Methodist Church sadly noted, "the entire colored charge have dissolved their connection with us and united with the African M. E. C."[9]

The September 1867 minutes of the Bainbridge District in southwestern Georgia demonstrate the frailty of the freedpeople's relationship to the southern Methodist church. The minutes state that on the Spring Hill and Camilla circuits and in Thomasville, the "colored people adhere to our church," and in the Ocklocknee mission they "adhere to our Church up to this time." However, in Bainbridge they were "not doing as well as desired." At Albany the black Methodists had withdrawn to the AME Church, while on the Blakely circuit, they were divided, "some of them gone over to the African Methodist Episcopal Church." That year the Bainbridge District reported 1,646 black members; the next year, 242. At the third session of the Georgia Conference of the AME Church in 1869, the assembled delegates received the "cheering news" from Fort Valley that "the colored Methodists there desired to give in their adherence to our church." Across the state throughout this period, black Methodists left the southern church and united with one of the three northern Methodist denominations — the Methodist Episcopal Church (MEC), the AME Church, and the African Methodist Episcopal Zion (AMEZ) Church.[10]

The experience of Hopewell Presbytery in Georgia illustrates the difficulties of reaching acceptable adjustments between the races in religious matters. This presbytery, located between Augusta and Macon, had 145 black communicants in 1863. Sixty-one of these were members of the Macon Church, which had appointed three black men, David Laney, Joseph Williams, and Robert Casters, to act as exhorters for them. In April 1866 the black members of the Macon Church petitioned the Hopewell Presbytery to be set apart as a separate congregation. The presbytery ordained the three black exhorters as "Presbyterian ministers, with power to preach the gospel, to administer the sacraments of the Church, to solemnize marriages, and to ordain ruling-elders and deacons," having agreed to ordain them with two provisions. First, they "shall be regarded as ordained ministers in the Presbyterian Church only in connection with their own people." Second, the presbytery "shall obtain, from them, previously, a public expression of their adhesion to the doctrines and discipline of the Presbyterian Church, and [be] . . . fully persuaded of their personal piety, and their competency to instruct colored congregations in religious matters." The presbytery also appointed David Laney pastor of the separate black First Church of Macon.[11]

Within a year the arrangement had become unsatisfactory to the black ministers. Joseph Williams wrote a protest to the presbytery, complaining that black ministers held an inferior position in that body and requesting that he be dismissed. The three black ministers had already organized Knox Presbytery, the first all-black presbytery in the nation, which later joined the northern Presbyterian church. In response, Hopewell Presbytery struck the names of the black ministers from their rolls. Other black Presbyterian congregations were established in Savannah, Macon, Dalton, Athens, Atlanta, and Newnan. In 1868 the presbyteries of Knox, Catawba (North Carolina), and Atlantic (South Carolina) united to form the Atlantic Synod of the northern Presbyterian church. This synod included all of the northern Presbyterian work along the Atlantic coast and in 1873 had 6,600 members.[12]

Southern white Christians responded to the black exodus with a mixture of dismay, relief, and irritation. Eliza Fain in eastern Tennessee prayed that God would "give us hearts to treat those who serve us as we should. . . . May we of the South still feel for the sons and daughters of Ham and do all that is consistent with thy will for their moral advancement." She found the freedpeople's desire to have the Bible "truly so gratifying. They are in great need of spiritual advice by those who have a just appreciation of the religion which a thorough acquaintance of Bible truth gives."[13]

In the face of black withdrawals and the threat of losing all influence in black religious life, white evangelicals were forced through five stages of accommodation in an attempt to retain at least some of their dwindling black membership. The adjustment did not take place at the same rate in all denominations and in all locations, nor did all individual churches with black members go through each of these five steps. In some areas, the process began during the war, proceeded rapidly, and was virtually complete by 1865. In other places, whites only gradually changed their attitudes in the 1870s. The larger pattern that emerges is one of whites' gradually relinquishing their control in response to black initiatives throughout the South, a process that was complete by the mid-1870s.

At first, white evangelicals insisted that emancipation need produce no change in blacks' ecclesiastical relationships. Moreover, any change would be unwise and perhaps dangerous. In 1865 the Bark Camp Church in Burke County, Georgia, sent a message to the Hephzibah Baptist Association, asking simply, "What is the proper status of the colored members of our churches?" Admittedly their political status had changed, but their social status "remains the same as during slavery," the association insisted; "ecclesiastically, their 'status' and church relations are unaffected." The General Assembly of the southern Presbyterian church, meeting in Macon, Georgia, in December 1865, received a similar query. The General Assembly resolved that "whereas experience has invariably proved the advantages of the colored people and the white being united together in the worship of God we see no reason why it should be otherwise, now that they are freedpeople and not slaves." Displaying a similar attitude, the Antioch Baptist Church in Savannah, Georgia, permitted blacks to attend its services as long as they remained in the rear section of the building they had occupied during slavery.[14]

Central to the assumption that antebellum relationships should persist was the belief that white southern Christians understood the freedpeople best and were also best prepared to help them. The first pastoral letter issued by southern Methodist bishops after the war urged southern Methodists to assure black members "that as heretofore we have been, so we will continue to be, their friends, and in every available way aid their moral development and religious welfare." The Memphis Annual Conference declared: "We are bold to assert that the best friends the black man ever had, or will have, are the Ministers of the Methodist Episcopal Church, South."[15]

White southern evangelicals feared that if they did not maintain religious contact with the freedpeople in their midst, black religion would deteriorate into superstition. As the Methodist Memphis Annual Conference warned, "if we do not provide amply for their religious wants, we fear that ignorant and superstitious men will rise up among them as teachers and guides, who will lead them into false notions of religion that will ultimately culminate in the worst forms of superstition, idolatry, and barbarism." Reeling from the loss of over ninety percent of its 1865 black membership, the Bethel Baptist Association in southwestern Georgia declared in 1870 that "with few exceptions, the colored population are not now commonly enjoying the preaching of a gospel sound either in doctrine or precept." Instead, "the religious meetings among them are generally becoming noted for extravagance and disorder, and often for performances violative of common decency."[16]

White Christians also feared that northern missionaries would gain undue influence among the freedpeople. The Southern Baptist Convention in 1866 expressed its concern over northern missionaries among them: "While we are not opposed to any right-minded man aiding in this important work, it is our decided conviction, from our knowledge of the character of these people, and of the feelings of our citizens, that this work must be done mainly by ourselves." By 1869 the editor of the Baptist *Christian Index* in Atlanta attributed the difficulties of evangelizing the freedpeople to "industrious and widespread efforts of political and fanatical emissaries to alienate Baptists 'of African descent' from their white brethren in the South — to induce their withdrawal from our churches — to lead them to forsake our ministry, and accept in lieu of it the ministry of ignorant persons of their own color, or of 'loyal' (and often irresponsible) adventurers from a distance." These northern missionaries persuaded the freedpeople that "they had never heard the 'full' or even the 'true' gospel from their old instructors" and created "in their minds a demand for 'social equality' as the condition of religious fraternity."[17]

The second stage of the white response to black restlessness was the provision of separate black churches with white ministers; these churches were to remain within the parent ecclesiastical organization. Methodist editor David S. Doggett, who would be elected bishop in 1866, wrote in the fall of 1865 that the southern Methodist church must organize its black members into independent congregations and supply their pulpits with "judicious white ministers." These white ministers were especially important because northern ministers "would inflict incurable damage upon these nascent churches."[18]

A closely related third stage was to provide black ministers to separate churches still under the authority of the local and regional white church bodies. Black ministers and other leaders quickly learned that they would not be accepted as equals in white ecclesiastical bodies. When a black Baptist church in La Grange, Georgia, petitioned for admission to the Western Baptist Association in 1866, a committee formed to consider the request recommended that the association "receive the colored Church at La Grange, under its watch-care." The association requested that the black congregation report their statistics each year "by letter," and urged them to forward funds for "missionary or other purposes" to the association. The association thereby subtly but firmly requested the black church not to send black representatives to the associational meeting. In 1868 two more black churches, Antioch and

Canaan, were admitted into the association "upon the basis the La Grange colored church was in 1866." At the same time, the La Grange black church, "having joined the African Association of Atlanta," was removed from the roll of churches.[19]

The Ebenezer Baptist Association made its demands more explicit; in 1867 it resolved to admit black churches into membership provided that they, "in all cases, represent themselves by some orderly white brethren of the nearest white church." If they failed to do so, "their connection [will] be dissolved." The Ebenezer Association made the racial proscription complete by insisting that any black association that wanted to correspond with them had to "represent themselves by white messengers." Unsatisfied with excluding blacks as voting members of the association, they wanted no blacks in their midst at all.[20]

In the fourth stage of white adjustment, white churches, in response to black demands for equal representation, more autonomy, and greater authority over their churches, encouraged the establishment of separate black associations, conferences, and presbyteries. Unwilling to admit blacks to equality in these bodies, southern white Christians advocated the formation of parallel organizations. In 1866 white Georgia Baptists in the Western Association recommended to their black brethren "the propriety of constituting churches of their own" and pledged their "assistance in organizing an Association, if they so desire." The sooner black Baptists were able to care for themselves, the association frankly admitted, "the better it will be for them and for us." In 1871 the Washington Baptist Association between Atlanta and Augusta, Georgia, resolved to "recommend to the colored churches in our midst to organize themselves into an association."[21] For black Baptists, the formation of associations generally marked their withdrawal from the southern body, if they had not already left as individual congregations. As early as February 1866, the *Christian Index* correctly predicted that black separation from the white Baptist churches was "only a question of time."[22]

As they gradually realized that their black members would not remain in biracial churches led by white ministers, southern Methodists moved toward the establishment of independent black conferences, which were to remain within the MECS. In the General Conference of 1866, southern Methodists adopted a plan for the organization of black churches, districts, annual conferences, and even a "separate Conference jurisdiction for themselves, if they so desire and the Bishops deem it expedient."[23] Over the next four years, southern Methodists organized five black annual conferences. In November 1867, Bishop Robert Paine organized the Memphis Colored Conference in Jackson, Tennessee. Some ten thousand members from the Memphis and Tennessee conferences of the southern Methodist church joined the new conference. Of fourteen presiding elders, only one, Isaac Lane, was black. In January 1869, Bishop George Foster Pierce organized the Georgia Colored Conference in Augusta with approximately thirteen thousand members. At least six of the sixteen districts in the conference had black presiding elders. Three other conferences, Kentucky, Mississippi, and Alabama, were also organized in 1868 and 1869.[24]

Cumberland Presbyterians began creating an entirely separate church structure for their black members in 1869. Responding to black claims for equal representation in the presbyteries, the General Assembly of 1869 approved the formation of black presbyteries. Over the next two years, black presbyteries were organized in

Middle Tennessee (Elk River), West Tennessee (Hopewell), and East Tennessee (Greenville). In November 1871 at Fayetteville, Tennessee, these presbyteries united with the Huntsville Presbytery of Alabama to form the first black synod.[25] Black Presbyterians in the PCUS followed suit after 1874. In response to appeals from the synods of Mississippi, Memphis, and South Carolina, along with the Presbytery of East Hanover in Virginia, the General Assembly of the PCUS urged its presbyteries and synods to organize black churches that would then be organized into black presbyteries and synods.[26]

Torn between genuine Christian concern for black southerners and their own pervasive racism, white southern evangelicals were sometimes uncertain of the will of God. Georgia Baptists in the Western Association, when faced with the request of a black church for admission, insisted that the questions involved were "grave and complicated in their character and exceedingly difficult of solution." The hesitancy of the 1869 General Assembly of the Cumberland Presbyterian Church to endorse black presbyteries stemmed from a broader uncertainty about how to treat its black membership, a subject "environed with no ordinary difficulties." However, Moses T. Weir, a black minister, forced the issue by requesting to be seated in the assembly as the representative of a newly formed black presbytery. In response to Weir's challenge and a request from black leaders for their own presbyteries, the General Assembly instructed its synods to form black presbyteries "whenever, in the judgment of the Synod, the best interests of the colored membership of the Church will be subserved thereby." The assembly declined to seat Weir because "it would not be for the advancement of the Church, among either the white or the colored race, for the ministers of the two races to meet together in the same judicatories." The assembly thought it "prudent for all our Church judicatures to confine themselves to such steps as are obviously necessary and proper for the present and await the further developments of Divine Providence before determining upon an ultimate policy."[27]

The fifth and final stage of white adjustment to the black exodus was the organization of entirely separate and independent denominations for black Christians. By the time the southern Methodist and Presbyterian churches and the Cumberland Presbyterian Church had reached this decision, most of their black members had departed. In 1870 the General Conference of the MECS approved the formation of a new denomination for its black members. The original plan in 1866 had provided for segregation, but the black jurisdiction was to remain under the authority of the General Conference, bishops, and Discipline of the MECS. In 1870 the bishops announced their intention of "organizing them into an entirely separate church, and thus enabling them to become their own guides and governors." It also provided for the transfer of church property once the new church had been established, and appointed a delegation to advise and assist the black members in the organization of their General Assembly.[28]

In December 1870, forty-one black ministers and laypeople from the southern Methodist church met in Jackson, Tennessee, to organize the Colored Methodist Episcopal (CME) Church. Six delegates, including Lucius H. Holsey, came from Georgia, and thirteen attended from Tennessee. The Organizing General Conference elected two bishops, William H. Miles of Kentucky and Richard H. Vanderhorst of Georgia, both born slaves. On the final day of the conference, Bishops Robert

Paine and Holland N. McTyeire officially consecrated the two black bishops. In a symbolic gesture fraught with more meaning than perhaps either pair of bishops realized, Paine called Miles to his chair, and McTyeire left his seat for Vanderhorst. Paine said, "The time has come for us to resign into your hands the presidency of this body, and the episcopal oversight of your people. . . . Henceforth, you are their guides and governors!" What none of these bishops recognized was that the formation of the CME Church marked the end of most white southern involvement in the religious lives of black Methodists.[29]

The culmination of the movement toward segregation in the Cumberland Presbyterian Church came in May 1874. At the Publishing House of the Cumberland Presbyterian Church in Nashville, delegates organized the General Assembly of the new Colored Cumberland Presbyterian Church, which had seven presbyteries with forty-six ministers and only three thousand communicants.[30] The PCUS waited even longer before organizing its black members into a separate church. By 1895 it had only seventy black churches with some seven hundred members scattered throughout its territory, including seven in Georgia and five in Tennessee. Three years later, on May 19, 1898, representatives of four independent presbyteries and two PCUS presbyteries, representing approximately 1,500 black Presbyterians, met in New Orleans and organized themselves into the Synod of the Colored Presbyterian Church in the United States and Canada. In 1899 the name of this church was changed to the Afro-American Presbyterian Synod, and in 1917 it quietly reentered the southern Presbyterian church.[31]

The five stages of white southerners' attitudes highlight several important aspects of religious reconstruction. Blacks were clearly the important historical actors in this movement; white evangelicals as they passed through these various phases were reacting to black demands. Not all black members left the biracial churches immediately, and white attempts to retain some degree of control over the religious lives of their former slaves were directed only at those who remained; those who left were beyond the reach of either white accommodation or control. Whites' varying attempts at accommodation also emphasize the gulf that separated black and white Christians. White southern evangelicals firmly refused to treat as equals their black members, who increasingly determined to accept nothing less.

Outside the official ecclesiastical reactions to black withdrawal, some southern whites violently opposed the establishment of independent black churches and schools, especially those having any association with northern denominations. Northern Presbyterians reported from Tennessee in 1866 that "four schoolhouses, two of them used as churches, erected by the freedpeople, were burned by lawless persons." In February 1869 the large AME church building in Macon, Georgia, was burned by an "incendiary." A few weeks later another arsonist burned the freedpeople's school in Clinton, Tennessee.[32] Although these acts of violence cannot be linked directly to southern churches, they tacitly encouraged such actions by insisting that independent bodies of black Christians or those linked with "radical" northern denominations were dangerous to southern society.[33] These attacks were most frequent during the late 1860s, when reconstruction governments controlled the southern states on the strength of black votes, and denominational competition for black members was especially intense.

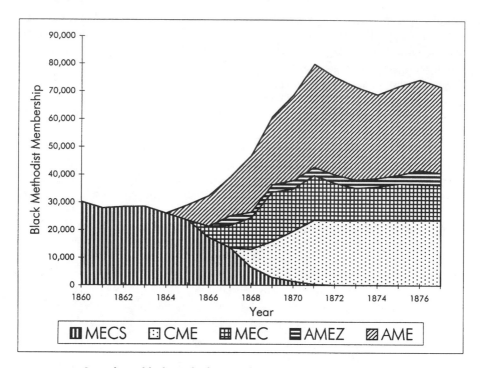

FIGURE 5-3 Cumulative black Methodist membership in Georgia, 1860–1877. Statistics include both members and probationers. Although not full members, probationers had made at least a tentative commitment to a particular church and were not likely to make a similar commitment simultaneously to another church.

As black members left the biracial churches and denominations behind, southern black Protestantism experienced a general revival. The freedom and hope born of emancipation led many freedpeople into the newly forming black churches. The AME missionary Henry M. Turner rejoiced that 1866 was "a year of revivals in Georgia, some of our churches have had as high as 450 probationers on the list, and as for conversions, they will only be known in eternity." In 1860, the Georgia Conference of the MECS and the churches of the Florida Annual Conference in southern Georgia had reported 30,246 black members. A decade later, the five Methodist denominations vying for the souls of Georgia's freedpeople reported over sixty-eight thousand black members, an increase of 125 percent (see fig. 5-3). By 1877 nearly seventy-two thousand black Georgians were members of Methodist churches. Georgia Baptist churches reported 26,192 black members in 1860; by 1870, six black Baptist associations had 38,878 members, an increase of 48 percent. In 1877, when better records were kept, black Georgia Baptist associations reported 91,868 members, or three and a half times the number of black Georgia Baptists in 1860.[34]

Black evangelicals who departed southern churches in the decade following the Civil War needed assistance in four major areas in order to establish a stable and independent religious life. First, they needed organizational help. For the independent-

minded Baptists, the establishment of a separate local congregation was often sufficient. However, most Christian freedpeople were illiterate and unfamiliar with the
procedures for constituting a government for a local church, so even black Baptists
often needed some assistance. For the more hierarchical Methodists and Presbyterians, whose organizations were in significant respects built from the top down, the
authority of bishops, conferences, assemblies, synods, and presbyteries was an important part of their religious life. Nevertheless, some congregations of black Methodists and Presbyterians became virtually independent during the disruptions of the
war and its immediate aftermath, and only later connected themselves with another
ecclesiastical organization.

Black Christians' second need, closely related to the first, was for the licensing
of their preachers and the ordination of their ministers, as mentioned in chapter 4.
Again, black Methodists and Presbyterians emphasized this requirement more than
did Baptists.[35] Third, the new black congregations needed church buildings; many
were shut out of the buildings they had formerly occupied once they bade fare-
well to the southern denominations. Although a church might have been built entirely by slave labor and used only for black worship services, the building itself
was owned by white trustees. Black Christians were rarely able to wrest control of a
church building from unwilling trustees through resort to military or judicial authorities.[36] Recently freed from bondage, they had few resources to devote to the erection of church buildings and therefore looked to others for help. As AME missionary
Thomas Crayton wrote from Lumpkin, Georgia, in 1867, "Our greatest want at present are houses of worship. Oh, that the Lord would send us help to fill that want!"[37]

The freedpeople's fourth need was for the education of their preachers and
teachers, as mentioned in chapter 4. Having been excluded from formal learning,
the ex-slaves coveted education for their children and a trained ministry for their
churches.

Black Baptists, Methodists, and Presbyterians all received some assistance from
the southern denominations they had departed and the white northern denominations that had sent missionaries among them. Black Baptists also enjoyed the support of the northern black Consolidated American Baptist Missionary Convention
(CABMC), and black Methodists likewise received additional benefits from two
northern black denominations, the AME and AMEZ churches. The federal government, through the agency of the Freedmen's Bureau, assisted all the denominations,
furnishing money and materials for schoolhouses and churches and for paying teachers.[38] Each of these particular groups also had its own priorities and, often, a different view of religious reconstruction that conflicted with those of others. The freedpeople's decision to ask for assistance and the responses of those asked were crucial
factors in determining the shape of black religious life in the post-war South.

Southern white denominations were the most readily available source of aid,
but black evangelicals were sometimes reluctant to accept advice and direction from
their former masters. Nevertheless, individual southern white ministers and congregations did provide vital assistance for local black congregations taking their first
steps toward organizing their own churches. In some cases blacks and whites shared
a genuine emotional attachment to each other, which manifested itself in a harmonious division and continued interaction after the separation.

White church organizations were eager to give counsel, still hoping to maintain some measure of control over black religious life. The Hephzibah Baptist Association, "knowing that our colored brethren are unacquainted with the mode of constituting and organizing a church, and believing that they will need the assistance of pastors and other brethren when such a work is undertaken," urged its member churches to "offer their services to the colored brethren to aid and assist them." Even after black churches were organized "they will still need counsel and advice in discipline, and in many other things." As late as 1873, Eliza Fain in eastern Tennessee wrote in her diary, "Let us rejoice ever in the advances of this people spiritually and do all we can to advance them intellectually and teach them the importance of striving to learn to take care of themselves. They are a helpless dependent people." Reflecting her estimation of black religion, Fain prayed that God would keep them from "spiritual pride, superstition and everything which will degrade and destroy them."[39]

The ministers and members of the CME Church relied more heavily than other Methodist freedpeople on paternalistic southern white assistance. After two bishops of the MECS helped to organize the CME Church as a separate denomination in 1870, Lucius H. Holsey continued to serve as one of its leading ministers. When Bishop Richard H. Vanderhorst died in July 1872, the fledgling denomination was left with only one bishop, William H. Miles. In response the CME Church held a called General Conference in March 1873 at Holsey's Trinity Church in Augusta, Georgia. The assembly elected three former slaves, including Holsey, as bishops of the CME Church. In less than a decade, Holsey had risen from slavery to the episcopacy; he was thirty years old. Bishop George Foster Pierce, Holsey's mentor in the MECS, preached the ordination sermon and aided Bishop Miles in ordaining the three new episcopal leaders. As bishop, Holsey presided over annual conferences across the South, and he both guided and represented the CME Church through his forceful oratorical and writing abilities.[40]

Local CME churches also received the use of or outright title to church property from white churches. Lacking a clear view of the fate of its black membership in December 1865, the Georgia Conference of the MECS declared that it had no right to transfer property held by trustees for black members. Even if only a handful of black members remained in the MECS, they generally received exclusive use of any property used by black members before the war. However, in cases where all of the local black membership left the southern Methodist church, the Georgia Conference recommended that the white trustees allow the black former members to use the church buildings for worship. The primary legacy of white southern Methodists to their black membership came five years later after the organization of the CME Church when white MECS trustees transferred church property valued at approximately $1,000,000 to black CME trustees. White Baptists in Darien, Georgia, displayed a similar mixture of benevolence and resignation to the new religious situation. After General Sherman's troops burned the Baptist church there during the war, white Baptists decided not to rebuild and gave the church lot to Baptist freedpeople.[41]

The transition of the First Colored Baptist Church of Nashville from slavery to freedom reflected the experience of many other black churches across the South. The black members of Nashville's First Baptist Church had begun to meet separately under a white minister in 1847. In 1853, the white congregation voted to license former slave Nelson Merry to preach; later in the year, the whites established the black congregation as a black mission church and appointed him its pastor, a position he held until his death in 1881. From 1863 to 1865, the black church doubled in size as refugees fled to Nashville and Federal protection from the surrounding countryside. In March 1865, the five hundred black members of the First Baptist Church requested their independence from their white brethren. Perhaps unwilling to offend Federal occupation troops, for fear that their church might be closed, the white membership acceded, and in September 1865 also transferred the deed to the property that the blacks were using.[47]

Although southern white evangelicals declared that they had a responsibility to provide education for black ministers and teachers, little aid actually was given. Early in the 1870s, the Southern Baptist Convention supported two black students in schools started by northern Baptists in the South; in 1875, the Southern Baptists discontinued this work, citing denominational poverty. In the 1880s Southern Baptists also held a limited number of ministers' institutes for the education of black pastors; interest in this venture soon failed as well. Although many Baptist state conventions acknowledged their responsibility for providing for evangelization and education among the freedpeople in the late 1860s, most said nothing about them after 1870. The Augusta Institute, a Baptist college for training black ministers, had been in intermittent operation since 1867, but the Georgia Baptist Convention ignored it until a native southerner, Dr. Joseph T. Robert, took the presidency of the school in 1871. Robert, a former slaveholder who had moved to the North in 1850, rapidly built up the institution, and in 1879 it moved to Atlanta and became the Atlanta Baptist Seminary. Beginning in 1872, the Georgia Baptist Convention passed several favorable resolutions praising the "sound and wholesome instruction" offered at the Augusta Institute. In 1876 the convention observed with pleasure that the school was, "as such enterprises in our midst should all be, under the immediate care of a Southern man." However, the southern state body offered no financial support for the struggling school. The Reverend Emanuel K. Love, a recent graduate of Robert's college who was to become a prominent denominational leader, testified in 1878 to the positive effects of Robert's efforts. Black churches that had ministers trained under Robert, Love declared, "are in better order, know more about the Holy Bible, have clearer ideas, less superstition, and yell less during preaching" than other churches. Robert had done a "great work" in teaching Georgia's blacks "the true manner of worshipping the great God."[43]

Southern Presbyterians and Methodists likewise paid lip service to the ideals of black education but produced little tangible support. Only in the 1880s did the MECS make any serious effort to educate southern blacks. In 1883, southern Methodists, belatedly responding to repeated appeals from Bishop Lucius H. Holsey of the CME Church, organized Paine Institute in Augusta, Georgia. The school was a joint educational venture sponsored by the two churches, where black ministers and teachers could get "the right kind of education," in Holsey's words. The first president of the institute, George W. Walker, was a white presiding elder from the South Carolina Conference of the MECS. In Jackson, Tennessee, the CME Church had begun its own school, Lane Institute, in 1882; in 1887 its new president was the Reverend Thomas F. Saunders, a member of the Memphis Conference of the MECS and a former Confederate soldier. These two white college presidents, whose salaries were paid by the southern Methodist church, imposed a measure of white southern control, but they also encouraged at least meager southern white financial support for these colleges, resources that would have been unavailable otherwise.[44]

Northern white denominations were perhaps a more important source of assistance for the freedpeople. Much to the consternation of white southern evangelicals, representatives of the American Baptist Home Mission Society, the MEC, and the Presbyterian Church in the United States of America entered the South on the heels of Union armies and continued to arrive throughout the 1860s and into the 1870s. Although initially these missionaries and their religious scalawag allies intended to minister to both black and white southerners, they soon found that their most fertile missionary field was among the freedpeople. Black Christians found northern denominations appealing because they represented the delivering power of the North, the tool God had chosen to humble the South and set its captives free. Northern missionaries also declared that their churches did not make distinctions on the basis of race. Eventually many black Christians came to understand that their northern brethren were only slightly less paternalistic and racist than southern evangelicals, but those northern brethren did help to organize black churches, provided the freed-people with ministers, and ordained those who already served them.

The most important service the northern white denominations performed was their ability to tap northern sources of financial assistance. This aid was directed at first toward acquiring land, erecting church/school buildings, and providing elementary education, and later toward the establishment of southern colleges that trained black preachers and teachers.[45]

The support that came from northern black denominations was less significant in terms of material help, but carried no weight of racism. Black Baptists in the South received some support from the CABMC, which was organized in 1866 in an attempt to unite the efforts of northern black Baptist associations organized before the war with the newly emerging southern black Baptist associations. Between 1866 and 1872, the CABMC supported 209 missionaries in twenty-four states; they organized ninety-five new congregations and forty-six new schools. Internal divisions, lack of funds, the political involvement of some of its missionaries, and the end of the Freemen's Bureau combined to cripple the CABMC's efforts by the mid-1870s, and it disbanded in 1879.[46]

Southern black Methodists received assistance from two northern black denominations, the AME and AMEZ churches. Organized in 1816 and 1821, respectively, both of these denominations grew out of local black congregations that had withdrawn from the MEC.[47] Prior to the Civil War, these denominations expanded slowly among the black population of the northern states. In 1866 the AME Church had approximately fifty thousand members, while ten years later it had over three hundred thousand members. The AMEZ Church had 4,600 members in 1860; by 1870 its ranks had swelled to 125,000. The vast majority of this growth was among the freedpeople of the South.[48]

Although these northern black denominations did not have the financial resources available to their white counterparts, they appealed to Methodist freedpeople because they were black and some of their missionaries had been born slaves. Lacking the resources initially to provide church buildings, the primary benefits the northern black Methodist denominations brought the freedpeople were organization and the authority of licensing and ordination.[49] Several of the earliest representatives of these denominations in the South had remarkable organizational abilities. Ministers and bishops such as James Lynch, Henry M. Turner, Daniel Payne, James W. Hood, and Joseph J. Clinton rapidly organized the black portion of southern Methodist congregations into self-sustaining churches. They recognized and authorized the existing leaders in most of these congregations and gathered hundreds of thousands of black Christians into their denominations. Having established local congregations, these missionaries aided them in appealing to the Freedmen's Bureau or northern benevolent sources for aid in buying a lot, building a church/schoolhouse, and securing the services of a teacher.

The AME chaplain Henry M. Turner continued his efforts for the religious reconstruction of the South after the war ended. When his regiment was mustered out of service, he received a commission as a regular army chaplain from President Andrew Johnson and was assigned to the Freedmen's Bureau in Georgia; he arrived in Atlanta in December 1865. A few weeks later, he resigned his army commission to devote himself wholly to the work of the AME Church in Georgia. The South Carolina Annual Conference of the AME Church appointed him as "superintendent" or presiding elder of the North Georgia mission in 1866, but he served more as an "unordained bishop," in the words of one of his contemporaries. Turner traveled throughout the state, preaching to black congregations and urging them to join the AME denomination. Thousands joined; in July 1866, Turner declared that he had received five hundred people into the AME Church in less than a month. After extensive involvement in Georgia reconstruction politics from 1866 to 1871, Turner accepted the pastorate of St. Philip's AME Church in Savannah, where he served from 1872 to 1876.[50]

The presence of so many denominations vying for members created much turmoil in religious reconstruction. The Methodist experience in Georgia amply illustrates the competition.[51] From 1866 forward, the MEC, the AME Church, and the AMEZ Church all competed for the black Methodists who were leaving the MECS. After 1869, the CME Church joined the fray as well. Figure 5-4 illustrates the numerical results of this rivalry, as well as the loss of black members by the MECS.

The highest prizes in the competition were the large semi-independent black congregations in the larger towns. Augusta had two such Methodist congregations — Bethel and Trinity. The Reverend Samuel Drayton, one of the few black ministers ordained before the war by the southern Methodist church, was pastor of Bethel; Edward S. West, only recently ordained, was the pastor of Trinity. In 1865, missionary James Lynch enrolled Drayton and his congregation in the AME Church. West's church, however, was divided, and West adhered to the MECS.[52]

The Committee on Colored Membership that met at the General Conference of the MECS in 1866, chaired by white minister James E. Evans of Columbus, Georgia, reported that it favored the channeling of those black members who desired to leave the southern church into the AME Church, to prevent them from joining the MEC. So bitter was the division among white Methodists that southern Methodists

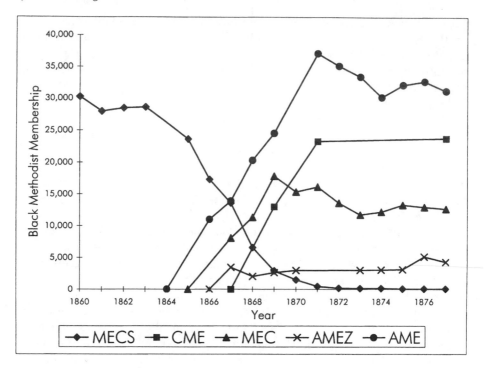

FIGURE 5-4 Black Methodist membership in Georgia, 1860–1877. See note fig. 5-3. Geor-gia's Methodist membership statistics differ from regional averages because the CME Church was comparatively strong in the state, while the AMEZ Church was particularly weak. The CME Church was strongest in the states of Georgia, Mississippi, Tennessee, and Alabama. The AMEZ Church was strongest in North Carolina, Alabama, and South Caro-lina. The strength of the AME Church was more evenly spread across the South.

preferred initially to encourage black members of the MECS to join an all-black de-nomination rather than ally with the MEC. From mid-1866 to late 1867 AME mis-sionaries and southern Methodist preachers cooperated, and whole black congrega-tions were transferred to the AME Church. In return, AME missionaries agreed not to attempt to break up congregations of black Methodists who wished to remain in the MECS and to adhere strictly to "the one work of preaching the gospel." The AME bishops asked the southern General Conference to cede church properties used by the freedpeople to their denomination; the southern white Methodists declined.[53]

In 1866 Fortune Robeson, an AME minister following the instructions of his presiding elder, Henry M. Turner, attempted to take charge of the black church in Lumpkin, Georgia. The white southern Methodist pastor, John C. Simmons, insist-ing that the black congregation had not requested to join the AME Church but ex-pected to become part of the black church structure within the MECS, as provided for by the 1866 General Conference, wrote to the *Southern Christian Advocate* for advice. The reply, from James E. Evans, declared that those who wanted to join the AME Church could do so, but the AME Church had pledged not to interfere with congregations that wished to remain in the MECS.[54]

Trying to abide by the agreement not to proselytize southern black Methodist congregations, Henry M. Turner did not attempt to recruit the large Trinity Methodist Church in Augusta for the AME Church, though he clearly disagreed with the course of its pastor, Edward S. West. In 1866 Turner wrote to his denominational newspaper that West, "the cat's paw of the Southern Church," was "old and ignorant, and I suppose he thinks he is doing right." Then on June 15, 1867, Bishop Joseph Jackson Clinton organized the Georgia Conference of the AMEZ Church with Trinity Methodist Church as the leading congregation. "With a flank move," Turner declared, "which certainly bespeaks considerable strategy for him, [Clinton] attacks this moral citadel, and with such a surprising pressure, that he carried everything before him." Clinton's victory was short-lived. Soon after the close of the organizational meeting, West and his church left the AMEZ Church and returned to the MECS. In 1869, West became the presiding elder of the Augusta District of the Georgia Colored Conference of the MECS, and in 1870 he went with that conference into the CME Church. Bishop Lucius H. Holsey of that church later referred to West as an "Old Christian hero." James W. Hood, a bishop and historian of the AMEZ Church, wrote about Trinity's departure, "our hopes for Georgia were lost. Augusta was one of the three important points in Georgia at that time. The Methodist Episcopal Church held Atlanta, the African Methodist Episcopal Church held Savannah, but if we could have held Augusta we should have been in as good fix as any of them; but we failed to hold Augusta, and so lost Georgia."[55]

Representatives of all the Methodist bodies frequently resorted to such military metaphors to describe the congregations they had captured, secured, or held for their particular branch of Methodism. For example, when Andrew W. Caldwell, a white religious scalawag in the Methodist Episcopal Church, was working among the freedpeople in Rome and Cartersville, an AME minister — with the support of the local MECS minister — was attempting to attract black Methodists in Cartersville to his denomination. Caldwell wrote to his supervisor, "our loss of Cartersville would be a signal triumph to our enemies, and this will be the result unless we give them aid speedily." Henry M. Turner wrote to his denomination's newspaper in Philadelphia that he was "happy to inform you that I have captured Griffin, Ga., and every one of the colored Methodists in it." The weapons of this warfare were promises of church buildings for worship and schoolhouses and teachers for education. The prizes were black congregations.[56]

Similar problems plagued black Methodists in Tennessee. In Nashville, the St. John's Chapel AME church, organized by Bishop Payne in December 1863, was afflicted with division. B. L. Brooks became pastor in November 1865, and by June 1866 he had increased the membership to around three hundred. However, thirty of the original members went back to the MECS, and then claimed the property because it was deeded to white trustees. In August "judgment was given" against the AME congregation; they had to leave the church building "simply because the people would not worship under the spiritual direction of the Methodist Church South. For this crime we were compelled to leave the house that we had built in the days of slavery." One year later, the AME congregation had purchased a lot on Capitol Hill for $3,000 and had completed the basement of their church.[57]

The critical assistance that black Christians received from northern and south-

ern denominations should not obscure their own contributions to the creation of
new religious identities and institutions for themselves. The freedpeople's intense
desire for a new religious life is best illustrated in their remarkable efforts to secure
church and school buildings and establish schools. From Lumpkin, Georgia, an
AME minister wrote in 1867, "Our people are earnest for education, and while much
is being done in many parts of this howling wilderness of sin and ignorance in this
country, not a dollar has been given by the Government, or from any other source,
yet we have from three hundred to three hundred and fifty attending day school in
this county." In 1867 John H. Caldwell, the religious scalawag and missionary of the
MEC in western Georgia, collected $300 from the freedpeople in Grantville and
$400 from those in Whitesville to establish a church and school building in each
community. The Missionary Society of the MEC agreed to provide $350 for the
former and $300 for the latter place; Caldwell then wrote to the superintendent of
education for the Freedmen's Bureau to request contributions of $350 and $300. The
bureau granted the money with the provision that the lot be deeded to black trustees. In 1870 Freedmen's Bureau superintendent John W. Alvord marveled when he
learned that freedpeople in Macon, Georgia, were erecting a brick church costing
$10,000, which was "planned and constructed by their own mechanics — tasteful in
style, and to be paid for wholly by themselves." He noted that the freedpeople "give
more liberally for church purposes than even towards the support of their school."
That black Georgians, only a few years out of slavery, could raise these sums attests
to their commitment to education and to a separate religious life for themselves.[58]

Not all black Christians had the resources to support either their churches or
schools. An AME minister wrote from Albany, Georgia, that although they had "a
very neat little church here," it was poorly furnished, "for the people all seem very
poor and therefore not able to contribute much for church purposes, and barely
able to pay the expenses of their pastor." Although these black Methodists were willing to "do their duty," the "necessities of life forbid their giving very largely."[59]

By 1870 most black southerners had withdrawn from the antebellum biracial
churches and had entered either a northern black or biracial denomination or a
separate organization established by southern churches for their black members.
However, such separations did not resolve the racial issues that confronted southern
religion. As late as 1878, the issue of race was still troubling a few white churches directly. In that year, the white minister Henry F. Hoyt and his congregation of seventy
in the Presbyterian church in Darien, Georgia, were forced "to decide definitely the
position of our colored members in our church." The church was divided over the
status of Mrs. Todd, a Hispanic member. Insisting that they would decide the question upon the "principle of *right*, not of *expediency*," one group offered a resolution
insisting that it was not right "to break down the social barriers between the white
and colored races, even in the house of worship or at the communion table." Therefore, "we deem it right to assign our colored members a subordinate position both
in the church and at the Lord's table." In a second resolution, however, the authors
declared they did not "class Mrs. Todd with the colored race, but on account of her
free birth, her Spanish parentage, her education, and her intimate association with
the whites," she was entitled to all the privileges of the white race in the church.
After reconsidering their broad declaration of religious and social subordination, the

congregation amended the resolution to state, "while we do not consider it right to endeavor to break down the social barriers between the white and colored races, still we do not deem it right to assign our colored members a subordinate position either in church or at the Lord's table." In light of this change, the resolution regarding Mrs. Todd was stricken out.[60]

Racial issues also plagued the operations of northern white denominations in the South and hampered efforts to reunite the sectional bodies of the major evangelical denominations. While southern black Christians were establishing a religious life for themselves separate from the domination of southern whites, northern and southern whites were acting out their own plans of religious reconstruction. At a crucial period in the establishment of independent black churches, northern and southern denominations offered both organizational and material assistance. Yet they did so without surrendering their own priorities and ideals for rebuilding the religious life of the South. Black Christians crossed the wilderness and the River Jordan in the years between 1865 and 1877, but the promised land they found was inhabited, and the contours of its religious life were contested.

6

Southern Churches Resurgent

Denominational Structures and Religious Newspapers

When the LORD shall build up Zion, he shall appear in his glory.

Psalm 102:16

To reinvigorate their sectional religious identity, white southerners had to reestablish their denominational organizations. In the late 1860s white congregations could barely sustain themselves, and they could do little for religious education or missions without uniting with other congregations. If southern denominations failed to reorganize themselves, local churches would either exist in isolation or be forced to accept an even worse fate — union with the northern denominational organizations. Fierce sectional loyalty insured that few churches or even individuals would choose the latter option. Revulsion at the idea of reunion with the haughty northern churches spurred white evangelicals to greater efforts to rebuild their religious institutions on an explicitly southern basis.

The religious life of whites in Georgia in the 1860s and 1870s was dominated by three denominations — the Georgia Annual Conference of the Methodist Episcopal Church, South (MECS), the Georgia Baptist Convention of the Southern Baptist Convention (SBC), and the Synod of Georgia of the Presbyterian Church in the United States (PCUS). In 1860, these three organizations had over 150,000 members in nearly two thousand local congregations. An additional twenty thousand members belonged to several hundred independent, mostly Baptist, churches unaffiliated with these three statewide organizations. The next largest denominational organization in the state, the Protestant Episcopal Church, had only two thousand members. Cumberland Presbyterians, though numerous in neighboring Tennessee, had only four churches in the northwestern corner of Georgia, with a total of fewer than five hundred members.

In Tennessee, 91 percent of the congregations belonged to four denominations — Baptist, Methodist, Presbyterian, and Cumberland Presbyterian. Tennessee Baptists had general organizations in each of the three major geographical divisions of the state: the West Tennessee Baptist Convention, the General Association of Middle Tennessee, and the East Tennessee Baptist General Association. The Methodists were also divided into three regional conferences — the Memphis Annual Conference in the west, the Tennessee Annual Conference in the central section, and the Holston Annual Conference in the east. The Presbyterians were divided into two synods — the Synod of Memphis in the west and the Synod of Nashville in the central and eastern sections. The more numerous Cumberland Presbyterians had four synods either wholly or partly in Tennessee — the West Tennessee Synod, the Middle Tennessee Synod, the East Tennessee Synod, and the Columbia Synod. Together, these four denominations in 1860 had some 175,000 Tennessee members in over two thousand local churches.

The principal statewide organizations consisted of smaller regional groups — Methodist quarterly conferences, Baptist associations, and Presbyterian presbyteries — each of which contained from five to fifty local churches. These organizational structures existed primarily to facilitate financial support for schools and the domestic and foreign missionary endeavors of the state or national organizations. For example, Georgia's locally oriented Baptists united in a common convention to support "Missions, Education, the Sunday School work, and the collection of funds for benevolent purposes."[1] In the more hierarchically organized Methodist and Presbyterian churches, church councils had greater disciplinary authority, but their activities demonstrated that educational and missionary activities were central to their existence as well.

When southern Christians began to reconstruct their religious lives in the mid-1860s, denominational structures were the logical foundations on which to build, but first they had to be repaired from the damage they had suffered during the dislocation of war and the devastating loss of black members. After recovering from the initial shock of defeat, southern religious leaders perceived in the destruction of the war a chance to rebuild their institutions, much as New South leaders saw that destruction as a chance to industrialize the South. From the start, denominational leaders understood the important role religious newspapers could play in uniting disparate churches behind the common goal of religious reconstruction. In the pages of these journals, southern editors proclaimed southern ideals and condemned northern denominations. They urged paternalism toward the freedpeople and garnered support for denominational colleges and Sunday schools. In short, these newspapers strengthened ties between individual churches and larger ecclesiastical bodies, while forging a distinctive southern religious identity, based on their understanding of God's providence in the great conflict just ended.

The largest share of responsibility for southern religious reconstruction fell to the ministers of the various denominations; they were the first line of defense against the devil and the North. The Western Baptist Association in Georgia solemnly declared in 1866, "we should be grateful to our God for protecting the lives of our preachers, for surely Zion has much need for watchmen on her walls." Sounding a note of caution, the 1865 meeting of the Synod of Memphis urged churches to fill their pulpits quickly, but only with "known and tried men." Presbyterian minister Robert Langdon Neely observed in his manuscript history of the synod, "the *caveat* was inserted on account of the uncertainty of men and things in those days."[2]

Ministers such as Presbyterian Thomas H. McCallie of Chattanooga worked tirelessly to rebuild southern religious life. In 1866 and 1867 McCallie preached eighty-seven sermons in neighboring towns, "beside my regular services twice each Sabbath and on Wednesday night." In 1869 and 1870, he continued the fervid pace, preaching in towns and cities from Knoxville, Tennessee, to Huntsville, Alabama. Between 1866 and 1870, he conducted nearly two hundred services each year. By early 1873, his "health was gone." In March of that year, he reluctantly resigned his pastorate in Chattanooga and became an evangelist for the Knoxville Presbytery.[3]

Some Confederates determined to enter the ministry in gratitude for their survival through the war. One of the most famous of their number was General Clement A. Evans from Lumpkin, Georgia. Having returned home in May 1865, on June 7 Evans wrote to the presiding elder of the Americus District seeking to join the Georgia Conference of the MECS. Sitting upon the battlefield immediately after the bloody conflict at Fredericksburg, Virginia, late in 1862, he had determined to become a Methodist preacher, realizing that "I should have devoted myself to the ministry in the beginning of life." Although he was struck by bullets five times, he felt that his life was "safe during the entire war." Certain that "God has graciously preserved me for a good purpose," he wrote, "the deep sense of gratitude, of obligation and of love I feel knows no bounds."[4] In December 1865, Bishop George F. Pierce appointed him to the Manassas Circuit in Bartow County, Georgia. General Sherman's army had desolated the area, and the people were "broken-down, broken-hearted, poverty-stricken." Evans "took pot-luck with them" and ministered to them for three years. He later reminisced that the appointment was "in some respects the *best I* ever had."[5]

For most men who were interested in entering the ministry, the obstacles were imposing. The *Southern Presbyterian* complained, "not a few of our pious young men would be glad to qualify themselves to preach the everlasting gospel, but have not the means to prosecute their studies." Tennessee Presbyterian Eliza Fain believed that the education of ministers was "at present . . . one of the most important matters of earth before us. We need men as heralds for the gospel but when they come we have no institutions to fit them for it." Only with denominational assistance and a sufficient number of seminaries could many young candidates ever hope to receive ministerial training.[6]

Even established ministers had difficulty devoting their attention to religious reconstruction in the immediate aftermath of the war. The *Southern Presbyterian* noted, "many of our best and most earnest preachers have been compelled to betake themselves to school-keeping, or some other secular employment, in order to provide the means of subsistence for their families." In January 1866, the Committee on the Narrative for the Synod of Nashville, chaired by Thomas H. McCallie, reported that "quite a number" of the synod's ministers "have been, and still are, engaged in teaching, while at the same time preaching from Sabbath to Sabbath. These exhausting labors they cannot long endure, nor will they be able to accomplish much in the vineyard of the Master while worn out with the duties of the school-room." "A school teaching ministry," the committee concluded, "is a hindrance to the progress of the gospel, which we deeply mourn." By 1868 the Synod of Georgia had recommended to the presbyteries to fix the minimum salary for ministers at $600 per year. In accordance with this plan, "no church should expect the services of a minister all his time that can not raise $600 for his support." As evidence that "the all-absorbing passion for personal welfare, and for individual safety" had captured the southern heart, the *Christian Index* in January 1866 called attention to "the number of ministers who are forced by want to embark in secular pursuits."[7] The Tennessee Conference of the southern Methodist church urged its members to support their pastors: "Where you cannot furnish your ministers with money, give them shelter, send them food; give them a portion of the products of your field, your shops, your trade." In 1873 the Holston Conference of the same church complained that only 69 percent of the preachers' claims had been paid in the previous year.[8]

Critical to the success of any effort for religious reconstruction was the revitalization of the local churches. Scattered, demoralized, and often without leadership, these individual congregations had to be secured to the southern denominations to prevent them from looking to northern denominations for support. The 1865 General Assembly of the PCUS instructed its Executive Committee of Domestic Missions to survey the churches and determine which needed financial help and which were in a position to aid other churches. The committee also arranged for the collection and dispersal of funds. However, during the year 1865–66, fewer than one-fifth of the churches contributed anything to the cause, and the vast majority of money contributed to domestic missions was designated specifically for the support of weak churches. In June 1865, Thomas H. McCallie "began taking up a collection every Sunday for church expenses" in Chattanooga. The first collection was $17; thereafter "church affairs, especially the financial part, moved along more smoothly." Previously, the church had collected funds "about once in three months, or on every sacramental occasion." As Thomas C. Johnson, a historian of the PCUS, wrote three decades later, "Her work for the time was not so much to establish new churches as to repair old ones. Jerusalem had to rebuild her own walls before she could dwell in safety and repossess the land."[9]

There were some signs of hope amidst the devastation. Revivals flourished in some areas, and many returning soldiers became more faithful to the churches in the aftermath of their wartime experiences. In the fall of 1865, the *Christian Index* noted that among the revivals in the country churches, "it has been pleasant to observe that our young men who had just returned from the army were among the first to manifest an interest for their souls, while great numbers of them have been converted and become praying members of the churches with which they united."[10]

Despite the devastation, ministers expected their congregations to rally to the cause of religious reconstruction and chastised them when they did not. The Executive Committee of the New Sunbury Association on the coast of Georgia reminded the churches in 1867 that since "the war has been past now for more than two years," it was "time to stop pleading it as a cause for neglecting to build meeting houses and to supply the Gospel." Their excuses only barely disguised their "selfishness" and "love of the world." If Christ's love "burns in our hearts," the committee reminded the association, His cause "may be carried forward in hard times." In the same year, the Bethel Baptist Association in southwest Georgia reported, "with sadness of heart, that the churches generally are in a very cold, declining state."[11]

Despite considerable progress in recovery in the years after the war, an 1869 survey of the condition of Baptists in Georgia found some areas still in need. The Reverend Sylvanus Landrum, pastor of Savannah's First Baptist Church, chaired a newly formed Committee on the State of Religion and Religious Destitution in the State. In the corner of Georgia north and east of Athens, the committee reported, "there is not a minister who is supported while preaching the gospel." North of Augusta for twenty miles, "there is much need of preaching." Around Knoxville in central Georgia the area was in a state of "most deplorable destitution — churches without preaching and general demoralization." On the coast the destitution was "well nigh universal," and the "flourishing town" of Thomasville was without a pastor. Most of the city churches had pastors, but "there is much complaint of theatre going, balls, worldliness, and also want of integrity in reference to promises and commercial honor." Landrum closed the report by insisting that among Georgia Baptists, there was "a great want of ministerial consecration and ministerial support," "much destitution in the churches, and many neighborhoods unprovided with the preached Word." The report called for prayer and self-denial, rather than the use of the war and poverty "as pleas for the love of the world and the idolatry of covetousness."[12]

By 1871 the Georgia Baptists were faring better. The Committee on the State of Religion happily declared that "there is a more general supply of preaching and fewer churches without pastors than existed two years ago." Church members displayed "a manifest improvement in the willingness to give," and "there is a decided improvement in morals." The committee urged the Baptists of the state to "carry forward, with conquering power, the banner, bearing the inscription: GEORGIA FOR JESUS!" Committee reports to the convention in 1874 and 1875 likewise reported the state of religion as "encouraging." By 1874, the state had "very nearly as many churches as are needed," and in some areas had too many. In some localities, the committee suggested, it would be wise for two or more weak churches to unite. In 1877 the committee noted thankfully that while the war "entailed calamities which might have been more ruinous than they are, our Lord has given us marvelous growth."[13]

Although southerners mounted an intensive effort for religious reconstruction in the late 1860s, much remained to be done in the 1870s. Many congregations had either rebuilt their damaged churches or built entirely new edifices. Yet in 1871, the North Georgia Annual Conference, "one of the most prosperous conferences of the Methodist Episcopal Church, South," reported that of its 606 church buildings, only 177 were ceiled or plastered and only 151 had stoves.[14]

Wartime devastation created postwar opportunities for denominational restructuring that eventually made southern churches more effective. The devastation of Sherman's march through Georgia and the complementary wreckage by retreating Confederates destroyed the Cherokee Baptist Convention in the northwestern section of the state. Many rural churches were left without ministers and with only a few members. As late as 1869, one minister was preaching to six different churches in this area. In 1866 the Middle Cherokee Baptist Association lamented, "many of our churches were destroyed and flocks scattered during the occupancy of the country by the enemy. Many of the ministers, formerly within our bounds, who sought safety during the late war in other sections, have not returned, and in consequence there is great want of ministerial labor." To meet this emergency, the association suggested the appointment of a missionary "to labor within our limits, to destitute churches and sections." The association also indefinitely postponed the election of delegates to the Cherokee Baptist Convention and "agreed to refer to the Churches composing this body the question of joining the Georgia Baptist Convention."[15] The Georgia Baptist Convention was receptive to the idea; the committee on the State of Religion and Religious Destitution in the State told the 1869 convention that if "the brethren of this section could be persuaded to identify themselves with this Convention and with Mercer University, your committee are of the opinion that mutual good would result."[16] The constituent associations of the Cherokee convention —Coosa, Middle Cherokee, and Tallapoosa — all joined the Georgia Baptist Convention between 1869 and 1875.

In the unsettled context of religious reconstruction, several ecclesiastical bodies reorganized. After a long discussion and two votes, Georgia Methodists narrowly decided in 1866 to divide the Georgia Annual Conference into two more manageable conferences. A Committee on the Division of the Conference recommended, "in view of all the circumstances connected therewith, and the general good of the church, that the division should take place." The conference, on November 30, voted 63 to 56 in favor of division, and three days later, after a motion for reconsideration, voted 65 to 51 to divide. Consequently, the Methodist churches in the state were divided along a line running just north of Columbus and Macon and just south of Augusta. The newly formed North Georgia Conference encompassed nine presiding elders' districts with nearly forty-five thousand members, while the South Georgia Conference had seven districts with 26,500 members.[17]

While Georgia Methodists divided, Tennessee Baptists moved toward greater unity. By 1873 each of the three regional associations had considered the possibility of a statewide union, and the associations appointed committees to discuss its viability. The committee from the East Tennessee Baptist General Association called for a meeting in Murfreesboro in April 1874, and forty delegates assembled there to consider unification. A Committee on Unification proposed a constitution for the "Tennessee Baptist Convention." After expressly forbidding ecclesiastical jurisdiction over the member churches, the Constitution declared that the purpose of the convention was to "promote the educational interests of the Baptists of Tennessee." This unification conference also appointed a committee of nine (three from each section) to consider the best location for a "well-endowed, thoroughly equipped University, of the highest order." Four months later, the committee chose Jackson, Tennessee, as the site of the new Southwestern Baptist University.[18]

Provincialism and suspicion of a strong state organization remained in some areas of Tennessee. After some debate, both the West Tennessee Baptist Convention and the General Baptist Association of Middle Tennessee and Northern Alabama dissolved in 1874, but the East Tennessee Baptist General Association did not vote to disband until 1885.[19]

While state religious bodies were regrouping and assessing the damages done by four years of strife, the sectional denominational bodies provided both inspiration and assistance. Both the Presbyterian General Assembly and the Methodist General Conference considered new names for their organizations in the wake of the failure of the Confederacy. The General Assembly of the Presbyterian Church in the Confederate States of America met in December 1865 at Macon, Georgia. After delegates had proposed sixteen different names and debated the issue thoroughly, they chose the name Presbyterian Church in the United States, which received forty-two votes. The name Presbyterian Church, South, came in a distant second with seven votes. The Reverend Dr. Frederick A. Ross proposed the latter name because it "expresses the truth" and "would harmonise different parts of our body." He insisted, "We are not going to unite with the Church North; let them, if they wish, unite with us." A majority of the General Assembly consciously avoided the use of the terms "South" or "Southern" both to woo border state Presbyterians and to avoid any misinterpretation "that we are contending for merely temporary and sectional ends." However, a strong element of sectional identity remained, as the delegates' attitude toward the Presbyterian Church in the United States of America made clear.[20]

The General Conference of the MECS met in New Orleans in April 1866 to consider the future of that church. Many believed the word "South" in the name dampened the appeal of the church among border state Methodists; after considering nine alternative names, the conference voted 111 to 21 to rename the organization The Methodist Church. After reconsidering this decision the next day, the conference decided on The Episcopal Methodist Church instead. The General Conference submitted the change to the annual conferences, three-fourths of which had to approve for the change to take place. Most annual conferences were less concerned about appealing to border state Methodists than was the General Conference, and in a triumph of sectional identification, the requisite number of conferences failed to approve the change in name.[21]

The 1866 General Conference gave impetus to a variety of efforts designed to rebuild southern Methodism. This first meeting of the entire church since 1858 "challenged and revived the confidence of the people, and sounded the keynote of the quadrennium for renewed activity and lofty endeavor. Preachers and people everywhere responded, and once more, after a long, dark period of decimation, demoralization, and depression, the church went forward." Since several of the bishops of the church were in feeble health, the General Conference elected four new bishops to supplement the ranks of the episcopacy and give it renewed vigor for the challenges of religious reconstruction.[22]

Georgian Edward H. Myers chaired a Committee on Changes of Economy, which reviewed the various proposals for changes in polity and submitted them in seven different reports to the conference. The subjects of these reports included changing the name of the church, changing the reception of members and the social meetings of the church, establishing district conferences, forming episcopal districts, instituting lay representation, extending the pastoral term, and adopting a new constitution for the church.[23]

After considering these various reports, the conference enacted a broad series of constitutional reforms that abolished class meetings, probationary periods for mem-

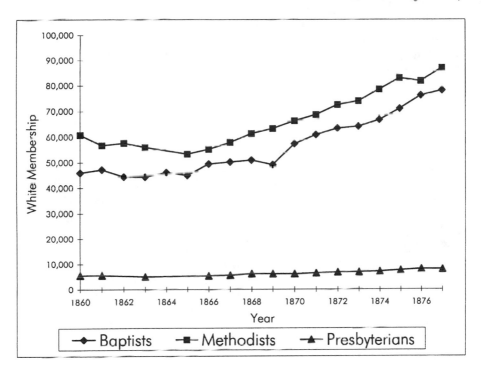

FIGURE 6-1 White membership in southern denominations in Georgia, 1860–1877

bership, gender segregation of church services, and the ban on pew rentals. It also extended the maximum pastoral term from two to four years. Most important, it provided for the election of lay delegates to the General Conference, a reform that meant that the church would reflect the social attitudes of all white southerners more closely than had its antebellum counterpart, which was led by a ministerial elite.[24]

The SBC was also active in providing both leadership and financial support for state conventions, associations, and local churches. Georgia Baptists in 1869 acknowledged the assistance they had received from the Domestic Mission Board of the SBC. Georgia had "received a liberal return" from the Board, and the state's "destitution has not been overlooked." Since 1865 seventeen Georgia Baptist ministers and several feeble churches had been aided by the Domestic Board. Georgia Baptists considered the Board "a necessity in the land," and believed it provided "evidence of our interest in the great work of Southern evangelization."[25]

Dramatic increases in membership were the most tangible manifestations of successful religious reconstruction. Patterns of membership growth also provide a unique glimpse of how average white southerners reacted to competing visions of religious reconstruction. Georgia's white population increased by 38 percent between 1860 and 1880, rising from 591,550 in the former year to 816,906 two decades later. As figure 6-1 illustrates, the white membership of each of Georgia's principal denominations grew steadily during these decades. Moreover, denominational growth exceeded the growth rate of the white population as a whole. The white membership of the Synod of Georgia grew by 55 percent in these two decades to number slightly over 8,600 communicants in 1880. Although the Methodist Georgia Annual Conference and the Georgia Baptist Convention lost virtually all their black members, their growth in white membership gave them a net increase over the two decades. According to its statistical reports, the white membership of the Georgia Baptist Convention grew from nearly forty-six thousand members in 1860 to over eighty-four thousand in 1880, an increase of 83 percent. White Methodist membership grew by 56 percent from a total of 60,753 in 1860 to 94,925 in 1880. In stark contrast, the missionary efforts of the Methodist Episcopal Church in Georgia never garnered more than four thousand white members in this period.

Although churches in the western two-thirds of Tennessee enjoyed a very similar recovery in membership, East Tennessee remained deeply divided.[26] Home to a large number of Unionists during the war and actively cultivated by northern missionaries, East Tennessee became notorious for religious strife. The statistical records of the MECS in Tennessee demonstrate the contrast between the Methodists of western and central Tennessee, who remained overwhelmingly loyal to the southern church, and those of eastern Tennessee, who were divided between the northern and southern churches. Figure 6-2 shows that the Memphis and Tennessee conferences rapidly recovered their prewar strength and grew steadily in the 1870s. Although the Holston Conference of the southern church doubled in size between 1867 and 1877, it was crippled by the initial loss of 21,161 (75 percent) of its members between 1865 and 1866.

Most evangelical Georgians and Tennesseeans remained in their southern churches, and many of their neighbors joined them there in the decade following Appomattox. Only in eastern Tennessee did large numbers of white Christians join northern denominations. The mountain Unionists there rejected the southern vision of religious reconstruction and embraced the northern vision instead.[27]

In this struggle for the religious loyalty of southern Christians and the maintenance of southern ecclesiastical organizations, the revival of the southern religious periodicals, which staunchly proclaimed the principles of the southern denominations, was crucial. The religious journals were the watchdogs against northern intrigues from without and lack of commitment from within. The Synod of Memphis in 1865 "keenly felt" the importance of religious literature. According to one member of this synod, Robert Langdon Neely, "the publication of religious papers in our church was scarcely established at this date, the mass of people never seeing one, and as for good new books of a religious character, no one expected to see them." Although "distant publishers" were willing to supply this demand, much of their material was "unfriendly and unsuitable." The synod exhorted all Presbyterian families to supply themselves with "reliable religious readings, and, in reference to papers, suggested that they patronize such papers as would truly and faithfully advocate and represent the interest and feelings of our church."[28]

The *Southern Presbyterian* served members of the PCUS in several states, including Georgia. The last wartime issue had been published in Augusta on April 6, 1865. A new editor, the Reverend James Woodrow, resumed publication of the newspaper in Columbia, South Carolina, on January 4, 1866. He made it clear in the inaugural issue that the *Southern Presbyterian* would remain thoroughly southern: "A

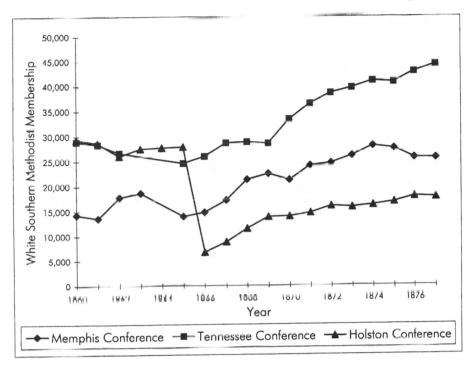

FIGURE 6-2 White southern Methodist membership in Tennessee, 1860–1877. *Sources: Minutes of the Annual Conferences of the Methodist Episcopal Church, South, 1860–1877* (Memphis Annual Conference, Tennessee Annual Conference, Holston Annual Conference). Each of these conferences included some churches located in neighboring states, but the figures here include only those presiding elder districts that were in Tennessee.

Presbyterian newspaper (published in the *South*, where there never has been a departure, by our ecclesiastical denomination, from the true doctrine of the *spirituality* of the Church . . .) is, in its very name, sufficiently distinctive." Although they emphasized the spirituality of the church, the editors did not pledge "to abstain from all allusion to public affairs" since "these affairs are frequently interlaced with grave ecclesiastical matters."[29]

Eliza Fain in eastern Tennessee found northern Presbyterian newspapers wholly unacceptable. When her husband brought her a copy of the northern New School *American Presbyterian* in June 1865, she wrote in her diary, "In it I find nothing, no nothing congenial with the Southern heart. Their whole enthusiasm and care is lavished upon the African race regardless of the feelings of the white Christian brother or sister who may from his view of Bible teaching see it to differ with them." Fain found the *Christian Observer*, edited by Amasa Converse in Richmond, much more "congenial." In December 1869, with "snow covering the ground and weighing down the lifeless looking trees," Fain's family gathered around their hearth with "our Bible, our religious papers and the life of the devoted martyrs before us filling the heart with a joy, a comfort which the dreariness of the outer world cannot take away."[30]

By the summer of 1866 southern Methodists had reestablished nine of their periodicals, including the *Southern Christian Advocate* in Macon, Georgia, and the *Christian Advocate* (Nashville) and *Memphis Christian Advocate* in Tennessee. Methodist James O. Andrew wrote to his fellow bishop Holland N. McTyeire, "Surely we have a fine array of newspapers if that be regarded as any proof of prosperity."[31]

The *Southern Christian Advocate*, edited by the northern-born but staunchly southern Edward H. Myers, returned to normal publication in Macon in August 1865 to circulate "those conservative and unifying opinions that the present time demands." Myers reasoned that the "conservative and harmonizing influence" of the religious press was never "more needed, than at a period of change such as that through which Southern society is now passing." Bishop Pierce proclaimed that the paper was "a church necessity." In the current state of the country, Methodists must have "a medium of communication with the preachers and the people, in order to conserve the great interests committed to our charge." What Myers and Pierce wanted the *Southern Christian Advocate* to help preserve was both religious and distinctively southern.[32]

Methodist preachers and laypeople in the churches also believed a religious newspaper was essential. The members of the Bainbridge District in south Georgia resolved to endeavor to increase the circulation of the *Southern Christian Advocate* because it was "eminently calculated to promote the Spirit of piety, zeal and earnest devotion to the Church and all its interests."[33]

Subscriptions to the *Southern Christian Advocate* did not meet the expenses of publication until 1868. In December of that year, the North Georgia Conference hailed it as "one of the very best religious periodicals in the country," which would soon "rival, if not exceed, its former capacity for usefulness." If the debts it had accumulated in the first years after the war could be paid, "the success of the paper will be secured beyond ordinary contingencies." In 1871, the North Georgia Conference was proud to proclaim that the *Southern Christian Advocate* had "overcome all the difficulties that once embarrassed its publication." If the preachers and laity "will but do their duty," the newspaper "will prove a power and a blessing to the Church."[34]

The *Christian Advocate* in Nashville reappeared in January 1866 after MECS book agent John B. McFerrin convinced President Johnson to return the Southern Methodist Publishing House seized by Federal troops in 1862. Once able to reoccupy the publishing house, McFerrin and the Publishing House's financial secretary Richard Abbey ran the press and published the *Christian Advocate* until Thomas O. Summers, the Publishing House's former book editor, returned to Nashville in the late spring of 1866 to begin editing the paper.[35]

The Georgia Baptists' *Christian Index*, published in Macon, did not resume regular publication until January 1866. In the fall of 1865, the Houston Baptist Association in central Georgia urged its members to read and support the *Baptist Banner*, published in Augusta, and the *Christian Index*, "soon to be resumed in Macon," because both "have ever been good and safe papers for the reading public."[36] "Safe" meant religious in content and southern in loyalty.

The *Christian Index* rendered valuable service to Georgia Baptists as they rebuilt their religious lives. In a trial issue in November 1865, the newspaper proclaimed its desire to "maintain and uphold the various enterprises of Christian Benevolence in which the Baptists of Georgia and the adjoining States are engaged." It promised that the "various educational interests of the denomination shall receive constant attention, and whatever we can do to foster and sustain them, shall be done." The publishing office of the *Christian Index*, now in Atlanta, would be the "Baptist Headquarters and Sanctum of the Brethren."[37]

The new editor of the newspaper, Henry H. Tucker, declared the *Christian Index* "a necessity to our denomination" that was "never more needed than now." Foremost among his qualifications as editor, Tucker proclaimed himself to be "a Southern man — Southern by birth — as were his ancestors before him for six or seven generations — Southern in all his habits of thought and sympathies." Nevertheless, he declared, he hoped to "elevate himself and his readers above sectional feelings." Although perhaps not as bitter in tone as some other religious periodicals, the *Christian Index* remained one of the most conservative southern Baptist newspapers, firmly upholding the Confederate vision of religious reconstruction.[38]

Tennessee Baptists had to wait longer for the reemergence of their paper, the *Tennessee Baptist* of Nashville, edited by the vociferous leader of Baptist Landmarkism, J. R. Graves, which was forced to suspend operations in 1862. On February 1, 1867, Graves resumed publishing the paper in Memphis with its original title, *The Baptist*. Conscious of his duty as a denominational spokesman, Graves immediately called Baptists' attention to the hardship suffered by pastors and their families who were not properly supported by their congregations.[39]

When the *Christian Index* resumed in Atlanta in January 1866, it also served as the periodical for Alabama Baptists. The *South-Western Baptist*, published until April 1865 in Tuskegee, Alabama, did not survive the war; rather than attempt to launch several small papers "upon the hazards of a not very promising future," Alabama Baptists agreed to unite with Georgia Baptists in the support of the *Index*. The Reverend Samuel Henderson, former editor of the *South-Western Baptist*, continued for a time to edit a page devoted to Alabama Baptist issues. He insisted, "the necessity for a religious newspaper has never been so extensively and imperatively felt as now." Pastors needed it "to encourage and sustain them." Churches needed it "as they emerge from that baptism of suffering which they have endured for more than four years." Baptist families needed it "to preserve them from the contagion of an alien literature that would lead them to repudiate the faith of their fathers." The denominational organizations needed it "to supplement their efforts to meet the demands which are upon them."[40]

The consolidation of newspapers was also evident in other denominations. In 1874 the Cumberland Presbyterian Board of Publication purchased the subscription lists of the *Banner of Peace* of Nashville, Tennessee, the *Cumberland Presbyterian* of Alton, Illinois, and the *Texas Cumberland Presbyterian* of Tehuacana, Texas; it then began to publish the *Cumberland Presbyterian* from Nashville.[41]

Other newspapers were not so fortunate. After the war destroyed the Cherokee Baptist Convention in northwest Georgia during the war, its *Baptist Banner* struggled on in Augusta for a short while and then dissolved. The *East Tennessee Baptist*, begun in November 1869, lasted less than a year. Despite the editor's plea that no newspaper outside of east Tennessee was satisfactory, the thirty-five thousand Baptists of the area did not respond. In February 1870, the editor insisted, "both labor and sacrifice will be necessary to carry on what we have begun." If "the friends of the paper" would do their part, he argued, "we believe we shall succeed." Two months later, he still condemned the "apathy" and "do-nothing spirit" of east Tennessee Baptists. Soon afterward the paper ceased publication.[42]

Southern evangelicals also restored other parts of their religious press. After the Southern Methodist Publishing House reopened in late 1865, the Nashville *Christian Advocate* stated, "No institution of the South suffered to a greater extent during the war . . . than did the Publishing House of the M.E. Church, South." By 1870, however, its immediate postwar debt of $71,000 had been reduced to $41,000.

Recovery ended abruptly in February 1872 when a fire destroyed most of the two buildings occupied by the Publishing House. Equipment, supplies, the stock of books, and denominational records were all destroyed.[43] Book agent Albert H. Redford determined immediately to rebuild the establishment and projected that $50,000 would be needed. After the expenditure of over $176,000, Southern Methodists had a four-story building that was the pride of the denomination, but by 1878 the high cost of rebuilding and Redford's financial mismanagement had driven the Publishing House deeply into debt. In that year the General Conference appointed a committee to investigate Redford's report about the organization. The committee discovered that instead of having $300,000 more in assets than debts, as Redford claimed, the Publishing House had $46,000 more in debts than assets. The Conference overwhelmingly appointed John B. McFerrin, then seventy-one, to attempt to sell $300,000 in bonds and save the Publishing House. Appealing to sectional pride, McFerrin asked Methodists across the South to consider the alternative if his mission failed: "The Bishops, the General Conference officers, the preachers, the people — men, women, and children — are gathered on the Public Square in Nashville, in front of the Publishing House, to witness the sad and shameful scene — the sale of the honor and good name of the Southern Methodist Church!" Among the Confederate Christians who had upheld a distinctively southern denomination during religious reconstruction, this appeal found a receptive audience; McFerrin sold all the bonds within two years.[44]

The Southern Methodist Publishing House supported the southern approach to religious reconstruction by publishing such works as *The Disruption of the Methodist Episcopal Church, 1844–1846* (1875), a history of the division of Methodism written by Edward H. Myers, the polemical editor of the *Southern Christian Advocate* from 1856 to 1871. Myers's interpretation upheld the constitutionality of the division and reinforced the belief that the political activities and radicalism of northern Methodists forced southern Methodists to withdraw from the corrupted MEC. In his introduction to the volume, Thomas O. Summers insisted that fraternal relations could not be established by a simple assertion to "let by-gones be bygones." Instead, the two churches had to delineate their current relationship carefully and then proceed to establish fraternity. Summers declared, "the South cannot recede from its platform," including its "views on slavery," nor did he "ask the North to recede from its." With such intransigence on both sides, reunion efforts had little chance for success. The Southern Methodist Publishing House and Summer's *Christian Advocate* (Nashville) defended at every point the maintenance of a separate

southern Methodist church and carefully surveyed their ranks for any sign of acqui-
escence to northern overtures.[45]

Southern Presbyterians supplemented their newspapers by resuming the publication of the quarterly *Southern Presbyterian Review*. It too upheld southern views
and institutions. In 1870, for example, the journal published an article originally
written in 1865 by Rev. Dr. A. W. Miller, the pastor of the First Presbyterian Church
in Charlotte, North Carolina, entitled "Southern Views and Principles Not 'Extinguished' by the War." In response to northern assertions that southerners "accepted
the situation," Miller declared that southerners did so only in one sense: "The providence of God has sorely smitten them, and humbled them, and they desire to bow
in submission to His holy will." However, "it does not follow that the providence of
God has decided against the justice of their cause." Miller insisted that "accepting
the situation" did not mean that southerners "abandoned their former distinctive
views and principles." Citing Old Testament accounts of the defeat of the Jews by
neighboring nations, Miller argued that "Providence, for wise ends, may permit an
ungodly nation to prosper for a time." To be victorious, both the cause and the people supporting it must be righteous. The South lost the war because "God frustrates
a righteous cause on account of the sins of those who espoused it." If southerners
had maintained a proper relationship with God, "Southern principles would have
been crowned with speedy victory." The people of the South, therefore, "whilst sub-
mitting humbly to the terrible rebukes of a holy God for their sins, do not thereby
surrender their well-established views and principles, political and moral: the first,
supported by the Constitution of the country; the last, protected by the Scriptures of
eternal truth." That the *Southern Presbyterian Review* chose to publish this article in
1870 demonstrates that the moral and ecclesiastical battles of religious reconstruction still raged.[46]

The speedy restoration of southern denominational institutions and religious
newspapers gave Confederate Christians a distinct advantage over northern missionaries who came south seeking Unionists and penitent rebels. Southern ministers
preached a different version of God's purposes in the war, and once denominational
mechanisms were again in working order, southern churches began to receive thousands of new members. Denominational periodicals zealously guarded against laxity
among southern Christians and mercilessly attacked northern denominations and
their missionaries. In the contest for white Christians, the southern churches won
an overwhelming victory as they grew far more rapidly than the northern churches
in the South. Their remarkable growth even outstripped that of the population in
general. Furthermore, southern evangelicals labored not only for the revival of
southern religion in the present, but also for its perpetuation into the future as well.
To ensure that the next generation of Southern Baptists, Methodists, and Presbyterians kept the southern faith, they worked tirelessly to revive and establish Sunday
schools and denominational colleges throughout the South.

7

Educating Confederate Christians

Sunday Schools and Denominational Colleges

Walk about Zion, and go round about her: tell the towers thereof.
    Mark ye well her bulwarks, consider her palaces; that ye may tell it to the generation following.

Psalm 48:12–13

The proper education of young southerners formed an integral part of white southern Christians' vision of religious reconstruction; they understood that the perpetuation of their distinctive religious identity depended on their success at transmitting cultural ideals to the next generation. The primary instruments used to accomplish this goal, other than the churches themselves, were Sunday schools and denominational colleges.

Both institutions existed in the antebellum South, and both were disrupted by the war. During religious reconstruction, however, Sunday schools appeared in more and more southern churches. In these schools young children could be taught both the basics of the Christian faith and devotion to the southern forms of American evangelicalism. Southern denominations also devoted extraordinary efforts to the reestablishment of their colleges. Their efforts revived a movement begun before the war as part of a growing tide of southern sectionalism. Fearing dependence on the North for the education of their youth, southerners had established several denominational colleges in the 1840s and 1850s.[1] As with other aspects of religious reconstruction, the postwar support for colleges stemmed from both a genuine concern over the religious and intellectual training of southern youth and a desire to educate them in the tenets of the southern interpretation of the nation's spiritual heritage and recent history. Southern colleges and seminaries were the training grounds for the

114

next generation of ministers who would uphold southern religious ideals against the world, the devil, and the northern denominations.

Even before the Civil War, southern Christians had established Sunday schools in a few of their larger churches. Most of their Sunday school materials came from the American Sunday School Union in Philadelphia; during the 1840s and 1850s, they became increasingly suspicious of this organization, fearing that it had become "an abolition society." In 1859 the Central Baptist Association in Georgia declared that it "regretted" that in most of its Sunday schools "the Union school books are retained." The following year, the Central Baptist Association affirmed, "the Word of God and the Hymn Book are the only necessary books" for Sunday schools, though "other works are sometimes used advantageously."[2]

During the Civil War, southerners began to publish their own Sunday school periodicals when possible. Samuel Boykin, a native Georgian and the editor of the Baptist *Christian Index*, began the *Child's Index* in 1862 with a salutation telling southern children, "Since we have been engaged in repelling our wicked invaders, you have been deprived of the neat and interesting papers you used to get from the North." The *Child's Index*, which became the *Child's Delight* after 1866, filled the demand for a southern Baptist children's periodical.[3]

An editorial in the *Southern Presbyterian* in the spring of 1861 contended that one of the "most indispensable" needs facing southern Presbyterians was that of a "religious paper for our Sunday-schools." They could no longer depend on their former sources in the North, because many of them "entertain a profound distrust of everything and everybody at the North," even more were determined to boycott northern businesses, and the mails were sure to be interrupted. Even if it were possible to continue receiving northern publications, the editors asserted, it would be undesirable, because one country should not depend on another and because "the Southern mind is now being injured by its condition of pupilage in things literary, benevolent, and religious." Furthermore, "the Sunday-school work has characteristics at the South which it has no where else; e.g., plantation Sunday Schools, and schools for the negroes in our churches." For all these reasons, the *Southern Presbyterian* supported the establishment of a southern Sunday school paper on a union basis with support from different denominations.[4]

Presbyterian efforts bore fruit in December 1861 when the General Assembly of the Presbyterian Church in the Confederate States of America ordered the publication of a Sunday school paper. The *Children's Friend*, which did not appear until August 1862 because of the difficulty of obtaining paper and a printer, was published by the Presbyterian Committee of Publication in Richmond, Virginia, and began publication with three thousand subscribers. Methodists began the publication of an illustrated Sunday school newspaper, entitled the *Children's Guide* and published by John W. Burke in Macon, Georgia.[5]

The standard fare of these Sunday school periodicals were religious stories and reports of Sunday school activities throughout the South. In keeping with the nineteenth-century preoccupation with death, the papers also included obituaries of children who had faced death bravely with Christian resignation. In some issues, editors sought to instruct their young readers on various aspects of the war and its consequences. An advertisement for the *Child's Index* boasted that the periodical included "instructive stories, pleasing anecdotes, illustrations of history and natural history, and, by its scriptural enigmas, sets the young to 'searching the Scriptures.'"6

To help children cope with the death of loved ones, the *Children's Friend* published "A Furlough and Discharge" in October 1862. In this story a brave little North Carolina girl, whose brother had died in a Richmond hospital after failing to secure a furlough to return home, tells her pastor that God gave her brother "a furlough and a discharge too!" The writer hoped that "every little girl and boy who reads these lines, and who has lost a dear brother since this war began, might be able to say what this little sister did, 'God gave him a furlough and discharge too.'" The readers should remember that "God will take care of all his people, and all his children, and take them away from this world of sorrow and trouble, to that peaceful home in heaven, where war, and the sin that makes it, shall never come."7

By July 1863, the *Children's Friend* declared that it was becoming "a favorite with the children, all over the Confederacy." Sunday schools of all denominations — Episcopalians, Methodists, Baptists, and Presbyterians — were using it for instruction. As it began its second year of publication the following month, the editors apologized that "we cannot give you those pictures, which we sent to England for, for we know children like to look at pictures." They feared that "our enemy's blockading ships have captured them." If the plates had fallen into enemy hands, "they will no doubt keep them, for what do they care for the children in the Confederacy? Have they not driven many little children with their dear mothers from their homes, and burned their houses, so that they have now no home?" Reflecting the Confederate understanding of the war, the editors continued, "How much we ought to pray that God would forgive the sins for which he is now chastening us, and put an end to this dreadful war." They urged all the children as well as adults to "pray for this, and many times every day." Turning to a spiritual application, the editors declared that another war existed in which all children should be soldiers: "that is the war against your sins, and against the world, and against the devil." Although the readers of the *Children's Friend* were too young to enter the armies of the Confederacy, "none are too young to enter the army of our Lord Jesus Christ." Children were fond of "playing soldiers," but if "you become Christians, you will be real soldiers; and you will be certain to get the victory."8

Near the end of the war, the *Child's Index* published the story "A Little Hero," written by a Mrs. M. J. M. As the story opens, Willie tries to comfort his mother after the Yankees have stolen all of their food and horses and killed their livestock. All they have left is some corn, but brave little Willie says, "Well, then, mother, we can live on parched corn and water." Beaming with pride, Willie's mother praises her "TRUE SOUTHERN BOY. The Yankees would soon throw down their arms if every mother had such a son." Willie and his brother Eddie have told the Yankees that they intend to be "'Federate soldiers" when they grow up, and the officer in command of the Union soldiers said to himself, "No reconstruction here." Puzzled, Willie later asks his mother what reconstruction is. His mother replies that reconstruction "is admitting we are wrong, to quit fighting, to give up our slaves and lands and to be in truth the slaves ourselves of the wicked Yankees." "But, mother, how can anyone do this," Willie asks. "We feel sure we are right; how then can we acknowledge we are wrong? Why this would be story in the sight of God." His mother agrees,

"No true soldier, no brave man, wants reconstruction." Defiant, Willie exclaims, "I'LL never go back to the Yankees. No, no, never; I'll eat parched corn all my days before ever I'll be for reconstruction." The author concluded her story by asking "who will emulate the spirit of Willie?" She hoped "all would take for your motto, 'NO RECONSTRUCTION.'"9

In another issue of the *Child's Index*, editor Samuel Boykin described the landing of the pilgrims and their early settlements but condemned their descendants, the "Yankee nation." The Yankees, who were trying to deprive southerners of "not only our religious liberty, but of every other kind of liberty," had forgotten what their ancestors had suffered for these same freedoms. They "refuse to let us have Bibles, prevent our getting them from Europe, and when they can they steal what we do bring." They have imprisoned southern preachers, and they "deprive us of our churches, and burn them or use them as stables and storehouses." If Yankees triumphed, they would "take away all our churches, stop the mouths of our preachers by law, and not even let us pray in our families as we wish." Boykin urged southern children to "pray to God to change their minds" for they were "blinded by fanaticism and infidelity." Southerners should also "pray to God to forgive them, for they know not what they do." Hopefully, God would soon allow southern armies to drive them from the South and establish the Confederate nation so that southerners could enjoy all of their "rights and liberties."10

At the 1862 meeting of the Southern Baptist Convention (SBC), Basil Manly Jr., a strong advocate of Sunday schools, chaired a Committee on the Need for a Sunday School Board. The committee proclaimed that the Sunday school was "the nursery of the Church, the camp of instruction for her young soldiers, the great Missionary to the Future." The time had come for Baptists in the Confederacy to move beyond cooperation with other denominations and "commence this work on our own account." Some might question the wisdom of making such an attempt in wartime. To them the committee declared, "the need of Sunday Schools is as great as ever, is even greater with us than heretofore." More children were orphans and destitute; more were ignorant and neglected. "These must grow up to vice and ruin — must poison the very roots of our young Confederacy — must infect the moral atmosphere in which we and our children shall live, unless met by early and vigorous efforts." Who would care for these "helpless ones" if not the "Churches of Christ"? Although many Christian workers were in the army, more than enough remained at home who were either too old or too young for military service. Furthermore, the Sunday schools could also expect aid from "that never failing and invincible corps of reserves, the sisterhood, who are ready for every good word and work, and need only to have the way opened and pointed out to them." The SBC formed a Sunday School Board in 1863 with Manly as president. By early 1865, the board was publishing several books "by Southern authors," including the new and enlarged *Confederate Sunday School Hymn Book*.11

The Civil War provided new opportunities for southern evangelical women to teach Sunday schools when male teachers left for the war. The Washington Baptist Association in Georgia described the work of Sunday school teachers as similar to that of ministers in its 1864 meeting: "Your committee consider the Sabbath School in connection with the Bible Class, second only to the preaching of the gospel as an instrument of good. . . . Every member of the church, both male and female, should feel the responsibility resting on him or her in this important work." Despite the importance attached to the Sunday school, women clearly remained in subordinate positions within the churches. The evangelical ideal of womanhood gave these teachers opportunities for social interaction beyond the family circle, but it also proscribed their autonomy and independence.[12]

When the war ended, southern evangelical leaders renewed their commitment to Sunday schools, lamenting their absence in many churches, especially rural ones. The Central Baptist Association complained in August 1865, "it is a painful fact that too many christian parents take no interest in the Sabbath Schools — a large number of our country churches have none at all." Baptists in western Tennessee admitted that they had not been "sufficiently careful to foster and promote Sunday Schools in our bounds." Sunday schools could be "a most efficient means of instilling moral and religious sentiments into the minds of children, and properly training the rising generations for the momentous responsibilities which must soon devolve upon them as members of society and of the church of God." Although several churches in the area had "large and flourishing" Sunday schools, "the large majority of the Churches in West Tennessee are without schools."[13]

Presbyterian Eliza Fain reflected her commitment to Sunday schools in her diary in July 1868: "I do feel I ought every Sabbath to be at my post as a teacher." Feeble health prevented her from teaching frequently, but "I loved the Sabbath School and one of the happiest winters of my life was that of 65 & 66 when I was hardly ever absent from that precious place where I met a large class of dear girls and some boys." On Christmas Eve, 1869, seven of Fain's children attended a Sunday school celebration in the nearby town of Rogersville: "A Christmas tree has been made and the means given to decorate with presents to the Sabbath school." Fain trusted that "good results may follow," though she had doubts "as to its propriety." She preferred that the money had been "expended in giving to the poor and needy children necessary comforts."[14]

Active Sunday schools made deliberate efforts to commemorate the Confederacy. At St. James Methodist Church in Augusta, Georgia, two leaders of the Sunday school began in October 1865 an effort to memorialize the church's Confederate dead. The Sunday school erected a monument directly in front of the church. On the side facing the church is the inscription, "St. James Sabbath School Dedicates this Tablet to her Fallen Heros," followed by twenty-four names. On another face, the monument declares, "These men died in defense of the principles of the Declaration of Independence."[15]

Southern churches attempted to organize and expand their Sunday school work in the aftermath of the war in various ways. In 1867, for example, the South Georgia Conference of the Methodist Episcopal Church, South, established a Sunday School Society, which, according to its constitution, was "to supervise the general interests of Sunday Schools within the bounds of the Conference, to devise ways and means for furnishing books to destitute Sabbath Schools, to suggest the best means of conducting Sunday Schools, and to do all in its power to increase the interest of our people in this most important agency of the church." During the 1860s and 1870s both state and denominational bodies appointed Sunday school missionaries. In 1867 octogenarian Lovick Pierce began his work as the Sunday school agent for the South Georgia Conference, a position he held for the next four years.[16]

From 1874 to 1894 Thomas C. Boykin likewise served as Sunday school evangelist for the Georgia Baptists, who had formed a Sunday School Association in April 1868 at a meeting in Augusta. With the motto "A Sunday School in Every Baptist Church Throughout the State," the new association urged pastors, deacons, and laity to organize and maintain Sunday schools in their churches. When the Tennessee Baptist Convention formed in 1874, many wanted a Sunday school evangelist for the state, but the new convention did not have the financial resources; in 1881 W. A. Therrell was appointed Tennessee's Sunday school evangelist through an agreement with the American Baptist Publication Society in Philadelphia.[17]

At the denominational level as well, the Sunday school attracted renewed attention after the war. In 1870 the southern Methodist General Conference appointed Atticus G. Haygood as its first denominational Sunday school secretary, and he moved from Georgia to Nashville, Tennessee, to begin his new work. He revised the *Sunday School Visitor* and began work on a series of lessons for different age groups drawn from the same scriptural text. Although successful at first, his system had come under considerable criticism by the time he resigned in the fall of 1875. His successor, W. G. E. Cunnyngham, began in 1876 to utilize the International Series of lessons, which were aimed at all American Protestants rather than emphasizing Methodist doctrines as Haygood had done. Despite this change, Haygood's energetic work as Sunday school secretary had vitalized the growing Sunday school movement in many Methodist churches across the South.[18]

Southern Baptists had a more difficult time. Their Sunday School Board, organized in 1863, moved to Memphis in 1868. The SBC in 1870 considered the possibility of closer cooperation with northern Baptists in Sunday school work, but determined that it was "eminently wise and proper to maintain our existing organization, and devote our energies to the development and nurture of our own resources."[19] Despite Southern Baptists' unwillingness to unite their Sunday School Board with northern efforts, doctrinal and publication controversies with Tennessee Baptist leader J. R. Graves and financial problems led the Convention to merge it with the Domestic Mission Board in 1873. Most of the denominational Sunday school work lapsed for two decades, except for the publication of a periodical, until the Convention formed a new Sunday School Board in 1891.

As part of their renewed commitment to Sunday schools, southern evangelicals resumed the publication of Sunday school periodicals started during the war and began others. The southern Presbyterian General Assembly in December 1865 instructed its Committee of Publication to resurrect the *Children's Friend*, which had been published for three years prior to the destruction of the Richmond offices in April 1865. The destruction of John W. Burke's Macon publishing house by Federal cavalry in April 1865 had ended the publication of the Methodist *Children's Guide*; although Burke promised to "commence the *Guide* again" when he got a suitable press, the periodical never reappeared. Other publishers revived the *Sunday School Visitor* for southern Methodist Sunday schools in 1869.[20]

Baptist Samuel Boykin, wartime editor of both the *Christian Index* and the *Child's Index*, sold his interest in the *Christian Index* but restarted his Sunday school periodical early in 1866 with the new title of *Child's Delight*. Southern Baptist seminary professors in Greenville, South Carolina, began to publish another periodical, *Kind Words*, in 1866 to meet the demand for southern Sunday school literature. In December 1866, the editors urged southern Baptists to "show *Kind Words* to everybody, circulate it everywhere, and send us *large* orders with money." Only $1.00 for ten copies per month for a year was a small price to pay for "our own Southern paper." During the summer of 1868, *Kind Words* moved to Memphis, Tennessee; Boykin's *Child's Delight* merged with it in 1870, and Boykin became one of its editors. He expressed his sincere hope that "all will continue to subscribe for KIND WORDS, THE CHILD'S DELIGHT. Their old editor will still write for them, and try his best to give them a good and profitable paper." Although the Sunday School Board ceased to exist as a separate entity in 1873, *Kind Words* continued publication; in 1891 the new Sunday School Board adopted and enlarged it, and Samuel Boykin continued to serve as editor and writer until his death in 1899.[21]

Southerners remained concerned in the postwar era about the corrupting influence that northern Sunday school literature might have on their children. The North Carolina Baptist *Biblical Recorder* warned in 1866 against purchasing Sunday school literature from northern publishers, because such publications might brand Confederates as "traitors and criminals." In 1869 the Committee on Sabbath Schools of the North Georgia Annual Conference admitted that the "Lesson Paper Systems (such as that published by Adams, Blackmer & Lyon, of Chicago) are great improvements," but they objected to "the locality where they are issued." The committee greatly preferred to have "all our *Sabbath School Books especially* written and published here at home." "Is this impossible?" the report asked. "Surely we might, at least, make selections and compilations from those which are not objectionable, and have them published at our own house." The ministers made their reasoning explicit: "Northern sentiments and interpretations do not always correspond with ours, and we prefer to have home books, and home teaching, and home publishers, if so it may be." The Sunday School Society of the South Georgia Annual Conference urged "all our Pastors to adopt the uniform system of lessons prepared and published by our Publishing House." The Methodist *Christian Advocate* of Nashville insisted that in conducting Sunday schools, "we wish to supersede the use of all such questionable helps as Barnes's Notes, Questions, etc. of the American Sunday-school Union, and Special Lessons gotten up by parties who are, as far as our Church is concerned, utterly irresponsible — Mimpriss, Chicago, and others, which we cannot indorse." The choice of textbooks for Sunday schools was "a very serious matter," and "our pastors ought not to sanction the introduction into our schools of books of instruction gotten up by Northern Houses and others over which we have no control."[22] As with so many other elements of religious reconstruction, Sunday schools needed southern teachers using southern materials to uphold southern ideals.

Southern Baptist Charles Manly's reaction to a poem in a northern Sunday school newspaper demonstrates southern sensitivity over what must have seemed to northerners rather innocuous materials. The cause of Manly's consternation was a poem entitled "Glad and Free" that appeared in the April 1, 1866, issue of the *Young Reaper*, published by the American Baptist Publication Society in Philadelphia. The poem celebrated the freedom of African Americans from slavery and proclaimed

"Oh! none in all the world before / Were e'er as glad as we; / We're free on Caro-lina's shore, / We're all at home, and free!" Manly wrote to the editor of the *Young Reaper*, "if he thought proper to publish any more such articles in the paper, I would prefer that he would not send them to us; as I should not distribute them and did not care to pay postage on what would be waste paper." The editor replied that he thought Manly was too sensitive about the freedpeople . Manly declared that while the editor could publish what he wanted, "even those things which he *knew* would be offensive to Christians at the South, we would also reserve to ourselves the right of not circulating papers which contained objectionable statements — especially when the objection to them was that they were *false* and *irritating*." The poem deeply troubled Manly because it attributed the end of slavery to the work of Christ, an idea utterly opposed to his understanding of the South's recent history.[23]

Southern Sunday school periodicals, in contrast, carefully upheld the ideals of the southern denominations and the memory of the Confederacy and its heroes. The content of these newspapers during the Reconstruction era was much the same as during the war. Their young readers continued to receive numerous stories about southern children who learned valuable moral lessons. Occasionally, Confederate heroes appeared. In "She Never Gave Me Aught But Pleasure," the author began, "So wrote General Lee of a daughter who died during the war." The lesson for young readers was clear: "I want you to live so as to give your dear father and mother plea-sure, and only pleasure. To do this you must obey them promptly, cheerfully, and at all times." The author associated the reverence due the great general with the obe-dience due to parents. In another article, "Tommy and His Rules" by John Broadus, Tommy asks his father for a set of rules to live by, and his father obliges by giving him a list. Every other rule on the list is "Tell the truth." Tommy wonders why this rule is repeated so often, and his father replies that he wants Tommy to be "like a man I read about, not long ago" — Colonel Coleman of Virginia, "who belonged to Lee's Army, and was killed during the war." The mother of this man "whom every-body admired and loved" had said that she had never known him to tell a lie in his whole life, except on one occasion; later, she found she was mistaken about that in-cident. Tommy's father declares, "Ah! Tommy, if only your dear mother could say when you are grown, that you never told a lie, from baby up to man!"[24] This story transforms a Confederate hero into a moral hero as well, a model for young south-erners like Tommy.

The efforts of denominational organs to increase both the number and quality of southern Sunday schools led one Georgia committee to declare, "We believe this to be emphatically a Sunday School era"; these initiatives enjoyed considerable suc-cess in the decade and a half after the war. The Georgia Baptist Association in 1866 voted to form a committee on Sunday schools and to ask its member churches for Sunday school statistics in their annual reports. By 1878 the association proudly re-ported that no church "is without a Sabbath School," and some had two or more. Evangelist Thomas C. Boykin reported to the Georgia Baptist Convention in 1876 that he had organized sixty-one new Sunday schools in the previous year, yielding a total of 567 schools with over twenty-one thousand students. The following year he declared that there were nearly seven hundred Sunday schools with approximately twenty-five thousand scholars.[25]

Southern Methodists also enjoyed considerable Sunday school gains. The number of Sunday schools in the Tennessee Conference doubled between 1866 and 1869; by 1877 it had 384 Sunday schools with 21,250 students. The North Georgia Conference reported 471 schools and 23,810 Sunday school scholars in 1867, and by 1877 the total had risen to 585 schools and 30,487 students. The South Georgia Conference also enjoyed considerable growth, reporting 221 schools and 10,049 students in 1867, and 322 schools with 12,619 scholars a decade later.[26]

The development of southern Sunday schools involved more changes than just numerical increase. Proponents of Sunday schools were troubled that many met for only part of the year, were union schools that served several denominations, or did not subscribe to denominational periodicals. In 1872, for example, the Methodist South Georgia Conference had 276 Sunday schools. However, only 141 were using Dr. Haygood's uniform lessons, only 162 were described as "successful," and only 94 met through the winter months. In 1873 the Americus District resolved to "establish Sunday Schools at each one of our appointments, upon a strictly methodistic basis, and discourage as much as possible, in a prudent way, the patronage of Union Schools." The following year, the pastor of the Sumter Circuit "deprecated the habit of S. Schools going into winter quarters." The Bainbridge District resolved in 1871 to "use our best exertions to establish a Sunday School in connexion with every church, if possible, in the bounds of the District"; it also recommended "the S. School Magazine, the S. S. Visitor, Our Little Folks, and Haygood's System of Uniform Lessons to the adoption of all our Sunday Schools, as valuable auxiliaries in the religious instruction of Children." By 1873 the district rejoiced because "our own series of Uniform Lessons & S. S. papers are being generally introduced" and urged all "to adopt & introduce into the schools our own literature." Even Sunday school statistics revealed much work yet to be done. In 1876, 428 Georgia Baptist churches did not have Sunday schools, and of 167 Presbyterian churches in the Synod of Georgia in 1875, only eighty-four had Sunday schools. Nevertheless, Sunday schools were gaining favor across the South among both the denominational leadership and laypeople, and many of these churches without schools would establish them in the next few years.[27]

By the 1880s most southern evangelical churches had Sunday schools that inculcated Christian, denominational, and specifically southern values in their students. These "nurseries of the church" were training the next generation of southern evangelicals whom their elders trusted to uphold the Confederate understanding of the war and the southern forms of evangelicalism into the next century. The training begun in the Sunday schools was continued in denominational colleges, where religious southerners could safely send their sons and daughters without fear of corruption.

The report of the trustees of Mercer University in 1866 manifested the guiding ideals behind the revival of southern denominational colleges in the 1860s and 1870s: "Knowledge is power. If the sons of the South are to possess that power and influence which will be demanded in their sunny clime, they must be educated. They will be the more useful and happy if their education is secured in their native State." The report on education from the same meeting of the Georgia Baptist Convention proclaimed, "the proper mental and moral training of all classes and conditions of our young people is the great desire of all christians and of all lovers of our race." Georgia's young men and women should be trained in the South by southern teachers to "meet the demands of the oncoming generation of our noble Commonwealth." At the 1867 meeting of the Georgia Baptist Convention, the Committee on Education urged all "faithful Christians who desire the purity of Zion" to support education. Baptists should, "as a denomination, looking not only to the political, but the religious future of our country, determine to do our part in wielding that powerful instrumentality for good — the education of the young." Furthermore, "let us see to it, that every year there shall go forth from our academies, colleges, and professional schools, increasing supplies of earnest, educated men, who will become centers of influence, and perpetuate our ideas in the political and religious institutions of the country." When political institutions were in the hands of others, southern evangelicals could educate their sons and daughters at denominational colleges that, unlike state schools, were free of Republican domination.[28]

The fortunes of Georgia's three principal denominational schools reveal the difficulties white southerners faced in rebuilding religious education in the 1860s and 1870s. Georgia Baptists were proud that their Mercer University at Penfield remained open throughout the war when virtually all other colleges suspended operations. However, thirty Mercer students died in the Civil War, and most of the rest served in the Confederate army. The four faculty members were paid very little during 1865, and the close of the war "left the University without income, and all our people without money for purposes of education." Under these circumstances, the president resigned to become president of a college in Kentucky. Denominational leaders had attempted several times in the 1850s to relocate the university to a more accessible town, but their efforts had failed. In August 1865, an Atlanta man resurrected the idea of moving the university when he offered forty-five acres of land on the Macon and Western Railroad in Atlanta if the school moved there within five years. Because of opposition to the move within the Georgia Baptist Convention, however, the college struggled on at the rural village of Penfield.[29]

In December 1866, the newly elected Georgia legislature attempted to aid the state's impoverished colleges by enacting a law to support the education of maimed or indigent soldiers at one of five colleges — the University of Georgia, Emory College, Mercer University, Oglethorpe University, and Bowdon Collegiate Institute. The law provided for the support of the soldier until his graduation; in return he had to teach in the state's schools for as many years as he had received support. The state would reimburse the school for the student's expenses up to a maximum of $300 annually. The University of Georgia received over $50,000 of the more than $100,000 expended by the state during the two years of the program. The $27,000 that Emory College received provided critical support to that Methodist institution in the difficult early postwar years; in the two years the law was in effect, Emory received more support from the state than from paying students. The other three colleges together received $27,000.[30]

Mercer President Henry H. Tucker complained in the spring of 1867 that he could not accept the state's offer because payment was tendered in "State bonds, of an inferior grade and of a character which I am sure must make them entirely worthless." Although the university had given and would continue to give free tuition to Confederate veterans, it could not provide them with board, clothing, and books "gratis, or . . . furnish them for unmarketable bonds, which amounts to the same thing." After Governor Charles J. Jenkins was removed from office in early 1868, President Tucker inquired of military commander General George Meade whether the state's appropriation for disabled soldiers would continue. Meade replied that the program would continue as long as black and Federal veterans were accepted on an equal footing with Confederate soldiers. Tucker and the faculty refused to accept students on these terms, which were not "in accordance with our own sense of duty or propriety." When the Georgia Baptist Convention met in April, however, the delegates had lost their patience. Undoubtedly envying Emory College's receipt of vital support from this source, the committee assigned to examine the report of Mercer's board of trustees grew irritated with the faculty and trustees. The university had "already suffered in public esteem, and must continue thus to suffer so long as other institutions render efficient this appropriation, and Mercer alone does not." The committee urged the trustees and faculty to "place Mercer in the same relation to disabled soldiers that is sustained by like institutions in the State." Despite this effort, Mercer probably received little support from the 1866 act, as the 1869 state legislature repealed it outright and appropriated funds only through the end of 1868.[31]

To overcome some of the financial difficulties the university faced, the board of trustees decided in the spring of 1867 to move Mercer and appointed a committee to investigate possible locations. This plan created an immediate storm of protest from several associations, led by the powerful Georgia Association in which Mercer was located; in response, the trustees stated that it was "inexpedient to attempt the removal of the University." The Georgia Baptist Convention in 1868 passed three resolutions that it hoped would settle the issue. The first expressed the convention's persuasion that Mercer's current lack of prosperity was not "exclusively attributable to location." The second resolution declared that the continued agitation of the subject injured the university, and the convention "earnestly and affectionately entreat our brethren to cease the agitation of the subject of its removal from the town of Penfield." The third resolution instructed the trustees to "put the University buildings and enclosures in a state of complete repair" in order to promote "the permanency and efficiency of the University."[32]

The controversy over Mercer's remote location arose again, however, in the Georgia Baptist Convention meeting of 1870; after discussing the issue for half of the three-day conference, the convention voted to move the university to a more suitable location. The decision did not go unchallenged; the Georgia Association condemned it as "unwise, injudicious, morally wrong, and necessarily tending to the destruction of the unity and the educational interests of the Baptists of Georgia." The primary reasons cited for removing Mercer from Penfield were that the town was too small to provide satisfactory public accommodations and patronage and that it was too far from the railroads. Chief among the virtues of Macon, Mercer's new home, were the $125,000 offered by the city and its central location, "of easy access by railroad from every part of the State." The relocation proved successful; Mercer was second only to the University of Georgia among the state's colleges in the 1870s.[33]

The Presbyterians' Oglethorpe University followed a much different course after the war. Located in the small village of Midway, near Milledgeville, Ogle-thorpe closed under the pressures of war. At the 1865 meeting of the Synod of Georgia in Augusta, the Committee on Oglethorpe University recommended that the university remain closed until more resources were available. The committee also "seriously doubted whether [Oglethorpe] can ever successfully accomplish its design where it now is, or till it shall be situated in a city or a large town." Fortunate that part of its endowment survived the war, the struggling university reopened in 1867, but the synod passed a resolution that it "should be removed from its present location to some point more favorable to its prosperity." In 1868 the synod considered the possibility of uniting the resources of Oglethorpe with Davidson College in North Carolina. At the end of 1869, Georgia Presbyterians narrowly passed a resolution to relocate Oglethorpe in Atlanta, with the promise that the city would donate ten acres of land and the citizens would raise $40,000; the relocated university opened in Atlanta in October 1870. Despite a promising start with about 120 students (including those in the "preparatory department"), the university had within two years consumed virtually its entire endowment. The Synod of Georgia in November 1872 ordered "the prompt and unconditional close of the exercises of the Institution." Central to Oglethorpe's failure was the small base of Presbyterians in Georgia. Although the college enjoyed sponsorship from the Synods of Alabama and South Carolina as well as the Synod of Georgia, the denominational base remained considerably smaller than that supporting either Mercer University or Emory College. The relocation to Atlanta had produced "disastrous results," and the synod soon lost its rights to the property donated by the city for Oglethorpe. In 1874 the synod lamented "the entire loss . . . of all the funds left by the war and which it took years of hard labor to accumulate, a fund which should have been held sacred."[34]

The relocations of Mercer and Oglethorpe universities from small, isolated villages to growing cities reflected the aggressiveness of southern evangelicals who were determined to redeem the South. No longer content to minister only to a rural membership or so determined to isolate students in a separate evangelical community, southern denominations moved several of their colleges to cities in the late-nineteenth century. Others, like Vanderbilt University, were begun in larger cities. The decisions to move both Mercer and Oglethorpe rested on the belief that more accessible locations near railroads would increase enrollment; and many towns and cities were willing to offer large sums of money and tracts of land for the social and economic benefits a college would bring. These offers were quite attractive to denominational colleges struggling for survival in the postwar South. The geographical movement paralleled a social transformation as the evangelical churches became increasingly influential in southern society, although as religious colleges moved from the safety of social and geographical isolation, the danger of assimilation in southern cities was real.[35]

The Georgia Methodists' Emory College in Oxford had closed in 1862, and its endowment had vanished with the failure of the Confederacy, but by the end of 1866 it was once again in operation and able to utilize, in 1867 and 1868, the Georgia legislature's program to educate disabled Confederate soldiers. Bishop George Foster Pierce also called for five hundred people to join him in pledging $20 per year to provide a temporary endowment. He announced that Emory had "risen from the dead." Although ravaged by the war, "her pulse of life is strong, her heart full of hope, and her future bright with promise." He warned his "friends and brethren" that if they did not rush to join him in supporting the college, "I shall be compelled to worry you with line upon line." In 1869 the North Georgia Annual Conference protested the repeal of the law providing education for disabled soldiers. It hoped that "a returning sense of justice and humanity may yet induce the General Assembly to reconsider their action and restore an appropriation at once just, humane, benevolent and patriotic." Despite this setback, Emory College continued to grow and remained the capstone of Methodist education in Georgia.[36]

During the Reconstruction era, Tennessee evangelicals sought to build major universities that would serve both their state and the entire South. During the 1870s they established three new universities in the state — Southwestern Presbyterian University in 1873 at Clarksville, Southwestern Baptist University in 1874 at Jackson, and Vanderbilt University (originally to be called the "Central University of the Methodist Episcopal Church, South") in 1875 at Nashville. Each institution achieved some success, but Vanderbilt became by far the most prominent in its brief career (1875–1914) as a Methodist institution.[37]

The origins of the Southwestern Presbyterian University lay in the difficulties many southern Presbyterian colleges faced in the aftermath of the Civil War. Early in 1866 the *Southern Presbyterian* was "pleased to learn that an effort is soon to be made" to unite the three Presbyterian colleges in La Grange, Tennessee, Oakland, Mississippi, and Midway, Georgia. None of these institutions was "now in a condition to stand alone." All three did soon fail; only the La Grange Synodical College joined in the effort to organize the university. The property of the Synod of Memphis, La Grange Synodical College lost most of its endowment during the war, but it still possessed valuable land in Arkansas. The synod mused in 1866, "six years ago its success seemed certain," but "today it lies prostrate in the dust and its glory has departed." The synod appointed a committee to examine the possibility of reviving the college.[38]

The Synod of Nashville faced a similar problem with Stewart College of Clarksville, Tennessee. After failing to gain support for Stewart from the Synod of Memphis, a committee employed an agent to raise funds, but he became so discouraged that he soon gave up. In October 1868 conditions were so bleak that the trustees of the college "desire finally to wind up and dispose of the College enterprize." Since there were "parties ready to take it off their hands," the trustees believed it was "a favorable time to close it up" since it was, "in its present condition, only a source of mortification and reproach." Unready to admit defeat, the Committee on Stewart College proposed a final effort to save the school. It assessed $6,000 on the various churches of the synod for the relief of the college with the understanding that if satisfactory progress were not made in three months, the trustees could dispose of the college property at their discretion. Immediately after the synod meeting adjourned, one member visited the Synod of Memphis then in session, which — after two years of consideration — was reluctantly concluding that it could not sustain La Grange College. It pledged $1,000 in aid to Stewart College and agreed to join the Synod of Nashville in its control and patronage. This support, together with the contributions from the churches of the Synod of Nashville and private donations, saved the college.[39]

The General Assembly of the Presbyterian Church in the United States considered the possibility of establishing a central southern Presbyterian university in 1867 and 1868, but in the latter year it indefinitely postponed the proposal. Prominent southern evangelicals James A. Lyon and Benjamin Morgan Palmer continued to advocate the idea, and the issue resurfaced at the General Assembly of 1871. Opposition was strong, however, and the General Assembly simply urged the synods not to begin any more colleges and to unite in the support of existing institutions. The Synod of Nashville seized on this idea and urged other synods in the southwest to unite with it in the support of a single university. In 1873 commissioners from the synods of Alabama, Arkansas, Memphis, Mississippi, and Nashville met to create the Southwestern Presbyterian University out of the assets of Stewart College in Clarksville. The Synod of Texas later joined the alliance. At the time Stewart was the only institution of higher learning in the entire Mississippi Valley that belonged to southern Presbyterians.[40]

Tennessee Baptists faced a similar dilemma with their Union University in Murfreesboro. This school did not resume classes until 1868, and the Tennessee Baptist Educational Society, which owned the college, closed it in 1873, citing too few students, the country's financial crisis, an epidemic of cholera, and strong competition from state schools as its reasons. When the Baptists of Tennessee united into the Tennessee Baptist Convention in April 1874, Article 5 of the new constitution they adopted pledged the convention to "promote the educational interests of the Baptists of Tennessee, as a special object." The Committee on Education of the convention insisted that it was "of vital importance to the denominational interests of the Baptists of the State" to establish a "well-endowed, thoroughly equipped University, of the highest order." A committee appointed to select a location for the proposed university met in July to consider Chattanooga, Jackson, McMinnville, and Murfreesboro; it chose Jackson because the town offered the campus and endowment of West Tennessee College and subscriptions of $150,000. The committee also recommended that the university's board of trustees include members from Tennessee, Alabama, Mississippi, Louisiana, Arkansas, and Texas. A special August meeting of the Tennessee Baptist Convention approved the committee's actions, and Southwestern Baptist University began operations in September 1874. In 1875 the Tennessee Baptist Educational Society voted to transfer all the assets of Union University to Southwestern Baptist University, but the trustees of Union University never transferred the property. Despite its goal of being a Baptist university for several states, Southwestern actually garnered little support outside of western Tennessee.[41]

The origins of Vanderbilt University lay in the 1860s and 1870s, when some southern Methodists increasingly favored the establishment of a theological school to train ministers. Conservatives, however, under the leadership of Bishop George F. Pierce, opposed a theological school as detrimental to "experiential religion" and successfully blocked the proposal for a theological school at the General Conference of 1870. Undaunted, advocates of theological training determined to achieve their goal by joining forces with those southern Methodists who wanted to erect a great central university. Prominent among those favoring the new institution were Bishops Holland N. McTyeire and Robert Paine. In January 1872 a convention of delegates from nine conferences in the states of Alabama, Arkansas, Louisiana, Mississippi, and Tennessee, met in Memphis to formulate plans for a large southern Methodist university. The Memphis Convention decided that the proposed university would need a minimum endowment of $1 million and should not begin operations until supporters had raised at least $500,000. Bishop Pierce once again led the opposition, declaring, "every dollar invested in a theological school will be a damage to Methodism." "Had I a million," he proclaimed, "I would not give a dime for such an object." Despite this division among the leaders of the church, the College of Bishops approved the proposed university in May 1872. The school remained only a plan, however, because efforts to raise the sum necessary to begin the enterprise yielded only modest returns. In March 1873 Commodore Cornelius Vanderbilt offered $500,000 to the university with the conditions that it be located "in or near Nashville" and that Bishop McTyeire be elected president of the board of trustees and equipped with broad veto powers. In accepting this offer, the board changed the name of the school to Vanderbilt University. Later gifts from the Vanderbilt family raised the wealth of the institution to $1.5 million by 1890. As historian Hunter D. Farish noted, Vanderbilt University in the latter part of the nineteenth century had "a financial independence enjoyed by no other Southern university."[42]

Denominational colleges for women also struggled to survive after the war and into the 1870s. Some recuperated quickly, like the Methodists' Wesleyan Female College in Macon, which resumed its career as a "dispenser of sanctified learning" soon after the war. Others, such as the Baptist Female College of South-western Georgia in Cuthbert, did not survive long. This college was suspended during the war, resumed in 1866, and in 1868 closed again with "dilapidated" buildings and no teachers. In 1871 it was revived again, but in 1875 closed forever; four years later the state took over the property for use as an agricultural school.[43]

Most religious colleges for women followed the course of the Methodists' Andrew Female College in Cuthbert, which strove to remain open and weathered the years of Reconstruction with a handful of college and preparatory students. The colleges that survived offered instruction to young women in a thoroughly southern atmosphere. In 1866 the Georgia Annual Conference commended the recently reopened Andrew Female College and its "corps of competent teachers, all of whom are graduates of Southern Institutions." The 1867 *Almanac* of that college boasted that the faculty were all "genuinely Southern" and the president, A. L. Hamilton, had been an officer in the Confederate army for four years. In Jackson, Tennessee, Amos B. Jones — Methodist minister, Confederate soldier, and Ku Klux Klan member — served as a professor and later president of the Memphis Conference Female Institute. The "thoroughly qualified president" of La Grange Female College in Georgia between 1870 and 1872 was the Reverend Morgan Callaway, who had served in the Confederate army; he was later a professor at Emory. Southern evangelicals could safely send their daughters to such schools with the assurance that they would receive proper religious — and southern — educations.[44]

Throughout religious reconstruction, southern ministers urged their congregations to educate their children at southern denominational colleges. The ministers of the Bainbridge District of the southern Methodist church resolved to impress upon all the importance of having their sons and daughters educated "where the better feelings of the heart, no less than the faculties of the mind, are trained and cultivated." The North Georgia Annual Conference could not "with too much emphasis express the conviction that Georgia Methodists should educate their sons and daughters, as far as possible, at our own institutions, and especially at those under the ownership and patronage of this Conference." Five years later, the conference still resolved to "urge upon Georgians to educate their children in Georgia, and upon Methodists to educate their children at our Conference schools." The West Tennessee Baptist Convention notified its members that "it is their duty to God, to truth, to their own families, and to posterity, to patronize their own schools and colleges." Fearing that "the late political revolution" would be followed by "greater revolutions in the social and religious world," Georgia Baptists insisted that "the proper education of the head and the heart is, perhaps, the best defence we can provide for posterity."[45]

Most southern Christians in the 1860s and 1870s agreed with Methodist Atticus Haygood, who in 1874 called evangelical higher education "the cause of the Church, and, therefore, the cause of God."[46] Out of their zeal for religious education, citadels of southern evangelicalism arose that formed a vital part of the Confederate vision of religious reconstruction. In these schools young southern men and women were to receive religious educations free from the corrupting influences rampant in the North and go forth to uphold the values of southern Christianity for future generations.

8

"A Pure and Loyal Gospel"

Northern Missionary
Efforts in the South

The spirit of the Lord GOD is upon me; because the LORD hath anointed me to preach good tidings unto the meek . . . to proclaim liberty to the captives. . . .

To proclaim the acceptable year of the LORD, and the day of vengeance of our God; to comfort all that mourn;

To appoint unto them that mourn in Zion, to give unto them beauty for ashes, the oil of joy for mourning. . . .

And they shall build the old wastes, they shall raise up the former desolations, and they shall repair the waste cities, the desolations of many generations.

Isaiah 61:1–4

While black and white southerners implemented their plans for religious reconstruction, northern evangelicals supported a major missionary effort in the South. Determined to spread "a pure and loyal gospel" in this benighted region, as northerners deemed it, hundreds of missionaries and teachers traveled south under the banners of their denominations. According to northern Church leaders, God had issued His stern decree upon slavery and had crushed the government and armies that upheld it and had given northern evangelicals a vast mission field to occupy. They would be disregarding His manifest will if they failed to meet the challenge. Initially, northern Christians approached religious reconstruction with much confidence, but their aspirations increasingly clashed with the competing visions held by black and white southerners. Ultimately, they had to reevaluate their mission in the South and concentrate on a few more limited goals.

Northern Baptist, Methodist, and Presbyterian missionaries moved rapidly into the South behind the advancing Union armies as early as 1861. They were joined in their ministrations by both freedpeople and religious scalawags. Northern preachers often occupied the prominent positions of authority and served the larger city churches, but southern converts played a vital and underappreciated role in this movement. Southern ministers who had left the southern denominations conducted most of the "northern" missionary labor in the South during religious reconstruction. For example, the ministerial ranks of the Tennessee, Holston, and Georgia Conferences of the Methodist Episcopal Church (MEC) consisted overwhelmingly of southern white and black preachers. Only a handful of presiding elders and pastors in centers like Nashville, Knoxville, Chattanooga, and Atlanta were from outside the South.

Northern missionaries had access to much of central and western Tennessee after the surrender of Nashville and Memphis in the first half of 1862, and work among the freedpeople in these two cities began in 1863 and 1864. Eastern Tennessee was not an open mission field for northerners until the end of the war, but southern Unionists began internal organization there early in 1864. With the ground thus prepared, northern denominations reaped a much greater harvest among whites there than in the rest of the state. Missionary endeavors began in Georgia on the coastal islands and in Savannah late in 1864, but the rest of the state was inaccessible until mid-1865.

By 1865 all four of the major northern evangelical denominations (Baptist, Methodist, New School Presbyterian, and Old School Presbyterian) had begun evangelistic and educational work in the South. In April 1865, the American Baptist Home Mission Society (ABHMS) already had 120 missionaries, teachers, and assistants in the South. The American Baptist Publication Society resolved in that year as well to raise a fund of $50,000 "to appoint Sunday School colporteurs or missionaries to traverse the Southern States; to reorganize Sunday-schools among the whites, and start them among the blacks." From 1866 to 1872, the ABHMS employed from sixty to one hundred missionaries in the southern states — one-third of its entire mission force. The society was particularly active in Tennessee, which ranked behind only Missouri and Virginia as a focus of northern Baptist missionary labor, with fourteen missionaries in 1866 and ten in 1868. Georgia had only three northern Baptist missionaries in 1866, seven in 1868, and five in 1871.[1]

In late 1866 the Board of Bishops of the MEC declared that emancipation had "opened at our very door a wide field calling alike for mission and educational work. . . . The school must be planted by the side of the Church; the teacher must go along with the missionary."[2] In August 1866 at Cincinnati, Ohio, several Methodist ministers and laypeople had organized the Freedmen's Aid Society of the Methodist Episcopal Church with Bishop Davis W. Clark as its president. Methodists had become increasingly distressed with the nonsectarian Freedmen's Commissions who insisted that educational and missionary work be conducted separately. Furthermore, other denominations were beginning their own efforts among the freedpeople, and the MEC sought to gain members through educational work. More northern Methodists began to agree with the minister who wrote that "from the start . . . Methodist hands should have handled Methodist funds . . . to found Methodist schools." The Freedmen's Aid Society handled the work of the MEC among the freedpeople, while the Missionary Society supported efforts among white southerners. During its first six years of existence, the Freedmen's Aid Society spent $315,100 in the South.[3]

Northern missionaries initially entered the South to minister to both whites and blacks. They urged white southerners to return to the northern denominational bodies just as the southern states were to return to the Union, and they expected to find many southern Christians sobered by God's judgment in the war and ready to repent of the sins of slavery and secession. They also anticipated finding many others who had never supported either but were trapped by geography within the Confederacy. Both groups would form a strong foundation on which to reestablish the northern denominations in the South. The early successes among religious scalawags, both clergy and laypeople, reinforced these optimistic assumptions. Northern missionaries did manage to raise their denominations' banners in areas populated by Unionists and in several of the larger cities where northern emigrants constituted the majority of their congregations. Elsewhere, as historian James Moorhead has observed, they were "almost universally shunned by the white people of the South."[4]

Despite the ensuing disappointments, the ABHMS remained committed as late as 1873 to meeting the needs "among millions of the poorer class of whites in the South, who cannot read and write." The society testified that no appointments were "voted through with greater heartiness or unanimity" than those for the benefit of white southerners. In some cases southern white missionaries were supported by the society: "brethren they are in some instances of rare worth and piety and devotion."[5]

One of the most successful efforts by the ABHMS in the South was its church edifice program, a plan that helped small churches build houses of worship; devastated churches in the postwar South eagerly participated. Statistics for the period of religious reconstruction are scarce, but both black and white churches received aid. In 1881 white churches in Georgia still owed the society $800, and black churches owed $1,750, on loans made during 1870–75. Also in 1881 in Tennessee, white churches owed $8,977 and black churches owed $1,000 for loans made between 1871 and 1876. Since churches applied for and received assistance on an individual basis, the Southern Baptist Convention (SBC) could do little to oppose this plan, though it did begin its own church building program in 1884.[6]

Nashville was one of the handful of southern cities where northern denominations were able to establish congregations among northern emigrants. The Presbyterian Church in the United States of America (PCUSA) (Old School) gained entrance into central Tennessee when three ministers and one elder of the southern Nashville Presbytery withdrew to form a separate Nashville Presbytery in connection with the northern Presbyterians. A representative of the northern Presbyterians offered Thomas H. McCallie of the Presbyterian church in Chattanooga "a salary of one thousand dollars a year if I would come to the General Assembly of the Northern Presbyterian Church and bring my church with me." When McCallie declined, the envoy "threatened me with evil consequences if I refused." By 1866 the PCUSA (Old School) had thirteen missionaries at work in the South, but the General Assembly was clearly displeased with the meager results of the Board of Domestic Mission's attempts "to secure a footing among our seceded southern churches. The only direct effort to reach our southern churches was made in Tennessee; but the attempt was a complete failure." In 1870 the Nashville Presbytery had only 122 members in two churches, one of which was a black church. In the same year, the corresponding southern presbytery had 2,074 adherents in twenty-three churches.[7]

The northern Methodists also established a congregation in Nashville. During the war, Methodist chaplain Michael J. Cramer appealed to his brother-in-law, General Ulysses S. Grant, for possession of McKendree Chapel, and it passed into the hands of the MEC early in 1864. Authority for this seizure came from the 1863 War Department order that granted northern Methodist missionaries the right to occupy all houses of worship "in which a loyal minister . . . appointed by a loyal bishop" did not officiate (see chapter 1). In January 1865, military governor Andrew Johnson ordered the church returned to the Methodist Episcopal Church, South (MECS), but various rear-guard tactics kept northern Methodists in possession of the edifice until August, much to the dismay of southern ministers. After the northern white congregation finally left the church, it built Union Chapel with $10,000 from the northern Methodist Church Extension Society. Northern Methodists also made some inroads among the white population in the surrounding countryside of middle Tennessee. When the Tennessee Conference was organized in October 1866, it counted nearly one thousand whites among its members, and by 1868 over three thousand white members.[8]

Most southerners viewed northern missionaries and religious scalawags with suspicion and contempt. When a group of northern teachers attended a local church with some of the "best citizens of the town" in Bainbridge, Georgia, nobody spoke to them. In four months the only white person who visited their quarters was the local Baptist pastor, "a man of Union sympathy." Other whites "carefully avoided them." One teacher who went south "disposed to be generous to the Southern people" quickly learned that southerners "would accept no sympathy that was not founded on the acknowledgement that right was and always had been on their side." Edward H. Myers, the editor of the *Southern Christian Advocate*, described John H. Caldwell and other Methodist religious scalawags as "miserable traitors to their brethren, their church, and their country." Caldwell's fellow religious scalawag, John W. Yarbrough, must have begun to understand the hostility he would face when a fellow minister in the southern church wrote him: "These northern missionaries are instigated of the devil and are in league with hell"—the author did not yet know of Yarbrough's impending pact with the devil.[9]

In some instances the Ku Klux Klan threatened northern ministers and southern religious scalawags, and it drove a few from their churches. In many areas the Klan and other vigilante groups burned schools and persecuted northern teachers. The *Southern Presbyterian Review* insisted that northern missionaries were simply political emissaries who preached politics rather than salvation. Even worse, the accusation went, they stirred racial antagonisms. They went to areas where southern churches had once striven hardest to Christianize the slaves, and they attempted to provoke divisions for their own aggrandizement.[10]

Southern Appalachia, especially eastern Tennessee, was the primary exception to the generally hostile reception of northern missionaries by white southerners. During the war and for long afterward, this area was deeply divided between Confederates and Unionists. Eastern Tennessee alone provided between thirty and forty thousand soldiers for the Federal armies during the Civil War.[11] Both during and after the war, eastern Tennessee's religious landscape was fractured along lines parallel to the political divisions in the region. Because of their particular forms of ecclesiastical government, which bound them closely to state and national organizations, southern Presbyterians and Methodists were the most bitterly divided. The rift produced dozens of lawsuits as contending parties laid claim to various church properties for themselves and the church to which they belonged.

In 1857 five synods seceded from the New School branch of the PCUSA and formed themselves into the United Synod of the South; the Synod of Tennessee, with its four constituent presbyteries, was a member. In 1864 the United Synod of the South joined with the Presbyterian Church in the Confederate States of America. However, the Union and Kingston presbyteries of the Synod of Tennessee met in September 1864 with the southern ministers absent and voted unanimously to reunite with the PCUSA (New School). In May 1865 the General Assembly of the PCUSA (New School). recognized these two presbyteries and accepted their commissioners as members. It also organized a new Holston Presbytery and combined the three presbyteries into its own Synod of Tennessee. After listening to reports from two Unionist ministers in the area, the assembly declared that the occupation of eastern Tennessee, "now reopened by Divine Providence, is the positive duty of the Presbyterian Church." The body requested its Home Mission Committee to send ten of its pastors to labor in that area for three months. In 1866 the Synod of Tennessee reported 2,260 members, and its membership remained between 2,200 and 2,750 for the rest of the decade.[12]

Ecclesiastical divisions at the national level also rent congregations at the local level. In August 1867, southern Presbyterians in Cleveland, Tennessee, urged the Reverend Thomas H. McCallie to travel from Chattanooga to assist them with difficulties in their local church. In Cleveland, McCallie found that "one David Nelson, with a crowd of 50 or 100 Negroes, armed with clubs" had proceeded to the Presbyterian church on Sunday morning and threatened "anybody and everybody with violence that dared preach there that day." McCallie "reckoned with said Nelson for awhile," after which Nelson withdrew and allowed the religious services to proceed.[13]

At Jonesboro, in the northeastern corner of Tennessee, two elders and a minority of the members of the Presbyterian church united with the Holston Presbytery of the PCUSA (New School) shortly after the war and claimed the local church property. After failing to regain possession of the property, southern Presbyterians formed their own church early in 1868 and connected it to the Holston Presbytery of the southern Presbyterian Church in the United States. By 1870 Jonesboro had a northern church with ninety members and a southern church with fifty members. In 1871 the southern church appealed to the county court for possession of the church building, and the court overruled the northern faction's bill of demurrer objecting to the southern group's claim. On appeal, the Tennessee Supreme Court upheld the lower court and remanded the case for further proceedings. In an unusual display of Christian charity during religious reconstruction, the two groups agreed in June 1873 to stop litigation and to use the building on alternate Sundays, with each group paying half the expenses of maintenance and repairs.[14]

In Athens, Tennessee, a missionary from the Home Missions Committee of the

PCUSA (New School) took possession of the Mars Hill Presbyterian Church in 1865 and ministered to Unionists there. When he left Athens in 1867, the pro-Confederate portion of the antebellum congregation signed a petition requesting that "as the church is unoccupied," the building be opened to allow Thomas H. McCallie of Chattanooga to preach once or twice a month. The elders and trustees, allied with the Unionist faction, denied the use of the church building for services by any disloyal minister, and near the end of that year, the PCUSA (New School) sent the Reverend David M. Wilson to preach at the Mars Hill Church. In January 1868, twenty members of the church who were southern in sympathies signed a petition requesting the use of the church building and preaching by a minister of their own choice. Wilson and the elders summarily dropped from the roll all those who had signed the petition, citing as reasons their sympathy with the Confederacy and their request for services by preachers forbidden by the northern General Assembly. The northern faction continued to use the building, and the southern group held meetings elsewhere. In 1870 the Mars Hill Church (northern) had fifty-seven members, and the Mars Hill Church (southern) had fifty-eight members. After several attempts at resolution, the southern group filed suit in May 1871 in the McMinn County Chancery Court for control of the property, and in May 1872 the court awarded the property to them. Wilson and the northern congregation appealed to the Tennessee Supreme Court, but it upheld the lower court's ruling.[15]

With the reorganization of the Synod of Tennessee, northern New School Presbyterians also gained control of the synod's school, Maryville College. Just days after the surrender of Fort Sumter, the college had closed as students left to join both armies; two professors had supported the Union, and the president and a tutor had favored the Confederacy. After the war one of the professors, Thomas Lamar, returned from the North and reopened the college with northern financial support. To the horror of the southern Presbyterian *Christian Observer*, "the doors and classes of this institution are now thrown open very widely for the admission of *both sexes and colors*." Despite southern hostility, the school continued to operate, though with a predominantly white student body.[16]

Southern Presbyterian Eliza Fain was deeply troubled by the actions of northern Presbyterians in East Tennessee. When the northern Holston Presbytery demanded the antebellum records of the once unified body from the southern Holston Presbytery, Fain wondered, "Have they a desire to bring down those who are today standing for the truth? O has that moral pollution which is sapping our civil structure to its very foundation been making insidious inroads upon our fair and once beautiful system of religious faith drawn and supported by the words of gospel truth." Viewing radical reconstruction as the end of civil liberty, Fain worried that religious liberty was likewise in jeopardy: "We fear, we tremble, may God in his infinite mercy and love preserve us from the fatal steps which would plunge us into a terrible persecution."[17]

Eastern Tennessee was also fertile ground for the MEC. Division within the Holston Conference of the southern Methodist church began with the purges of 1862, 1863, and 1864. A large majority of the ministers favored the Confederacy, but a sizable minority supported the Union. During these three annual meetings, a total of thirty-five ministers were charged with disloyalty to the Confederacy or the MECS. Ten were expelled or suspended.[18]

In response to these tactics, "Parson" William G. Brownlow began recruiting preachers and laypeople into the MEC early in 1864. He insisted through the columns of his newspaper, the *Whig and Rebel Ventilator*, that "God's retribution" was being visited upon southern Methodists. As a religious scalawag, he adopted most of the northern understanding of the war and acted accordingly, with considerably more ardor than most. In July 1864 he led a convention of Unionist Methodists to proclaim their loyalty to the Federal government. They also declared themselves the true Holston Annual Conference and insisted that they were "entitled in law to all property belonging to said ecclesiastical organization." With God's help, they intended "to claim and hold the same and rebuild the waste places of Zion." In response to the activities of Brownlow and others, Bishop Davis W. Clark in June 1865 officially organized the Holston Annual Conference of the MEC in Athens, Tennessee. Thirty-three former ministers of the MECS and six transfers from other conferences of the MEC formed the new conference, with 5,146 members; the defections from the southern Methodist church continued over the next three years. By May 1866, the northern Holston Conference's membership had climbed to 13,918; eighteen months later it had 18,897 members. By 1868, most of the movement of members between the two Methodisms in eastern Tennessee had ceased. The Holston Conference of the MEC had 20,790 full members, including 1,277 black members; the Holston Conference of the MECS enrolled 26,180 white, but only 172 black, and 75 Indian members.[19]

Athens Female College, an institution of the southern Methodist church in Athens, Tennessee, closed under the pressures of war in 1863; in 1865 the president of the college, the Reverend Erastus Rowley, joined the northern Holston Conference. Rowley filed a claim in chancery court requesting that the property be sold to satisfy a debt of $6,000 owed him by the college. At the forced sale, representatives of the MEC purchased the property and established East Tennessee Wesleyan College for white students. In 1868, the institution, now with 120 students, was renamed East Tennessee Wesleyan University; in 1871 it added theological and law departments.[20]

Throughout eastern Tennessee the two Holston Conferences appointed preachers to the same charges. Both conferences assigned ministers to Athens, Chattanooga, Cleveland, Decatur, Kingston, and several other towns; both northern and southern Methodists were committed to maintaining their church in this section of the state. Conflicts over church buildings and parsonages inevitably erupted. In local congregations that were divided in their loyalties between northern and southern Methodism, both groups claimed the right to exclusive use of the church property. Members of the MEC were quite successful at gaining control; as late as 1869, that church still held forty-six churches and three parsonages in eastern Tennessee that had belonged to the MECS before the war. Negotiations between the two Holston conferences on property issues proceeded diplomatically but fruitlessly. While "we deplore the necessity of going to law with brethren," southern Methodists asserted, in some areas they resorted to the civil courts to assert their claims to these properties. In 1880 a court awarded the parsonage of the Jonesboro Circuit to southern Methodists and required northern Methodist trustees to pay them $800 for past rent. Northern Methodists also occupied the southern Methodist church on Church Street in Knoxville for ten years before a threatened lawsuit compelled them to give up the property.[21]

Like the northern Baptists, the MEC established a Church Extension Society in 1864 to aid in the erection and repair of church buildings. East Tennessee Methodists made full use of this service, as the Church Extension Society appropriated $10,000 for the Holston Conference in 1866. Half that amount went toward the construction of a church at Knoxville, while other funds were used for building and paying building debts in Cleveland, Chattanooga, Athens, Loudon, Jonesboro, and elsewhere.[22]

Despite some limited successes among whites in cities, in Appalachia, and in border states, northern denominations were most successful among the southern black population. Reflecting a common theme in northern missionary efforts, the General Assembly of the PCUSA (New School) concluded in 1867: "The work at the South has been more encouraging among the freedpeople, wherever they have been able to send missionaries, than among the whites." There were few black missionaries available, however, and "the prejudice against all Northern men, among the whites at the South, both loyal and rebel, is such as to hinder the usefulness and comfort of missionaries sent from the North."[23]

Northern missionaries devoted much of their early attention to providing educational assistance to the freedpeople. In its first year of operations in the South, the Freedmen's Aid Society of the MEC began schools in nine southern states, with fifty-two teachers and five thousand enrolled pupils. In its second year, the society had fifty-nine schools with seven thousand students, including seventeen schools in Tennessee and eleven in Georgia. In the fall of 1865 northern Methodist missionaries in Nashville began a school in the basement of the blacks' Andrew Chapel. Within a few months, they had 180 pupils, and soon the number climbed to 610. By 1867 the school had eight hundred students of all ages. In Georgia, the Methodist Freedmen's Aid Society sponsored thirty-one teachers between 1865 and 1873. Several Methodist religious scalawags also started schools for freedpeople in conjunction with their missionary efforts. Northern Presbyterians and Baptists also supported schools for freedpeople throughout the South. The Committee on Freedmen of the PCUSA (Old School) employed three teachers for Georgia freedpeople in 1869, while the New School's Home Missionary Committee had one in the state. During the period from 1865 to 1873, northern Baptists through the ABHMS supported eleven teachers for freedmen in Georgia.[24]

The northern denominations also began to organize presbyteries, associations, and conferences among the freedpeople in the South. Northern Presbyterian organization in the South began in 1866 when the Catawba Presbytery of the Old School church was organized in the Carolinas and Georgia. Knox Presbytery was established in Georgia the following year, and in 1869 these two presbyteries and the Atlantic Presbytery united to form the Synod of the Atlantic.[25] With their looser denominational structures, northern Baptists were less likely to organize associations among the freedpeople, but they eagerly sought cooperation with the associations the freedpeople themselves formed in the 1860s and 1870s.

Northern Methodists were the most active in establishing conferences among the freedpeople. When the Tennessee Conference began in 1866 in the middle and western portions of the state, three-quarters of the membership was black. By 1869 the conference had 5,493 black members, but its membership declined in the early

1870s, probably due to the formation of the Colored Methodist Episcopal Church. By 1879 the MEC claimed 6,117 black members in middle and western Tennessee.[26]

The formation of the Georgia Annual Conference (MEC) in 1866 and 1867 demonstrates how northern and southern preachers worked together to enact the northern vision of religious reconstruction. Bishop Davis W. Clark created the Georgia and Alabama Mission District in January 1866 when he met in Atlanta with John H. Caldwell and six other religious scalawags, who had been ministers in the MECS. Clark appointed the Reverend James F. Chalfant of Cincinnati as superintendent of the mission district, and over the next year and a half these preachers, joined by other religious scalawags and black preachers, gathered together congregations from Macon to the Tennessee border. Several white congregations in the mountains of north Georgia joined the new organization, but the majority of members came from the black population. Large black congregations transferred from the southern to the northern Methodist church in Rome, Newnan, La Grange, Griffin, Jonesboro, Oxford, and elsewhere in central and northern Georgia. Despite harsh opposition from native whites, religious scalawags also began schools for the freedpeople in each of these towns with assistance from the Freedmen's Bureau and the Freedmen's Aid Society of the MEC. Throughout religious reconstruction, the Georgia Conference had a few prominent northern ministers such as Erasmus Q. Fuller and Nelson E. Cobleigh as members, and Atlanta even served as the home of Bishop Gilbert Haven after 1872. However, the principal troops for northern Methodism in the conflicts of religious reconstruction were the religious scalawags and black preachers who manned the various charges around the state and experienced firsthand the hostility of white southerners. At the formal organization of the Georgia Annual Conference in October 1867, approximately 8,000 blacks and 2,300 whites had been gathered into the MEC. By 1877, the denomination had 12,600 black and 2,800 white members in Georgia.[27]

The MEC had several advantages over its primary rivals, the African Methodist Episcopal and African Methodist Episcopal Zion churches. Well-organized and well-supported, the Freedmen's Aid Society was able to carry on simultaneous evangelistic and educational programs over a large part of the South; the northern Methodist church gained many adherents in the South through promises of support for building churches and paying teachers. In Griffin, Georgia, for example, a group of blacks voted to join the northern Methodist church after a representative promised that "they should have help to build a church, [buy] Sunday School books, and [pay] a teacher." The MEC also appealed to southern blacks through its claims to color blindness. Many missionaries echoed the call of Timothy W. Lewis, who, when presenting his church to freedpeople in Charleston insisted, "there will be no galleries in heaven [and] those who are willing to go with a church that makes no distinction as to race or color, follow me."[28]

After the Executive Board of the ABHMS declared in 1863 that soon "the entire South would be one vast home mission field," missionaries immediately went to work among the freedpeople in Tennessee. The Reverend Isaac C. Hoile and six other workers began missionary work in Memphis; the Reverend Simon Quackenbush and three assistants represented northern Baptists in Nashville; others labored in Chattanooga and Knoxville. From these centers, northern Baptists organized churches and schools among black Baptists across the state. Throughout the South between 1862 and 1894, the ABHMS spent $2,452,000 on black evangelization and education.[29]

In Georgia, northern Baptist missionaries had begun work among freedpeople by the end of 1865. By 1871, thirty ABHMS missionaries had labored in Georgia for a total of more than three thousand weeks, delivered almost three thousand sermons, and participated in the conversion of nearly one thousand black men, women, and children. At the end of 1865, one of the society's missionaries wrote, "If there were seven times as many Sabbaths as there are, I could find work abundant. I have numerous calls upon me to preach in places I have not been able to answer." Even in 1878 a black missionary appointed by the ABHMS concluded, "many places — in fact, most places, are as dark as midnight." He complained that in some churches a person could not be baptized unless he or she "has seen God, been to hell, seen the devil, heard a voice, or felt a mysterious shock." Others claimed they had a Bible in their hearts, which they could read at any time. These doctrines were "preached from the pulpit." Although the state was in "a pretty dilapidated condition," he concluded, it was not "beyond the reach of Divine grace."[30]

One of the society's principal methods of promoting black education was through the holding of "Ministers' Institutes." The practice originated with the efforts of southern Baptist Ebenezer W. Warren, pastor of the First Baptist Church in Atlanta, Georgia. In the early 1870s, Warren gathered uneducated black ministers and deacons from the surrounding area together and provided them with a study of fundamental doctrines for about ten days. The program was so effective that the SBC endorsed it in 1875, and the next year its Domestic Mission Board began sponsoring institutes. In 1878 the ABHMS voted to cooperate with the SBC in conducting ministers' institutes for the freedpeople, and S. W. Marston was appointed superintendent of missions to the freedpeople. In the first year of operation, this joint effort was responsible for thirty-three institutes, which were attended by 1,119 black ministers and deacons. In 1881 the ABHMS reorganized its participation, holding newly renamed "Biblical Institutes" in connection with its freedpeople's schools in the South. The society also hoped to cooperate with the Baptist conventions in each of the southern states for the appointment of a general missionary to the freedpeople of that state, so cooperation in biblical institutes now meant participation in all of the activities of the society in the South. Under these conditions, most southern state conventions recoiled from further cooperation. The Tennessee Baptist Convention, however, did seriously consider cooperating formally with the ABHMS in mission work. After one minister proposed the appointment of a committee to explore the issue with the society, another objected that such an alliance would be humiliating to the Domestic Mission Board of the SBC. The motion was defeated, but the convention appointed messengers to attend the society's jubilee convention in 1882.[31]

In 1878, the ABHMS began limited cooperation with the Georgia Baptist Convention. Although the society had been active in missionary work among Georgia freedpeople since 1865, the Georgia Baptist Convention had taken no official notice of it until 1872; in 1877, after James H. DeVotie was elected corresponding secretary of the newly organized Georgia Baptist State Mission Board, he received a request from Corresponding Secretary S. S. Cutting of the society suggesting a "fraternal talk" regarding missionary efforts in Georgia. DeVotie hoped that the society could help in evangelizing the freedpeople. Georgia Baptists could not do the work alone, but, DeVotie confided, "You can help us if you find a safe way." The Georgia Baptist Convention could not enter into a direct alliance with the ABHMS because "we would lose more at home than we would receive from you." DeVotie suggested that the society provide $1,000 and allow the convention's board to appoint missionaries who would report to the society. In 1878 one white and three black missionaries began work, with the society paying two-thirds of their salaries. Later, the society and the convention modified the plan so that the society, the convention, and the Georgia Missionary Baptist State Convention (black) each contributed one-third of the salaries of two missionaries to Georgia freedpeople. Cooperation between the ABHMS and white Georgia Baptists ended early in the 1880s, and the SBC reasserted its interests in Georgia in 1883, when it appointed W. H. McIntosh to conduct ministers' institutes in the state.[32]

Northern Baptist women became independently involved in the cause of evangelizing the South through the Women's Baptist Home Mission Society, organized in February 1877. The society immediately commissioned as its first missionary Joanna P. Moore, who was then at work in New Orleans and had been a missionary to the freedpeople for over a decade. In addition to financial support, the society sent Moore young women to assist her. Within a decade, it was supporting one hundred female missionaries throughout the South.[33]

Both northern and southern blacks contributed substantially to the work of freedmen's aid organizations, in many cases organizing schools for their children, and increasingly making donations. Between 1862 and 1874, blacks contributed $478,995 to the total of nearly $4 million spent by these organizations. As early as 1865, Savannah blacks contributed $1,000 for their first teachers. Of the 236 schools for freedpeople in Georgia in 1867, 152 were entirely or partially supported by blacks, and blacks owned thirty-nine of the buildings.[34]

With the demise of the Freedmen's Bureau in 1870 and waning support from private sources, northern Christians had to reevaluate their southern evangelistic and educational plans. By the early 1870s most areas of the South lay within a network of associations, conferences, and presbyteries affiliated with northern denominations, so fewer missionaries were necessary. Northern evangelicals also determined to focus their attention on a few colleges and universities to train black preachers and teachers, leaving elementary instruction to the southern states. Northern white denominations commanded the resources necessary to establish colleges for blacks in the 1860s and 1870s. Northern Baptists founded the Nashville Normal and Theological Institute at Nashville and the Augusta Institute at Augusta, Georgia, in 1867; the MEC began Central Tennessee College at Nashville in 1865 and Clark University at Atlanta in 1870; and northern Presbyterians concentrated most of their attention on the establishment of Biddle Memorial Institute at Charlotte, North Carolina, begun in 1867.[35]

Central Tennessee College began in 1865 in the basement of Clark Chapel in Nashville. After a brief tenure in an old gun factory and unsuccessful attempts to purchase property, the college finally moved to a dilapidated two-story mansion that was repaired with funds from the Freedmen's Bureau. In 1876 the college created a medical department, and during the next two years, the five Meharry brothers, farmers in Indiana and Illinois, gave more than $30,000 for the new Meharry Medical College. For many years thereafter Meharry trained over half of all black American doctors and dentists.[36]

The origins of Clark University in Atlanta lay in a primary school that northern Methodist minister J. W. Lee and his wife started in Clark Chapel in early 1869. Its success prompted the Freedmen's Aid Society to adopt it, and it moved to another building in 1870. In 1872 it opened a theological department, which, after a substantial gift from northern Methodist minister Elijah H. Gammon in 1883, became Gammon Theological Seminary. However, Clark did not begin regular college-level instruction until 1879. The institution was named for Bishop Davis W. Clark because of his participation in southern evangelism and because of his daughter's gifts after his death in 1872.[37]

In its early years of operation in the South, the ABHMS supported many schools that provided elementary instruction, but in the 1870s it devoted its primary attention to institutions of higher learning. The Augusta Institute (later Morehouse College) began in February 1867 at the Springfield Baptist Church in Augusta with forty students. Three women missionaries were the first teachers. For the next four years, a variety of northern white leaders tried to run the school without success. In August 1871, the Reverend Joseph T. Robert, a southerner who had lived in the North since before the war, assumed control of the school; in 1872, he and one assistant taught forty-four students. By 1877 the student body had grown to eighty-four, including fifty-one studying for the ministry. Robert moved the school to Atlanta in 1879 and renamed it Atlanta Baptist Seminary. Although it was designed to train preachers and teachers, President Robert found that "ministers, indeed, with but few exceptions, were entirely untaught, and unable to read the scriptures." Therefore, the college was forced to begin with primary departments that taught basic skills.[38]

The Baptists' Nashville Institute declared that its "primary object" was "to prepare young men for the ministry and both men and women for teachers." The school began when British minister Dr. Daniel W. Phillips came from Boston to Knoxville in 1864. The following year he moved to Nashville and began a class in his home for young black men intending to become ministers; later in the year, the class was transferred to the basement of the black First Baptist Church. Also in 1865 the ABHMS bought an abandoned government building for $1,000, took it down, and rebuilt it on a lot northwest of the city; there the Nashville Institute continued for nearly a decade. In the 1873–74 school year, Phillips and four unmarried women taught seventy-nine male and twenty-nine female students. In that year, the school moved to an estate southwest of the city — a brick "mansion house" and thirty acres of land, which had been purchased for $30,000. By 1877 the institute had expanded to accommodate six teachers and 129 pupils. The school's catalog for that year reminded its patrons, "a good pastor or preacher must needs have, first, common sense; second, piety; third, a call from God; fourth, education." The catalog also promoted its expanded Ladies' Department, where young women would be educated. "Every reason for the education of young men demands equally the education of young women," the Nashville Institute declared; "educated [C]hristian mothers educate, [C]hristianize and elevate the whole people."[39]

Religious colleges sponsored by northern denominations did not train large numbers of students. Neither Clark University nor Atlanta Baptist Seminary ever had more than ten students at one time in their college departments until the end of the century. The first college class was formed at Central Tennessee College in 1874 with two students. In 1878 the college had its first graduate.[40] However, black men and women trained at these colleges wielded an influence over black education in the region out of proportion to their number.

Northern evangelicals' initial enthusiasm for the evangelization and education of the South began to fade in the 1870s. In response to declining resources, the Freedmen's Aid Society of the MEC applied for recognition as one of the approved organizations of the denomination. The Methodist General Conference of 1872 consented to the request and urged northern Methodists to support the society and in 1876 granted it "a very large increase" in its annual budget. Despite the official recognition, however, the apathy of many northern Methodists continued to hamper the operations of the Freedmen's Aid Society.[41]

Apathy among the laypeople stemmed in part from declining interest in the pulpit. In his study of northern Protestant sermons during Reconstruction, Paul Brownlow found only seventeen sermons in the period from 1869 to 1877 that discussed reconstruction problems. All but one of the eleven preachers who discussed the freedpeople shared two assumptions — that blacks were unequal and that God was taking care of black southerners. In sharp contrast to the far greater number of sermons on reconstruction in the years 1865–68, none of these sermons demanded punishment for the South or its leaders. Northern clergy were now more interested in promoting sectional reconciliation. Brownlow concludes, "general lack of pulpit interest in the whole subject of reconstruction indicates that many preachers may have no longer cared what happened to the South."[42]

The retreat from religious reconstruction meant fewer missionaries and less financial support for evangelizing and educating southerners. The ABHMS had supported sixty to one hundred missionaries in the South in the late 1860s and early 1870s; after 1872, it sponsored only thirty to fifty workers. Part of the decrease stemmed from the decision not to employ students during summer vacations after 1872. However, the decline also reflected a redirection of the society's efforts toward the West. In 1877, twelve of the society's thirty-eight missionaries in the South labored in Indian Territory. Only one to five missionaries worked in each of the former states of the Confederacy. By 1881, thirty-one of the sixty missionaries working in the South were in Indian Territory, Texas, and New Mexico; outside of Texas, only seventeen worked in former Confederate states.[43]

Contribution statistics reveal a small base of financial support among northern Christians even at the height of religious reconstruction — a base that grew even smaller in the 1870s and 1880s. In 1867, among Old School Presbyterian churches, only 526 (21 percent) contributed to evangelical work among the freedpeople; 1,982 did not. The Committee on Freedmen complained that missionary work among southern blacks "has not been sustained in a manner at all commensurate with its importance." In 1872, after reunion with the strongly antislavery New School Presbyterians, still only 1,120 local churches (24 percent) supported freedpeople's work; 3,469 made no contribution. A greater percentage of northern Methodists churches supported the Freedman's Aid Society of the MEC, but in the 1870s nearly half took no collection for this purpose. In 1875, there were 5,124 local congregations (56 percent) that contributed; 4,050 did not.[44]

Some northern Christians rightly believed that their efforts to evangelize the freedpeople interfered with the process of reunification with the southern denominations. Presbyterian leaders in 1871 professed their desire to avoid "all unpleasant collision with the Southern churches" over the issue of evangelizing the freedpeople. In their attempts to evangelize southern whites, members of northern denominations, especially religious scalawags, became increasingly willing to sacrifice the interests of the freedpeople.[45]

Even as northern Methodist missionary work in the South was taking shape, racial separation became the norm. Segregated congregations soon gave rise to segregated presiding elders' districts, so that blacks and whites met only at the annual and general conferences. Even there, among ministers of the gospel, racial antagonisms sometimes erupted. When Bishop Calvin Kingsley tried to administer the sacrament simultaneously to both black and white ministers at the 1867 meeting of the Holston Conference, whites denounced the practice as "an unnatural and disgusting practice" and "a strike for Negro equality." When Bishop Gilbert Haven tried the same experiment in Georgia, the white ministers refused to partake of the sacrament and left the meeting. The racial antagonism also extended to the ordination of ministers. A preacher in eastern Tennessee complained about "Negro equality" after he was "ordained to deacon's orders . . . with . . . the colored brethren." One Georgian in a similar circumstance "refused to be ordained" and left the conference without ordination. He insisted that "he could never meet the opposition at home should he be thus ordained." For many white southerners, their desire to unite with northern denominations had little to do with race and much to do with loyalty and politics.[46]

As early as 1869, black members of the Holston Conference requested that they be organized into a separate body. The conference did not set them apart, but it did create three districts with black presiding elders and preachers; in 1874 it resolved that when the "growth of this work shall make it desirable on their part, to organize a separate Conference for the benefit of this people, we will cheerfully give our influence in favor of such a measure." At the 1875 meeting, the conference instructed its delegates to the General Conference of 1876 "to give their votes and influence for the establishment of all such separate Conferences as the interests of the Church among the white and colored races may require, and as both races may desire." Within the Holston Conference, the cause of freedpeople's aid met with indifference. In 1877 the conference determined in the next year to present the cause in all the churches and to collect an offering; the collections totaled $36.75.[47]

In 1869 the fledgling Georgia Conference was also beginning to polarize along racial lines. The physical setting of its annual conference that year illustrated a trend toward segregation. Originally scheduled for Lloyd Street Church in Atlanta, the conference was transformed into a camp-meeting at Rataree's Grove, five miles from Atlanta. Two large brush arbors were built on the campgrounds about a quarter of a mile apart. "Two services per day were held in each so that the races worshipped simultaneously, but separate. Business sessions were attended by the two races jointly in a rude building mid-way between the two camps." At this conference, nine black preachers introduced a petition requesting that "districts be manned by colored ministers, and that as soon as may be proper in your judgment, we be organized into a separate conference." The conference gave some sanction to the plan by organizing one black district with Adam Palmer, a black preacher, as presiding elder.[48]

During the October 1871 meeting of the Georgia Conference, two religious scalawags introduced a resolution to instruct their delegates to the 1872 General Conference "to move that Body to authorize the setting off of a colored annual conference in Georgia" and that the preachers in Georgia discuss the issue among themselves and come to the next conference prepared to take action; after discussion the resolution was adopted. The 1872 General Conference, meeting in Brooklyn, New York, in May, authorized the Missouri and St. Louis Conferences to establish racially separate conferences if the bishops felt "the interests of the work required it," but declined to separate other conferences. Erasmus Q. Fuller, the editor of the *Methodist Advocate* in Atlanta, complained that the General Conference "practically took no action upon the question of the colored conferences." Many conferences that had requested division had few white members and were practically black conferences, he argued, and "they have never felt many of the embarrassments found in some localities," like the Georgia Conference had.[49]

The subsequent October meeting of the Georgia Annual Conference and those in 1873 and 1874 again passed resolutions requesting a racial separation of the conference. The 1875 session contemplated the racial segregation of the Georgia work, but some black members and northern preachers voted down a proposal by other blacks and white religious scalawags for a racial division of the conference. The two sides compromised on asking for a geographical rather than racial division. Opponents of segregation also passed a resolution disclaiming "any movement which looks to the separation of our work into a white and colored conference."[50]

However, the 1876 General Conference approved the separation of the southern conferences provided that the action was "requested by a majority of the white members, and also a majority of the colored members." The Georgia work of the MEC was immediately split into the Georgia Conference and the Savannah Conference, presumably along geographical lines.[51] In the midst of the fall meetings of these new conferences, however, a commission of ministers from both met in Augusta to adjust the boundaries of the two bodies. Citing the fact that "the conference lines are irregular and inconvenient, giving much needless travel to ministers in the work," and the desire of many black ministers and congregations in the Georgia Conference to transfer to the Savannah Conference, the commission voted to transfer the La Grange district from the Georgia to the Savannah Conference. It also declared that the Savannah Conference "shall have free access to all the people of color throughout the State of Georgia without regard to geographical lines," and that the Georgia Conference would have charge of all white Georgians. No person could be denied membership, however, on the basis of "race, color or previous condition." Presiding bishop Levi Scott approved the action of the joint commission, and the racial division of the MEC in Georgia was completed.[52]

At the 1876 meeting of the Tennessee Conference, white ministers asked for a racial division because of the "effect of the present condition of the Conference on the white work." Fifty-one white clergy supported division; forty-four black preachers opposed it. Only a handful of white ministers were willing to oppose separation, including John Braden, who wrote, "Not a single colored man would have voted for division on the merits of the question." The conference postponed the decision for a year, but black members agreed to divide the conference if a majority of whites continued to desire it. In 1877 whites withdrew and formed the Central Tennessee Conference with some 4,400 members.[53]

By 1884, twenty-five of the twenty-eight conferences of the MEC in the former slave states contained only black or only white ministers and members. The efforts of northern Methodist missionaries to minister to the freedpeople and their commitment to a measure of ecclesiastical equality drew many black southerners to their church but dampened its appeal among white southerners. In a capitulation to southern mores and an expression of their own spirit of caste, the southern members of the MEC appealed for the racial division of their conferences. This futile bid for respectability failed to draw more white members to the MEC and undermined much of northern Methodism's critique of the southern church's attitude toward the freedpeople. It did, however, seem to have some positive effects on the efforts to establish fraternal relations with the MECS.[54]

Armed with the belief that God had judged the South for the sins of "menstealing" and rebellion, northern missionaries had moved southward behind Union armies to gather wayward white southerners and vulnerable freedpeople into the folds of their churches. Unfortunately for their plans, these groups had other ideas about what was necessary for religious reconstruction. Freedpeople welcomed the financial, organizational, and educational support northern Christians offered them, but they resented the "spirit of caste" that continued in ecclesiastical bodies and denominational schools. By the end of religious reconstruction, black evangelicals were organizationally isolated. Both the southern churches from which they had withdrawn and, to a lesser extent, the northern churches they had joined had been unwilling to accept their assertions of religious equality. White southern evangelicals loathed the northern missionaries and teachers who, in their minds, came only to steal their churches, engender strife among the races, and destroy the southern social order. Perhaps even worse were those traitors to the South, the religious scalawags, who joined the invaders in their unholy work. Worse still for religious ex-Confederates, northern evangelicals and their southern allies entered the secular political arena to press their demands for the reformation of southern society.

9

Voting the Bible

*Religion and Politics in the
Reconstruction South*

And Jesus answering said unto them, Render to Caesar the things that are
Caesar's, and to God the things that are God's. And they marvelled at
him.

Mark 12:17

A s with religious reconstruction, the three major groups of Christians had different
attitudes toward political reconstruction in the aftermath of the Civil War. White
southerners urged the rapid restoration of the antebellum patterns in southern political, as well as religious, life. The resumption of political "home rule," they believed,
would enhance the viability of their sectional religious organizations. White northerners believed that the sins of slavery and secession had corrupted southern political
institutions as well as southern churches and deemed it necessary to rebuild the South
politically to protect the reunited nation from further treasonous activities. A politically reconstructed South would protect the civil and religious liberties of the freedpeople, southern Unionists, and northerners who had immigrated into the South.
Most freedpeople likewise felt that political reconstruction was crucial to the survival
of their new freedoms, both civil and religious. Acquiring basic civil rights would
allow them to protect the religious liberties they had gained through emancipation.

Political activism was hardly a novel concept for American Christians in 1865.
Recent scholarship has demonstrated just how important a role religion played in
antebellum American politics. Richard J. Carwardine, for example, argues that "the
Republicans acquired their essential moral energy from evangelical Protestantism,
and their unique fusion of religion and politics drew on established modes of mobilizing revivalist enthusiasm." He also maintains that Republicans "drew on the public discourse of evangelicals as it had been elaborated over a quarter of a century."
Although not as "apolitical as most of them publicly insisted," southern evangelicals,

in contrast, "resisted the explicit fusing of politics and religion, and remained divided in their partisan allegiances."[1]

Likewise, Mitchell Snay, while agreeing that Southern ministers accepted the formal separation of church and state, insists that "if a political issue was perceived as possessing any kind of moral significance, . . . Southern clergymen claimed that it fell within their jurisdiction and justified their attention." During the antebellum ecclesiastical struggles over slavery, southern Protestants "freely borrowed constitutional discourse from the political sphere" and later, "denominational schism, in turn, gave added depth and meaning to political discourse" over the conflict between "majority tyranny and minority rights." By the time of the secession crisis, Snay argues, northern and southern ministers "shared the same rhetorical world," and their discourse displayed striking similarities. "Both groups of clergy," Snay concludes, "used the same language and set of assumptions to explain and interpret the sectional controversy between North and South."[2]

Similarly, during the Civil War northern and southern evangelicals actively supported their respective administrations. Clergymen in both sections recruited soldiers, served as chaplains, and proclaimed from the pulpit that God favored their political and military leaders. Laypeople prayed for the success of their armies, quelled dissent, and assured themselves and others that the clergy understood God's estimate of their leaders. Many evangelical Protestants in the North were fervent Republicans, and many devout white southerners were equally committed to the Davis administration. God's purposes were to be accomplished through these leaders, and some Christians in each section came to view political dissent as comparable to a lack of religious faith.[3]

During the Reconstruction era, Christians continued to participate in the political process when they believed important moral issues were at stake. However, not all groups of Christians were equally active politically, nor did their past political activity dictate their attitudes toward political reconstruction. In marked contrast to their enthusiastic public support for secession and the Confederacy, for example, southern ministers and denominational newspapers devoted relatively little attention to political reconstruction. In 1859 the influential southern Presbyterian minister Thomas Smyth had written that the "connection between true religion and sound politics is very intimate." During the war itself, the southern Presbyterian General Assembly and denominational newspapers supported the Confederacy and sought to make it a Christian nation. In the wake of emancipation and Confederate defeat, however, southern Presbyterians adopted the apolitical stance that had been prevalent among border state Presbyterians during the sectional crisis. In their 1866 General Assembly, they proclaimed the "non-secular and non-political character of the Church of Jesus Christ." In keeping with their new emphasis on the "spirituality of the Church," southern Presbyterian journals commented little on the politics of Reconstruction. However, as historian Jack P. Maddex has perceptively observed, southern Presbyterians "made their ecclesiastical rivalry with Northern Presbyterians a surrogate for politics." In that conflict (examined more fully in chapter 10) they debated in theological and ecclesiological terms the issues that divided northerners and southerners in the realm of politics.[4]

Southern Baptists and Methodists likewise avoided frequent comment on political affairs. Although they occasionally spoke out against what they believed to be the excesses of radical Republican state governments in the South, Baptist and Methodist denominational newspapers, like their Presbyterian counterparts, devoted more attention to condemning the political activities of northern missionaries and religious scalawags. While avoiding frequent commentary on political issues, southern religious newspapers occasionally made their opposition to Radical Reconstruction and their support for the Democrats clear. After Democratic victories in several states in the 1874 elections, the editor of the *Christian Index* in Georgia proclaimed that "every Christian in the Southern States should devoutly thank God for His mercies bestowed in the political victories of the last week." The "trials" and "oppressions" of the past decade had been so great that "many of our people — otherwise good citizens — have been led to doubt the overruling Providence of God." A week later, the editor admitted that "this paper is devoted to *Religion*, and not to *Politics*." However, this "political revolution" was "a Christian triumph," which had been "wrought by the hand of an All-wise and merciful Providence." He regarded it his "religious duty to point the event to the Christian world . . . [for] universal thanksgiving." The editor of the *Religious Herald* in Virginia likewise could not contain his enthusiasm: the results of the elections "filled us with the most sincere delight and inspired us with bright hopes for the future of the country."[5]

Individual white southern evangelicals clung to their faith that God still ruled the world and that He would overrule the designs of their political and religious enemies. Although many white southern Christians viewed President Johnson as a traitor and an infidel, they welcomed his lenient policy toward the South and hoped for a speedy return of the old political order. On March 4, 1865, Eliza Fain writing in her diary about the inauguration, labeled Vice-president Johnson "traitor, traitor." By the end of April, however, she rethought her attitude toward Johnson, the new president: "a man whose character we have all regarded as a very dark one." He reached the White House by "being a traitor to his own native section." However, "the party who placed him there I do believe are trembling with anxious fear as he has done away with the taking of that accursed oath which was an outrage upon the feelings of every Christian man." Fain thought that perhaps Johnson "may now seek to do something which will wipe away the stigma of traitor." When told a few weeks later that Johnson intended to conciliate the white South, Fain wrote in her diary, "If this is true of that man I feel from my inmost soul God has done it. He had his heart in his hand and he can do no more and go no further than the Father of the Southern Christian will permit him."[6]

When Congress, led by the radical Republicans, assumed charge of Reconstruction over Johnson's protests and vetoes, white southern evangelicals were appalled. However, they remained confident that God continued to rule over the affairs of men as they prayed for deliverance from this new trial. "For several years we were kept in a state of unrest and of apprehension of evils that were coming on the country," Presbyterian minister Thomas H. McCallie later remembered. Each time Congress met, "its very first meeting filled the minds of the people with foreboding of evil." God, the ruler of nations, finally intervened to deliver His southern Zion: "But God ruled and when He took away Hon. Thad Stevens, of Pennsylvania, the great strong, destructive leader, the whole South breathed freer."[7]

If white southern Christians were ambivalent about their proper role in postbellum politics, northern evangelicals and their religious scalawag allies were confident that political action was essential to the successful reconstruction of southern society. "Next to a sound theology," wrote the editor of the northern Methodist *Central Christian Advocate*, "the thing we most need in this country is correct political teaching." Georgia Methodist religious scalawag John H. Caldwell insisted that political reconstruction was linked intimately to religious reconstruction. "My experience, as well as observation," he wrote, "taught me months ago, that if the Southern States should be admitted to their full share of political power in the Union without such constitutional guarantee as would place the whole question which had occasioned all our troubles, both in Church and State, forever beyond the reach of factions and corrupt majorities, our Church would have a long and desperate struggle, if, indeed, she could succeed at all, in planting herself permanently upon this soil." The results of the recent 1866 Congressional elections assured Caldwell that the Thirteenth Amendment would be passed, and "the door will be effectively opened for our Church all through the South, never again to be shut by all the powers of earth and hell."[8]

As southern Christians rethought their negative estimation of Johnson the "traitor" during Presidential Reconstruction, northern Christian opinion moved in the opposite direction. Northern evangelicals worried that Johnson would undermine northern victory; "Southern politicians hope to win in Congress what the confederate generals lost on the field. Shall they have the opportunity?" a northern Methodist editor asked. By mid-1867, when it became clear that Johnson would attempt to thwart Radical Reconstruction, northern religious journals openly called for his impeachment. The Methodist *Zion's Herald* in Boston published an editorial entitled "The Traitorous President" and later drew attention to his "crimes as a politician and a magistrate against the peace and welfare of the country." When the General Conference of the Methodist Episcopal Church (MEC) met in the spring of 1868 during Johnson's trial by the Senate, the assembled clergy set aside an hour of prayer "to invoke the mercy of God upon our nation and to beseech Him to save our Senators from error, and so influence them that their decision shall be in truth and righteousness." After Johnson's impeachment, Methodist bishop Matthew Simpson actively canvassed among wavering senators, urging them to convict the president. Two days later, shortly before the Senate acquitted him by one vote, a Johnson supporter sent a telegram to George Pendleton in Cincinnati, which read "We have beaten the Methodist Episcopal Church North, hell, Ben Butler, John Logan, Geo. Wilkes, and Impeachment. President Johnson will be acquitted if a vote is had today."[9]

Northern evangelicals also avidly supported the passage of the Thirteenth, Fourteenth, and Fifteenth Amendments to the Constitution, both as morally appropriate and as a means of assuring the permanence of political reconstruction. Gilbert Haven, the editor of *Zion's Herald*, wrote in November 1866 that equal suffrage was "as much a moral and religious, as a political question." A year later, he feared that "the political revival is seemingly at an end. The people are getting tired of being virtuous." However, he continued to support the cause of equal suffrage until the passage of the Fifteenth Amendment in February 1869. Northern Baptist missionary Joanna Patterson Moore shared the common attitude among northern evangelicals toward this important amendment. She recalled in her autobiography that she had once said that "the black man had no means of protection." However, she concluded, "I was wrong, *he had the ballot*. Thank God for that. He could not have been a real free man without it."[10]

Freedpeople likewise believed that political activity was essential to their future. Their providential understanding of history gave them a foundation for political activism by assuring them that God would reward their efforts. It also rendered the end of reconstruction all the more devastating. From the beginning of reconstruction during the war until the passage of the Fifteenth Amendment in 1869, African Americans pressed their claims for all the political and legal rights associated with citizenship. Within local African-American communities, black missionaries and preachers frequently formed the political as well as the religious leadership. Over one hundred served in constitutional conventions and state legislatures during Reconstruction. In Mississippi, black voters elected African Methodist Episcopal (AME) missionary Hiram R. Revels to fill Jefferson Davis's seat in the United States Senate. From South Carolina, African Methodist Episcopal Zion (AMEZ) missionary Richard H. Cain served two terms in Congress.[11]

In their roles as spokesmen within emerging black communities, these religious leaders saw no impropriety in acting as political leaders as well; they viewed the two roles as complementary and essential to the freedpeople's welfare. William H. Banks, a black Baptist pastor in Wilmington, North Carolina, insisted, "a minister has to preach politics — not party, but *personal* politics. . . . Every minister should preach politics as are necessary for good government." If a minister "sees a national trouble approaching, such as would depress him, as well as all others," Banks asked, "would it not be in his line of pulpit duties to give the alarm?" When he does so, however, "evil ones begin to try to kill his influence and usefulness as a minister of the Gospel, by charging him with preaching politics in the pulpit." Rufus Lewis Perry, corresponding secretary of the black Consolidated American Baptist Missionary Convention (CABMC) and editor of several periodicals, insisted that black leaders must protest to Congress "against the political outrages to which they are subject." The best way to "make the ballot a blessing," he said, was to "educate and Christianize the voter." Bishop Daniel Payne of the AME Church declared in 1868, "when a Christian approaches the poll he is morally bound to cast his vote for no one, but an open and fearless advocate of liberty, justice and all righteousness."[12]

In an editorial entitled "The Religious Bearing of the Fifteenth Amendment," AME minister and editor Benjamin T. Tanner declared, "with the ratification of this Amendment, the religious character of the negro can be brought to bear upon the government." In the great issues of the day, he declared, "the negro votes the Bible." Northern black Baptist pastor and missionary William E. Walker made clear what black Christians wanted: "Equality of rights in a Republican form of government, is the lifeblood of human existence; it is the apex of man's ambition to attain — without it life is but a myth at best. Man is not free after leaving the land of Egypt until he reaches Canaan." For this black evangelical, freedom without political rights left African Americans in the Wilderness.[13]

When the ministers of the CABMC assembled in St. Louis in October 1872, they addressed political as well as religious issues. Less than three weeks before the presidential election, these black preachers resolved, "we will honor God . . . by urging our colored fellow-citizens to cast their ballots for President U. S. Grant and for Hon. Henry Wilson, for the Vice-Presidency of these United States." The convention also urged Congress to pass a supplementary civil rights bill to end discrimination in public accommodations.[14]

Unlike most freedpeople, the conservative black Christians of the Colored Methodist Episcopal (CME) Church strenuously avoided political entanglements during Reconstruction. At its organizing conference in December 1870, the assembled delegates adopted the Discipline of the Methodist Episcopal Church, South (MECS), as their own, with some revisions. Among the changes was one to the section entitled "Of Building Churches." The original passage declared, "Let our churches be plain and decent, and with free seats, as far as practicable." The leaders of the new CME Church also added the provision, "And they shall in no wise be used for political purposes or assemblages." In part, these black Methodists added this provision in deference to white southern Methodists, who still owned and controlled the church property used by the CME congregations. However, it also reflected a nonpolitical stance that set the CME Church apart from and at odds with the AME, AMEZ, and northern Methodist churches in their advocacy of black political and civil rights. Bishop Lucious H. Holsey later explained, "as ministers of the Gospel, we make no stump speeches and fight no battles of the politicians." In response, representatives of other denominations frequently denounced the CME Church as the "Rebel church" and its adherents as "Democrats."[15]

Despite their official position of avoiding involvement in politics, individual CME members and ministers shared with their black brethren in other denominations a concern for the political and civil rights of the freedpeople. Although he refused to speak publicly on political issues, Holsey apparently voted for Republican candidates. Monroe F. Jamison, a CME minister from Texas, wrote in his autobiography that in 1872, "we voted for General Grant and the Republican State ticket." The CME historian Othal Hawthorne Lakey concludes that most of the members of the CME Church were "staunch Republicans in their political persuasions."[16]

When the CME General Conference met in Augusta in 1873, Dr. Richard Abbey of the MECS presented a memorial requesting the CME to support the southern Methodists' claim against the United States government for damages to their publishing house in Nashville. After some delegates raised objections to this "political" action, newly elected Bishop Holsey, "in some eminently conservative remarks," urged the conference to adopt the memorial "as much from gratitude to the M. E. Church South as to prove their own individuality." With no apparent sense of contradiction, he insisted that "they should pay no attention to enmities born of Politics but adhere strictly to Religion. There was no Politics in the establishment of their Church by their white brethren in the South. They are only to follow Jesus Christ and his Religion." Isaac H. Anderson, also from Georgia, insisted that "there was a General hue and cry to cast Politics out from the Church and he himself had been threatened with expulsion from his own Church for asserting his civil and legal rights." Anderson argued that the memorial was "a Political document as it asked for the settlement of a Claim from a Political body where Party lines were strictly drawn. [H]e never would sign such a paper." Although the minutes conclude that the memorial was "adopted and passed by the General Conference," the *Southern*

Christian Advocate reported that the CME General Conference had "voted that under prevailing circumstances, it could not see its way clear to present such a document to the United States Congress." Ironically, the members of the CME denomination, whom white southerners had hoped to keep out of politics, had done so with a vengeance, refusing even to aid the southern Methodist church on a matter that the black Methodists deemed to be political.[17]

A closer examination of political reconstruction in Georgia and Tennessee illuminates how northern missionaries, religious scalawags, and Christian freedpeople were involved in the process. In Georgia, political reconstruction began with a civilian political vacuum in the spring of 1865, after Federal authorities arrested Governor Joseph E. Brown early in May and dispersed other Confederate leaders. Military rule replaced the toppled Confederate government, until President Johnson appointed James Johnson as Georgia's provisional governor in mid-June. Presidential pardons and oaths of allegiance allowed many ex-Confederates to vote again in October 1865 for delegates to a new constitutional convention. The convention met in October and November and quickly abolished slavery and repealed the state's secession ordinance; it also provided for new civil elections on November 15 to replace the provisional government. Only after intense prodding by President Johnson and Governor Johnson did the convention repudiate the Confederate war debt. In the November 1865 elections, Georgians chose many ex-Confederates to represent them in the state legislature and in the United States House of Representatives. In January 1866, the new General Assembly elected former Confederate vice-president Alexander Stephens and former Confederate senator Herschel V. Johnson to the United States Senate. Congress refused to seat any of Georgia's representatives, and it soon seized control of Reconstruction from Andrew Johnson.[18]

Across the South, northern missionaries, southern religious scalawags, and black ministers watched the contest between Johnson and Congress with anxiety. Georgia religious scalawag John H. Caldwell declared as early as April 1866 his belief that the president's policy would ruin the country. He saw "no hope for the negro, no hope for true liberty but in the success of the radicals." "The Union reconstructed with the present rulers of the South," he feared, "would extinguish the last ray of hope for the amelioration and advancement of the negro." In August 1866, Caldwell wrote, "my only hope of permanent success is in the success of Congress in the fall elections in the North." If the radicals emerged victorious, "we shall have a certainty of protection and success." For Caldwell, as for other black and white ministers and missionaries in the South, hope for the religious reconstruction of the South depended on the political fortunes of the radical Republicans.[19]

To enhance their prospects for success, therefore, Christians who subscribed to the northern or freedpeople's visions of religious reconstruction mobilized support for the Republican party. In the spring of 1867, several Methodist religious scalawags participated in the organization of Union or Loyal Leagues. Cornelius Parker in Griffin wrote to G. L. Eberhart, superintendent of education for the Freedmen's Bureau in Georgia, "we initiated 20 colored men into the Union League Saturday night. . . . They are pleased." The Union Leagues also drew in black support for the MEC. Richard Waters in Jonesboro boasted, "We have the biggest Union League in the least time in this town perhaps you ever saw and yet they come by companies. Now with the right sort of management the whole Methodist fraternity is ours." Religious scalawag John Murphy in Fairburn declared, "the Union League works admirable for our Church." In La Grange, where John H. Caldwell organized the freedpeople both religiously and politically, "the Republican Party, through the League, became practically supreme."[20]

Henry M. Turner of the AME Church and Tunis Campbell of the AMEZ Church likewise organized freedpeople into local voting blocs. After Congress passed a series of reconstruction acts in the spring and summer of 1867, Turner began to organize the freedpeople to support the Republican party. With characteristic modesty, he later boasted, "I first organized the Republican Party in this state. . . . I have put more men in the field, made more speeches, organized more Union Leagues, Political Associations, Clubs, and have written more campaign documents that received larger circulation than any other man in the state." In McIntosh County on the coast of Georgia, Campbell served as a registrar in addition to his duties as a missionary. While registering voters, registrars like Campbell had the opportunity and the duty to explain to the freedpeople their political rights and privileges. At a Republican rally in April 1867, Campbell deftly combined his roles as religious and political leader; after offering an opening prayer, he delivered an hour-long speech on the merits of Radical Reconstruction.[21]

As historian Edmund L. Drago has observed, "the church became the focal point of black political life during Reconstruction. It was the only black institution capable of providing the organization and leadership necessary to mobilize black voters." Churches hosted political rallies, registered voters, and provided black political leaders during Reconstruction. Of the thirty-nine black legislators in Georgia from 1867 to 1872 whose occupation Drago could identify, twenty-five were ministers.[22]

After months of experience in mobilizing black voters for the Republican party, several ministers became natural candidates for public office. John H. Caldwell became the most politically active among Methodist religious scalawags in Georgia. Although he felt that the MEC should address certain issues in the South such as common schools and labor relations, he declared, "I am not for uniting Church & state nor secularizing our work, but for securing to Methodism the fruits of her victory for which she has fought for 100 years." In early September 1867, he wrote to the superintendent of the Georgia and Alabama mission district of the MEC to explore the possibility of campaigning for a political office. Several Union men had approached him and asked him to serve as a delegate to the constitutional convention. He noted with pride that the freedpeople intended to vote for him, "no matter who else may run." While he claimed no "political aspirations" and wanted to do "nothing that would in any way compromise my position of usefulness in the ministry," he clearly desired to run for the office. For Caldwell and others, the proper reconstruction of the civil government was essential to the prosperity of loyal Methodism in Georgia. In this attempt to "secure both civil and religious liberty," Caldwell later explained, "I felt as truly called of God to enter the political arena for the reconstruction of the State government as I ever felt called to my ministerial office and functions." Henry M. Turner likewise described himself as a "minister of the gospel and a kind of politician — both."[23]

John H. Caldwell, Henry M. Turner, Tunis Campbell, and at least fourteen other ministers were elected in October 1867 as delegates to the constitutional convention. John Emory Bryant, a Methodist layman from Maine, also became a delegate. The convention met in Atlanta from December 1867 to March 1868, and the minister-politicians generally pursued a moderate course. Turner even urged leniency for ex-Confederates and a pardon for Jefferson Davis. The convention produced a new constitution, which formed the basis for new elections. In April 1868 Georgians ratified the constitution, elected a new legislature with a Republican majority in the Senate and a closely divided lower house, and chose Republican Rufus B. Bullock as their governor. Among those elected to the new state legislature were Caldwell, Turner, Campbell, and other ministers. Bryant also returned, and Georgians elected Jefferson F. Long, an AME layman from Macon, as Georgia's only black delegate to the U.S. House of Representatives. The new legislature included three black senators and twenty-five black and four mulatto representatives.[24]

Because the new state constitution did not explicitly guarantee the right of African Americans to hold political office, their seats in the legislature were insecure after the April elections. During the constitutional convention Turner himself had voted against inserting a provision in the constitution stating that blacks could hold office. He had believed the assurances of white Republicans that such a clause was unnecessary. Now the former Confederate governor Joseph E. Brown publicly declared that the new constitution permitted the prohibition of black officeholding. In the summer of 1868, the General Assembly, with the support of Turner and other black legislators, seated Brown and other ex-Confederates who had been elected in April; once seated, these delegates challenged the right of blacks to seats in the legislature. By early September, Democrats in the legislature had garnered enough white Republican support to expel the black legislators from their midst. On September 3, Turner delivered a speech filled with religious rhetoric to oppose the expulsion proposal. The resolution, he insisted, was "a thrust at the Bible — a thrust at the God of the Universe for making a man and not finishing him; it is simply calling the great Jehovah a fool." He warned the legislators to remember that an omniscient God "never fails to vindicate the cause of Justice, and the sanctity of his own handiwork." Shortly afterward on the same day, the legislature voted eighty-three to twenty-three to expel its black members; they were not allowed to vote on the matter. At Turner's request, the Georgia House of Representatives remained seated as he and the other black representatives walked out. In a final religious-political gesture, Turner declared that "in imitation of Christ, he would brush the dust off his feet (suiting the action to the word)."[25]

During the move to expel the black legislators, Caldwell, who had opposed the measure, wrote to a national Republican leader, "it is astonishing to see, notwithstanding they are certain of being expelled, the calmness . . . and the faith which they have, that although they may be expelled now, they will come back again, and come to stay." The African-American legislators would return in January 1870, but only after Congress once again intervened in the political reconstruction of Georgia.[26]

After the crushing defeat of Republican candidates in Georgia in the November 1868 presidential elections, Governor Rufus Bullock charged that the state had not been reconstructed under the terms established by Congress. The legislature had seated ex-Confederate members incapable of taking the test oath and had unconstitutionally expelled black members from its ranks. This "illegal" legislature's vote to ratify the Fourteenth Amendment was therefore invalid, and Georgia could not be legally readmitted to the Union. Bullock requested that Congress remand Georgia to military rule until it complied with the congressional mandates for readmission. On December 24, 1869, President Grant and Congress returned Georgia to military rule until the legislature of April 1868, purged of its ineligible members, could reconvene and ratify the Fifteenth Amendment.[27]

The old legislature reassembled in Atlanta on January 10, 1870, and the black legislators retook their seats. General Alfred Terry, commanding general of the District of Georgia, barred from the legislature those unable to take the test oath or ineligible under the provisions of the Fourteenth Amendment. "Terry's purge" gave the Republicans solid majorities in both houses; the restored legislature ratified the Fifteenth Amendment and reratified the Fourteenth Amendment, and Congress voted in July 1870 to readmit Georgia to the Union. However, Congress, tiring of the issue of reconstructing Georgia, decided to seat the two U.S. Senators elected by the legislature that had expelled its black members rather than those elected by the restored legislature earlier in 1870. State elections in December 1870, again marred by violence and intimidation, gave the Democrats overwhelming majorities in both houses of the state legislature, which was to convene in November 1871. In October 1871, Governor Bullock resigned to avoid impeachment and fled the state. The president of the Senate, Republican Benjamin F. Conley, served as Georgia's governor until Democrat James M. Smith was elected without opposition in December 1871. Reconstruction in Georgia was over; Democrats had reasserted white southern control over state governments; they had "redeemed" the state.[28]

White southern evangelicals described the end of Reconstruction as a "redemption," a term that evoked a sense of regaining control of their political destinies, which had for too long been in the hands of usurpers. This "favorite euphemism of the white Democrats," as Kenneth M. Stampp described it, had distinctively religious overtones. Southerners drew on their religious heritage to find a term that would describe adequately their conception of this political transformation. In choosing "redemption," they rejected European historical alternatives such as "restoration" and "Bourbonism," though the latter was sometimes used. Although the first usage of the term remains obscure, southerners were employing it at least from the time that the first southern state, Tennessee, was redeemed in 1869–70. In January 1871, for example, John Forsyth, the editor of the Mobile, Alabama, *Register*, warned his fellow Democrats against courting black votes. "The road to redemption," Forsyth boldly declared, "is under the white banner." This rhetorical merger of race, religion, and politics was common during the 1870s as white southerners sought to regain control of their political institutions.[29]

The bitter legacy of political reconstruction continued to influence the religious life of Georgia long after white southerners regained political control of the state. As late as the 1880s, the religious scalawags of the Georgia Annual Conference were still trying to overcome the persistent southern belief that the MEC was an intensely political organization allied with the Republican party. In 1882 they passed a resolution that their denomination, "while mainly supporting the great Government of the United States, is in no sense allied to any political party, nor will it allow its policy to be dictated by the views and interests of political parties or leaders." Instead, they continued, "our work in the South is simply to preach the law of God and the gospel of Christ clearly, fully and simply, with an aim at the conversion and salvation of men, leaving our members and friends to determine upon the political relations and course of action which they ought to choose and hold." The Georgia Annual Conference reprinted this resolution for several years after 1882 in its annual *Minutes.* The political activism that Caldwell and others believed essential to the success of religious reconstruction in the 1860s had become a severe liability for northern missionaries and their religious scalawag allies in the 1880s.[30]

In Tennessee, reconstruction took a different form. The last state to leave the Union, Tennessee became a battleground early in the war; Federal forces occupied much of its central and western portions in 1862 and 1863. As wartime military governor from March 1862 to March 1865, Andrew Johnson several times attempted without success to restore civilian government. After his election as Lincoln's vice-president in November 1864, Johnson renewed his determination to end the military government of Tennessee. He issued a call for a constitutional convention, which assembled early in January in Nashville. The convention passed amendments abolishing slavery and repealing the state's secession ordinance and alliance with the Confederacy. It also called for elections for a governor and legislature on March 4; a popular referendum in February 1865 endorsed its actions. Johnson left the state for Washington, D.C., in February, and in March, Tennessee Unionists elected a new legislature and William G. Brownlow as the new civilian governor.[31]

From 1865 to 1869, the dominant figure in Tennessee politics was the most prominent of all southern religious scalawags, William G. "Parson" Brownlow. Born in 1805 in Virginia, Brownlow became an orphan at age eleven. He lived with an uncle and farmed for several years, then moved to another uncle's home where he learned the carpenter's trade. In 1825 he was converted in a Methodist camp meeting; the following year, he became a minister in the Holston Conference of the MEC. For the next ten years, he traveled the circuits of the Holston Conference, preaching in Virginia, North Carolina, South Carolina, Georgia, and Tennessee. In 1836 he began his long career as a newspaper editor and publisher. Over the next three decades, he published a newspaper under various titles, which always included *Whig,* in three East Tennessee towns; in these newspapers he upheld the Whig party and the Methodist church against all opponents. He moved his operations in 1849 to Knoxville, where he published the *Knoxville Whig and Independent Journal* until Confederate authorities suppressed it in October 1861.[32]

A determined supporter of slavery, Brownlow declared in May 1861 that "the Redeemer of the world smiles alike upon the devout master and the pious slave!" However, he was also deeply committed to the American Union and vigorously opposed secession as unnecessary and dangerous.[33] In July 1861, Brownlow condemned southern ministers for supporting secession: "The South is now full of these reverend traitors and every branch of the Christian Church is cursed with their labors." In October he fled Knoxville for the countryside of East Tennessee; early in December, he presented himself to Confederate authorities, but civilian authorities arrested him before he could leave for the North. Imprisoned for three weeks, he was transferred to his home because of severe illness, where he remained under house arrest for another ten weeks. Early in March 1862, he was transported to Union lines in Kentucky. For nearly a year, Brownlow spoke to large and enthusiastic crowds across the North and published a book recounting his persecution at the hands of Confederates. He told his audiences, "the worst class of men in the Southern Confederacy are the Episcopalian, Methodist, Baptist and Presbyterian Preachers." To demonstrate that God wore blue, he employed the common evangelical language of providence: "In a review of the battles lost and won in this war, it is plain to be seen which army has the approbation of Providence." Northern armies had won seventeen battles in 1861 and twelve in 1862, while "with the Lord's *permission*," they had captured fifty-six towns and cities and twenty-five forts. In stark contrast, by Brownlow's estimation, southern forces had won only seven battles since the conflict began.[34]

Brownlow returned to Tennessee in February 1863 and accepted a post as United States treasury agent in Nashville. By November 1863, he was once again in Knoxville and had resurrected his newspaper, newly christened the *Knoxville Whig and Rebel Ventilator*. Eighteen months later, Tennessee Unionists elected him their governor. Having suffered at the hands of Confederates, he was determined to pursue a radical reconstruction policy; on his recommendation, the legislature quickly approved the Thirteenth Amendment and disfranchised all Confederates. A former champion of slavery and deeply racist, Brownlow had a dim view of the political abilities of black southerners, but radical Republican attitudes toward the freedpeople moved him toward a more liberal position on black capabilities. By the summer of 1865, he believed that when it came to wielding the ballot, "a loyal Negro is more worthy than a disloyal white man." After the Tennessee legislature passed the Fourteenth Amendment in July 1866, Congress quickly readmitted Tennessee to the Union. In December 1866, Brownlow urged the legislature to extend the franchise to the freedpeople, and in February 1867, Tennessee became the only southern state to allow its black citizens to vote.[35]

After the freedpeople were enfranchised, they proved a "potent force in politics" in Tennessee. Prior to the elections of August 1867, Unionists and freedpeople held mass meetings throughout the state. At a meeting outside the Capitol in Nashville, Abraham Smith told the crowd, "if it had not been for the Radicals we would have been slaves today, and our prayers should ever ascend to Heaven for the good cause. The Radicals fought four years to free you, and the Rebels fought four years to enslave you. All the Radicals in the Tennessee Legislature voted to give you the right of suffrage and the Rebels voted against it." The assembly adopted resolutions endorsing Brownlow for reelection and criticizing President Johnson for his defection.[36]

In the August election, Tennesseeans overwhelmingly reelected Brownlow, largely on the strength of black votes. A few days earlier, on August 1, Eliza Fain's "thoughts turned upon the great events of this day in the political issues of our state government. My heart is troubled as we appear to be standing upon a rather roaring volcano which seems to threaten the complete overthrow of the mighty fabric of American liberty. . . . Will there be brought upon this country a war of races," she wondered. Between Emerson Etheridge, the conservative candidate, and Brownlow, the radical candidate, "we as a people so far as I know stand for the conservative believing that they are the party now rising in the government who will stand shoulder to shoulder with us who have borne the heat of the day for sustaining constitutional liberty as was once enjoyed by us as a people." On July 23, Etheridge and Horace Maynard, one of Brownlow's supporters, had spoken in Rogersville. A riot broke out between rival groups and two people were killed. Fain had described the nearby fray as "the white man standing with the white man for the sustaining of the principles of true liberty. The black man in heart standing with the black in skin for the pulling down of every thing which had been sacred upon the foundations laid by the Fathers of the past." Fain had no doubt that many freedpeople would have been killed, but "the Southern heart who has ever had sympathy for the poor Negro still felt it." After the turmoil of the elections had abated, the state legislature in January 1868 passed a bill granting blacks the right to sit on juries and to hold political office.[37]

Presbyterian minister Thomas H. McCallie viewed the political situation in Tennessee during the early years of Reconstruction as did many other white southerners: "The country was in a deplorable political condition. Radicals were in office, such as William G. Brownlow. The white citizens who had been in the war or sympathized with the South were disfranchised. The ignorant Negroes were clothed with this privilege. Carpetbaggers swarmed in the country, and ministers, missionaries from the North, inflamed the minds of the colored people against their white neighbors."[38]

Southern white Christians were quick to link northern missionaries with any political persecution of former Confederates. The Synod of Nashville in January 1866 deplored the "lawlessness" that had been "sadly prevalent" within a portion of its boundaries. Some of its ministers and many of its church members had been "driven from their homes for no other reason than that their political sentiments were not pleasing to the mob." The synod was "sorry to say that some of the missionaries of the Northern General Assembly have excited and encouraged this lawless spirit. Some of our churches have been utterly broken up by this persecution."[39]

While Brownlow was actively engaged in governing the state, his role as spokesman for East Tennessee Unionist Methodists passed to Thomas H. Pearne, an influential northern Methodist from Oregon, who had campaigned widely for Republican candidates. Pearne also became editor of the *Knoxville Whig*, from which post he loyally supported Brownlow and the radical Republicans. Pearne denied that the MEC was a "political church," but northern Methodists did "believe treason against the Government of the United States . . . is sin against God." However, he continued, "we do not believe in bringing partisan politics into the pulpit or into the Church. They have no right there." He declared that in thirty years, no one had heard him "preach or pray party politics in the pulpit." Pearne outlined his vision for the political and religious reconstruction of the South in an editorial: "Religious Patriotism will grow in the South, and so, also, will the church that cherishes this element in society."[40]

Brownlow resigned as governor of Tennessee in February 1869 to accept a seat in the United States Senate, to which he had been elected by the state legislature sixteen months earlier. He mistakenly believed that his successor, DeWitt C. Senter, would continue his policies and strengthen the Republican party in Tennessee. When the Republican State Convention met in Nashville in May 1869, it was so deeply divided that the meeting dissolved before it could be organized. One faction nominated Senter for governor, and the other nominated William B. Stokes, representative of Tennessee's third district in Congress. Seeking to broaden his base of support, Senter appealed to conservatives by promising to repeal restrictions on the franchise; Stokes, who represented the radical Republican views, opposed the immediate restoration of the ballot to ex-Confederates. Brownlow supported Senter in the August election, declaring that he was "a true man," who stood "squarely upon the Republican platform." An increased electorate dramatically changed the balance of power. Eliza Fain's husband, Richard Fain, an ex-Confederate officer, "voted for the first time since the surrender." Eliza Fain noted in her diary, "What a farce this government has appeared to me to be for the past 4 years." Hill, one of their former slaves, also voted, but Fain was troubled by his use of the ballot: "He voted all right, poor negro, poor negro, how little do you seem to know about your own good." Senter overwhelmingly won the election in August 1869, and the state legislature passed firmly into the control of the Democrats.[41]

The new legislature considered and rejected the Fifteenth Amendment, and it repealed much of the legislation passed by the previous Republican legislatures. A constitutional convention convened in January 1870 to draft a new constitution for the state, which Tennessee voters adopted in March. The election of a Democratic governor in the autumn of 1870 completed the process of the "redemption" of Tennessee. Unlike the situation in Georgia, no blacks served in the state legislature during Radical Reconstruction, though Sampson W. Keeble, a black Nashville barber, was elected in 1872. As if to confirm that Tennessee had been irreversibly redeemed, ex-Confederate Joseph A. Mabry purchased Brownlow's interest in the *Knoxville Whig* after the election of August 1869 and replaced Pearne with C. W. Charlton, a southern Methodist minister, as editor.[42]

In many areas of the South, including portions of Georgia and Tennessee, white southerners resorted to violence to oppose Radical Reconstruction. While the terrorist activities of the Ku Klux Klan lacked the coordination necessary to topple the Republican state governments of Tennessee and Georgia, they did effectively disfranchise blacks in many local areas.[43] Furthermore, Democrats in the mid-1870s used coordinated violence and intimidation in new ways to wrest control from black majorities in Lower South states such as South Carolina and Louisiana. Appealing to racial pride, Democrats used aggression against blacks to unify whites behind their political goals. Although white southern evangelicals undoubtedly participated in these assaults, the southern churches remained remarkably silent on the entire matter. Displaying the compatibility of religious zeal and allegiance to secret societies, one Tennessee Confederate veteran proudly declared on his tombstone: "Belonged to the Ku Klux Klan, a deacon in the Baptist Church and a Master Mason for forty years." While conducting the trials of Ku Klux Klan members in South Carolina in 1871, federal judge Hugh Bond repeatedly asked witnesses whether white ministers of the Gospel had spoken out against the Klan. He was appalled to learn that they had not, although the members of the churches "pretty much" all belonged to the Klan. Reflecting the common northern Christian vision for religious and political reconstruction, Bond wrote his wife that the freedpeople would never obtain equal rights until "we have added to the power of our political truth the energy of religious fervor."[44]

Reconstruction ended on the state level in Georgia and Tennessee in 1870 and 1871, but the process persisted in other states into the mid-1870s. The presidential election of 1876 and its aftermath, however, proved fatal to political reconstruction.

The narrow electoral victory of Rutherford B. Hayes in November and his with-drawal of United States troops from Florida, Louisiana, and South Carolina in April 1877 ended the prospects for further Republican control in those states. Evangelicals responded to the collapse of Reconstruction as either a blessing or a calamity, based on their vision for the future of the South. Republican evangelicals were pleased to learn that Hayes had won by a slim electoral margin over Democrat Samuel J. Tilden, but those committed to Radical Reconstruction soon became despondent when Hayes removed federal troops from the South. Conversely, southern Demo-crats were disappointed by the election of Hayes, but the removal of federal troops mitigated their discouragement and presaged better days ahead.[45]

In November 1876, Hugh Mitchell came to Eliza Fain's home outside Rogers-ville, Tennessee, to repair her clock. While there, he told her that he had voted, but had "gone back home feeling little interest in elections." Fain was troubled by his atti-tude and told him that she had "felt much about the presidential race, feeling it was an important one in our country's history." She feared that a war might result because Tilden had won the popular vote, "which was the voice of the people." "Why," she asked, "had the states of Florida, South Carolina and Louisiana been robbed of their liberty at the ballot box?" She told Mitchell, "we are I fear treading upon the very threshold of our Republic's overthrow," and she prayed that God would "bring forth a leader who shall be able as a human instrument to lead us to victory." The follow-ing week Fain noted that the day was set aside as a day of Thanksgiving by "a presi-dent whom we cannot honor whose whole career has been marked by wickedness and usurpation of power." She believed that "the destinies of nations as well as indi-viduals" were in God's hands and thanked God that He had "thus far shielded us from the enemies who have sought our overthrow."[46]

Georgia AME minister Henry M. Turner, in contrast, supported Hayes's bid for the presidency. In defense of his political involvement, Turner wrote that he had al-ways doubted "any man's religion or worth, who was so holy that he could sit quietly and see his country go to the devil because he wanted to go to heaven." Turner and other blacks were somewhat optimistic when Hayes won in the electoral college, but in April 1877, when Hayes withdrew the federal troops from South Carolina and Louisiana, Turner proclaimed the death of the Republican party. Tearfully, he wrote an "obituary" for it, telling his fellow black Christians, "the great Republican Party, hero of many battles and author of National Sovereignty, American Freedom, Civil and Political rights and many other world renowned and heaven approved works, was slaughtered in the house of his friends, April 24, 1877."[47]

By 1877 many religious scalawags had followed the lead of their Georgia Meth-odist fellows in disavowing any political intentions and prohibiting ministers from running for public office. Many of their northern missionary allies had become dis-illusioned by 1877, and northern Christian support for the political and religious re-construction of the South had waned considerably. By the time political reconstruc-tion ended throughout the South, religious reconstruction was likewise drawing to a close. Both processes fell victim to waning northern commitment and persistent southern recalcitrance.[48]

Thus, as political and religious reconstruction proceeded simultaneously in the postwar South, the mingling of religious and political rhetoric, common both in the

antebellum and wartime eras, continued. Northern missionaries and religious scalawags drew on their vision of religious reconstruction to justify their extensive political involvement. Only when black and white southerners enjoyed basic civil and political rights, they reasoned, could the moral regeneration of the region proceed.
African Americans likewise blended religious and political aspirations and leadership. When black ministers organized the freedpeople into churches away from the
oversight of their former masters, they also informed these congregations of their
new political rights and responsibilities. The efforts of northern black and white missionaries among the freedpeople provided invaluable support for the Republican
party during Reconstruction. Conversely, the political revolution embodied in the
Thirteenth, Fourteenth and Fifteenth Amendments opened new religious opportunities for the freedpeople and the missionaries who labored among them. For white
southerners, religion provided solace and confidence of God's ultimate sovereignty
when "interlopers" controlled their political fortunes, along with the confidence
necessary to effect the political "redemption" of their beloved Zion. In such a cli-
mate of political and ecclesiastical warfare, proposals for the sectional reunion of the
major evangelical denominations had little hope for success.

10

One Nation under God?

Efforts toward Sectional Reunion

Behold, how good and how pleasant it is for brethren to dwell together in
unity!

Psalm 133:1

No other issue reflected so well the divergence of the Confederate and northern
visions of religious reconstruction as the question of denominational reunion.
In no area was southern identity more pronounced. Georgia and Tennessee Baptists,
Methodists, and Presbyterians vehemently rejected any plans for reunion with their
counterparts in the North. The sectional rancor of the postwar period might seem
unavoidable, but for the example of other denominations: northern and southern
Episcopalians quickly healed the de facto breach in their organization; even the
Cumberland Presbyterians were able to restore their national unity in 1866. Yet each
of the three largest evangelical denominations remained bitterly divided in the aftermath of the war.

Even as political and cultural reunion progressed, Paul H. Buck has argued, the
clergy stood as the most "radical of sectionalists," and "the churches remained sectional bodies, an antagonistic element in the integration of national life." As a number of scholars have demonstrated, the movement for greater political and cultural
unity between the North and the South came only at the expense of African Americans' civil rights and freedoms. Although the major evangelical Protestant denominations did not reunite in the nineteenth century, even their halting efforts to establish
fraternal relations displayed a similar disregard for the religious lives of black southerners. To pacify uneasy southern ministers, northern evangelicals bowed to southern racial norms and segregated their ecclesiastical structures at the expense of black
Christians.[1]

The northern and southern wings of the Baptist, Methodist, and Presbyterian
churches remained separate because each insisted that their interpretation of the

Civil War was correct and, therefore, their policies toward religious reconstruction should be implemented. Even before the war ended, southerners made it clear that they wanted little to do with their coreligionists from the North. One North Carolina minister declared, "You may put me down as one of the number that will never, no never, consent to a union with the Yankees. I hope that this is the sentiment of every Presbyterian."[2]

Soon after the war ended, most southern clergy and laity proclaimed their determination to maintain their sectional denominations. Bishops James O. Andrew, Robert Paine, and George F. Pierce met in Columbus, Georgia, in August 1865 to prepare a "Pastoral Address" to the ministers and members of their church. In discussing the issue of reunion with the Methodist Episcopal Church (MEC), the southern bishops wrote, "we must express, with regret, our apprehension that a large proportion, if not a majority of northern Methodists have become incurably radical." They "teach for doctrine the commandments of man," "preach another gospel," and "have incorporated social dogmas and political tests into their church creeds." Northern pulpits were "perverted to agitations and questions not healthful to personal piety; but promotive of political and ecclesiastical discord, rather than of those ends for which the church of the Lord Jesus Christ was instituted." Given this view of the northern church, the bishops could "anticipate no good result from even entertaining the subject of re-union with them." The duty of the Methodist Episcopal Church, South (MECS), to maintain itself as a bulwark of southernness was clear: "Fidelity to what seems our providential mission requires that we preserve our church in all its vigor and integrity, free from entangling alliances with those whose notions of philanthropy and politics and social economy are liable to give an ever varying complexion to their theology."[3]

During the same month, a group of Methodist laypeople in Macon, Georgia, demonstrated their loyalty to the southern church. By reuniting with the MEC, they insisted, southern Methodists would "yield the position we have so often taken, admit the charges we have so often refuted, and by accepting political tests of church fellowship stultify ourselves and compromise the essential principles of the Gospel."[4]

A few southern Methodists did desire union with the MEC, but their plans, too, were influenced by the southern vision of religious reconstruction. Prominent among those initially desiring Methodist reunion was Braxton Craven, the president of Trinity College (now Duke University) and a pastor in Raleigh, North Carolina. His letter to northern Methodist bishop Edward R. Ames in July 1865 offers interesting insights into both the prospects for and limitations of Methodist fraternity. Craven insisted that the northern Methodist bishops "did too much, or not enough" in their meeting in June 1865. There the bishops determined "to occupy, as far as practicable, those fields in the Southern states which may be opened and which give promise of success." Craven feared that "time will inevitably increase the difficulties in the way of a successful operation or adjustment."[5]

With a prophetic voice, Craven warned Bishop Ames not to be overconfident of the northern church's chances of success in the South: "The action of the Holston Conference, St. Louis, and some other localities, may seem like the dawn of a glorious day to the M. E. Church, and to the unobservant may promise easy and rapid success, but clouds, darkness and storm will usher in and continue with a day commenced on that plan." Southern Methodism was "neither dead in sin, nor corrupt in the practices of the traitor." Two paths lay ahead: "it will either move on to great and lasting good within its own regular organization, or go back in a body to its former position." Insisting that "I do zealously favor *reconstruction*," Craven wrote that the "vast majority" of southern Methodists agreed. Ecclesiastical divisions and denominational quarrels "manifestly impede the work of God," and the separation of the two branches of American Methodism *"ought not* to continue." However, the conditions of reconstruction that had been proposed by northern Methodists were "neither Methodistic nor desirable." No church in history, he argued, has made "articles of faith or tests of membership" out of "political questions." Here he joined other white southern Christians in insisting that slavery and secession were fundamentally political rather than moral issues. To effect Methodist reconstruction, Craven proposed that the churches revoke the separation of 1844, that southerners adopt the discipline of the MEC, and that southern Methodists enter the church "as we now are, including conferences, Bishops, appointments, and all other things." On this point as well, northern and southern visions of religious reconstruction clashed. Northerners insisted on receiving southern Methodists individually or in small groups, while southerners desired a merger of equal bodies.[6]

Craven optimistically assured Bishop Ames, "reconstruction is practicable, easy, and Christian; it is every way desirable, and I believe, very generally desired, if it can be accomplished in the mode and spirit above indicated." Nevertheless, he wrote, many southerners thought "that the church North does not desire reconstruction on any basis whatever." He disagreed, for he did not believe northern Methodists were so self-righteous, self-confident, or intolerant as to reject fellowship with their southern brethren. "Why," he asked, "should not Methodism be reconstructed on fair Christian terms?" After expressing the hope, "May wise councils prevail, and may the work of God prosper in our hands," Craven closed his letter, "I remain respectfully your brother in Christ." This letter and its author represent a small group of moderates in both branches of Methodism who desired to restore the national denomination. Even in this conciliatory document, however, the contrast between the northern and southern visions of religious reconstruction stands out in bold relief. Craven was willing to admit much of the northern interpretation of the war when he wrote, "We of the South have erred, we have been punished, and I trust we have repented." Yet his plan for reunion remained firmly within the southern vision of reconstruction. The northern denominations had to readmit southerners as a body without inquiring into their views about slavery or secession. The northern vision of religious reconstruction prohibited such terms, and the prospects for an early reunion evaporated.[7]

Only one southern Methodist conference made a serious attempt to pass resolutions in favor of a speedy reunion: the Kentucky Conference, located in the eastern section of the state, considered the issue in its September 1865 meeting. The majority of a committee on the state of the church presented a report calling on the MECS to initiate steps toward reunion. The conference, however, rejected this report and instead adopted minority resolutions that declared, "we hold ourselves ready to consider," through the agency of the General Conference, any terms presented by the MEC that would initiate "a union of the two great coordinate branches of Episcopal Methodism in the United States." In the meantime, the Kentucky Conference would "earnestly maintain our present relation." Most of the dissenters soon withdrew and joined the MEC, followed by several thousand members. Thereafter, the Kentucky Conference was firmly entrenched in the southern Methodist fold.[8]

The southern Methodist bishops assured their church, "Whatever cause has been lost, that of Southern Methodism has survived." Addressing the General Conference of 1866 "in respect to the separate and distinct organization of our church," they asserted, "no reasons have appeared to alter our views as expressed in August last. No proposal of fraternal relations has come to us from others."[9] Unwilling to initiate an attempt at reunion, southern Methodists awaited an offer that would not come for two more generations — the merger of the two churches as corporate bodies. In the summer of 1866, the aging bishop James O. Andrew wrote to the newly elected bishop Holland N. McTyeire about the issue of reunion. Andrew, whose slaveholding was the spark that had divided the Methodist Episcopal Church in 1844, wrote to the stridently southern and progressive junior bishop about a speech by Dr. Daniel Curry, the editor of the *Christian Advocate and Journal* in New York. Andrew mused: "He is certainly coming round. He seems willing to let each church do its in its own way [sic] no formal union of the two churches yet maintain fraternal relations and kindly intercourse with each other individually. I think that is pretty near the right ground but possibly I may not have properly understood him but I leave the whole matter in the hands of God."[10]

Southern Presbyterians also intended to maintain their ecclesiastical separation. The *North Carolina Presbyterian* declared: "Better, far better, would it be for our future spiritual welfare, to be even subjugated by their civil power, if so be that we keep ourselves distinct in matters of faith and church government, than ever to strike hands with them again in common ecclesiastical association." When their General Assembly met in Macon in December 1865, southern Presbyterians made it clear to their northern brethren that they had no intentions of reuniting. When discussing its relations to other churches, the General Assembly insisted that the ministers of the Presbyterian Church in the United States of America (PCUSA) had "no further or higher claims on our courtesy than any other churches of the same section of country, which hold to the same symbols of faith and order with ourselves." The General Assembly issued a pastoral letter to the churches that exhorted southern Presbyterians "to walk in love towards all your fellow Christians," but to be "on your guard against attempts to disturb and divide your congregations." The Presbyterian Church in the United States (PCUS), they insisted, was "a branch of the Church as complete in our organization, as thoroughly distinct and harmonious, and as secure in our prospects as any other in the land." Southern Presbyterians, like their Methodist counterparts, repudiated any suggestions of reunion with northern denominations on virtually any terms.[11]

In January 1866 the editors of the *Southern Presbyterian* advised their readers that they should "expect no help from the Northern church. Thus far Northern Christians (the great mass of them, at least,) have showed no real sympathy in our behalf." If they were to offer any help, the editors warned, "it will be sure to come in a way and through channels that it will be neither safe, wise, nor honorable for us to accept." In response to the criticism of northern Presbyterian newspapers about southerners' unwillingness to consider reunion, the *Southern Presbyterian* insisted in February that the acts of the northern church had "compelled us to take up and maintain an attitude of independence." In effect, "the door of readmission has been violently closed in our faces, and then we are reproached for remaining outside." If the evil of schism applied to the perpetuation of two branches of the church, "the sin lies at the door of the Northern Assembly, and not at ours." However, in a later issue, the editors of the *Southern Presbyterian* considered the question, "would it be desirable for us to accede to a reunion, even if it could be effected on the most honorable terms?" If the northern Presbyterian church had remained where it stood in 1861, "we would feel no special repugnance to the resumption of our former relationship." But that church had "gone far astray" on matters of doctrine, discipline, constitutional principles, and the proper province of the church. It had repeatedly acted "as the hand-maid of the State," "violated the Constitution of the Church" by legislating on nonecclesiastical matters, and adopted "new and unwarranted terms of communion." For all these reasons, southern Presbyterians could not reunite with their northern brethren without "imperilling our own purity and safety, and doing dishonor to the Great Head of the Church." In other words, even if the hand of fraternity were offered by the northern General Assembly, some southern Presbyterians felt morally obligated to refuse it.[12]

Among independent-minded Baptist associations, the primary motive for cooperation was the support of educational and missionary endeavors. At the end of the war, northern Baptist associations expressed a desire to unite the efforts of the American Baptist Home Mission Society (ABHMS) with those of the Southern Baptist Convention (SBC). However, those southern associations that met in 1865 "were unanimous in favor of continuing their former separate societies, and against fraternization with the Northern societies." The Virginia General Association urged its churches "to decline any co-operation or fellowship with any of the missionaries, ministers, or agents of the American Baptist Home Mission Society." They feared that "radical" northern missionaries would alienate the freedpeople from southern whites by preaching "politics rather than religion" and "equal suffrage rather than repentance." Southern Baptists were particularly outraged over the society's seizure of southern church property during the war. Both at the state level and in the SBC, they expressed their determination to maintain separate southern organizations and missionary efforts.[13]

In stark contrast to their evangelical brethren, Cumberland Presbyterians managed to reunite their organization with a minimum of sectional bitterness. They enjoyed two distinct advantages over their fellows in other denominations. First, their denomination was concentrated geographically in the border states of the Upper South. They had no churches in the Northeast beyond Pennsylvania and few in the states of the Lower South. Second, their leadership deliberately tried to avoid both debates on slavery before the war and the formal division of the church during the war.[14]

When the General Assembly of the Cumberland Presbyterian Church met in Saint Louis in May 1861, only thirty-seven of the ninety-seven presbyteries were represented. The Reverend Milton Bird delivered the opening sermon and insisted that in heaven "there is no Northern and Southern religion." At the 1862 meeting, when no southerners were present, the General Assembly resolved to "allay and not exasperate the feelings of those who differ from us, and we most earnestly and affectionately advise our ministers and members to cultivate forbearance and conciliation." At the next two annual meetings, radical Unionists had stronger representation, and during the 1864 conference in Lebanon, Ohio, they passed resolutions against slavery and secession — in effect, an attempt to excommunicate all those who had voluntarily supported the Confederacy. Only after "repentance and humiliation before God and the Church" could those who had aided rebellion be allowed to reenter it. The 1865 assembly, which met in Evansville, Indiana, in May, accepted several delegates from the Unionist areas of East Tennessee. During the 1864 and 1865 conventions, staunch Unionists were in firm control of the General Assembly and supported the northern vision of religious reconstruction. They expected repentance from the erring southern members of their denomination as a condition for readmission.[15]

What the northern Cumberland Presbyterians failed to foresee, however, was the willingness of some northern and many border state conservatives to compromise in order to restore the unity of the church. During the war, southern Cumberland Presbyterians remained remarkably committed to an undivided church. At a convention held in August 1863 in Chattanooga, Tennessee, one member of the assembly had proposed the organization of a separate southern church. At this suggestion the Reverend W. M. Reed, a Confederate colonel, rose to address the body, and complained that while the world wanted ecclesiastical "deliverances," it failed to recognize that "the whole manhood of our Southern churches is giving its deliverances, with muskets in the trenches, not on paper in church judicatures." Those who wanted more, who asked "in addition that we put Caesar above Christ, and rend Christ's body, in order to show our patriotism, are not entitled to our respect." Instead, the proper course was to "wait, and pray, and hope." Reed believed that the Cumberland Presbyterian Church "will remain undivided, no matter what comes of this bitter civil struggle." When the motion came to a vote, even its author voted no. Throughout the rest of the war, southern Cumberland Presbyterians expressed their determination "stedfastly to resist any movement which looked toward the division of the church."[16]

In May 1866, the General Assembly met in Owensboro, Kentucky, with Milton Bird as the clerk of the conference. Bird enrolled southern delegates without questioning them on their loyalties during the war. Once enrolled, together with border state conservatives, they formed a majority against the northern faction. The Committee on War and Slavery returned to the entire conference with a majority report and two minority reports. None of the reports, however, was acceptable to the body as a whole, and Milton Bird offered a substitute that the assembly amended and adopted. The bland resolutions in this report condemned any movement that would tend to unite church and state, opposed the prostitution of the pulpit for political or sectional purposes, and insisted that the expression of political sentiment was "no part of the legitimate business of an Ecclesiastical Court." This resolution effectively negated those passed in 1864 and 1865 by the northern controlled General Assembly. The final resolution declared, "nothing in the foregoing shall be construed as an expression of opinion upon Slavery or Rebellion."[17]

Understanding that church newspapers would play an important role in successfully healing the breach in the Cumberland Presbyterian Church, the General Assembly adopted a proposal by Reverend G. W. Mitchell of Tennessee. The resolution "earnestly recommended" that the editors of the church newspapers "exclude from their columns such articles as may manifestly engender unholy strifes and divisions among brethren, and mar the peace and unity of our beloved Zion." The united church continued to grow throughout the rest of the nineteenth century; between 1860 and 1900, the membership and the clergy approximately doubled.[18]

Instead of following the Cumberland Presbyterian example and reuniting, as some members in both North and South desired, Baptists, Methodists, and Presbyterians remained divided. From the end of the war through the end of the 1860s, members of these denominations on both sides of the Mason-Dixon line insisted that their fellow clergy of the other side favored continued separation for specious and selfish reasons. Each side identified several barriers erected by the other that precluded reunion.

Northerners accused southerners of desiring to perpetuate organizations based on slavery and rebellion. Theodore Tilton, the editor of the New York *Independent*, contended that the spirit of rebellion remained "potent and insolent in its civic and religious forms." Northern churches had to work independently of the "unregenerate and apostate" southern denominations. "The Presbyterian, Methodist, and Baptist, will not soon resign their independent form for Northern fraternity," he concluded. "They will indulge their rancor and pride in the safe walls of their ecclesiastical fold."[19]

Furthermore, southern Churches and clergy, stained with terrible sins, were unfit to serve as agents of religious reconstruction in the South. The *Central Christian Advocate* of St. Louis declared in 1865, the "only true theory of Methodist reconstruction is to *push on our work.*" The MEC must "*occupy the territory*, whether there be a Church South or not, and we shall soon find that we have restored the unity of Methodism in a manner honorable to ourselves, and eminently beneficial to all loyal men, black or white, in the Southern States." The *Northwestern Christian Advocate* in Chicago was particularly disturbed by "decided secessionist" southern Methodist bishops George F. Pierce and Robert Paine. While willing to do "everything honorable and righteous for a united Methodism," the editors "would hesitate long before consenting to do business under such men." In October 1865, the West Wisconsin Conference of the MEC resolved that because the members and ministers of the southern church, "after instigating treason and rebellion, have not shown evidence of penitence and reformation," allowing them to return "would be countenancing sin, and tend to the impurity of the Church."[20]

Southern evangelicals, in turn, rejected any discussion of reunion because their northern coreligionists had become "incurably radical" in their political activities. Northern Christians had added political tests to their conditions for membership by insisting that southern ministers and members confess and renounce the sins of rebellion and slaveholding. The *Southern Presbyterian* proclaimed, "Christian men of the South" could "do neither without perjuring their consciences in the sight of God." The editor of the Baptist *Christian Index* assured his readers that if reunion with the northern Baptists depended on the South's humbling herself, "there can be neither union nor communion between us this side of eternity." Only if northerners were willing to put away these political tests and accept southerners as equals could reunion take place. Otherwise the sin of schism lay at their door, "not at ours."[21]

Furthermore, northern missionary efforts constituted an "invasion" of southern ecclesiastical territory, complete with the capture of church properties. Southern Methodists were particularly outraged by the policy of "disintegration and absorption" that the northern church adopted in the South. This hostile invasion must cease, and southern church property had to be restored, before southern evangelicals would consider merging the sectional religious bodies into common national churches. In 1867 southern Methodist editor Thomas O. Summers declared the terms on which southern Methodists might consider fraternity and union: "Let Northern Methodists repent of the wrongs they have done us; let them cease the defamations of the living and the dead; let them restore the property they have taken from us; let them suspend their schismatical movements on our territory; let them abrogate all their political lists of membership." If, after doing so, they proposed terms for reunion, Summers was confident that the southern General Conference would give them "a candid and courteous consideration."[22]

Finally, the status of black church members posed a barrier to reunion that grew more serious over time. By the 1870s southern churches were virtually bereft of black members, and many of those members had joined northern biracial denominations. Ever fearful of the specter of social equality, white southern Christians opposed such integration. Although they continually voiced their commitment to black evangelization, southern Baptists refused to allow blacks the full privileges of membership; southern Presbyterians resisted the idea of black ministers in their synods and assemblies; and southern Methodists shuddered at the thought of a black bishop presiding over their conferences. Even after blacks were relegated to their own conferences within the MEC, the issue of race continued to be a significant obstacle to Methodist reunion.

Although the sectional bitterness of the 1860s waned in the 1870s as political reconstruction drew to a close, the prospects for denominational reunion did not improve. The northern and southern wings of the three major evangelical bodies gradually established fraternal relations in the closing decades of the nineteenth century, but southern Christians remained steadfastly committed to their sectional organizations. The negotiations over the proper relationship of the two churches in each denomination clarify the issues at stake in religious reconstruction and demonstrate how the results of that process continued to influence southern religious life into the twentieth century.

Unlike the Baptists and Methodists, who divided in the 1840s, American Presbyterians had split into sectional camps only in 1861.[23] Despite the short separation, prospects for sectional reunion were no brighter among them in 1865 than within the other major evangelical denominations. During the conflict, the General Assembly of the PCUSA passed resolutions condemning slavery and secession; shortly after Appomattox, it voiced its commitment to "pass over and help to rebuild that part of the American Zion which has been so sadly laid waste by the rebellion and civil war." After pronouncing southern Presbyterians "schismatical," it declared it was ready to receive into "ecclesiastical fellowship" any who would "properly acknowledge and renounce their errors."[24]

Northern Presbyterians opened the way for fraternity in 1868 when the northern General Assembly formally acknowledged the separate and independent existence of the PCUS. In 1869 the northern General Assembly sent Christian salutations to the southern General Assembly, and in 1870 the first General Assembly of the reunited Old and New School Presbyterians in the North expressed its desire to restore fraternal relations with the southern church "on terms of mutual confidence, respect, Christian honor and love." To this end, it appointed a committee to confer on the issue of opening friendly correspondence.[25]

The General Assembly of the PCUS met this proposal with hostility. Dr. Benjamin M. Palmer, who chaired the committee to which the proposal was referred, was personally opposed to the appointment of a committee, fearing that fraternal relations might lead to reunion. Others were somewhat more conciliatory, so the General Assembly appointed a committee to confer with the northern Presbyterians. However, under the leadership of Palmer, Robert L. Dabney, and Stuart Robinson, the assembly gave the committee specific instructions that "the difficulties which lie in the way of cordial correspondence between the two bodies must be distinctly met and removed." The General Assembly went on to list the specific barriers to fraternity, including political declarations by the northern assembly, the "total surrender of all the great testimonies of the Church" in the union of the Old School General Assembly with the New School General Assembly, the treatment of ministers in Missouri and Kentucky who were expelled from the northern church, and accusations against the entire southern Presbyterian church of heresy, blasphemy, schism, and treason. To this list might be added the conflicting claims to church property and the status of black church members, important obstacles in later negotiations. On learning that the southern committee had very specific instructions, the northern General Assembly discharged its committee.[26]

Eliza Fain was troubled by her denominational leaders' intransigence. When reading the proceedings of the southern assembly, she was "grieved to see there what I do not think is the spirit of the Master." She admired the "spirit" of the men who came as a delegation from the northern assembly and could not believe that they were "spies sent in to view our land with a desire to dispossess us of it." She wrote, "I cannot see where we would in any way injure ourselves by holding fraternal correspondence. I do not see how it would be a giving up or a renunciation of any of the great principles of the truth as it is in Jesus but minds of the highest intellectual (and I do trust Christian) magnitude see otherwise." She prayed that God would help the southern church, whom He had given "a proud position." She reiterated her belief that the Civil War was a struggle "not only for civil but religious liberty." "A terrible wild fanaticism" had governed the North, "which if carried out would destroy the peace of our beloved Zion, but a bound was set over which they could not pass." Though Fain likely would not have approved of sectional reunion, she did question the judgment of leading southern clergy like Palmer and Dabney, who refused any sort of fraternal correspondence.[27]

In 1873 the northern assembly tendered the olive branch once again. Delegates passed a resolution declaring that "all action touching the brethren adhering to the body popularly known as the Southern General Assembly" had been, since the re-union of northern Presbyterians in 1869, "null and void." In 1874 the southern assembly appointed a committee without specific instructions to confer with a northern Presbyterian committee, not on the issue of union, but on fraternal correspondence. A significant minority opposed the appointment of a committee, but they were satisfied when the moderator appointed to the committee only men who were committed to the southern vision of religious reconstruction, including Palmer.[28]

The two committees met in Baltimore in January 1875. Southern representatives insisted that the two groups meet separately and communicate in writing. They demanded the removal of two major obstacles before fraternal relations could be established: first, the "unjust accusations" made against the southern church; second, "the course pursued in regard to Church property." Northern commissioners reminded the southerners that the northern General Assembly had declared "null and void" all statements derogatory to the southern church, and they promised to refer the property questions to the next General Assembly. The Baltimore conference closed without establishing fraternal correspondence.[29]

For the next seven years, the cause of fraternal relations made little progress. In 1882, however, movement came from an unexpected source. Four southern presbyteries, including Holston in eastern Tennessee, sent overtures to the General Assembly of the PCUS, requesting the formal interchange of delegates with the PCUSA, and a minister from Washington, D.C., moved that the assembly appoint a committee to bear greetings to the northern assembly and pledge cooperation in missionary endeavors. Most of these initiatives came from areas of the Upper South where southern and northern Presbyterian churches existed side by side. Southern Presbyterians there hoped to gain official recognition of growing fraternity in those areas. Opposition was centered in the Deep South, especially among the older members who had fought the battles of religious reconstruction. The proposed overtures and resolution were referred to the Committee on Foreign Correspondence, which presented a report recommending that they not be enacted. For two days, the assembly debated the issue and members took strong stands on both sides. Then, in a remarkable turn of events, a new motion was referred to the committee that it unanimously approved. In essence, the motion requested each assembly "to remove aspersions cast upon the Christian character of the other" and then to exchange delegates. The following resolution was adopted by a nearly unanimous vote and telegraphed to the northern General Assembly in session at Springfield, Illinois: "That while receding from no principle, we do hereby declare our regret for and withdrawal of all expressions of our Assembly which may be regarded as reflecting upon, or offensive to, the General Assembly of the Presbyterian Church in the United States of America." Two days later, northern Presbyterians sent a telegram informing the southern body that their General Assembly had adopted the same resolution in reference to the PCUS. Both General Assemblies immediately elected fraternal delegates.[30]

The decision in 1882 to establish fraternal relations, which marked the end of an era of bitterness between northern and southern Presbyterians, did not signal the end of sectionalism in the southern Presbyterian church. Led by Benjamin M. Palmer and Richmond K. Smoot, a substantial group of southerners wanted relations with the PCUSA to go no further. When the Upper Missouri Presbytery petitioned the southern General Assembly of 1883 to appoint a commission to discuss organic union with the northern Presbyterians, the answer was emphatic: "The question of organic union is not to be entertained as a subject before the church." In 1887, when more overtures appeared favoring closer relations with the PCUSA, the assembly appointed a committee to discuss with a northern committee all subjects "now regarded as obstacles in the way of united effort or the propagation of the Gospel." Prominent among these barriers was the status of black members in the northern church, and opposition to the committee in the southern General Assembly came principally from the synods of Virginia, North Carolina, and South Carolina. The PCUSA had established seven black presbyteries in these states, and white southern Presbyterians wanted no part of closer cooperation with a church that raised the specter of black equality and interracial cooperation.[31]

The two committees met in Louisville, Kentucky, in December 1887 to discuss their differences. In addition to the status of black members, the committees discussed the spirituality of the church, ecclesiastical boards, and doctrine. The southern commissioners discovered that the two churches were closer on these points than they had expected. On the most serious question, the status of the black churches, the northern committee declared that their church was "not in favor of setting off its colored members into a separate, independent organization." Several months before the joint commission met, prominent leaders of the PCUS, including Dabney, Palmer, and Smoot, cited the race issue as "an insuperable barrier to union with the Northern Church." On no other topic were "the Southern people more sensitive, to no danger are they more alive, than this of the amalgamation of the two races thrown so closely together and threatening the deterioration of both." This "peril" confronted southern Presbyterians "in the proposal to reintegrate in the Northern Church, as being one of the early steps leading surely to that final result."[32]

Even if all other difficulties could be resolved, the matter of black members proved insurmountable. After the southern committee reported to the General Assembly of 1888, that body proclaimed that the obstacles to reunion had not to any considerable extent been removed. The General Assembly of the PCUS approved this report and voted to discontinue negotiations by a vote of eighty-four to forty-three. A protest signed by thirty-eight delegates who desired to continue negotiations revealed a growing sentiment toward closer cooperation with the PCUSA. However, the older generation of ministers who had fought the battles of religious reconstruction, together with some younger recruits, effectively blocked every effort to resurrect the issue.[33] When the PCUSA and three southern presbyteries requested the appointment of a committee of conference in 1894, the southern General Assembly declined by a vote of ninety-one to sixty-seven, once again raising the old issues of the proper relation of church and state, the status of black members, and church property disputes. To these were added the status of women in the church and the disruption that would result from discussing reunion. Although the issue resurfaced periodically, the relationship established between the churches in the 1880s — fraternal relations and cooperation, but no union — persisted well into the twentieth century.[34]

Despite the initial barriers to reunion, northern Methodists continued to seek out common ground with their southern counterparts. At virtually every point southern Methodists, intent on maintaining their separate, sectional organization, re-buffed them. Two northern conferences, the New York and the New York East, sent messages to the southern General Conference of 1866 requesting that it appoint commissioners to discuss the subject of reunion. That conference, although willing to unite in prayer for the restoration of "Christian love and sympathy" between the churches, emphatically rejected any such discussion.[35]

Undaunted by this refusal, the northern Methodist bishops appointed three of their number in April 1869 to meet with the southern bishops. Early in May, Bishop Edmund S. Janes and Bishop Matthew Simpson[36] traveled to St. Louis to discuss "the propriety, practicability, and methods of reunion" with the southern bishops at their annual meeting. Janes and Simpson delivered a communication from the northern bishops that declared that since the division of the churches had "been productive of evil, so the reunion of them would be productive of good." Because "the main cause of separation has been removed, so has the chief obstacle to the restoration."[37]

The southern Methodist bishops replied a week later "at sufficient length to be understood," as one of them later reported. They declared that fraternal relations must be restored before any question of union could be considered. Furthermore, they insisted that they had no authority to act on the issues of the "propriety, practicability, and methods of reunion." They reminded the northern bishops of the obstacles that hindered any such discussion. They were particularly outraged by the "avowed purpose" of northern missionaries to "disintegrate and absorb our societies, that otherwise dwelt quietly." Their practice of "taking possession of some of our houses of worship" had "inflicted both grief and loss on us" and appeared to the world as not only "a breach of charity, but an invasion of the plainest rights of property." Perhaps most important, the southern bishops rejected the idea that "the main cause of separation has been removed." Slavery, they contended, "was not, in any proper sense, the cause, but the occasion only of that separation, the necessity of which we regretted as much as you."[38]

When the General Conference of the MECS assembled at Memphis in 1870, Bishop Edmund S. Janes and Dr. William L. Harris of the northern church appeared bearing fraternal greetings. They requested that the conference appoint a commission to meet with a similar group from the northern church to discuss reunion. In response, the conference endorsed the 1869 actions of its bishops, declined to appoint a commission, and resolved, "the true interests of the Church of Christ require and demand the maintenance of our separate and distinct organizations."[39]

In 1872 the General Conference of the MEC elected delegates who bore fraternal greetings to the southern General Conference in May 1874 at Louisville, Kentucky, as the first official fraternal delegates elected since the division of 1844. After listening to the northern delegates, the General Conference appointed a committee of nine ministers and laymen to consider relations between the churches; their report insisted that while corporate union was "undesirable and impracticable," they welcomed "measures looking to the removal of obstacles in the way of amity and peace." The General Conference appointed delegates to bear fraternal greetings to the 1876 northern General Conference. Among those chosen was the ninety-year-old Dr. Lovick Pierce, who in 1848 had been turned away by the northern General

Conference in his mission as a fraternal messenger from the southern church. The 1874 General Conference also selected a commission to meet with a similar commission from the northern church "to adjust all existing difficulties."[40]

After the northern General Conference designated a commission "to settle disturbing questions," the two delegations, each consisting of three ministers and two laymen, met at Cape May, New Jersey, in August 1876. They discussed several issues that hindered the establishment of formal fraternity. Southern representatives insisted that northern Methodists officially recognize the legitimacy of the MECS, and they requested northern commissioners to acknowledge that the two general conferences were "each rightfully and historically integral parts of the original Methodist Episcopal Church constituted in 1784." The northern delegates quickly declared that each of the churches was "a legitimate Branch of Episcopal Methodism in the United States." The joint commission also adopted a "Declaration and Basis of Fraternity," established guidelines for settling church property disputes, and investigated fourteen cases. Of the ten cases the conference decided, nine favored local societies of the MECS, as did the general rules adopted to settle property claims.[41]

The Cape May conference marked the end of religious reconstruction for Methodists. Northern Methodists recognized the permanence and legitimacy of the southern church, which they had hoped in 1865 would disintegrate in the face of their intensive missionary efforts. At every general conference after 1876, northern and southern Methodists exchanged fraternal delegates. However, none of these visitors proposed a union of the two churches.

Not coincidentally, the Cape May conference occurred just months after the MEC capitulated to the idea of segregated conferences in the South. In 1874 southern Methodists had identified the northern church's "mixed Conferences, mixed congregations, and mixed schools" as one of several barriers to reunion. At the request of both black and white ministers in the South, the northern General Conference of 1876 approved the racial division of the southern work. Critics of this plan maintained that the conference was ready to offer "the dark brother as a sacrifice for the fraternal fellowship of the Methodist Episcopal Church, South." The African Methodist Episcopal *Christian Recorder* lamented, "with repentance or without it, the [Church] South must be appeased."[42]

On the local level, the tensions of religious reconstruction gradually relaxed. In Carroll County, Georgia, southern Methodist Frank Robinson accepted the invitation of a nearby northern Methodist church to bring his Sunday school class to a local gathering. Previously "full of bitterness" toward northern Methodists, Robinson reported, he would have "felt myself disgraced to have been seen entering your Church." However, the kind invitation "has melted my heart and driven this bitterness out."[43]

For sixty years after the end of religious reconstruction, northern and southern Methodists made only halting progress toward reunion. In 1898 a Joint Commission on Federation met for the first time; by the time it closed its work in 1916, it had promoted cooperation in foreign missions and created a common hymnal, catechism, and order of worship to be used by both churches. In 1916 the Joint Commission on Unification began efforts to reunite the two churches; in 1923 it developed a plan for reunion, which the northern church adopted in its 1924 General Conference. A special General Conference of the MECS also met in 1924 and approved the plan. However, the southern annual conferences also had to approve the plan by a three-fourths majority for it to take effect, and while unification won a majority of the votes, it was far short of the necessary three-fourths. Importantly, five southern bishops had opposed the plan. Although black members were relegated to a separate regional conference, some southerners feared losing their identity and their church property in a united church where they would be a minority; others opposed the modernism in the northern church.[44]

However, on the local level, fraternity and unity of spirit continued to grow. In Tennessee and elsewhere in the South, southern Methodists sometimes visited nearby northern Methodist conferences, and northern ministers returned the favor. When the MEC dissolved its Central German Conference in 1932, Barth Methodist Church in Nashville returned to the southern church. Even more remarkably, northern and southern Methodists also exchanged several other churches in central Tennessee to improve flexibility among their charges. When the vote for reunion came in 1937, southern Methodists in the Tennessee Conference voted 187 to 72 in favor of it.[45]

Even in the 1930s, the issue of black members continued to cripple reunion negotiations. Some northern Methodists wanted equal representation in the merged conferences in the South; southern whites sought a union of whites only after the northern church had given its black members independence or turned them over to the Colored Methodist Episcopal Church. Compromisers settled upon the creation of a racially separate Central Jurisdiction for black members of the MEC. The creation of the Central Jurisdiction insulated blacks from the rest of the united church except at the highest levels. Although it perpetuated segregation and geographical overlapping, the arrangement did allow blacks to elect their own bishops and presiding elders.[46]

By 1935 commissioners from the MEC, the MECS, and the Methodist Protestant Church had devised a new plan for unification into "The Methodist Church." This time all three general conferences approved the plan, the annual conferences ratified these decisions, and the three churches merged into one in the spring of 1939. Ninety-five years after the division of 1844, northern and southern Methodists were once again in the same church. The issues that had prevented reunion during religious reconstruction had remained strong enough in 1925 to foil a unification plan, but by the late 1930s a new generation of Methodists in both sections overcame the old animosities and joined together.

Like their Presbyterian and Methodist brethren, southern Baptists staunchly resisted the idea of uniting with their northern counterparts. The primary vehicle for northern Baptist efforts in the South was the ABHMS, which reentered the South in 1862 to work among the freedpeople. Considering these missionary efforts an invasion of their territory, southern Baptists were very critical of the society.

At the 1867 meeting of the SBC, southern Baptists outlined what they considered to be the basis for cooperation with the ABHMS. Since the ABHMS wanted to aid in the religious instruction of the freedpeople, the SBC instructed its Domestic Mission Board to "make known to that Society our willingness to receive aid in this work, by appropriations made to the Boards of this Convention." In 1868, when the

ABHMS sent delegates bearing "Christian greeting" to the SBC meeting in Baltimore, the convention declared, "as we ask no concession of principle, we make none" in receiving the northern Baptist delegates. Southern Baptists also reiterated their desire for financial assistance, insisting that the Domestic Mission Board had "peculiar advantages for prosecuting this work — experience, proximity to the field, interest in the people — and they are willing to receive aid in its conduct." Southern Baptists wanted the ABHMS to recognize the South as a territorial unit in which only they could work.[47]

The convention also appointed a committee to confer with the ABHMS at its meeting later in 1868; the committee included some of the most prominent ministers in the convention, including J. B. Jeter, John A. Broadus, Richard Fuller, Basil Manly Jr., J. R. Graves, and H. A. Tupper. Broadus requested that the southern Baptist Domestic Mission Board be permitted to approve any missionaries sent among the freedpeople by the ABHMS. Northern Baptists rejected this proposal as an unreasonable restraint on their ability to appoint whom they wished. In turn, the ABHMS presented a formal plan for cooperative efforts to "lift up the millions of freedmen to the exercise of all the rights and duties of citizenship and Christian brotherhood." Believing that this statement implied social equality between the races, the southern delegates rejected the proposal because of its "political" objectives.[48]

In 1870 the SBC considered the possibility of an organic union with the ABHMS, and after discussion declined to pursue reunion. J. B. Jeter chaired a special committee instructed to consider the whole issue of cooperation with northern Baptists; its report declared, "All are agreed that the Convention and its Boards should be maintained in their integrity. No measures which endanger their existence or diminish their efficiency, are to be tolerated. All the energies of Southern Baptists should be directed to their support and the increase of their usefulness." Moreover, the committee concluded, "the further agitation of a subject which has absorbed so much of the valuable time of this body, at its last three sessions, tends only to disturb our own harmony, without promoting fraternal relations with other bodies."[49]

Despite the SBC official hostility to reunion, in the 1870s individual state conventions began to cooperate closely with the ABHMS's evangelistic efforts among southern blacks; in 1879, for example, the Georgia Baptist Convention entered into an agreement with the society for conducting missions among the freedpeople. Once again in 1879 the SBC considered cooperation with the society, and Isaac Taylor Tichenor, president of the Alabama Agricultural and Mechanical College at Auburn, proposed that the convention appoint fraternal delegates to the society at its upcoming meeting, approve a meeting of Baptists of all sections "to devise and propose . . . plans of co-operation," and allow the fraternal delegates to arrange such a meeting. John A. Broadus immediately objected to any overtures of cooperation, which he feared would lead inexorably to "union and consolidation." The ensuing "battle of the giants" is notable only for its narrowness. Neither Tichenor nor Broadus favored reunion with northern Baptists. After lengthy debate over the resolutions for a cooperative meeting, the convention rejected them; it only sent fraternal delegates to the ABHMS meeting in 1879. Finally, in 1882 Baptist bodies in fifteen southern states and territories sent representatives to the Jubilee meeting of the ABHMS to discuss plans for future cooperative work, and afterward both black and white local southern Baptist congregations increasingly looked to the society for financial assistance in building church edifices.[50]

By the early 1880s, the ABHMS had clearly overwhelmed the efforts of the Southern Baptist Convention's Home Mission Board. The northern force of sixty-seven missionaries in the South was triple the Home Mission Board's number, while the ABHMS spent $85,900 in the region annually, compared to the southern board's budget of $28,000. Many southern Baptists feared that the life of the SBC itself was at stake; the solution was to revive its domestic missionary activities. In 1881 it moved its Domestic Mission Board from Marion, Alabama, to Atlanta, Georgia. With a new name and a new executive secretary, the Home Mission Board under Isaac Taylor Tichenor reasserted the territorial conception of missionary work and fostered a growing denominational consciousness. During the 1880s the Home Mission Board increasingly challenged the supremacy of the ABHMS in the South. In Georgia, for example, the cooperation between the northern society and the state convention, which had begun in 1877 as an effort to support missionaries to blacks in Georgia, had ceased by 1885. At the 1881 meeting of the Tennessee Baptist Convention, a minister proposed that a committee be appointed to confer with the ABHMS about cooperative efforts in mission work, but another minister argued that such a move would be humiliating to the Home Mission Board. Accordingly, Tennessee Baptists declined to work with the northern society and determined instead to cooperate with the southern board.[51]

In 1894 the SBC asked the ABHMS to allow it greater participation in black evangelization, "believing that the time has come when it should enlarge its work among the colored people of the South"; it appointed a committee to meet with a similar one from the ABHMS. The two groups met at Fortress Monroe, Virginia, in September 1894, and after two days of deliberation unanimously adopted two resolutions and considered a third. The first proposed that the convention appoint local advisory committees where black schools existed to advise the ABHMS on changes it considered desirable. Southerners pledged to support the schools morally and financially and to encourage young blacks to attend them. The second resolution proposed that the convention and the society jointly appoint missionaries to black southerners, conduct ministers' and deacons' training institutes, and strengthen black Baptist missionary organizations. The third item proposed by southern delegates involved territorial limits on new missionary efforts; the society's representatives had no instructions on this matter and promised to present it to the society. Both the society and the convention later approved all three proposals.[52]

The Fortress Monroe agreement marked the end of religious reconstruction for Baptists. Southern Baptists won a major victory for their vision of religious reconstruction when the society formally recognized the territorial unity of the South and the SBC as its representative. The ABHMS did not immediately withdraw, but it did begin to curtail its operations in the South. Southern Baptists pledged greater financial support for evangelistic and educational efforts among black southerners, but the plan for greater coordination of missionary efforts clearly failed, because the white Baptist state conventions had refused to support it. By the turn of the century, southern Baptists had won the field. The formation of the Northern Baptist Convention in 1907 gave further impetus to the idea of sectional boundaries in Baptist missionary work, and northern Baptists increasingly focused on the Northwest and northern cities in their missionary endeavors.[53]

During the last quarter of the nineteenth century, northern and southern evangelicals slowly withdrew from the battles of religious reconstruction and achieved a measure of intersectional peace. These settlements came only after each side had once again aired its grievances. Although some southerners were anxious to restore harmony and even unity, most of the initiatives for fraternity and reunion came from northern bodies. Most southerners were intent on retaining their sectional identity and upholding the Confederate vision of religious reconstruction, and their ability to prevent the reunion of the denominations that many northerners and some southerners desired attests to the success of that vision in this area. Methodists were able to effect a sectional reunion, but this reconciliation came only after three-quarters of a century of negotiations. Even after the southern ecclesiastical warriors of religious reconstruction died, their successors upheld the propriety and necessity of separate southern organizations. Northern evangelicals achieved a measure of success in establishing fraternal relations at all, but they did so only by mollifying southern ecclesiastical pride and slighting their own black members. In the discussions of reunion, as elsewhere, the southern vision prevailed through its unyielding commitment to the Confederate interpretation of the Civil War.

Conclusion

The Shape of Religious Reconstruction

Then said I unto them, Ye see the distress that we are in, how Jerusalem lieth waste, and the gates thereof are burned with fire: come, and let us build up the wall of Jerusalem, that we be no more a reproach. . . . And they said, Let us rise up and build.

So they strengthened their hands for this good work.

Nehemiah 2:17–18

When Stonewall Jackson lay mortally wounded near Chancellorsville in 1863, the religious life of the South was still immersed in the preoccupations of the antebellum era. By 1877 the foundations of southern faith had been shaken, both by the outcome of the war itself and by the emerging forces that the war unleashed. The failure of the Confederacy's bid for independence opened the South to new opportunities, though hardly ones that were welcomed by white southern evangelicals. Southern Baptist, Methodist, and Presbyterian organizations were by no means dead, and they all reasserted themselves as guardians of sectional identity and religious purity in the postwar period. The impulse was to return as quickly as possible to the old conventions and familiar issues, but circumstances required considerable readjustment.

The three principal competitors in the southern religious economy of the 1860s and 1870s were white southerners, white northerners, and freedpeople. The small number of northern black missionaries from the African Methodist Episcopal (AME) and African Methodist Episcopal Zion (AMEZ) churches shared many of the attitudes and outlooks of the freedpeople to whom they ministered and therefore must be included in that group. A larger number of southern white ministers and laypeople openly repudiated the southern denominations and joined northern churches at their first opportunity; these religious scalawags shared much of the northern view of the war, and they played an important role in reinforcing northerners' preconceptions about the South and its people.

Each of these three groups interpreted God's purposes in the Civil War differently. White southern evangelicals believed Appomattox to be a severe chastisement by their heavenly Father who continued to love them in spite of their numerous sins. The sins for which God was punishing them included "extortion" or greed, reliance on men rather than God, and even several wrongs — reluctantly acknowledged — associated with the system of slavery. These shortcomings included the failure to recognize slave marriages or to respect family ties among slaves, restrictions on black preachers and religious meetings, and prohibitions against teaching slaves to read, a proscription that had prevented them from reading the Bible. At the same time, southerners emphatically rejected the Yankee conviction that slavery was inherently sinful. Nor could they accept even the milder suggestion of John H. Caldwell that slavery as it had been practiced in the South had been wrong.

Adopting this conception of the providential meaning of southern defeat, Confederate Christians proceeded to formulate a plan for rebuilding their religious lives. Since, on the whole, their treatment of slaves had been governed by the laws of God as contained in Scripture, they saw little reason for change in southern racial practices. Black Christians should remain quietly in the galleries and the rear of churches where they could continue to receive wholesome instruction from their "best friends." Although slavery had been eradicated in the war, white southerners insisted that the peculiar institution was not the issue over which they had separated from their northern brethren before the war. Disputes over church governance and the proper purview of ecclesiastical bodies were the real causes of division, and northern Christians' actions during the war only made these differences more difficult to remedy. To southern Christians, the northern denominations had become increasingly politicized and radical, and their seizure of southern church property under War Department orders especially rankled. They could not accept northern offers for reunion without surrendering their beliefs and their sense of regional identity.

Northern evangelicals interpreted Confederate defeat as God's just judgment on white southerners for the crimes of human bondage and political treason. Because of the southern clergy's active participation in these crimes, reasoned the victors, they were unfit to serve as agents of moral regeneration. "Hopelessly debauched with proslaveryism and tainted with treason," as one northern editor described their condition, the southern churches could not minister effectively to either white southerners or the former slaves.[1] Furthermore, northern clergy believed, many white southerners had never really supported the Confederacy or, for a time, had been misled by scheming leaders. At heart, they longed for the return of the "national denominations" from which they had been unwillingly separated. At first such opinions seemed to be verified by the emergence of the religious scalawags, whose numbers were thought to be greater than they actually were. These southerners who accepted the northern interpretation of the war returned to the northern denominations at their first opportunity. Concentrated in the border states and Appalachia, many had been Unionists throughout the war, but a few had supported the Confederacy and now repented of this error. In an era when church discipline was an important part of religious life, northern evangelicals demanded similar displays of repentance from all southerners as a condition for readmission into the northern denominations. Wartime missionary labors among black contrabands within Union lines also convinced northern Christians that they had a providential duty in the South. In the closing years of the war, northerners vowed to enter the South to preach a "pure and loyal gospel" to whites and to minister to the spiritual and educational needs of the freedpeople.

Armed with this understanding of the religious meaning of the war, northern evangelicals vigorously prosecuted an ecclesiastical "invasion" of the South. Missionaries organized congregations of southern Unionists in some areas, and in other places they welcomed freedpeople eager to leave the southern churches. Northern teachers also went south to staff schools for southern blacks. This educational effort served as an important implement of northern evangelistic efforts; wherever they organized a school, northern Christians were able to establish a local congregation for their denomination as well. While northern missionaries and teachers were moving southward to erect churches and schools, northern denominations also sought reunion with their southern counterparts. Believing that slavery was the primary cause of separation, they saw in the death of slavery an opportunity for renewed unity. However, they continued to demand repentance as a condition of reunion.

For black southerners and northern black missionaries, the real meaning of the war lay in the deliverance of four million people from bondage. God had heard their prayers, and He had been faithful. He used northern armies to set His children free by overthrowing the government erected to preserve slavery. In the terms of their favorite biblical narrative, the freedpeople had been delivered from Egyptian slavery as a result of the war, but a wilderness remained before them. They would need help to cross the River Jordan to reach the Promised Land. Black southern Christians quickly withdrew from the churches of their masters, despite the laments and warnings of their former brethren. They then turned to northern missionaries for organizational, educational, and financial aid. In return they offered themselves as members in the numbers-conscious northern denominations.

The competition among these three visions of religious reconstruction shaped the southern spiritual landscape into the twentieth century. The new alternatives in religious affiliation, coupled with a general religious revival in the postwar South, led to rapid expansion in the number of local churches in the 1860s. In 1870 Georgia Baptists, Methodists, and Presbyterians had thirty-one thousand more church seats and 450 more congregations than in 1860. In the same period, while general property values fell dramatically, the church property of these denominations rose in value by nearly a million dollars.[2] Tennessee's churches grew even faster. Between 1860 and 1870, Baptists, Methodists, Presbyterians, and Cumberland Presbyterians in Tennessee provided space for 122,000 more people and formed nearly eight hundred new local churches.[3] Although the 1880 census did not report statistics on church organizations or capacities, other evidence indicates that the proliferation of churches continued in the 1870s. The natural increase of the population and a greater tendency to join organizations of all sorts accounted for some of the growth, but the establishment of northern white and freedpeople's churches was primarily responsible for this expansion. In many areas of Georgia and of middle and western Tennessee, towns with one Baptist church in 1860 had two in 1870, one black and one white. In eastern Tennessee, localities with one Methodist church in 1860 had two or perhaps three in 1870, one southern white, one northern white, and one black. In some areas black Methodists also divided among themselves, and two or more churches sprang up to compete with the parent congregation. These patterns were repeated across the South and in all three denominations.

By 1870 southern churches were segregated to a far greater degree than they had been before the war. Shortly after departing the southern biracial churches, black Baptists began to form associations and often cooperated with the American Baptist Home Mission Society in evangelistic endeavors. In 1895 many of these black Baptist organizations united to form the National Baptist Convention. Black Presbyterians united with one of the northern Presbyterian churches (who themselves united in 1869) and were organized into presbyteries and synods, which were rarely biracial. Black Methodists enjoyed a greater variety of choices. The Methodist Episcopal Church (MEC) was attractive because it provided funds to build churches and schoolhouses and pay preachers and teachers. It also proclaimed itself the only racially inclusive Methodist church — a claim, however, increasingly divorced from reality as it became internally segregated in the 1870s. The AME and AMEZ churches appealed to racial pride and won hundreds of thousands of southern adherents in the postwar South. The Colored Methodist Episcopal (CME) Church, organized by the southern Methodist church in 1870, received the remaining black members in the southern church and drew others away from the three northern organizations. The competition among these four churches for black members was fierce in the 1860s and 1870s, but when religious reconstruction ended, the era of proselytizing efforts had largely passed.

Conflicts over white members also raged in portions of Appalachia and the border South during religious reconstruction. In eastern Tennessee and elsewhere, both churches waged a relentless war in the late 1860s over members and church property. Many southern evangelicals changed loyalties during the period; a few changed twice. By the late 1870s, thousands of white southerners belonged to "northern" denominations.

In response to these assaults, southern white churches marshaled their considerable organizational, educational, and cultural resources in an attempt to reassert dominance over the religious life of the region. Shortly after the war ended, each southern denomination declared its determination to rebuild and continue its antebellum mission, one that included a defiant sectionalism. The Confederacy had died, but the South remained, and white southern Christians committed themselves to perpetuating this self-conscious section within the larger nation. During reconstruction, religion served as a bulwark of sectional identity for southerners when the South's political and economic fortunes were to some extent outside of their control.

Within a year after Appomattox, most southern religious newspapers had revived, and many of the denominational organizations had convened to assess the damages. Some associations, conferences, and presbyteries held their first meeting in several years. From this moment forward, they began to rebuild their institutions. Some newspapers failed and some denominational boundaries had to be redrawn, but given the general poverty in the section, the recovery was swift and dramatic. Prominent among southern evangelicals' plans for religious reconstruction was the transmission of their values to the next generation. Accordingly, they devoted much time and many resources to developing a strong system of Sunday schools and a network of denominational colleges: in both, young southerners could be taught reverence for the South, its institutions, and its leaders. Taught by southern teachers and supplied with materials written by southern authors, students would come to appreciate their spiritual heritage and learn to defend it against any and all foes — including northern Christians.

As religious reconstruction progressed, northern clergy softened their earlier demands for repentance and tried repeatedly to arrange an organic merger between the sectional wings of each denomination. Each time, southern representatives adamantly refused. Only Cumberland Presbyterians were able to effect a reunion, and their ability to do so was in part a reflection of their strength in border states, rather than in the more ideologically polarized Deep South and New England areas. Southern Baptists, Methodists, and Presbyterians insisted that their northern counterparts had become incurably radical and had prostituted their churches for political purposes. Furthermore, they had violated the constitutions of their respective denominations and tyrannized southern minorities. In the clash over reunion, the southern denominations won a resounding victory by opposing reunion and by agreeing to the establishment of fraternal relations only after northern Christians had yielded to all of their demands.

Despite the successes of the Confederate vision of religious reconstruction, its triumph was incomplete. Most important, black southerners did not remain under the spiritual oversight of their former masters; nor did the northern denominations respect the exclusive territorial claims the southern denominations put forward. Instead, they launched a massive missionary and educational campaign in the former Confederacy. Although never as successful as northerners had hoped, hundreds of thousands of black and white adherents to the northern denominations by the late 1870s testified to the success of this operation. The northern vision's most enduring legacies, however, were the dozens of black colleges that northern missionaries founded, staffed, and supported through the difficult, early years of their existence. These institutions provided higher education for thousands of African Americans in the South and provided critical support for black communities well into the twentieth century.

The process of religious reconstruction proceeded at a different pace in the various denominations and localities, but the results were strikingly similar. Although Baptists, Methodists, and Presbyterians within each section continued to debate among themselves such issues as infant baptism and the proper form of church government, they largely agreed about the main features of religious reconstruction. A few variations in practice arose between the locally autonomous Baptists on one hand and the more hierarchical Presbyterians and Methodists on the other, but remarkable agreement existed on most major issues. All three southern denominations initially sought to retain their black membership, and all went through a similar process of adjustment to black demands for more religious autonomy. All three refused reunion with the northern denominations and instead committed themselves to rebuilding their own organizations. All four northern denominations (three after 1869) believed that they were chosen by God to evangelize and educate the freedpeople and, to a lesser degree, southern whites as well. All initially demanded repentance as a condition of readmission to membership but later sought closer relations with their southern counterparts on virtually any terms. They also gradually retreated from providing elementary education for the freedpeople and concentrated instead on supporting a few black colleges. On every major issue of religious reconstruction, racial and sectional affinities and animosities proved stronger than denominational distinctions.

Comparisons between the states of Tennessee and Georgia also reveal more similarities than differences. The two states experienced religious reconstruction in slightly different ways. The process began in Tennessee during the war but did not commence in Georgia until the summer of 1865. Eastern Tennessee, with its large contingent of Unionist residents, provided a far more fertile ground for northern missionary efforts among whites than any section of Georgia, though some whites in the mountains of northern Georgia did join northern denominations. Otherwise, religious reconstruction proceeded in both states with striking similarity. The strategies employed by all three groups in these two states had much in common, and evidence suggests that the pattern in other southern states was comparable.

Religious reconstruction profoundly affected the lives of many individual Christians. Eliza Fain continued to live on her farm near Rogersville, Tennessee. While weathering the trials of religious reconstruction, she retained her stern Calvinist faith in God and continued to pray frequently for the conversion of her family and friends. She also maintained a paternalistic interest in the religious life of her black servants and expressed relief when the "fanaticism" of radical reconstruction ended. She never wavered in her belief in the righteousness of slavery nor in the South's struggle for "civil and religious liberty." On George Washington's birthday in 1885, she reflected on the development of "a grand republic." "Having passed through a severe civil struggle," she wrote, "the South having sustained herself as conquered, but not a crushed people. Our God has not forsaken us, she is beginning to see the heavy clouds of despotism which have been so long heavy over her drifting away, and a brighter day dawning upon us." With the aid and comfort of her deep faith, she endured repeated personal tragedies; her husband of nearly forty-five years, Richard, died in 1878, and she buried six of her adult children between 1869 and 1882. She remained active in the Rogersville Presbyterian Church, and she continued to keep her diary until nine days before her death in January 1892. A former pastor described her in an obituary as "a true mother in Israel," who was "always in full sympathy with the messenger of God as he taught the people from Sabbath to Sabbath." He also noted, "the enlargement of Zion was to her a matter of continual rejoicing."[4]

Lucius H. Holsey was a slave at the beginning of religious reconstruction; by its end he was the youngest bishop in the new and expanding CME Church. For two decades after the end of religious reconstruction, Holsey guided his denomination in its conservative policies toward southern whites. By the 1890s, however, he had become increasingly disillusioned with the restrictive nature of the new paternalism he had so long endorsed, and he even abandoned his apolitical stance in 1896 to support the Populists against the Democrats. As Glenn T. Eskew has perceptively argued, Holsey's worldview unraveled in the 1890s in the face of increasing discrimination, segregation, lynchings, and the convict lease system: "Holsey's hopes for assimilation achieved through Christianity and education foundered on the reality of white racism in the late nineteenth century." By the turn of the century, Holsey was openly calling for a separate black state within the United States. Ironically, his ideas shared many similarities with those that his old rival, Henry M. Turner, had advocated for decades. Holsey died in August 1920, on the Golden Anniversary of the denomination he had done so much to establish.[5]

Thomas H. McCallie devoted the most productive years of his ministerial career to rebuilding the southern Zion. Immediately after the war, he rejected the offer of a substantial salary if he would rejoin the Presbyterian Church in the United States of America and bring his congregation with him. From 1865 to 1873, he worked passionately to help reconstruct southern Presbyterianism in eastern Tennessee. In 1873, his health broken, he resigned his Chattanooga pastorate; for the next nine years he served as an evangelist for the Presbytery of Knoxville as frequently as his health allowed. In 1882, he moved to the side of Missionary Ridge outside of Chattanooga, where he pastored a church for a few years. McCallie died in April 1912, widely revered as the pastor who had guided Chattanooga Presbyterians through the Civil War and its aftermath.[6]

After the Democrats redeemed Georgia in 1871, John H. Caldwell left the state, feeling that "reconstruction both in Church and State was accomplished." He transferred to the Wilmington Conference of the MEC, where he served as a pastor and presiding elder of churches in Maryland and Delaware for two decades; from 1885 to 1888 he was the president of Delaware College, which later became the University of Delaware. In the 1890s, a fellow religious scalawag from Georgia asked Caldwell to recount his role in the reestablishment of the MEC in Georgia after the Civil War; in response, he wrote a pamphlet entitled *Reminiscences of the Reconstruction of Church and State in Georgia*, in which he told the story of his career as a religious and political scalawag. Caldwell died in March 1899 in Dover, Delaware.[7]

Henry M. Turner grew increasingly bitter in the late 1870s over the failure of the Republican party to uphold black rights. Despairing of equitable treatment in the United States and believing that God wanted African Americans to evangelize Africa, he began to advocate emigration as early as the 1870s, when he spent four years in Philadelphia as manager of his denomination's publishing department, which included both its Book Concern and the AME Church's influential newspaper, the *Christian Recorder*. In recognition of his abilities, the General Conference of 1880 chose Turner as one of three new bishops of the AME Church. For the next three decades, he encouraged the denomination's educational ventures, soothed sectional divisions, and championed the role of women within the church. As a public figure, he strongly opposed the erosion of black civil rights in the late nineteenth century. In the 1890s, he was the first AME bishop to visit Africa to encourage the church's missionary efforts there. He also continued to urge African Americans to emigrate; by 1904, however, he seemed to have accepted the fact that few black Americans would heed his call, and he ceased to advocate emigration publicly. In 1906 at the Georgia Equal Rights Convention, Turner pronounced his verdict upon America: "I used to love what I thought was the grand old flag, and sing with ecstasy about the Stars and Stripes, but to the Negro in this country the American flag is a dirty and contemptible rag. Not a star in it can the colored man claim." The senior bishop in the AME Church since 1895, Turner died in May 1915 on his way to preside over a church conference in Ontario. Representatives of all of the major black denominations eulogized him for his role in religious reconstruction, and both Booker T. Washington and W. E. B. DuBois praised him for providing southern black churches with a firm foundation in the immediate postwar era.[8]

Joanna Patterson Moore served as a missionary to the freedpeople in New Orleans and in Little Rock, Arkansas, from 1873 to 1893. In 1884, while in Little Rock, she began her Fireside School program, which encouraged parents to read the Bible and religious literature daily to their children. The Fireside School movement quickly spread among African Americans in Arkansas and throughout the South. In 1885, she began the publication of *Hope*, a family religious newspaper that circulated across the South; in 1895, she moved to Nashville, Tennessee, where she continued to promote Fireside Schools and publish *Hope*. Joanna P. Moore died in 1916 and was buried in Greenwood Cemetery outside Nashville, "among the colored people whom she had loved and served so long." The National Baptist Publishing Board, the Baptist Ministers and Pastors' Alliance, and the AME Ministers' Alliance each sent resolutions of appreciation for her life's work on behalf of southern blacks.[9]

Better than any minister or theologian, Abraham Lincoln captured the tragedy of the Civil War in his Second Inaugural Address, delivered on March 4, 1865. His words were equally, perhaps prophetically, applicable to religious reconstruction: "Both read the same Bible, and pray to the same God; and each invokes His aid against the other. . . . The prayers of both could not be answered; that of neither has been answered fully." American Christians, north and south, black and white, looking back over religious reconstruction, would have agreed with Lincoln when he concluded, "The Almighty has His own purposes."[10]

The contest for the soul of the South between 1863 and 1877 reaffirmed the importance of religion in southern public and private life. As Edward L. Ayers has written in his history of the New South, even those indifferent or hostile to the churches "could not escape the images, the assumptions, the power of faith."[11] The contested process of religious reconstruction in the South forced black and white southerners and northerners to confront the meaning of the Civil War for their religious lives and to act upon that understanding. The decisions they made dramatically changed the religious landscape of the South and continued to affect the section and the nation into the twentieth century.

Notes

Introduction

1. R. E. Wilbourn to John Esten Cooke, 12 December 1863, John Esten Cooke Scrapbook, #5295-E, John Esten Cooke Collection, Alderman Library, University of Virginia, Charlottesville, VA.

2. R. E. Lee to Thomas J. Jackson, 4 May 1863, *The Wartime Papers of R. E. Lee*, ed. Clifford Dowdey (Boston: Little, Brown, 1961), 452–53.

My account of Jackson's wounding and death is based on Hunter McGuire, "The Death of Stonewall Jackson," in *The Confederate Soldier in the Civil War*, ed. John S. Blay (Princeton, NJ: Pageant Books, 1959), 158–60; Mary Anna Jackson, *Memoirs of Stonewall Jackson* (Louisville, KY: Prentice Press, 1895), 427–64; Charles Royster, *The Destructive War: William Tecumseh Sherman, Stonewall Jackson, and the Americans* (New York: Knopf, 1991), 193–231; Byron Farwell, *Stonewall: A Biography of General Thomas J. Jackson* (New York: Norton, 1992), 506–30; Ernest B. Furgurson, *Chancellorsville, 1863: The Souls of the Brave* (New York: Knopf, 1992), 212–15, 307–9, 324–29; and Robert K. Krick, "The Smoothbore Valley That Doomed the Confederacy," in *Chancellorsville: The Battle and Its Aftermath*, ed. Gary W. Gallagher (Chapel Hill: University of North Carolina Press, 1996), 107–42.

3. R. E. Lee to Mrs. Lee, 11 May 1863, in Robert E. Lee, *Recollections and Letters of General Robert E. Lee* (Garden City, NJ: Garden City Publishing, 1924), 94; Mrs. Mary Jones to Col. Charles C. Jones, Jr., 19 May 1863, in *The Children of Pride: A True Story of Georgia and the Civil War*, ed. Robert Manson Myers (New Haven: Yale University Press, 1972), 1063.

4. Information on the funeral is from "Funeral of Lieut. General T. J. Jackson," *Lexington* (Virginia) *Gazette*, 20 May 1863, and Jackson, *Memoirs of Stonewall Jackson*, 463–64; Elizabeth Preston Allan, *The Life and Letters of Margaret Junkin Preston* (New York: Houghton Mifflin, 1903), 166 ("Sincerer mourning" quotation).

5. James B. Ramsey, *True Eminence Founded on Holiness: A Discourse Occasioned by the Death of Lieut. Gen. T. J. Jackson* (Lynchburg, VA: n.p., 1863), 9, 18, 19. See also George William White, "On the Death of Stonewall Jackson," sermon delivered in May 1863, George William White Collection, Historical Foundation of the Presbyterian and Reformed Churches, Montreat, NC.

6. Robert Lewis Dabney, *True Courage: A Discourse Commemorative of Lieut. General Thomas J. Jackson* (Richmond, VA: Presbyterian Committee of Publication of the Confeder-

ate States, 1863), 22–23. For the personal turmoil that overwhelmed Dabney with Confederate defeat, see Charles Reagan Wilson, "Robert Lewis Dabney: Religion and the Southern Holocaust," *Virginia Magazine of History and Biography* 89 (January 1981): 79–89.

7. A Virginian [John Esten Cooke], *The Life of Stonewall Jackson* (Richmond, VA: Ayers and Wade, 1863), 1 ("chosen standard bearer" and "anointed of God" quotations); Ramsey, *True Eminence Founded on Holiness,* 19 ("The very time" quotation); Robert Lewis Dabney, *The Life and Campaigns of Lieut.-Gen. Thomas J. Jackson* (New York: Blelock, 1866), 727–28 ("Men were everywhere speculating" and "taken the good man" quotations).

For a recent evaluation of the broad implications of Stonewall Jackson's death, see Charles Royster, *The Destructive War,* 193–231.

For a more detailed consideration of the religious meaning of Jackson's death for white southern Christians, see Daniel W. Stowell, "Stonewall Jackson and the Providence of God," in *Religion and the American Civil War,* ed. Randall Miller, Harry S. Stout, and Charles Reagan Wilson (New York: Oxford University Press, forthcoming).

8. Oliver Otis Howard to Roland B. Howard, 16 May 1863, Howard Papers, Bowdoin College, Brunswick, ME, quoted in Royster, *The Destructive War,* 213; Oliver O. Howard, "The Eleventh Corps at Chancellorsville," in *Battles and Leaders of the Civil War,* ed. Robert Underwood Johnson and Clarence Clough Buel, 4 vols. (New York: Century, 1884–88), 3:202; *Independent,* 14 May 1863.

9. For reviews of the literature on class divisions among white southerners, see Randolph B. Campbell, "Planters and Plain Folks: The Social Structure of the Antebellum South" and Joe Gray Taylor, "The White South from Secession to Redemption," in *Interpreting Southern History: Essays in Honor of Sanford W. Higginbotham,* ed. John B. Boles and Evelyn Thomas Nolen (Baton Rouge: Louisiana State University Press, 1987), 48–77, 162–98. For works that stress class differences, see Michael P. Johnson, *Toward a Patriarchal Republic: The Secession of Georgia* (Baton Rouge: Louisiana State University Press, 1977) and Fred Arthur Bailey, *Class and Tennessee's Confederate Generation* (Chapel Hill: University of North Carolina Press, 1987). For denominational and class divisions among the freedpeople, see Reginald F. Hildebrand, *The Times Were Strange and Stirring: Methodist Preachers and the Crisis of Emancipation* (Durham, NC: Duke University Press, 1995).

10. Several scholars have produced excellent studies of the role of gender in the Civil War and Reconstruction. See Catherine Clinton and Nina Silber, eds., *Divided Houses: Gender and the Civil War* (New York: Oxford University Press, 1992); LeeAnn Whites, *The Civil War as a Crisis in Gender: Augusta, Georgia, 1860–1890* (Athens: University of Georgia Press, 1995); Drew Gilpin Faust, *Mothers of Invention: Women of the Slaveholding South in the American Civil War* (Chapel Hill: University of North Carolina Press, 1996); Elizabeth D. Leonard, *Yankee Women: Gender Battles in the Civil War* (New York: Norton, 1994); George C. Rable, *Civil Wars: Women and the Crisis of Southern Nationalism* (Urbana: University of Illinois Press, 1989); Ted Ownby, *Subduing Satan: Religion, Recreation, and Manhood in the Rural South, 1865–1920* (Chapel Hill: University of North Carolina Press, 1990). For the expanded public role of women later in the nineteenth century, see Evelyn Brooks Higginbotham, *Righteous Discontent: The Women's Movement in the Black Baptist Church, 1880–1920* (Cambridge: Harvard University Press, 1993) and John Patrick McDowell, *The Social Gospel in the South: The Woman's Home Mission Movement in the Methodist Episcopal Church, South, 1886–1939* (Baton Rouge: Louisiana State University Press, 1982).

11. On the unity of southern classes in "an essentially solid Southern society," which became the Confederacy, see Emory M. Thomas, *The Confederate Nation, 1861–1865* (New York: Harper and Row, 1979), 6–10, 233–34 (quotation, 10). George C. Rable observes: "few white women could transcend barriers of race and class to develop a sympathetic understanding of the slave's plight." Instead, they united with southern men in upholding the peculiar institution. Randall C. Jimerson, in his study of popular thought during the Civil War,

found that "sectional consciousness . . . constitutes the most pervasive and significant dividing line in popular thought during the war." However, Jimerson also admitted that social class was one of several factors that "limited sectional cohesiveness to varying degrees." Rable, *Civil Wars*, 31–32; Randall C. Jimerson, *The Private Civil War: Popular Thought during the Sectional Conflict* (Baton Rouge: Louisiana State University Press, 1988), 180–81, 191–98 (quotation, 181).

12. Lewis O. Saum, *The Popular Mood of Pre–Civil War America* (Westport, CT: Greenwood Press, 1980), xxii, 3–26; Samuel S. Hill Jr., *The South and the North in American Religion* (Athens: University of Georgia Press, 1980), 46–47. See also Ernest Lee Tuveson, *Redeemer Nation: The Idea of America's Millennial Role* (Chicago: University of Chicago Press, 1968), 187–208; Peter J. Parish, "The Instruments of Providence: Slavery, Civil War and the American Churches," in *The Church and War,* ed. W. J. Sheils (Oxford: Basil Blackwell, 1983), 291–320; Ronald Glenn Lee, "Exploded Graces: Providence and the Confederate Israel in Evangelical Southern Sermons, 1861–1865" (M.A. thesis, Rice University, 1990), 3–4, 202–10.

In his study of popular thought during the Civil War, Randall C. Jimerson notes that the American people were "bound by common political ideas and loyalties, reinforced by a common culture and a common tradition. . . . The sectional cleavage ran deep, but not deep enough to eliminate all traces of common American characteristics. The war thus reveals not two different civilizations, but one people divided by conflicting interpretations of common American values." Prominent among those values were religious beliefs and ideals, topics Jimerson does not address. Jimerson, *The Private Civil War*, 180.

13. Entry for 17 May 1863, Eliza Rhea Fain Diaries, John N. Fain Collection, McClung Historical Collection, Knox County Public Library System, Knoxville, TN.

14. Lucius Henry Holsey, *Autobiography, Sermons, Addresses, and Essays*, 2d ed. (Atlanta, GA: Franklin Printing and Publishing, 1899), 9–18; John Brother Cade, *Holsey—The Incomparable* (New York: Pageant Press, 1964), 1–7; Glenn T. Eskew, "Black Elitism and the Failure of Paternalism in Postbellum Georgia: The Case of Bishop Lucius Henry Holsey," *Journal of Southern History* 58 (November 1992), 639–40; William Pope Harrison, ed., *The Gospel among the Slaves* (Nashville, TN: Publishing House of the Methodist Episcopal Church, South, 1893; reprint, New York: AMS Press, 1973), 384–87.

15. Memoirs of Thomas Hooke McCallie (1901–12), McCallie Family Papers, McCallie School, Chattanooga, TN.

16. Elizabeth Caldwell to John H. Caldwell, 23 May 1849, in private possession of Marion T. Caldwell, Lookout Mountain, TN. For Caldwell's antebellum career, see Daniel W. Stowell, "'We Have Sinned and God Has Smitten Us!' John H. Caldwell and the Religious Meaning of Confederate Defeat," *Georgia Historical Quarterly* 78 (Spring 1994): 5–7; Andrew Leary O'Brien, *The Journal of Andrew Leary O'Brien; Including an Account of the Origin of Andrew College* (Athens: University of Georgia Press, 1946), 54; *Minutes of the Annual Conferences of the Methodist Episcopal Church, South, 1845–1865* (Nashville, TN: Methodist Publishing House, 1846–70),

17. *Christian Recorder*, 14 March 1863. For Turner's antebellum career, see Stephen Ward Angell, *Bishop Henry McNeal Turner and African-American Religion in the South* (Knoxville: University of Tennessee Press, 1992), 7–33, 56; Clarence E. Walker, *A Rock in a Weary Land: The African Methodist Episcopal Church during the Civil War and Reconstruction* (Baton Rouge: Louisiana State University Press, 1982), 122–23.

18. Joanna P. Moore, *"In Christ's Stead": Autobiographical Sketches* (Chicago: Women's Baptist Home Mission Society, 1903), 1–22; Grace M. Eaton, *A Heroine of the Cross: Sketches of the Life and Work of Miss Joanna P. Moore* (n. p., n. d.), 18–27.

19. James M. McPherson, *Battle Cry of Freedom: The Civil War Era* (New York: Oxford University Press, 1988); Eric Foner, *Reconstruction: America's Unfinished Revolution,*

1863–1877 (New York: Harper and Row, 1988), 88–95. Kenneth M. Stampp's classic revisionist synthesis gives no attention to religion. Kenneth M. Stampp, *The Era of Reconstruction, 1865–1877* (New York: Knopf, 1965).

20. Drew Gilpin Faust, *The Creation of Confederate Nationalism: Ideology and Identity in the Civil War South* (Baton Rouge: Louisiana State University Press, 1988); Richard E. Beringer et al., *Why the South Lost the Civil War* (Athens: University of Georgia Press, 1986); James H. Moorhead, *American Apocalypse: Yankee Protestants and the Civil War, 1860–1869* (New Haven: Yale University Press, 1978); Phillip Shaw Paludan, *"A People's Contest": The Union and the Civil War, 1861–1865* (New York: Harper and Row, 1988), 339–74; Gardiner H. Shattuck Jr., *A Shield and Hiding Place: The Religious Life of the Civil War Armies* (Macon, GA: Mercer University Press, 1987); Drew Gilpin Faust, "Christian Soldiers: The Meaning of Revivalism in the Confederate Army," *Journal of Southern History* 53 (February 1987): 63–90; Reid Mitchell, *The Vacant Chair: The Northern Soldier Leaves Home* (New York: Oxford University Press, 1993); Charles Reagan Wilson, *Baptized in Blood: The Religion of the Lost Cause, 1865–1920* (Athens: University of Georgia Press, 1980); Gaines M. Foster, *Ghosts of the Confederacy: Defeat, the Lost Cause, and the Emergence of the New South* (New York: Oxford University Press, 1987). See also Thomas L. Connelly and Barbara L. Bellows, *God and General Longstreet: The Lost Cause and the Southern Mind* (Baton Rouge: Louisiana State University Press, 1982) and Gregory J. W. Urwin, "'The Lord Has Not Forsaken Me and I Won't Forsake Him': Religion in Frederick Steele's Union Army, 1863–1864," *Arkansas Historical Quarterly* 52 (Autumn 1993), 318–40.

21. Rufus B. Spain, *At Ease in Zion: A Social History of Southern Baptists, 1865–1900* (Nashville, TN: Vanderbilt University Press, 1967); John Lee Eighmy, *Churches in Cultural Captivity: A History of the Social Attitudes of Southern Baptists*, rev. ed. (Knoxville: University of Tennessee Press, 1987); Hunter Dickinson Farish, *The Circuit Rider Dismounts: A Social History of Southern Methodism, 1865-1900* (Richmond, VA: Dietz Press, 1938); Ralph E. Morrow, *Northern Methodism and Reconstruction* (East Lansing: Michigan State University Press, 1956); Donald G. Jones, *The Sectional Crisis and Northern Methodism: A Study in Piety, Political Ethics, and Civil Religion* (Metuchen, NJ: Scarecrow Press, 1979); Lewis G. Vander Velde, *The Presbyterian Churches and the Federal Union, 1861–1869* (Cambridge: Harvard University Press, 1932); Ernest Trice Thompson, *Presbyterians in the South*, 3 vols. (Richmond, VA: John Knox Press, 1963–73).

22. Walker, *A Rock in a Weary Land*; Angell, *Bishop Henry McNeal Turner*; Katharine L. Dvorak, *An African-American Exodus: The Segregation of the Southern Churches* (Brooklyn, NY: Carlson Publishing, 1991); James Melvin Washington, *Frustrated Fellowship: The Black Baptist Quest for Social Power* (Macon, GA: Mercer University Press, 1986); William E. Montgomery, *Under Their Own Vine and Fig Tree: The African-American Church in the South, 1865–1900* (Baton Rouge: Louisiana State University Press, 1993).

23. Hildebrand, *The Times Were Strange and Stirring*, xviii.

24. United States, Census Office, *Statistics of the United States, in 1860; Compiled from the Original Returns and Being the Final Exhibit of the Eighth Census, under the Direction of the Secretary of the Interior* (Washington, DC: Government Printing Office, 1866), 365–70, 465–70; Edwin S. Gaustad, *Historical Atlas of Religion in America* (New York: Harper and Row, 1962), 58.

1 God's Wrath

1. For an exploration of life in the occupied South during the war, see Stephen V. Ash, *When the Yankees Came: Conflict and Chaos in the Occupied South, 1861–1865* (Chapel Hill: University of North Carolina Press, 1995).

2. Robert L. Neely, Manuscript Historical Sketch of the Synod of Memphis, 1880, Robert Langdon Neely Collection, Historical Foundation of the Presbyterian and Reformed Churches, Montreat, NC (quotations); W. Harrison Daniel, "The Effects of the Civil War on Southern Protestantism," *Maryland Historical Magazine* 69 (Spring 1974): 57–58.

3. Daniel, "The Effects of the Civil War on Southern Protestantism," 57; George F. Pierce to his son Lovick Pierce Jr., 15 October 1861, quoted in George Gilman Smith, *The Life and Times of George Foster Pierce* (Sparta, GA: Hancock Publishing, 1888), 444.

4. Daniel, "The Effects of the Civil War on Southern Protestantism," 58, Jesse L. Boyd, *A Popular History of the Baptists in Mississippi* (Jackson, MS: Baptist Press, 1930), 111; W. Fred Kendall, *A History of the Tennessee Baptist Convention* (Brentwood, TN: Executive Board of the Tennessee Baptist Convention, 1974), 135; Georgia Baptist Convention, *Minutes, 1866*; James Pickett Jones, *Yankee Blitzkrieg: Wilson's Raid through Alabama and Georgia* (Athens: University of Georgia Press, 1976), 136–38.

5. Memoirs of Thomas Hooke McCallie (1901–12), McCallie Family Papers, McCallie School, Chattanooga, TN. For religious life in occupied areas of the South, see Stephen V. Ash, *Middle Tennessee Society Transformed, 1860–1870: War and Peace in the Upper South* (Baton Rouge: Louisiana State University Press, 1988), 101–5; Ash, *When the Yankees Came,* 89–90, 97–98; Walter T. Durham, *Nashville: The Occupied City, The First Seventeen Months, February 16, 1862, to June 30, 1863* (Nashville: Tennessee Historical Society, 1985), 154–58; Walter T. Durham, *Reluctant Partners: Nashville and the Union, July 1, 1863, to June 30, 1865* (Nashville: Tennessee Historical Society, 1987), 49–51, 137–41.

6. Minute Book, Candays Creek Baptist Church, Bradley County, Tennessee, 1846–1866, 1st Saturday in June 1864, Tennessee State Library and Archives, Nashville, TN; Session Book, Monticello Presbyterian Church, Jasper County, Georgia, 1829–1904, 23 November 1863, Georgia Department of Archives and History, Atlanta, GA; Quarterly Conference Minutes, Port Gibson Station, Mississippi, 1848–1872, 18 June 1864, Mississippi Conference Historical Society, quoted in Willard Eugene Wight, "Churches in the Confederacy" (Ph.D. diss., Emory University, 1957), 86, Dolly Sumner Lunt Burge, *A Woman's Wartime Journal: An Account of the Passage over a Georgia Plantation of Sherman's Army on the March to the Sea* (Macon, GA: J. W. Burke, 1927), 19–20 (journal entry of 24 July 1864); Record Book, St. Paul's Presbyterian Church, Hamblen County, Tennessee, 1858–1875, 2 April 1865, Tennessee State Library and Archives.

For religious life in the expanding "no-man's-land" of the South that was regularly patrolled by Union forces from garrisoned towns, see Ash, *When the Yankees Came,* 104–5.

7. Wesley Norton, "The Role of a Religious Newspaper in Georgia during the Civil War," *Georgia Historical Quarterly* 48 (June 1964): 125–26; *Christian Observer,* 3 January 1861, 12 August 1863, 5 May 1864, 5 January 1865; Joseph Mitchell, "Southern Methodist Newspapers during the Civil War," *Methodist History* 11 (January 1973): 23; *Southern Presbyterian* 16 April 1863 (quotation); 17 December 1863; 16 June 1864 (quotation); 20 October 1864.

The Georgia Baptist *Christian Index* raised its subscription rate to $20 per year on January 12, 1865; two weeks later the price rose to $15 for six months. *Christian Index,* 12, 26 January 1865.

William E. Pell, editor of the *North Carolina Christian Advocate,* lamented the burning in 1863 of the paper mill at Bath, North Carolina, and urged his readers to sell their rags to the remaining mills. *North Carolina Christian Advocate,* 16 April 1863; Henry Smith Stroupe, *The Religious Press in the South Atlantic States, 1802–1865* (Durham, NC: Duke University Press, 1956; reprint, New York: AMS Press, 1970), 36, 93.

8. Mitchell, "Southern Methodist Newspapers during the Civil War," 20–23; Macum Phelan, *A History of Early Methodism in Texas, 1817–1866* (Nashville, TN: Cokesbury Press, 1924), 463; *Southern Christian Advocate,* 29 June 1865. Macon surrendered to the vanguard of General Wilson's cavalry on April 20. Jones, *Yankee Blitzkrieg,* 167.

According to W. Harrison Daniel, "inflation, a shortage of materials, and federal occupation forced the suspension of one-half of the religious weeklies in the South by the end of 1862." All Southern religious newspapers faced occasional suspensions during the war. Daniel, "The Effects of the Civil War on Southern Protestantism," 50–51; W. Harrison Daniel, *Southern Protestantism in the Confederacy* (Bedford, VA: Print Shop, 1989), 154.

9. John Abernathy Smith, *Cross and Flame: Two Centuries of United Methodism in Middle Tennessee* (Nashville, TN: Commission on Archives and History of the Tennessee Conference, 1984), 142–43; *Southern Christian Advocate*, March 1862, quoted in J. J. Tigert IV, *Bishop Holland Nimmons McTyeire: Ecclesiastical and Educational Architect* (Nashville, TN: Vanderbilt University Press, 1955), 124. See also James Penn Pilkington, *The Methodist Publishing House, A History, Volume I: Beginnings to 1870* (Nashville, TN: Abindgon Press, 1968).

10. *Southern Presbyterian*, 16 June, 20 October 1864, 4 January 1866; Arnold Shankman, "Converse, *The Christian Observer*, and Civil War Censorship," *Journal of Presbyterian History* 52 (1974): 240; Ernest Trice Thompson, *Presbyterians in the South*, 3 vols. (Richmond, VA: John Knox Press, 1963–73), 2:85, 435–39; Haskell M. Monroe Jr., "The Presbyterian Church in the Confederate States of America" (Ph.D. diss., Rice University, 1961), 326, 328; *Christian Index*, 9 November 1865, 6 January 1866; Norton, "The Role of a Religious Newspaper in Georgia," 139.

11. George B. Taylor, *Life and Times of James B. Taylor* (Philadelphia: Bible and Publication Society, 1872), 265; Jesse C. Fletcher, "A History of the Foreign Mission Board of the Southern Baptist Convention during the Civil War," *Baptist History and Heritage* 10 (October 1975): 205–6, 213–14.

12. Charles E. Taylor, *The Story of Yates the Missionary, As Told in His Letters and Reminiscences* (Nashville, TN: Sunday School Board, 1898), 147, 150; Fletcher, "A History of the Foreign Mission Board," 217–19 (quotations on 217, 218); Holland N. McTyeire, *History of Methodism* (Nashville, TN: Southern Methodist Publishing House, 1884), 665; Edith M. Jeter, "Under the Banner of King Jesus: Foreign Missions and the Civil War," *Baptist History and Heritage* 32 (July/October 1997): 89–99; Daniel, "The Effects of the Civil War on Southern Protestantism," 44.

13. Thompson, *Presbyterians in the South*, 2:20–22; Monroe, "The Presbyterian Church in the Confederate States of America," 294, 305, 309; McTyeire, *History of Methodism*, 665–66.

14. James F. Sulzby Jr., *Toward a History of Samford University*, 2 vols. (Birmingham, AL: Samford University Press, 1986), 1:44; Centenary College Faculty Minutes, 17 October 1861, quoted in Ralph Eugene Reed Jr., "Fortresses of Faith: Design and Experience at Southern Evangelical Colleges, 1830–1900" (Ph.D. diss., Emory University, 1991), 257; Reed, "Fortresses of Faith," 255–57; Charles Finney Ogilvie, "Alabama Baptists during the Civil War and Reconstruction" (Th.M. thesis, Southwestern Baptist Theological Seminary, 1956), 27–28; Comer Hastings, "The Methodist Episcopal Church, South during the Reconstruction Period" (M.A. thesis, Duke University, 1932), 16; Daniel, "The Effects of the Civil War on Southern Protestantism," 54; Samuel Luttrell Akers, *The First Hundred Years of Wesleyan College, 1836–1936* (Macon, GA: Beehive Press, 1976), 74; B. D. Ragsdale, *Story of Georgia Baptists*, 3 vols. (Macon, GA: Mercer University Press, 1935–38), 2:177, 3:106; Bethel Baptist Association, *Minutes*, 1865, 6.

Dr. George W. Carter, president of Soule University in Texas, became a colonel in the Confederate army and led his students to battle. Phelan, *A History of Early Methodism in Texas*, 464–67.

15. Spright Dowell, *A History of Mercer University, 1833–1953* (Macon, GA: Mercer University Press, 1958), 409; Charles F. Pitts, *Chaplains in Gray: The Confederate Chaplains' Story* (Nashville, TN: Broadman Press, 1957), 28; Waller Raymond Cooper, *Southwestern at*

Memphis, 1848–1948 (Richmond, VA: John Knox Press, 1949), 30–31; Winstead Paine Bone, *A History of Cumberland University* (Lebanon, TN: published by the author, 1935), 82; Georgia Baptist Convention, *Minutes*, 1866, 18 (quotation); *List of War Claims, Confined Entirely to Claims for Use and Occupation or Rent of Church Buildings, College Buildings, and Other Public Buildings, by the Military Forces of the United States During the War, Coupled in Some Cases with a Claim for Damages Done to the Building During the Occupancy With a Statement of Each Case Compiled for Convenience of Members of the Senate Committee on Claims in Connection with an Examination of H. R. 19115* (Washington, DC: Government Printing Office, 1912), 35.

16. *Southern Presbyterian,* 4 January 1866; W. Harrison Daniel, "Southern Presbyterians in the Confederacy," *North Carolina Historical Review* 44 (Summer 1967): 253. Presbyterian minister James A. Lyon wrote in his diary that he warned the treasurer of the seminary that investing in Confederate bonds was unwise, because even if the Confederacy succeeded, he believed all Confederate money and bonds would be repudiated. James Adair Lyon, Diary, 1861–1870, entry for May 1863, Historical Foundation of the Presbyterian and Reformed Churches, Montreat, NC; Synod of Georgia, *Minutes*, 1865, 12–13.

17. Reed, "Fortresses of Faith," 272–73; Daniel, "The Effects of the Civil War on Southern Protestantism," 52; Hastings, "The Methodist Episcopal Church, South during the Reconstruction Period," 15–16; Thompson, *Presbyterians in the South,* 2:97.

Even the Baptist trustees of the small Hearn School in Rome, Georgia, invested its endowment of $4,000 in Confederate bonds. Georgia Baptist Convention, *Minutes*, 1866, 18.

18. William H. Nelson, *A Burning Torch and a Flaming Fire: The Story of Centenary College of Louisiana* (Nashville, TN: Methodist Publishing House, 1931), 177–82; Daniel, "The Effects of the Civil War on Southern Protestantism," 54; George J. Stevenson, *Increase in Excellence: A History of Emory and Henry College* (New York: Appleton-Century-Crofts, 1963), 92–96; Allen Tankersley, *College Life at Old Oglethorpe* (Athens: University of Georgia Press, 1951), 108–13; Henry M. Bullock, *A History of Emory University* (Nashville, TN: Parthenon Press, 1936), 149; George V. Irons, "Howard College as a Confederate Military Hospital," *Alabama Review* 9 (January 1956): 22–23; Bethel Baptist Association, *Minutes*, 1865, 6; Irby D. Engram, "A History of Andrew College" (M.A. thesis, Emory University, 1939), 26–27.

19. Cooper, *Southwestern at Memphis, 1848–1948,* 30–31 (quotation); Synod of Memphis, *Minutes*, 1860–1865, meeting of 1862, Historical Foundation of the Presbyterian and Reformed Churches, Montreat, NC; John N. Waddel, *Memorials of Academic Life* (Richmond, VA: Presbyterian Committee of Publication, 1891), 365; *Churches and Institutions of Learning Destroyed by the United States Military Forces During the Civil War, But Not as an Act of Military Necessity, The Materials Having Been Appropriated and Used* (Washington, DC: Government Printing Office, 1912), 12; J. Barien Lindsley, "Outline History of Cumberland University at Lebanon, Tennessee, 1842–1876," *Theological Medium* 12 (October 1876): 437–38; Bone, *A History of Cumberland University,* 82, 87; *List of War Claims, Confined Entirely to Claims for Use and Occupation or Rent,* 34; Ragsdale, *Story of Georgia Baptists,* 3:106; Bainbridge District Conference, Minutes, 1867–1878, April 1868 meeting, South Georgia Conference Archives, Epworth-by-the-Sea, GA; Ogilvie, "Alabama Baptists during the Civil War and Reconstruction," 28.

20. Memoirs of Thomas Hooke McCallie (Chattanooga quotation); Fannie A. Beers, *Memories: A Record of Personal Experience and Adventure during Four Years of War* (Philadelphia: J. B. Lippincott, 1889), 80; Kate Cumming, *Kate: The Journal of a Confederate Nurse,* ed. Richard Barksdale Harwell (Baton Rouge: Louisiana State University Press, 1959), 144, 207; Glenn A. Toomey, *Jubilee Three: History of the Sweetwater Baptist Association and its Affiliated Churches, 1830–1980* (Madisonville, TN: n.p., 1980), 77 (Sweetwater quotation); *List of War Claims, Confined Entirely to Claims for Use and Occupation or Rent,* 29, 33 (Franklin

quotation, 33); Fred T. Wooten Jr., "Religious Activities in Civil War Memphis," *Tennessee Historical Quarterly* 3 (September 1944): 261–62 (Memphis quotation).

The United States government later reimbursed some churches for the use of their buildings by the Union army. The Presbyterian Church in Chattanooga received $4,590 for damages through the influence of the wife of a prominent local Unionist. *Chattanooga Daily Gazette*, 23 September 1865; Zella Armstrong, *History of the First Presbyterian Church of Chattanooga* (Chattanooga, TN: n.p., 1945), reprinted in David Cooper, *Catalyst for Christ, 150 Years: First Presbyterian Church, Chattanooga, Tennessee* (Chattanooga, TN: Chattanooga News-Free Press, 1990), 23.

21. Beers, *Memories*, 80; Cumming, *Kate*, 144; *Southern Presbyterian*, 5 November 1863.

22. *List of War Claims Including a Few Exceptional Cases for Churches; Also List of Other Claims to Which Objections Appear, Such as Laches, No Proof of Loyalty, Insufficient Evidence as to Facts, Evidence of Payment and Statutory Bars, With a Statement of Each Case Compiled for the Convenience of Members of the Senate Committee on Claims in Connection With an Examination of H.R. 19115* (Washington, DC: Government Printing Office, 1912), 11; Daniel, "The Effects of the Civil War on Southern Protestantism," 48–49; *List of War Claims, Confined Entirely to Claims for Use and Occupation or Rent*, 31–32, 36; *Churches and Institutions of Learning Destroyed*, 7; Hunter Dickinson Farish, *The Circuit Rider Dismounts: A Social History of Southern Methodism, 1865–1900* (Richmond, VA: Dietz Press, 1938), 29; Dover Baptist Association, *Minutes*, 1864, 20, quoted in Bell Irvin Wiley, *Southern Negroes, 1861–1865* (New Haven: Yale University Press, 1938), 101; Monroe, "The Presbyterian Church in the Confederate States of America," 312.

The Central Presbyterian Church in Atlanta was, according to its returning pastor, "very little injured" in its use by the Federal troops. Robert Quarterman Mallard Papers, Pastoral Record, 1855–1865, entry of May 14, 1865, Historical Foundation of the Presbyterian and Reformed Churches, Montreat NC.

23. Garnett Ryland, *The Baptists of Virginia, 1699–1926* (Richmond, VA: Baptist Board of Missions and Education, 1955), 297; *American Annual Cyclopaedia and Register of Important Events* 6, 1866 (New York: Appleton, 1870), 625; Stephen F. Fleharty, *Our Regiment. A History of the 102nd Illinois Infantry Volunteers* (Chicago: Brewster and Hanscom, 1865), 132; *List of War Claims, Confined Entirely to Claims for Use and Occupation or Rent*, 29 (Bolivar quotation); *List of War Claims Including a Few Exceptional Cases for Churches*, 11.

24. William Warren Sweet, *The Methodist Episcopal Church and the Civil War* (Cincinnati: Methodist Book Concern Press, 1912), 222–24; Pitts, *Chaplains in Gray*, 28–29; Gerald J. Smith, *Smite Them Hip and Thigh! Georgia Methodist Ministers in the Confederate Military* (Augusta, GA: published by the author, 1993), x, 172; Monroe, "The Presbyterian Church in the Confederate States of America," 336–38; Daniel, *Southern Protestantism in the Confederacy*, 32; James Stacy, *A History of the Presbyterian Church in Georgia* (Elberton, GA: Press of the Star, 1912), 181–82 (Alabama Presbyterian quotation); *Christian Advocate* (Nashville, TN), 8 May 1861 (New Orleans Methodist quotation). See also Sidney J. Romero, "Louisiana Clergy and the Confederate Army," *Louisiana History* 2 (Summer 1961): 277–300, and James W. Silver, "The Confederate Preacher Goes to War," *North Carolina Historical Review* 33 (October 1956): 499–509.

For further discussion of Confederate chaplains and religion in the Confederate armies, see Sidney J. Romero, *Religion in the Rebel Ranks* (Lanham, MD: University Press of America, 1983); Daniel, *Southern Protestantism in the Confederacy*; and Gardiner H. Shattuck Jr., *A Shield and Hiding Place: The Religious Life of the Civil War Armies* (Macon, GA: Mercer University Press, 1987).

25. W. Stanley Hoole, "The Diary of Dr. Basil Manly, 1858–1867," pt. 2, *Alabama Review* 4 (July 1951): 223.

26. Smith, *The Life and Times of George Foster Pierce*, 482; V. C. Clarke to James E. Bradley, 12 July 1864, James E. Bradley and Family Papers, Louisiana State University Archives, Baton Rouge, LA, quoted in Willard E. Wight, ed., "Pay the Preacher! Two Letters from Louisiana, 1864," *Louisiana History* 1 (Summer 1960): 255–56 (Louisiana Methodist quotations); J. L. M. Curry to Basil Manly II, 26 October 1866, Manly Collection of Manuscripts, Southern Baptist Historical Library and Archives, Nashville, TN; John C. Ley, *Fifty-Two Years in Florida* (Nashville, TN: Publishing House of the Methodist Episcopal Church, South, 1899), 90–91, 94 (Florida Methodist quotation, 90); *Southern Presbyterian*, 25 January 1866; Thomas W. Caskey, *Caskey's Last Book, Containing an Autobiographical Sketch of His Ministerial Life, with Essays and Sermons* (Nashville, TN: Messenger Publishing, 1896), 48; Smith, *The Life and Times of George Foster Pierce*, 491 (Methodist minister and historian quotations).

27. J. L. M. Curry to Basil Manly II, 26 October 1866, Manly Collection of Manuscripts. (Basil Manly Sr. is also Basil Manly II. Although his father was Basil Manly, Basil Manly Sr. named his oldest son Basil Manly Jr. Both Basil Sr. and Basil Jr. were active in the Southern Baptist Convention.)

Gerald J. Smith's careful study of Methodist and Confederate records reveals that at least 138 local preachers, exhorters, licensed preachers, and ordained deacons and elders from the Georgia Conference entered Confederate service as soldiers, officers, or chaplains. Twenty-two (16 percent) died in battle or of wounds or disease sustained while in Confederate service. Smith, *Smite Them Hip and Thigh*, 103–62, 172.

28. *Memorials of Methodism in Macon, Georgia, from 1828 to 1878* (Macon, GA: J. W. Burke, 1879), 34; Memoirs of Thomas Hooke McCallie; Daniel, "The Effects of the Civil War on Southern Protestantism," 60. Although the membership statistics given in table 1-1 are undoubtedly inaccurate because of the breakdown of ecclesiastical structures in the later years of the war, they do reveal the general trend. More important, they reflect the perception of southern evangelicals when they considered their denominations in 1865 and 1866.

29. Georgia Baptist Convention, *Minutes*, 1860, 1867; Georgia Annual Conference (MECS), *Minutes*, 1860, 1866; General Assembly of the Presbyterian Church in the United States of America (PCUSA) (Old School), *Minutes*, 1860; General Assembly of the Presbyterian Church in the United States (PCUS), *Minutes*, 1866. Once again, the figures are not completely accurate, though it is difficult to determine if membership as a whole is overestimated by the use of previous years' figures or underestimated by the failure of some associations, quarterly conferences, and presbyteries to report their statistics.

The Baptist figures are those reported at the April 1867 meeting of the Georgia Baptist Convention; they were reported to the various associations in the fall of 1866. These totals include all associations that were members of the Georgia Baptist Convention in 1877. They do not include the many primitive and the nonaligned missionary Baptists; the Georgia Baptist Convention represented approximately two-thirds of the Baptists in the state in this period. Of the twenty-eight associations extant in 1866, the data for fourteen were interpolated from known endpoints for each association. In several cases, the data were interpolated over only two years, but in others the range of missing data was much longer. Interpolation, therefore, smooths what was probably a large loss of membership in 1864–65 and a recovery thereafter.

Several Methodist churches in southern Georgia were in the Florida Annual Conference until 1866; the figures presented here include only those churches in the Georgia Annual Conference.

The Presbytery of Florida was one of the five presbyteries that made up the Synod of Georgia in this period.

30. By the spring of 1867, Georgia churches had begun to recover from the losses of the war, although many black members were yet to leave. The Georgia Association of the Georgia Baptist Convention, for example, lost 2,219 members between 1867 and 1868, most of them

freedpeople. Georgia Baptist Convention, *Minutes,* 1860, 1867; Robert G. Gardner et al., *A History of the Georgia Baptist Association,* 1784–1984 (Atlanta: Georgia Baptist Historical Society, 1988), 204, 213, 219.

31. Phelan, *A History of Early Methodism in Texas,* 467; *Cincinnati Gazette,* 16 June 1865; John N. Waddel Diary, 1 December 1863, 12 December 1864, John N. Waddel Papers, Library of Congress, quoted in Reed, "Fortresses of Faith," 264; *Southern Presbyterian,* 22 December 1864; *Central Presbyterian,* 27 August 1863.

32. Mary Jones to Joseph Jones, 2 May 1865, Joseph Jones Papers, Hill Memorial Library, Louisiana State University, Baton Rouge, quoted in Gaines M. Foster, *Ghosts of the Confederacy: Defeat, the Lost Cause, and the Emergence of the New South* (New York: Oxford University Press, 1987), 13; Entry for 10 May 1865, Grace Elmore Brown Diary, South Caroliniana Library, Columbia, quoted in Foster, *Ghosts of the Confederacy,* 13; Entries for 21 April, 21 May 1865, Eliza Rhea Fain Diaries, John N. Fain Collection, McClung Historical Collection, Knox County Public Library System, Knoxville, TN. See also Drew Gilpin Faust, *Mothers of Invention: Women of the Slaveholding South in the American Civil War* (Chapel Hill: University of North Carolina Press, 1996), 187–95, and George C. Rable, *Civil Wars: Women and the Crisis of Southern Nationalism* (Urbana: University of Illinois Press, 1989), 221–39.

33. South Carolina Presbytery, Minutes, September 1865, Historical Foundation of the Presbyterian and Reformed Churches, Montreat, NC; William Safford to Mrs. Mary Thompson, 26 December 1865, Safford Family Papers, Correspondence, 1863–1877, Historical Foundation of the Presbyterian and Reformed Churches, Montreat, NC; J. W. Kincheloe to Joseph Holt, 20 September 1865, Joseph Holt Papers, L, 6605–a, Library of Congress, quoted in E. Merton Coulter, *The Civil War and Readjustment in Kentucky* (Chapel Hill: University of North Carolina Press, 1926), 395; S. H. Ford, "Duty of Southern Churches," *Christian Repository and Family Visitor: A Southern Religious and Literary Monthly* 10 (June 1866): 65.

A correspondent to the *Christian Index* in January 1866 wrote:

> the providence of God, in this unexpected consummation, is to us an unfathomable mystery — we do not comprehend, and we have no right to comprehend it. Who are we, that we should arraign the wisdom of the great God? . . . It is our duty to submit, and to believe that the Lord of all the earth will do right. Yet by this mysterious providence the faith of some good men, in the justice of God, has been shaken; against this evil effect they, doubtless, struggle; but the harm is, it deadens the zeal and excuses inertness. ("Religious Literature for the South," *Christian Index,* 13 January 1866.)

The feeling that God had deserted them manifested itself in the army as well. One Presbyterian chaplain on hand for the surrender of the Confederate Army "wondered what had happened. Why had defeat finally overtaken the people of the South? Had God forgotten His flock?" William E. Boggs, *The Secession of South Carolina and Her Ten Sister States* (Columbia, SC: n.p., 1915), 3, quoted in Monroe, "The Presbyterian Church in the Confederate States of America," 330.

Jack P. Maddex Jr. writes that the downfall of the Confederacy turned southern Calvinists' "progressive millennialist confidence" into "millenarian desperation." The loss "crushed the very structure of their hopes and plunged them into a crisis of faith." Jack P. Maddex Jr., "Proslavery Millenialism: Social Eschatology in Antebellum Southern Calvinism," *American Quarterly* 31 (Spring 1979): 59.

34. Virginia Ingraham Burr, ed., *The Secret Eye: The Journal of Ella Gertrude Clanton Thomas, 1848–1889* (Chapel Hill: University of North Carolina Press, 1990), 276–77; Alfred Mann Pierce, *Lest Faith Forget: The Story of Methodism in Georgia* (Atlanta: Georgia Methodist Information, 1951), 111.

35. American Baptist Home Mission Society (ABHMS), *Annual Report*, 1862, 50–51 (quotations); Robert Andrew Baker, *Relations between Northern and Southern Baptists* (n.p., 1954; reprint, New York: Arno Press, 1980), 90; Oliver Saxon Heckman, "Northern Church Penetration of the South, 1860 to 1880" (Ph.D. diss., Duke University, 1939), 232. The 1864 figure includes only missionaries; the 1865 figure includes both missionaries and teachers.

36. Sweet, *The Methodist Episcopal Church and the Civil War*, 100, 139; General Conference of the Methodist Episcopal Church, *Journal*, 1864, 278–79; Frank K. Pool, "The Southern Negro in the Methodist Episcopal Church" (Ph.D. diss., Duke University, 1939), 45; "Rev. Dr. Newman's Address in New Orleans," *True Delta*, 28 March 1864, quoted in Edward McPherson, *The Political History of the United States of America During the Great Rebellion*, 2d ed. (Washington, DC: Philip and Solomons, 1865), 523; Isaac Patton Martin, *Methodism in Holston* (Knoxville, TN: Methodist Historical Society, 1945), 81–87; Smith, *The Life and Times of George Foster Pierce*, 490.

37. General Assembly of the PCUSA (New School), *Minutes*, 1864, 545 (quotation); Harold M. Parker Jr., *The United Synod of the South: The Southern New School Presbyterian Church* (Westport, CT: Greenwood Press, 1988), 271–74; General Assembly of the PCUSA (New School), *Minutes*, 1866, 77 (quotation); General Assembly of the PCUSA (Old School), *Minutes*, 1865, 553–54 (quotations).

38. Ralph E. Morrow, *Northern Methodism and Reconstruction* (East Lansing: Michigan State University Press, 1956), 155–56; Franklin C. Talmage, *The Story of the Synod of Georgia* (n.p., 1961), 75.

39. *Christian Recorder*, 30 May 1863; Clarence E. Walker, *A Rock in a Weary Land: The African Methodist Episcopal Church during the Civil War and Reconstruction* (Baton Rouge: Louisiana State University Press, 1982), 49–50, 64; Daniel A. Payne, *A History of the African Methodist Episcopal Church*, ed. C. S. Smith (Nashville, TN: Publishing House of the AME Sunday School Union, 1891), 471–72; David Henry Bradley Sr., *A History of the AME Zion Church, 1796–1872* (Nashville, TN: Parthenon Press, 1956), 160–62.

40. Sweet, *The Methodist Episcopal Church and the Civil War*, 96; S. Reed to Matthew Simpson, 23 November 1863, quoted in Robert D. Clark, *The Life of Matthew Simpson* (New York: Macmillan, 1956), 230; McPherson, *The Political History of the United States of America*, 521 (War Department order quotations). See also Circular, 12 February 1864, in *The War of the Rebellion: A Compilation of the Official Records of the Union and Confederate Armies*, 128 vols. (Washington, DC: Government Printing Office, 1881–1901), ser. 1, vol. 34, part 2, p. 311.

41. McPherson, *The Political History of the United States of America*, 521–22; Baker, *Relations between Northern and Southern Baptists*, 88–89.
The radically abolitionist American Baptist Free Mission Society harshly denounced the ABHMS for violating the separation of church and state and for ousting black majorities as well as white minorities when they seized many southern church buildings. The American Baptist Free Mission Society preferred that title to the confiscated buildings be transferred to the black majorities of local churches. James Melvin Washington, *Frustrated Fellowship: The Black Baptist Quest for Social Power* (Macon, GA: Mercer University Press, 1986), 65–70.

42. *Christian Advocate and Journal*, 4 February 1864 (quotation); Clark, *The Life of Matthew Simpson*, 232–33; Morrow, *Northern Methodism and Reconstruction*, 34–35.

43. R. W. Kennon to O. M. Addison, 4 June 1865, quoted in Phelan, *A History of Early Methodism in Texas*, 486; McPherson, *The Political History of the United States of America*, 522 (Kentucky Presbyterian quotation); *American Annual Cyclopaedia and Register of Important Events 4*, 1864 (New York: Appleton, 1870), 515 (Kentucky Methodist quotation); Morrow, *Northern Methodism and Reconstruction*, 37–39.

44. Smith, *The Life and Times of George Foster Pierce*, 492.

45. *Methodist*, 19 December 1863.

2   God's Chastisement

1. Benjamin Morgan Palmer, *The South: Her Peril and Her Duty. A Discourse delivered in the First Presbyterian Church, New Orleans, on Thursday, November 29, 1860* (New Orleans: n.p., 1860), 6–16; Haskell Monroe, "Bishop Palmer's Thanksgiving Day Address," *Louisiana History* 4 (Spring 1963): 105–18.

2. Thaddeus W. McRae, typescript autobiography, 1880, Thaddeus W. McRae Papers, Historical Foundation of the Presbyterian and Reformed Churches, Montreat, NC. For more on the widespread dissemination and reaction to Palmer's sermon, see Wayne C. Eubank, "Benjamin Morgan Palmer's Thanksgiving Sermon, 1860," in *Antislavery and Disunion, 1858–1861: Studies in the Rhetoric of Compromise and Conflict*, ed. J. Jeffery Auer, (New York: Harper and Row, 1963), 305–8.

3. Benjamin F. Riley, *History of the Baptists of Alabama* (Birmingham, AL: Roberts and Son, 1895), 280 (quotations); James W. Silver, *Confederate Morale and Church Propaganda* (Tuscaloosa, AL: Confederate Publishing, 1957), 16–19; C. C. Goen, *Broken Churches, Broken Nation: Denominational Schisms and the Coming of the Civil War* (Macon, GA: Mercer University Press, 1985), 170–74; Mitchell Snay, *Gospel of Disunion: Religion and Separatism in the Antebellum South* (New York: Cambridge University Press, 1993), 151–80.

The Georgia Baptist Convention, meeting in April 1861, declared: "We declare it to be a pleasure and a duty to avow that, both in feeling and in principle, we approve, endorse, and support the government of the Confederate States of America." Georgia Baptist Convention, *Minutes*, 1861.

Eighteen ministers served as delegates to secession conventions. All opposed remaining in the Union as it was then constituted; ten were immediate secessionists. Ralph A. Wooster, "An Analysis of the Membership of Secession Conventions in the Lower South," *Journal of Southern History* 24 (August 1958): 366.

4. Memoirs of Thomas Hooke McCallie (1901–12), McCallie Family Papers, McCallie School, Chattanooga, TN. For an analysis of Unionists' responses to secession in Upper South states including Tennessee, see Daniel W. Crofts, *Reluctant Confederates: Upper South Unionists in the Secession Crisis* (Chapel Hill: University of North Carolina Press, 1989).

5. Silver, *Confederate Morale*, 25–101; Drew Gilpin Faust, *The Creation of Confederate Nationalism: Ideology and Identity in the Civil War South* (Baton Rouge: Louisiana State University Press, 1988); Richard E. Beringer et al., *Why the South Lost the Civil War* (Athens: University of Georgia Press, 1986), 82–102, 268–76; Willard E. Wight, "The Churches and the Confederate Cause," *Civil War History* 6 (December 1960): 361–73; W. Harrison Daniel, "Protestantism and Patriotism in the Confederacy," *Mississippi Quarterly* 24 (Spring 1971): 117–34; David B. Chesebrough, "A Holy War: The Defense and Support of the Confederacy by Southern Baptists," *American Baptist Quarterly* 6 (March 1987): 17–30.

6. Thomas Smyth, "The Battle of Fort Sumter: Its Mystery and Miracle — God's Mastery and Mercy," *Southern Presbyterian Review* 14 (October 1861): 392; "The New Phase of Our Contest," *Southern Presbyterian*, 29 January 1863; George Foster Pierce and Benjamin Morgan Palmer, *Sermons of Bishop Pierce and Rev. B. M. Palmer, D.D. Delivered Before the General Assembly at Milledgeville, Ga., on Fast Day, March 27, 1863* (Milledgeville, GA: Boughton, Nisbet and Barnes, 1863), 3–5, 39–40; Benjamin Morgan Palmer, *A Discourse Before the General Assembly of South Carolina on December 10, 1863, Appointed by the Legislature as a Day of Fasting, Humiliation and Prayer* (Columbia, SC: Charles P. Pelham, State Printer, 1864). For similar sentiments, see J. J. D. Renfroe, *The Battle Is God's: A Sermon Preached Before Wilcox's Brigade on Fast Day, the 21st of August, 1863, Near Orange Court-House, Va.* (Richmond, VA: MacFarlane and Fergusson, 1863); John Randolph Tucker, *The Southern Church Justified in Its Support of the South in the Present War* (Richmond, VA: n.p.,

1863); and William A. Hall, *The Historic Significance of the Southern Revolution: A Lecture Delivered by Invitation in Petersburg, Va , March 14th and April 29th, 1864, and in Richmond, Va., April 7th and April 21st, 1864* (Petersburg, VA: A. F. Crutchfield, 1864).

7. John H. Caldwell, *A Fast Day Sermon, Preached in Newnan, Ga., April 8, 1864, On the Occasion of the President's Proclamation* (LaGrange, GA: Daily Bulletin Office, 1864), 10–14.

8. *The Army Songster. Dedicated to the Army of Northern Virginia* (Richmond, VA, 1864), 65, quoted in H. Shelton Smith, *In His Image, But . . . : Racism in Southern Religion, 1780–1910* (Durham, NC: Duke University Press, 1972), 191.

9. Augustus Baldwin Longstreet, *Fast-Day Sermon* (Columbia, SC: Townsend and North, 1861), 9–10. On Longstreet, see John D. Wade, *Augustus Baldwin Longstreet: A Study of the Development of Culture in the South* (New York: Macmillan, 1924; reprint, Athens: University of Georgia Press, 1969).

10. Robert Partin, "The Sustaining Faith of an Alabama Soldier," *Civil War History* 6 (December 1960): 435–37; see also Drew Gilpin Faust, "Christian Soldiers: The Meaning of Revivalism in the Confederate Army," *Journal of Southern History* 53 (February 1987): 63–90; Gardiner H. Shattuck Jr., *A Shield and Hiding Place: The Religious Life of the Civil War Armies* (Macon, GA: Mercer University Press, 1987), 35–50, 95–110.

11. Morgan Callaway to Leila Callaway, undated fragment from 1864, Morgan Callaway Papers, Special Collections, Robert W. Woodruff Library, Emory University, Atlanta, GA; William Thomas Conn to Mrs. M. A. Brantley, 25 July 1861, William Thomas Conn Papers, Duke University, quoted in Christopher Hendrick Owen, "Sanctity, Slavery, and Segregation: Methodists and Society in Nineteenth-Century Georgia" (Ph.D. diss., Emory University, 1991), 340.

Private Robert C. Beck also found solace in his religious beliefs. After being wounded in the foot on June 1, 1864, he crawled to the foot of a tree and waited for the battle to end "Oh how comforting was prayer to me then in my time of distress. Oh who so dear a friend as Jesus in time of trouble." Beck's foot was amputated two days later, and he died on July 22, 1864. Undated entry, Diary of Robert C. Beck, April–July 1864, Robert Alexander Webb Papers, Historical Foundation of the Presbyterian and Reformed Churches, Montreat, NC.

12. Sarah M. Manly to her sons, 15 February 1862, Basil Manly II to his sons, Charles, James, and Fuller, 16 February 1862, Manly Collection of Manuscripts, Southern Baptist Historical Library and Archives, Nashville, TN.

13. Basil Manly Jr. to Charles Manly, 15 July 1863, Manly Collection of Manuscripts; Leroy Madison Lee, *Our Country—Our Dangers—Our Duty. A Discourse in Centenary Church, Lynchburg, Va , on the National Fast Day, August 21, 1863*. (Richmond, VA: Soldiers' Tract Association, 1863), 12; Calvin H. Wiley, *Scriptural Views of National Trials: Or the True Road to Independence and Peace of the Confederate States of America* (Greensboro, NC: Sterling, Campbell and Albright, 1863), 191. See also Pierce and Palmer, *Sermons of Bishop Pierce and Rev. B. M. Palmer*, 14–15, and Bell Irvin Wiley, "The Movement to Humanize the Institution of Slavery during the Confederacy," *Emory University Quarterly* 5 (December 1949): 207–20.

In his analysis of Wiley's views on slavery, Paul M Ford concluded that, for Wiley, "the South's great sin, the sin which she had not recognized or had recognized and not dared repent of, was her treatment of the Negro." According to Ford, Wiley believed that "This War was not just a case of God punishing a South that had sinned; it was a case of God continuing the punishment of His children until they recognized their sin and ceased to commit it." Unless and until southerners recognized slave marriages and provided religious instruction for slaves, the war would continue. Wiley's book was quite successful; within months he sold more than four thousand copies in North Carolina. Paul M. Ford, "Calvin H. Wiley's View of the Negro," *North Carolina Historical Review* 41 (January 1964): 12.

14. Beringer et al., *Why the South Lost the Civil War*, 98.

See Gaines M. Foster, "Guilt over Slavery: A Historiographical Analysis," *Journal of Southern History* 56 (November 1990): 665–94; Eugene D. Genovese and Elizabeth Fox-Genovese, "The Religious Ideals of Southern Slave Society," *Georgia Historical Quarterly* 70 (Spring 1986): 1–16. Foster notes that "In an evangelical culture, given to public or at least to private confession of sin, southerners with a conscious sense of failing to live up to religious ideals by owning slaves would have confessed that sin more readily than surviving evidence indicates," 687–88.

15. W. Stanley Hoole, "The Diary of Dr. Basil Manly, 1858–1867," pt. 4, *Alabama Review* 5 (January 1952): 72.

16. Daniel R. Hundley, *Prison Echoes of the Late Rebellion* (New York: S. W. Green, 1874), 44; Ebenezer Baptist Association, *Minutes*, 1864, 2; H. C. Hornady, "Sermon," *Christian Index*, 12 January 1865. See Fred Hobson, *Tell about the South: The Southern Rage to Explain* (Baton Rouge: Louisiana State University Press, 1983), 63–80.

17. "A Voice from the People: 'A Citizen's Meeting of Coweta Co., Ga.,'" *Tri-Weekly Telegraph*, 4 March 1865.

18. "Have Faith in God," *Christian Index*, 23 February 1865.

This confidence in Confederate victory was not limited to civilians. See Reid Mitchell, *Civil War Soldiers: Their Expectations and Their Experiences* (New York: Viking Penguin, 1988), 173–74.

19. Entries for 4 March, 7, 13 April 1865, Eliza Rhea Fain Diaries, John N. Fain Collection, McClung Historical Collection, Knox County Public Library System, Knoxville, TN. See also entries for 14, 15, 17 April 1865.

20. "Keep in Good Heart," *Central Presbyterian* reprinted in the *Southern Presbyterian*, 23 March 1865; "Words of Cheer," *Christian Index*, 30 March 1865.

21. "The Scepticism Engendered by the War," *Christian Index*, 13 January 1866; Earl Schenck Miers, ed., *When the World Ended: The Diary of Emma LeConte* (Lincoln: University of Nebraska Press, 1987), 90, 99.

Presbyterian Anna Safford wrote in her diary, "When the news of Lee's surrender reached us, we could not believe it. It seemed such a tragic, thoroughly unbelieved-in termination — so dreadful — that we thought it incredible." Anna C. Safford diary, Safford Family Papers, Historical Foundation of the Presbyterian and Reformed Churches, Montreat, NC.

Joseph Addison Turner wrote from Putnam County, Georgia, in May 1865: "The news of the surrender of General Lee's Army came upon us like a clap of thunder from a cloudless sky. We were altogether unprepared for such a denouement . . . this fact paralyzed us." *Countryman*, 23 May 1865, 286, quoted in Gerald J. Smith, *Smite Them Hip and Thigh! Georgia Methodist Ministers in the Confederate Military* (Augusta, GA: published by the author, 1993), 170.

22. Peyton Harrison Hoge, *Moses Drury Hoge: Life and Letters* (Richmond, VA: Presbyterian Committee of Publication, 1899), 235–37.

Confederate Vice President Alexander H. Stephens, imprisoned in the North, also drew comfort from the biblical account of Job's struggle to understand why God was allowing such affliction to befall him. In late June he wrote in his prison journal, "My before-breakfast reading was from Job — a favourite book with me. I have read Job oftener than any other book in the Bible, except perhaps St. John." Myrta Lockett Avary, ed., *Recollections of Alexander H. Stephens* (New York: Doubleday, Page, 1910), 262.

23. Rappahannock Baptist Association, Mss. Minutes, 1865, Virginia Baptist Historical Society, Richmond, VA, quoted in W. Harrison Daniel, "Southern Protestantism —1861 and After," *Civil War History* 5 (September 1959): 276–82.

24. See "Religious Literature for the South," *Christian Index*, 13 January 1866.

25. Hobson, *Tell about the South*, 81.

26. Rufus B. Spain, *At Ease in Zion: A Social History of Southern Baptists, 1865–1900* (Nashville, TN: Vanderbilt University Press, 1967), 17.

27. Thomas S. Dunaway, *A Sermon Delivered by Elder Thomas S. Dunaway, of Lancaster County Virginia, before Coan Baptist Church, in Connection with a Day of National Fasting, Humiliation and Prayer, April, 1864* (Richmond, VA: Enquirer Book and Job Press, 1864), 18.

28. "The Scepticism Engendered by the War," *Religious Herald*, reprinted in *Christian Index*, 13 January 1866.

29. "Narrative of the State of Religion," General Assembly of the PCUS, *Minutes*, 1865, 380–81; S. G. Hillyer, "To the Baptists of Georgia," *Christian Index*, 9 November 1865.

30. "All Things Work Together for Good to Them that Love God," *Christian Index*, 13 January 1866. In November 1865, the *Christian Index* reported revivals among Georgia's country churches and concluded, "We should feel grateful for this evidence that the Divine favor is still graciously left to us." "Revivals in Georgia," *Christian Index*, 9 November 1865.

31. Miers, *When the World Ended*, 95; Entry for 19 April 1865, Fain Diaries. See also Charles Reagan Wilson, *Baptized in Blood: The Religion of the Lost Cause, 1865–1920* (Athens: University of Georgia Press, 1980), 73–74.

32. Southern clergy in the antebellum period had developed a sophisticated defense of slavery, which, for most of them, the results of the war did not destroy. For the antebellum defense of slavery, see Eugene D. Genovese, *"Slavery Ordained of God": The Southern Slaveholders' View of Biblical History and Modern Politics* (Gettysburg, PA: Gettysburg College, 1985); Mitchell Snay, "American Thought and Southern Distinctiveness: The Southern Clergy and the Sanctification of Slavery," *Civil War History* 35 (December 1989): 311–28; Elizabeth Fox-Genovese and Eugene D. Genovese, "The Divine Sanction of the Social Order: Religious Foundations of the Southern Slaveholders' World View," *Journal of the American Academy of Religion* 55 (Summer 1987): 211–33.

For a discussion of the "religious logic of secession," see Snay, *Gospel of Disunion*, 151–80. On the compatibility of southern evangelicalism and notions of honor, see Edward R. Crowther, "Holy Honor: Sacred and Secular in the Old South," *Journal of Southern History* 58 (November 1992): 619–36. For a contrasting view of honor and evangelicalism as competing ideologies, neither of which triumphed, leaving the South with a "divided soul," see Bertram Wyatt-Brown, "Religion and the 'Civilizing Process' in the Early American South, 1600–1860," in *Religion and American Politics: From the Colonial Period to the 1980s*, ed. Mark A. Noll (New York: Oxford University Press, 1990), 172–95.

33. Entry for 17 May 1865, Fain Diaries. Fain did believe that "God is pouring out his wrath upon the South" for a sin associated with slavery: "the amalgamated race who have been born in a state of slavery." "Oh white man of the South," she wrote in her diary, "has it ever entered in thy soul to count the cost of this terrible sin." The bloody battlefields of the Civil War demonstrated "what it is for a nation favored of God as no other has been to mix blood with a race whom God for reasons unknown to us has doomed to a state of servitude." Entry for 22 May 1865, Fain Diaries. See also entry for 19 November 1865.

34. "A Pastoral Letter from the General Assembly to the Churches Under Their Care," General Assembly of the PCUS, *Minutes*, 1865, 385.

For Southern Presbyterians' views on political involvement, see Jack P. Maddex, "From Theocracy to Spirituality: The Southern Presbyterian Reversal on Church and State," *Journal of Presbyterian History* 54 (Winter 1976): 438–57 and James Oscar Farmer Jr., *The Metaphysical Confederacy: James Henley Thornwell and the Synthesis of Southern Values* (Macon, GA: Mercer University Press, 1986).

35. John Leland, "The War—God's Design to Abolish Slavery," *Religious Herald*, 22 February 1866.

36. Robert Lewis Dabney, *A Defence of Virginia, and Through Her, of the South* (New York: E. J. Hale and Son, 1867), 6, 22; Hobson, *Tell about the South*, 85–105; David Henry Overy, "Robert Lewis Dabney: Apostle of the Old South" (Ph.D. diss., University of Wisconsin, 1967).

Gardiner H. Shattuck Jr. rightly highlights a group of conservatives in the New South, of whom Dabney was one of the most prominent, who "utterly refused to compromise their antebellum principles." They, unlike fellow evangelicals such as J. William Jones and Atticus Haygood, were never able to embrace the optimistic New South creed of racial peace, sectional reconciliation, and economic progress based on industry and scientific agriculture. Shattuck concludes, "Defeat in the war, after all, triggered much soul-searching among religious southern whites." Most southerners, however, seem to have embraced parts of both schools of thought. Few brooded as long or as deeply about Confederate defeat as did Dabney. Most considered defeat to be divine chastisement, and they moved on to reconstruct the South politically, socially, economically, and religiously. They did not thereby reject the righteousness of either slavery or secession. Gardiner H. Shattuck Jr., "'Appomattox as a Day of Blessing': Religious Interpretations of Confederate Defeat in the New South Era," *Journal of Confederate History* 7 (1991): 3. On the New South creed, see Paul M. Gaston, *The New South Creed: A Study in Southern Mythmaking* (New York: Knopf, 1970).

37. *Christian Advocate*, 13 August 1875; "Report of the Home Mission Board," Southern Baptist Convention, *Proceedings*, 1892, iv. The Home Mission Board also insisted that since emancipation the freedman had found white southerners to be "his truest friends and his most efficient helpers."

In November 1871, J. L. Reynolds assured South Carolina Baptists that the Southern Baptist Convention had "never receded" from its views on slavery. It had "no confession to make" and "no repentance to offer" for its views. South Carolina Baptist Convention, *Minutes*, 1871, Appendix, 36.

38. Memoirs of Thomas Hooke McCallie.

39. "Who Has Prevented Reconstruction?" *Southern Presbyterian*, 8 February 1866; Thomas Smyth, "The War of the South Vindicated," *Southern Presbyterian Review* 15 (April 1863): 499; Smith, *In His Image, But . . .*, 213–16; Spain, *At Ease in Zion*, 19–20; Gaines M. Foster, *Ghosts of the Confederacy: Defeat, the Lost Cause, and the Emergence of the New South* (New York: Oxford University Press, 1987), 22–23.

For postwar defenses of secession, see Methodist Albert Taylor Bledsoe's *Is Davis a Traitor; or Was Secession a Constitutional Right Previous to the War of 1861?* (Baltimore: Innes, 1866); Presbyterian Robert Lewis Dabney's *The Life and Campaigns of Lieut.-Gen. Thomas J. Jackson* (New York: Blelock, 1866); and Baptist John William Jones's *The Davis Memorial; or Our Dead President, Jefferson Davis* (Richmond, VA: B. F. Johnson, 1890). For an analysis of the postwar southern apologia, see Richard M. Weaver, *The Southern Tradition at Bay: A History of Postbellum Thought*, ed. George Core and M. E. Bradford (New Rochelle, NY: Arlington House, 1968).

40. Bishop Leonidas K. Polk to Bishop Stephen Elliott, 20 August 1856, Leonidas Polk Papers, Southern Historical Collection, University of North Carolina at Chapel Hill, quoted in John McCardell, *The Idea of a Southern Nation: Southern Nationalists and Southern Nationalism, 1830–1860* (New York: Norton, 1979), 218; Robert H. Crozier, *The Confederate Spy: A History of the War of 1861* (Gallatin, TN: R. B. Harmon, 1866), 5. Crozier's defiant plea appears in the preface to his novel; the preface was written on May 27, 1865.

41. Hunter Dickinson Farish, *The Circuit Rider Dismounts: A Social History of Southern Methodism, 1865–1900* (Richmond, VA: Dietz Press, 1938), 52–54.

42. "Pastoral Address of the Southern Methodist Bishops," *Southern Christian Advocate*, 31 August 1865.

Ironically, twenty years earlier, a young George Foster Pierce proclaimed at the organizational meeting of the MECS in Louisville, Kentucky, that the door should remain open for fraternal relations and even reunion when northern Methodists "are convinced of their sins." When northern Methodists reversed the invitation in 1865 on the same basis, Pierce spurned the offer. Luther Lee and E. Smith, *The Debates of the General Conference of the M. E. Church, May, 1844, to which is added a review of the proceedings of said conference* (New York: O. Scott for the Wesleyan Methodist Connection of America, 1845), 442.

43. Memphis Annual Conference, Minutes, 1865, 97, Luther L. Gobbell Library, Lambuth College, Jackson, TN.

44. "A Pastoral Letter from the General Assembly to the Churches Under Their Care," General Assembly of the PCUS, *Minutes,* 1865, 384; "Is Reunion with the Northern Church Desirable?" *Southern Presbyterian,* 22 February 1866.

45. Robert G. Gardner et al., *A History of the Georgia Baptist Association, 1784–1984* (Atlanta: Georgia Baptist Historical Society, 1988), 209.

46. *Christian Index,* 6, 13 January 1866. See also 20 January, 22 March, 3 May 1866.

47. "The Condition and Wants of the Church," *Southern Presbyterian,* 25 January 1866; Farish, *The Circuit Rider Dismounts,* 22–61; Ernest Trice Thompson, *Presbyterians in the South,* 3 vols. (Richmond, VA: John Knox Press, 1963–73), 2:89–115.

48. North Carolina Baptist Convention, *Minutes,* 1865, 16; F. M. Law, "Duty of Southern Christians to Furnish Religious Instruction to the Freedmen," *Texas Baptist Herald,* 3 October 1866.

49. A writer to the *Christian Index* insisted that God had changed the relationship between the races in the South because southerners had not fulfilled their duties as masters. The correspondent urged his fellow Christians to "labor so to form and regulate the new relations which are to arise, that the two races which God has brought together in this good land, may partake together of God's bounty, and may live together in such a manner as to secure his approbation." "Our Chastisement," *Christian Index,* 10 February 1866.

Rufus Spain concluded in his study of the social attitudes of southern Baptists: "The Protestant churches of the South closed ranks after the Civil War in defense of the traditional relationship of the races. Except for recognizing the personal freedom of the Negroes, Southern churches exhibited no appreciable change of attitude as a result of emancipation." Spain, *At Ease in Zion,* 44.

50. Alabama Baptist Convention, *Minutes,* 1865, 10.

51. Basil Manly II to Jane Smith, 16 November 1865, Manly Collection of Manuscripts.

52. Gardner et al., *A History of the Georgia Baptist Association,* 199, 201, 209.

53. Synod of Georgia, *Minutes,* 1865, 14–15.

54. "Narrative of the State of Religion," General Assembly of the PCUS, *Minutes,* 1865, 380.

55. Georgia Annual Conference (MECS), *Minutes,* 1865, 11–13.

56. William B. Gravely, "The Social, Political and Religious Significance of the Formation of the Colored Methodist Episcopal Church (1870)," *Methodist History* 18 (October 1979): 3–25; Othal Hawthorne Lakey, *The History of the CME Church* (Memphis, TN: CME Publishing, 1985), 189–223.

3   God's Judgment

1. James H. Moorhead, *American Apocalypse: Yankee Protestants and the Civil War, 1860–1869* (New Haven: Yale University Press, 1978). See also Peter J. Parish, "The Instruments of Providence: Slavery, Civil War and the American Churches," in *The Church and War,* ed. W. J. Sheils (Oxford: Basil Blackwell, 1983), 291–320; Ernest Lee Tuveson, *Redeemer*

Nation: The Idea of America's Millennial Role (Chicago: University of Chicago Press, 1968). Parish qualifies Moorhead by arguing that northern clergy often used apocalyptic language to "dramatise a more prosaic message." In Parish's view, northern ministers saw the war as "a process of purification, which would restore both republican and Christian virtue to their pristine American glory."

2. Phillip Shaw Paludan, *"A People's Contest": The Union and Civil War, 1861–1865* (New York: Harper and Row, 1988), 339.

3. Ibid., 344; Chester Forrestor Dunham, *The Attitude of the Northern Clergy toward the South, 1860–1865* (Toledo, OH: Gray, 1942), 71–80; Oliver Saxon Heckman, "Northern Church Penetration of the South, 1860 to 1880" (Ph.D. diss., Duke University, 1939), 42.

4. Detroit Annual Conference, *Minutes*, 1861, 35; Edward McPherson, *The Political History of the United States of America during the Great Rebellion*, 2d ed. (Washington, DC: Philip and Solomons, 1865), 468 (New School Presbyterian quotation), 475 (ABHMS quotation).

5. Lewis G. Vander Velde, *The Presbyterian Churches and the Federal Union, 1861–1869* (Cambridge: Harvard University Press, 1932), 42–63, 93–95, 102; James Oscar Farmer Jr., *The Metaphysical Confederacy: James Henley Thornwell and the Synthesis of Southern Values* (Macon, GA: Mercer University Press, 1986), 274–81.

6. Paludan, *"A People's Contest,"* 351; "Asbury Guards," *Western Christian Advocate*, 15 May 1861.

For the influence of religion on northern soldiers, see Reid Mitchell, *The Vacant Chair: The Northern Soldier Leaves Home* (New York: Oxford University Press, 1993), 118–20, 138–40, 150; Gardiner H. Shattuck Jr., *A Shield and Hiding Place: The Religious Life of the Civil War Armies* (Macon, GA: Mercer University Press, 1987), 13–34, 73–94.

7. "Tendencies," *Western Christian Advocate*, 24 June 1863; McPherson, *The Political History of the United States of America*, 477. See Victor B. Howard, *Religion and the Radical Republican Movement, 1860–1870* (Lexington: University Press of Kentucky, 1990), 52–55.

8. John R. McKivigan has examined the efforts of northern abolitionists to convert northern denominations to their cause. Except for a few small denominations, he argues, northern churches remained indifferent or even hostile to an immediate emancipation program even into the Civil War. Rather than leading public sentiment against slavery, northern churches only belatedly and carefully embraced abolitionism. John R. McKivigan, *The War against Proslavery Religion: Abolitionism and the Northern Churches, 1830–1865* (Ithaca, NY: Cornell University Press, 1984), 183–201.

9. Vander Velde, *The Presbyterian Churches and the Federal Union*, 25 (1818 quotations), 123–24; McPherson, *The Political History of the United States of America*, 466 (1864 quotation).

10. Paludan, *"A People's Contest,"* 339, 349; Shattuck, *A Shield and Hiding Place*, 13–33.

11. Joanna P. Moore, *"In Christ's Stead": Autobiographical Sketches* (Chicago: Women's Baptist Home Mission Society, 1903), 22–25. For celebrations in the North on January 1, 1863, see John Hope Franklin, *The Emancipation Proclamation* (Garden City, NY: Doubleday, 1963; reprint, Wheeling, IL: Harlan Davidson, 1995), 85–98.

Other young northern women were likewise drawn to educational and missionary work in the South by a sense of religious duty. Carrie E. Waugh attributed her initial interest in aiding the freedpeople to her strongly abolitionist father and the publication of the "soul stirring" *Uncle Tom's Cabin*. Then "the Civil War came and the smoke of battle had not cleared away when the Lord called me to go to the freedmen." Although she was reluctant to leave her recently widowed mother, "the call grew louder and stronger and God's Word continually rang in my heart." Appointed in the fall of 1865, Waugh began her first school in Raleigh, North Carolina, in March 1866. After several years of teaching in North Carolina and Georgia, she resigned and "entered on definite mission work under the Woman's American Baptist

Home Mission Society, whose policy it was to carry the gospel into every home and to help the women and children." *Service in Fruition: The Story of the Work for the Betterment of the Colored People of James City and Newbern, North Carolina* (Chicago: Woman's American Baptist Home Mission Society, 1916), 4–5. See also Jacqueline Jones, *Soldiers of Light and Love: Northern Teachers and Georgia Blacks, 1865–1873* (Chapel Hill: University of North Carolina Press, 1980), 39–48, for a discussion of religious and other motivations among northern teachers.

12. Moore, "In Christ's Stead," 26–37. After the war ended, Moore taught the freedpeople in Little Rock, Arkansas, until 1868, when she returned to Illinois to care for her ailing mother.

13. *Christian Advocate and Journal*, 5 February 1863; New York East Conference, *Minutes*, 1864, 41; R. L. Stanton, *The Church and the Rebellion* (New York: Derby and Miller, 1864; reprint, Freeport, NY: Books for Libraries Press, 1971), 303–5, 362.

14. David B. Chesebrough, "No Sorrow Like Our Sorrow": *Northern Protestant Ministers and the Assassination of Lincoln* (Kent, OH: Kent State University Press, 1994), 53–78; Thomas Reed Turner, *Beware the People Weeping: Public Opinion and the Assassination of Abraham Lincoln* (Baton Rouge: Louisiana State University Press, 1982), 77–89.

15. Howard, *Religion and the Radical Republican Movement*, 2–3, 90–105; Dunham, *The Attitude of the Northern Clergy*, 239.

Like their southern counterparts, northern ministers turned to the Bible for support of their understanding of the war and their plans for religious reconstruction. Baptist minister Alfred Patton of Utica, New York, declared on April 23, 1865: "Plainly, God is saying to us, by his providences to-day, what he said to his people of old, 'Execute judgment upon them speedily, whether it be unto death, or to banishment, or to confiscation of goods, or to imprisonment.'" Patton insisted that this passage from Ezra 7:26 was God's solution to the problem of reconstruction. Alfred S. Patton, *The Nation's Loss and Its Lessons* (Utica, NY: Curtiss and White, 1865), 13; Paul Clyde Brownlow, "The Northern Protestant Pulpit on Reconstruction, 1865–1877" (Ph.D. diss., Purdue University, 1970), 27

16. "The Churches and Reconstruction," *New York Times*, 29 September 1865; "The Religious Condition of the South," *Nation*, 12 July 1866.

17. For contemporary criticism, see *New York Times*, 18 September 1865, and *New York Express*, quoted in *Mobile Daily Register*, 14 September 1865. The editors of the *Nation* observed:

> there is nothing which irritates the Southern people so outrageously as the assumption, on which nearly all our offers of reconciliation are based, that they have not only sinned, but sinned with the full knowledge that they were sinning — that they went into the war well knowing that they were about to commit a great crime. We accordingly not only look on their defeat as a piece of retribution, but we expect to them to see it in the same light, and to meet us as penitents in sackcloth and ashes, and take our advances to them as proof of our magnanimity and forgivingness.

Northern evangelicals certainly believed that southerners had sinned in rebelling and in upholding slavery, though they did not believe that southerners deliberately defied God in doing so: many had simply been terribly misled into the war. What northerners did expect was for southern Christians to acknowledge in the outcome of the war God's disapproval of their actions, to admit that they had been wrong, and to express a desire to live differently in the future — in short, repentance. Despite the *Nation's* criticisms, the position of northern evangelicals was not irrational, based on *their* understanding of the war. "The Religious Condition of the South," *Nation*, 12 July 1866.

For historians' evaluations, see, for example, Dunham, *The Attitude of the Northern*

Clergy, 218–19; Robert Andrew Baker, *Relations between Northern and Southern Baptists* (n.p., 1954; reprint, New York: Arno Press, 1980), 172; Hunter Dickinson Farish, *The Circuit Rider Dismounts: A Social History of Southern Methodism, 1865–1900* (Richmond, VA: Dietz Press, 1938), 40–41, 54–55; Ralph E. Morrow, *Northern Methodism and Reconstruction* (East Lansing: Michigan State University Press, 1956), 69–70; Ernest Trice Thompson, *Presbyterians in the South,* 3 vols. (Richmond, VA: John Knox Press, 1963–73), 2:140–42; and Heckman, "Northern Church Penetration of the South," 186–87, 361–62. Donald G. Jones has protested the "carpetbagger" interpretation of northern Methodism presented in Morrow, emphasizing instead northern guilt over complicity in the perpetuation of slavery. While Jones properly rescues northern Methodists from the reputation of being vindictive zealots, his emphasis on guilt feelings obscures their firm belief that God had favored the North and had judged the South. Those northern Methodists involved in religious reconstruction neither hated all southerners nor brooded over their part in slavery. They confidently sought to reestablish a national Methodist Episcopal Church and to minister to southerners of both races, endeavors that they were certain had God's blessing. Donald G. Jones, *The Sectional Crisis and Northern Methodism: A Study in Piety, Political Ethics, and Civil Religion* (Metuchen, NJ: Scarecrow Press, 1979), 91–94, 256–65.

18. *American Annual Cyclopaedia and Register of Important Events* 5 (1865) (New York: Appleton, 1870), 704; *Independent,* 27 July 1865; "Our Next Duty," *Christian Advocate and Journal,* 13 April 1865.

19. J. S. Hurlburt, *History of the Rebellion in Bradley County, East Tennessee* (Indianapolis: n.p., 1866; reprint, n.p.: Sink-Moore, 1988), 21–25.

20. "The Rebel Prisoners," *Christian Times and Illinois Baptist,* 26 February 1862; "The Prospect," *Western Christian Advocate,* 1 April 1863; "A Change of the General Rule on Slavery," *Western Christian Advocate,* 20 April 1864; General Assembly of the PCUSA (New School), *Minutes,* 1866, 314. See also Thomas H. Pearne, *An Address on the Two Churches* (Cincinnati, OH: Methodist Book Concern, 1867), 25; H. S. Foote, "Review of the War of the Rebellion," *Methodist Quarterly Review* 48 (April 1866), 306–7; George Lansing Taylor, "Methodist Reconstruction," *Christian Advocate and Journal,* 8 June 1865; and "Methodism in the South, From a Southern Standpoint," *Western Christian Advocate,* 24 May 1865. In April 1865, the *Western Christian Advocate* declared, "We have never for a moment doubted that everywhere in Southern society a thorough but silent Union sentiment has prevailed. Nor have we doubted that at the practical division of the Church, in 1846, thousands parted from the old Church with heartbreaking reluctance." "The Spirit of the South," *Western Christian Advocate,* 19 April 1865.

21. "Report of Committee on the Reconstruction of the Church, New England Conference," *Christian Advocate and Journal,* 27 April 1865; John Lanahan, "Southern Reconstruction," *Christian Advocate and Journal,* 6 April 1865; "Methodism in the South," *Christian Advocate and Journal,* 11 May 1865; *Christian Herald and Presbyterian Observer,* May 1865, quoted in Dunham, *The Attitude of the Northern Clergy,* 208–9; *Christian Secretary,* September 1865, quoted in Dunham, *The Attitude of the Northern Clergy,* 195. A contributor to the Methodist *Zion's Herald* insisted that the "folly and sin" of the "proslavery and rebellious clergy" had "forever unfitted them for official position in a loyal church." They were "unfit to be teachers, as much as any other criminals." "The Methodist Church and the South," *Zion's Herald,* 24 May 1865.

The northern New School General Assembly proclaimed in 1865 that "to disobey the civil law, unless required to do so by the law of God, is alike a crime against the State and a sin against God; rendering the offender justly amenable to punishment." General Assembly of the PCUSA (New School), *Minutes,* 1865, 19–20.

Some southern Methodist ministers carried in their pockets a copy of the Report on

Church Reconstruction by the New England Conference, and used it as a "campaign document" against any plans for reunion between the two churches. *Zion's Herald*, 12 July 1865.

22. "Methodist Reconstruction in the South," *Christian Advocate and Journal*, 16 March 1865.

23. *New York Examiner and Chronicle*, February 1866, quoted in Baker, *Relations between Northern and Southern Baptists*, 96; General Assembly of the PCUSA (Old School), *Minutes*, 1865, 562–63; *Presbyter*, 17 May 1865; *Doctrine and Discipline of the Methodist Episcopal Church*, 1864 (Cincinnati, OH: Poe and Hitchcock, 1864), 84; "Action of the Bishops," *Western Christian Advocate*, 28 June 1865. For Pendleton's experiences as a Unionist in Confederate Tennessee early in the war, see J. M. Pendleton, *Reminiscences of a Long Life* (Louisville, KY: Press Baptist Book Concern, 1891), 108–38. See also Vander Velde, *The Presbyterian Churches and the Federal Union*, 499–501.

Henry Lee Swint declared that the Yankee teachers who went south "believed that the people of the South had sinned, both in holding to that abominable institution, slavery, and in rebelling against the Union. . . . The people of the South were not only sinners, but defeated sinners, who refused to be properly humble and abject, and who, worst of all, refused to repent of the error of their ways." Swint's sarcastic tone reveals his own judgment of northern missionary teachers. His interpretation is perhaps more accurate than he realized. In the eyes of northerners, southerners' sin was worse not because they had been defeated but because they had been *judged* and still refused to repent. A sinner of any sort who behaved in this manner would be considered especially recalcitrant by a nineteenth-century evangelical. Henry Lee Swint, *The Northern Teacher in the South, 1862–1870* (Nashville, TN: Vanderbilt University Press, 1941; reprint, New York: Octagon Books, 1967), 56.

24. New York *Examiner and Chronicle*, January 1866, quoted in Baker, *Relations between Northern and Southern Baptists*, 95–96; "The True Policy of Southern Methodism," *Western Christian Advocate*, 23 August 1865; "Church Reconstruction in Rebeldom," *Christian Advocate and Journal*, 9 February 1865; "Reconstruction," *Christian Advocate and Journal*, 25 May 1865; "Our Policy in the South," *Christian Advocate and Journal*, 25 April 1867.

25. "The True Policy of Southern Methodism," *Western Christian Advocate*, 23 August 1865; "Church Reconstruction in Rebeldom," *Christian Advocate and Journal*, 9 February 1865.

26. ABHMS, *Annual Report*, 1862, 50–51; Heckman, "Northern Church Penetration of the South," 232.

27. Daniel Curry, *Life-Story of Rev. Davis Wasgatt Clark* (New York: Nelson and Phillips, 1874), 213.

28. The phrase "religious scalawag," as a descriptive term for white southern ministers and laypeople who joined northern denominations, is useful for three reasons. The mass of southern whites viewed these ministers much as they did southern whites who joined the Republican party — as traitors to their section and to the memory of the Confederacy. The term also easily distinguishes this group from northern ministers who came into the South after the war. Finally, the title emphasizes the political orientation of most southern members of northern denominations; many religious scalawags were active political scalawags as well. My use of this label is not intended to be derogatory, though the label "scalawag" was applied at the time as an epithet.

29. For a discussion of Unionist sentiments among southern clergy during the war, see W. Harrison Daniel, "Protestant Clergy and Union Sentiment in the Confederacy," *Tennessee Historical Quarterly* 23 (September 1964): 284–90.

30. Isaac Patton Martin, *Methodism in Holston* (Knoxville, TN: Methodist Historical Society, 1945), 72–78; R. N. Price, *Holston Methodism: From Its Origin to the Present Time*, 5 vols. (Nashville, TN: Publishing House of the Methodist Episcopal Church, South, 1913), 4:297–399.

31. *Knoxville Whig and Rebel Ventilator*, 27 May 1864, quoted (81) in Martin, *Methodism in Holston*, 81–85; Price, *Holston Methodism*, 4:353–58; E. Merton Coulter, *William G. Brownlow: Fighting Parson of the Southern Highlands* (Chapel Hill: University of North Carolina Press, 1937; reprint, Knoxville: University of Tennessee Press, 1971), 296–97.

32. W. B. Hesseltine, "Methodism and Reconstruction in East Tennessee," *East Tennessee Historical Society's Publications* 3 (1931): 50–53; Morrow, *Northern Methodism and Reconstruction*, 42–43; Thomas H. Pearne, letter, *Christian Advocate and Journal*, 29 June 1865. See "The Holston Conference," *Western Christian Advocate*, 14 June 1865.

33. "A New Star in Kentucky," *Western Christian Advocate*, 20 September 1865; *Western Christian Advocate*, 27 September 1865.

34. Jedidiah Foster, "Reasons for Changing My Church Relations," *Western Christian Advocate*, 18 April 1866.

35. "Georgia Conference Documents—On the State of the Country," *Southern Christian Advocate*, 11 December 1862 (quotation); John H. Caldwell, *A Fast Day Sermon, Preached in Newnan, Ga., April 8, 1864, On the Occasion of the President's Proclamation* (La Grange, GA: Daily Bulletin Office, 1864); "A Voice from the People: 'A Citizen's Meeting of Coweta Co., Ga.,'" *Tri-Weekly Telegraph*, 4 March 1865.

36. John H. Caldwell, *Reminiscences of the Reconstruction of Church and State in Georgia* (Wilmington, DE: J. Miller Thomas, 1895), 3; John H. Caldwell, *Slavery and Southern Methodism: Two Sermons Preached in the Methodist Church in Newnan, Georgia* (New York: published by the author, 1865), 18–20, 64–66, 74–75 (emphasis in the original).

37. Daniel W. Stowell, "'We Have Sinned, and God Has Smitten Us!' John H. Caldwell and the Religious Meaning of Confederate Defeat," *Georgia Historical Quarterly* 78 (Spring 1994): 1–38; Daniel W. Stowell, "The Failure of Religious Reconstruction: The Methodist Episcopal Church in Georgia, 1865–1871" (M. A. thesis, University of Georgia, 1988).

38. *Christian Advocate and Journal*, 24 August 1865; *Methodist Quarterly Review* (New York), October 1865, 624–25.

Religious scalawags spoke out in other areas of the Deep South as well. John Jackson Brasher, father of the prominent holiness leader John Lakin Brasher, was a Methodist religious scalawag in Alabama. After the war, John Jackson Brasher "determined to sever my connection with the Church South, unless they struck from their discipline the word 'South.'" Reflecting the northern religious understanding of the war, he continued, "The cause of the separation had been removed, and consequently there was no further necessity for this distinction." He and four other ministers, with three hundred and fifty laypeople, formed a separate organization; "one of the tests of membership among us was loyalty to the Government of the United States." Later this group united with the newly organized conference of the Methodist Episcopal Church in Alabama. J. Lawrence Brasher, *The Sanctified South: John Lakin Brasher and the Holiness Movement* (Urbana: University of Illinois Press, 1994), 13.

39. Steven Edwards Brooks, "Out of the Galleries: The Northern Presbyterian Mission in Reconstruction North Carolina" (M.A. thesis, University of North Carolina at Chapel Hill, 1974), 31, 45, 99; Thompson, *Presbyterians in the South*, 2:146–50.

40. Thaddeus W. McRae, typescript autobiography, 1880, Thaddeus W. McRae Papers, Historical Foundation of the Presbyterian and Reformed Churches, Montreat, NC; Thompson, *Presbyterians in the South*, 2:151–52.

41. Thomas L. Janeway, "Our Position," *Home and Foreign Record*, November 1865, quoted in Thompson, *Presbyterians in the South*, 2:144–45; Report of the Board of Domestic Missions, General Assembly of the PCUSA, *Minutes*, 1866, 144.

42. Union Presbytery, "Minutes" (April 1865 and Fall 1865), McClung Room, Lawson McGhee Library, Knoxville, TN, quoted in Harold M. Parker Jr., *The United Synod of the*

South: The Southern *New School Presbyterian Church* (Westport, CT; Greenwood Press, 1988), 271–73; General Assembly of the PCUSA (New School), *Minutes*, 1865, 12, 15–16.

1 God's Deliverance

1. Northern black evangelicals took part in the religious reconstruction of the South primarily through the activities of missionaries from the AME Church, the AMEZ Church, and the Consolidated American Baptist Missionary Convention (CABMC). Many of these missionaries were born free, and they shared with northern white missionaries some of the same religious ideals and attitudes. In fact, southern blacks did not always welcome black missionaries; old slave preachers and exhorters jealously guarded their positions in the changing black communities. Nonetheless, northern blacks' view of the significance of the war, religious reconstruction, and their race ensured that they had more in common with the freedpeople than with white missionaries. Like the freedpeople, they believed that emancipation was the central providential fact of the war. Furthermore, black missionaries from the North were always a small minority of the clergy of churches affiliated with these denominations. Between 1864 and 1872, only six AME ministers from the North labored in Georgia, and most of them stayed only a short time. Therefore, for the purpose of this study, these northern black missionaries are grouped with the freedpeople with whom they shared similar views rather than with their white counterparts from the North. Stephen Ward Angell, *Bishop Henry McNeal Turner and African-American Religion in the South* (Knoxville: University of Tennessee Press, 1992), 72.

In April 1866 the AME denominational newspaper, the *Christian Recorder*, reported, "the religion of the South is debauched. With many the failure of the cause has led to infidelity in God's providence. In no instance did any one express the idea that the South had done wrong on slavery and rebellion. Even in the revivals lately reported, there has been no confession of sorrow for their sins." By accepting these statements, which were made by Joseph E. Roy, an agent of the ABHMS, the AME Church united with northern white denominations in a dim view of the state of southern religion. However, the AME also entered into fraternal negotiations with the MECS to receive its black members who wanted to leave, a step which was unthinkable for the MEC, which considered the southern church "debauched." "Religious Condition of the South," *Christian Recorder*, 28 April 1866; Reginald F. Hildebrand, *The Times Were Strange and Stirring: Methodist Preachers and the Crisis of Emancipation* (Durham, NC: Duke University Press, 1995), 12–13, 43; Leon F. Litwack, *Been in the Storm So Long: The Aftermath of Slavery* (New York: Random House, 1980), 4.

2. Katharine L. Dvorak, *An African-American Exodus: The Segregation of the Southern Churches* (Brooklyn, NY: Carlson Publishing, 1991), 2, 69 -119. See also Eric Foner, *Reconstruction: America's Unfinished Revolution, 1863–1877* (New York: Harper and Row, 1988), 93–94.

3. Strife developed between black and northern white Baptists when whites tried to control black Baptist associations and conventions. Blacks were not allowed to participate in the management of the ABHMS. When the American Baptist Publication Society, at the behest of southerners, refused to accept black contributions to its Sunday school literature, blacks Baptists were outraged. In Atlanta in 1895, they organized the National Baptist Convention, and soon the National Baptist Publishing Board under the leadership of Richard Henry Boyd began to publish its own Sunday school literature. John Hope Franklin, *From Slavery to Freedom: A History of American Negroes*, 2d ed. (New York: Knopf, 1965), 398; James Melvin Washington, *Frustrated Fellowship: The Black Baptist Quest for Social Power* (Macon, GA: Mercer University Press, 1986), 159–70, 190–91; Paul Harvey, *Redeeming the South: Religious Cultures and Racial Identities among Southern Baptists, 1865–1925* (Chapel Hill: University of North Carolina Press, 1997), 227–55.

4. Albert J. Raboteau, *Slave Religion: The "Invisible Institution" in the Antebellum South* (New York: Oxford University Press, 1978); Mechal Sobel, *Trabelin' On: The Slave Journey to an Afro-Baptist Faith* (Westport, CT: Greenwood Press, 1979), 99–180; Mechal Sobel, *The World They Made Together: Black and White Values in Eighteenth-Century Virginia* (Princeton: Princeton University Press, 1987), 178–213; Lawrence W. Levine, *Black Culture and Black Consciousness: Afro-American Folk Thought from Slavery to Freedom* (New York: Oxford University Press, 1977), 3–80; Donald G. Mathews, *Religion in the Old South* (Chicago: University of Chicago Press, 1977), 185–236; John B. Boles, ed., *Masters and Slaves in the House of the Lord: Race and Religion in the American South, 1740–1870* (Lexington: University Press of Kentucky, 1988); Erskine Clarke, *Wrestlin' Jacob: A Portrait of Religion in the Old South* (Atlanta, GA: John Knox Press, 1979).

5. Raboteau, *Slave Religion*, 309–10.

6. Eugene D. Genovese, *Roll, Jordan, Roll: The World the Slaves Made* (New York: Pantheon Books, 1974), 232–55; Mathews, *Religion in the Old South*, 248–50; Raboteau, *Slave Religion*, 152–288; John B. Boles, *Black Southerners, 1619–1869* (Lexington: University Press of Kentucky, 1984), 157–68; William E. Montgomery, *Under Their Own Vine and Fig Tree: The African-American Church in the South, 1865–1900* (Baton Rouge: Louisiana State University Press, 1993), 19–27.

In an 1877 sermon on the "Destined Superiority of the Negro," African-American Episcopal minister Alexander Crummell wrote:

> We have seen, to-day, the great truth, that when God does not destroy a people, but, on the contrary, trains and disciplines it, it is an indication that He intends to make something of them, and to do something for them. It signifies that He is graciously interested in such a people. In a sense, not equal, indeed, to the case of the Jews, but parallel, in a lower degree, such a people are a "chosen people" of the Lord. There is, so to speak, a *covenant* relation which God has established between Himself and them. (In J. R. Oldfield, ed., *Civilization and Black Progress: Selected Writings of Alexander Crummell on the South* (Charlottesville: University of Virginia Press, 1995), 52.)

7. W. E. B. DuBois, *The Souls of Black Folk* (New York: Penguin Books, 1989), 163.

8. Norman R. Yetman, ed., *Life under the "Peculiar Institution": Selections from the Slave Narrative Collection* (New York: Holt, Rinehart and Winston, 1970), 95.

By 1860, the MECS had 171,857 "colored" members, the Southern Baptist Convention had at least 150,000 (probably many more) "colored" members, and the PCUSA had, in the South, as many as 30,000 "colored" members. These totals do not include the black members of Baptist churches that were not affiliated with the Southern Baptist Convention or churches that were part of smaller denominations like the Cumberland Presbyterian Church. *Minutes of the Annual Conferences of the Methodist Episcopal Church, South*, 1860 (Nashville, TN: Methodist Publishing House, 1861), 293; Southern Baptist Convention, *Proceedings*, 1859, 60–61; Ernest Trice Thompson, *Presbyterians in the South*, 3 vols. (Richmond, VA: John Knox Press, 1963–73), 1:443.

Mechal Sobel estimates that nearly seven hundred thousand blacks, north and south, were members of Baptist, Methodist, or Presbyterian churches in 1860. Sobel, *Trabelin' On*, 182–83.

9. Joel Williamson, *After Slavery: The Negro in South Carolina during Reconstruction, 1861–1877* (Chapel Hill: University of North Carolina Press, 1965), 201; Peter Kolchin, *First Freedom: The Responses of Alabama's Blacks to Emancipation and Reconstruction* (Westport, CT: Greenwood Press, 1972), 120; Raboteau, *Slave Religion*; Levine, *Black Culture and Black Consciousness*; Sterling Stuckey, *Slave Culture: Nationalist Theory and the Foundations of Black America* (New York: Oxford University Press, 1987); John W. Blassingame, *The Slave Community: Plantation Life in the Antebellum South* (New York: Oxford University Press,

1972); Boles, *Black Southerners*; and the essays in Boles, *Masters and Slaves in the House of the Lord*.

Boles insists that the underground church is an "insufficiently understood and greatly exaggerated aspect of slave religion," and that the meetings in the slave quarters and brush arbors supplemented rather than supplanted worship in biracial churches. Boles, *Black Southerners*, 163–64.

This recent debate parallels in important respects the earlier disagreement between E. Franklin Frazier and Melville J. Herskovits about the survival of Africanisms in black culture in America. Frazier insisted that slaves were stripped of most of their culture by the process of enslavement, while Herskovits maintained that many Africanisms survived and had an important influence on African-American culture in the United States. E. Franklin Frazier, *The Negro Church in America* (New York: Schocken Books, 1964); Melville J. Herskovits, *The Myth of the Negro Past* (Boston: Beacon Press, 1958).

10. Montgomery, *Under Their Own Vine and Fig Tree*, 36–37. For differences among black Methodists, see Hildebrand, *The Times Were Strange and Stirring*.

11. Dvorak, *An African-American Exodus*, 1–48; Boles, *Black Southerners*, 165.

12. George P. Rawick, ed., *The American Slave: A Composite Autobiography*, 39 vols. (Westport, CT: Greenwood Press, 1972–79), vol. 6, pt. 2, *Indiana Narratives*, 158–59; vol. 17, *Florida Narratives*, 142.

13. W. E. B. DuBois, *Black Reconstruction: An Essay toward a History of the Part Which Black Folk Played in the Attempt to Reconstruct Democracy in America, 1860–1880* (New York: Russell and Russell, 1935), 124; John W. Blassingame, ed., *Slave Testimony: Two Centuries of Letters, Speeches, Interviews, and Autobiographies* (Baton Rouge: Louisiana State University Press, 1977), 661.

14. Rawick, *The American Slave*, vol. 2, pt. 1, *South Carolina Narratives*, 151. Some northern black evangelicals shared Lincoln's conviction, expressed in his Second Inaugural Address, that the war was a judgment on both the North and the South. James Lynch, an AME minister, insisted, "the head of this rebellion was in the South and its tail was in the North and that God intended to punish the whole due to its unnumbered crimes." *Christian Recorder*, 14 March 1863.

15. *Christian Recorder*, 29 August 1863; Angell, *Bishop Henry McNeal Turner*, 33–59.

16. Daniel A. Payne, *Recollections of Seventy Years* (Nashville, TN: Publishing House of the AME Sunday School Union, 1888), 162; "South Carolina Correspondence," *Christian Recorder*, 27 May 1865.

17. Rawick, *The American Slave*, vol. 4, pt. 2, *Texas Narratives*, 92; Claude Bowers, *The Tragic Era* (Cambridge, MA: Riverside Press, 1922), 49–50; Austa M. French, *Slavery in South Carolina and the Ex-Slaves; or, The Port Royal Mission* (New York: W. M. French, 1862), 133–34.

Although the following catechism, used at a freedpeople's school in Richmond, Virginia, was probably written by a northern white teacher, the ideas that it expresses were common among the freedpeople themselves:

"Are you glad you are free?"
"Yes, indeed."
"Who gave you your freedom?"
"God."
"Through whom?"
"Abraham Lincoln." (*National Freedman*, 1 (1 June 1865), 162.)

18. Thomas L. Johnson, *Twenty-Eight Years a Slave* (Bournemouth, England: W. Mate and Sons, 1909), 29–30.

19. For a sweeping interpretation of white churches, north and south, as hopelessly cor-

rupted by "the inherent racism of American Christianity," see Forrest G. Wood, *The Arrogance of Faith: Christianity and Race in America from the Colonial Era to the Twentieth Century* (New York: Knopf, 1990), especially 288–338.

20. Carter G. Woodson, *The History of the Negro Church*, 2d ed. (Washington, DC: Associated Publishers, 1945), 165.

21. Leon F. Litwack, *Been in the Storm So Long*, 464; Rappahannock Baptist Association, *Minutes*, 1864, 10; John W. Blassingame, *Black New Orleans, 1860–1880* (Chicago: University of Chicago Press, 1973), 148.

22. Payne, *Recollections of Seventy Years*, 156; James W. Hood, *One Hundred Years of the African Methodist Episcopal Zion Church: The Centennial of African Methodism* (New York: AME Zion Book Concern, 1895), 85–86, 290–91.

23. Montgomery, *Under Their Own Vine and Fig Tree*, 68, 86; Clarence L. Mohr, "Slaves and White Churches in Confederate Georgia," in Boles, *Masters and Slaves in the House of the Lord*, 156; George A. Singleton, *The Romance of African Methodism: A Study of the African Methodist Episcopal Church* (New York: Exposition Press, 1952), 105–6; Wesley J. Gaines, *African Methodism in the South, or Twenty Five Years of Freedom* (Atlanta, GA: Franklin Publishing, 1890), 5–6 (Andrew Chapel quotations); Haygood S. Bowden, *History of Savannah Methodism from John Wesley to Silas Johnson* (Macon, GA: J. W. Burke, 1929), 127–28 (Quarterly Conference quotation, 128). See also Edward J. Cashin, *Old Springfield: Race and Religion in Augusta, Georgia* (Augusta, GA: Springfield Village Park Foundation, 1995).

24. Thomas O. Fuller, *History of the Negro Baptists of Tennessee* (Memphis, TN: Haskins Printing, 1936), 64; Alrutheus A. Taylor, *The Negro in the Reconstruction of Virginia* (Washington, DC: Association for the Study of Negro Life and History, 1926), 189; Montgomery, *Under Their Own Vine and Fig Tree*, 86; Morgan Callaway to Leila Callaway, September 1863, Morgan Callaway Papers, Special Collections, Robert W. Woodruff Library, Emory University, Atlanta, GA.

25. Lucius H. Holsey, *Autobiography, Sermons, Addresses, and Essays*, 2d ed. (Atlanta, GA: Franklin Printing and Publishing, 1899), 11–12; John Brother Cade, *Holsey—The Incomparable* (New York: Pageant Press, 1964), 11–12.

26. Holsey, *Autobiography*, 10 ("no complaint" quotation); Cade, *Holsey*, 14–15, 49–50 ("first church" quotation), 60–61 ("always been impressed" quotation); Othal Hawthorne Lakey, *The History of the CME Church* (Memphis, TN: CME Publishing, 1985), 114–29; Hildebrand, *The Times Were Strange and Stirring*, 15–27.

27. David Henry Bradley Sr., *A History of the AME Zion Church, 1796–1872* (Nashville, TN: Parthenon Press, 1956), 162; Montgomery, *Under Their Own Vine and Fig Tree*, 99.

28. French, *Slavery in South Carolina and the Ex-Slaves*, 127; entry for 21 October 1866, Charles James Oliver Diary, Charles James Oliver Collection, Special Collections, Robert W. Woodruff Library, Emory University, Atlanta, GA. For an analysis of the various types of labor contracts in "agricultural reconstruction," see Roger L. Ransom and Richard Sutch, *One Kind of Freedom: The Economic Consequences of Emancipation* (New York: Cambridge University Press, 1977), 81–99.

29. *Daily Advertiser* (Montgomery, AL), 22 August 1865; Robert E. Perdue, *The Negro in Savannah, 1865–1900* (New York: Exposition Press, 1973), 29; J. W. Smith, "A History of the Seventh Street Presbyterian Church of Charlotte, North Carolina" (B.D. thesis, Theological Seminary, J. C. Smith University, 1948), 10.

30. Basil Manly II to Jane Smith, 16 November 1865, Manly Collection of Manuscripts, Southern Baptist Historical Library and Archives, Nashville, TN. For an examination of Manly's antebellum paternalistic attitudes toward blacks, see Harold Wilson, "Basil Manly, Apologist for Slavocracy," *Alabama Review* 15 (January 1962): 38–53.

31. Clarence M. Wagner, *Profiles of Black Georgia Baptists* (Gainesville, GA: privately published, 1980), 54; J. R. Huddlestun and Charles O. Walker, *From Heretics to Heroes: A Study of Religious Groups in Georgia with Primary Emphasis on the Baptists* (Jasper, GA: Pickens Tech Press, 1976), 168; Charles Octavius Boothe, *The Cyclopedia of the Colored Baptists of Alabama: Their Leaders and Their Work* (Birmingham: Alabama Publishing, 1895), 111–13; Woodson, *The History of the Negro Church*, 170.

32. United States, Congress, *Report of the Joint Select Committee to Inquire into the Condition of Affairs in the Late Insurrectionary States*, 13 vols., 42d Congress, 2d Session, 1870–1871 (Washington, DC: Government Printing Office, 1872), *Georgia Testimony*, 2:616; "Letter from H. M. Turner," *Christian Recorder*, 30 December 1865; Christopher Hendrick Owen, "Sanctity, Slavery, and Segregation: Methodists and Society in Nineteenth-Century Georgia" (Ph.D. diss., Emory University, 1991), 411.

33. Harry V. Richardson, *Dark Salvation: The Story of Methodism as It Developed among Blacks in America* (Garden City, NJ: Anchor Press, 1976), 197.

34. David Sullins, *Recollections of an Old Man: Seventy Years in Dixie, 1827–1897* (Bristol, TN: King Printing, 1910), 327. For a similar scenario in the Methodist church of Griffin, Georgia, see *Christian Recorder*, 7 July 1866.

Apparently, either Sullins also wrote to the AME Church or his *Recollections* are mistaken about which denomination received the black membership of his church. In the fall of 1866, he wrote to the journal of the AME that freedpeople in Wytheville were "very anxious, indeed, to see a minister of your Church, and learn from him what they had better do as to church relations. The most intelligent and reliable among them want to connect themselves with you, and desire to hold the congregation together until they may have an opportunity to do so. . . . But without authority and no one to give it, they can do nothing while others are busy." Perhaps Sullins wrote to both the AME and AMEZ denominations, and the first one to send a representative won the black members. D. Sullins, "Macedonian Cry," *Christian Recorder*, 1 September 1866.

35. J. Knowles to J. F. Chalfant, 3 January 1866, J. W. Yarbrough to J. F. Chalfant, 27 January, 26 February 1866, Methodist Episcopal Church, Records of the Tennessee Conference, The Georgia and Alabama Mission District, The Reverend James F. Chalfant, Superintendent, 1865–1867, Incoming Letters to the Reverend James F. Chalfant, 1865–1878, Atlanta University Center Woodruff Library, Archives Department, Atlanta, GA.

36. Coosa River Baptist Association, *Minutes*, 1866; Josephus Shackleford, *History of the Muscle Shoals Baptist Association* (Trinity, AL: published by the author, 1891), 84. See also Kolchin, *First Freedom*, 111–12.

37. L. S. Burkhead, "History of the Difficulties of the Pastorate of the Front Street Methodist Church, Wilmington, N.C., for the Year 1865," *Historical Papers* (Durham, NC: Historical Society of Trinity College, 1909; reprint, New York: AMS Press, 1970), 56, 75, 84–85.

38. Albany Baptist Church Records, 1860–1899, Mercer University Library, Special Collections, Macon, GA.

39. Genovese, *Roll, Jordan, Roll*, 257, 261–64; Rawick, *The American Slave*, vol. 4, pt. 2, *Texas Narratives*, 9 (Edwards quotation); Yetman, *Life under the "Peculiar Institution,"* 337; Rawick, *American Slave*, vol. 6, pt. 2, *Indiana Narratives*, 56 (Childress quotation); vol. 6, pt. 1, *Alabama Narratives*, 52 (Calloway quotation); Charles Raymond, "The Religious Life of the Negro Slave," *Harper's New Monthly Magazine* 27 (1863): 485, 677, quoted in Raboteau, *Slave Religion*, 234–35.

40. Litwack, *Been in the Storm So Long*, 461; *Clarke County Journal*, 18 October 1866, quoted in Kolchin, *First Freedom*, 119; *American Baptist*, 4 October 1864 (DeBaptiste quotation). See also Washington, *Frustrated Fellowship*, 62.

41. L. C. Matlack, "The Methodist Episcopal Church in the Southern States," *Meth-*

odist Review (January 1872):108 (Methodist missionary quotation); Thomas J. Kirkland and Robert M. Kennedy, *Historic Camden* (Columbia, SC: State, 1926), 279; Williamson, *After Slavery*, 194–95; Boothe, *The Cyclopedia of the Colored Baptists of Alabama*, 111–13; PCUS, Charleston Presbytery, "Minutes," (12 April 1867), quoted in Montgomery, *Under Their Own Vine and Fig Tree*, 75 (Presbyterian missionary quotation).

42. George B. Tindall, *South Carolina Negroes, 1870–1900* (Baton Rouge: Louisiana State University Press, 1966), 187; "Macedonian Cry," *Christian Recorder*, 1 September 1866; Williamson, *After Slavery*, 194; James Lynch, "The Beaufort, SC Correspondence," *Christian Recorder*, 25 July 1863; W. Stanley Hoole, "The Diary of Dr. Basil Manly, 1858–1867," pt. 5, *Alabama Review* 5 (April 1952): 152.

43. Raboteau, *Slave Religion*, 178; Robert L. Hall, "Black and White Christians in Florida, 1822–1861," in Boles, *Masters and Slaves in the House of the Lord*, 85.

44. Quotations from Gaines, *African Methodism in the South*, 9–10. The pattern was similar among Presbyterians. The PCUSA enlisted black congregations in Savannah, Macon, Dalton, Athens, Atlanta, and Newnan, Georgia. See Franklin C. Talmage, *The Story of the Synod of Georgia* (n.p., 1961), 75.

45. Wagner, *Profiles of Black Georgia Baptists*, 48; A. W. Caldwell to G. L. Eberhart, 9 April 1867, United States, Department of War, Bureau of Refugees, Freedmen, and Abandoned Lands, Record Group 105, Records of the Superintendent of Education for the State of Georgia, 1865–1870, available on microfilm (M-799, National Archives, Washington, DC); ABHMS, *Annual Report*, 1866, 33–34 (Grimes quotation); Washington, *Frustrated Fellowship*, 61–62.

In addition to his duties as chaplain of the First United States Colored Troops, northern black minister Henry M. Turner actively assisted black Union troops in learning to read and write. Angell, *Bishop Henry McNeal Turner*, 56.

46. For examinations of northern educational efforts among the freedpeople, see Jacqueline Jones, *Soldiers of Light and Love: Northern Teachers and Georgia Blacks, 1865–1873* (Chapel Hill: University of North Carolina Press, 1980); Robert C. Morris, *Reading, 'Riting, and Reconstruction: The Education of Freedmen in the South, 1861–1870* (Chicago: University of Chicago Press, 1981); Joe M. Richardson, *Christian Reconstruction: The American Missionary Association and Southern Blacks, 1861–1890* (Athens: University of Georgia Press, 1986); and Ronald E. Butchart, *Northern Schools, Southern Blacks, and Reconstruction: Freedmen's Education, 1862–1875* (Westport, CT: Greenwood Press, 1980).

47. Dvorak, *An African-American Exodus*, 160–68. For an exploration of class and sectional differences among black Baptists, see Washington, *Frustrated Fellowship*, 108–12. On the distinctive contributions of black women, see Kathleen C. Berkeley, "'Colored Ladies Also Contributed': Black Women's Activities from Benevolence to Social Welfare, 1866–1896," in *The Web of Southern Social Relations: Women, Family, and Education*, ed. Walter J. Fraser Jr., R. Frank Saunders Jr., and Jon L. Wakelyn (Athens: University of Georgia Press, 1985), 181–203, and Evelyn Brooks Higginbotham, *Righteous Discontent: The Women's Movement in the Black Baptist Church, 1880–1920* (Cambridge: Harvard University Press, 1993).

For a contrasting interpretation that views class and sectional differences as critical, see Hildebrand, *The Times Were Strange and Stirring*.

48. Armistead L. Robinson, "Plans Dat Comed from God: Institution Building and the Emergence of Black Leadership in Reconstruction Memphis," in *Toward a New South? Studies in Post–Civil War Southern Communities*, ed. Orville Vernon Burton and Robert C. McMath, Jr., (Westport, CT: Greenwood Press, 1982), 71–102.

49. Raboteau, *Slave Religion*, 320; Frazier, *The Negro Church in America*, 45.

5 *Crossing Jordan*

1. For African Americans' use of the Exodus narrative, see Albert J. Raboteau, "African-Americans, Exodus, and the American Israel," in Raboteau, *A Fire in the Bones: Reflections on African-American Religious History* (Boston: Beacon Press, 1995), 17–36; and Katharine L. Dvorak, *An African-American Exodus: The Segregation of the Southern Churches* (Brooklyn, NY: Carlson Publishing, 1991), 25–27.

2. Eric Foner, *Reconstruction: America's Unfinished Revolution, 1863–1877* (New York: Harper and Row, 1988), 88–91.

3. The Baptist statistics in figure 5-1, based on the thirty-five associations that were members of the Georgia Baptist Convention in 1877, are not inclusive of all black Baptists in biracial churches; antimissionary, primitive, and black associations are excluded. Of the 107 Baptist associations in the state in 1877, thirty-five were affiliated with the Georgia Baptist Convention, forty-six were primitive or neutral toward missions, and twenty-six were black associations. The convention reported no statistics in 1865 and 1866. These data were reconstructed from a survey of all extant associational minutes. Missing associational data for some years were interpolated from known end points. Approximately 18 percent of the annual figures for the entire period are interpolations. Because associations met in the fall, and the Georgia Baptist Convention met in April, the figures reported are from the previous year. This schedule produces a one-year lag in the statistics. This effect does not occur with the statistics for Georgia Methodists and Presbyterians because the Georgia Annual Conference and the Synod of Georgia met late in each year.

4. *Minutes of the Annual Conferences of the Methodist Episcopal Church, South, 1860–1877* (Nashville, TN: Methodist Publishing House, 1860–77); General Assembly of the PCUSA (Old School), *Minutes,* 1860; General Assembly of the PCUS, *Minutes,* 1866, Stephen V. Ash, *Middle Tennessee Society Transformed, 1860–1870: War and Peace in the Upper South* (Baton Rouge: Louisiana State University Press, 1988), 200–01, 211–13.

5. Georgia Baptist Convention, *Minutes,* 1865, 1867, 1875; Clifton Judson Allen et al., eds., *Encyclopedia of Southern Baptists,* 2 vols. (Nashville, TN: Broadman Press, 1958), s.v. "Georgia Associations," by Arthur Hinson; Clarence M. Wagner, *Profiles of Black Georgia Baptists* (Gainesville, GA: privately published, 1980), 54; J. R. Huddlestun and Charles O. Walker, *From Heretics to Heroes: A Study of Religious Groups in Georgia with Primary Emphasis on the Baptists* (Jasper, GA: Pickens Tech Press, 1976), 168.

Blacks departed the six churches of the original Sunbury Association that entered the New Sunbury Association even more swiftly: in 1866 these churches had only 432 white members and 72 black members, and by the following year, they had only one black member New Sunbury Association, *Minutes,* 1866, 1867.

6. Robert G. Gardner et al., *A History of the Georgia Baptist Association, 1784–1984* (Atlanta: Georgia Baptist Historical Society, 1988), 198–201, 268–70, 275. By 1880 the Georgia Association had only 570 black members, though this number was still larger than the black membership of all the other associations in the Georgia Baptist Convention combined.

7. Frederick A. Bode, "The Formation of Evangelical Communities in Middle Georgia: Twiggs County, 1820–1861," *Journal of Southern History* 60 (November 1994): 733–35. Stone Creek never licensed a black preacher before the Civil War, though other Twiggs County Baptist churches did. Contrary to its attitude after the war, Stone Creek in the antebellum period had "insisted on the maximum degree of white supervision and control, while Jeffersonville and Richland allowed at least a limited degree of black participation and autonomy." Bode, "The Formation of Evangelical Communities in Middle Georgia," 733.

8. Wagner, *Profiles of Black Georgia Baptists*, 48, 54, 66; Georgia Baptist Convention, *Minutes*, 1877; James Melvin Washington, *Frustrated Fellowship: The Black Baptist Quest for Social Power* (Macon, GA: Mercer University Press, 1986), 113–14.

9. Georgia Annual Conference (MECS), *Minutes*, 1864; Haygood S. Bowden, *History of Savannah Methodism from John Wesley to Silas Johnson* (Macon, GA: J. W. Burke, 1929), 128; Eatonton Methodist Church, Quarterly Conference Minutes, 29 June 1867, Georgia Department of Archives and History, Atlanta, GA.

10. Bainbridge District Conference, Minutes, September 1867, South Georgia Conference Archives, Epworth-by-the-Sea, GA; South Georgia Annual Conference (MECS), *Minutes*, 1867, 1868; Wesley J. Gaines, *African Methodism in the South, or Twenty Five Years of Freedom* (Atlanta, GA: Franklin Publishing, 1890), 22.

In 1870 the Bainbridge District reported 137 black members in three circuits or charges; beginning in 1871 it reported none. South Georgia Annual Conference (MECS), *Minutes*, 1870.

11. *North Carolina Presbyterian*, 30 May 1866 (quotations); Andrew E. Murray, *Presbyterians and the Negro—A History* (Philadelphia: Presbyterian Historical Society, 1966), 146–47; Synod of Georgia, *Minutes*, 1867, 12–13.

12. Murray, *Presbyterians and the Negro*, 147, 179; Franklin C. Talmage, *The Story of the Synod of Georgia* (n.p., 1961), 75; Ernest Trice Thompson, *Presbyterians in the South*, 3 vols. (Richmond, VA: John Knox Press, 1963–73), 2:148; Atlantic Synod, *Minutes*, 1873.

13. Entries for 5 January 1867, 16 April 1866, Eliza Rhea Fain Diaries, John N. Fain Collection, McClung Historical Collection, Knox County Public Library System, Knoxville, TN.

Other members of Fain's family did not share her paternalistic concern for the freedpeople; her son Ike Fain told her that he "did not believe they had souls." Shocked, she told him "they would rise in judgment against him." Entry for 4 May 1870, Fain Diaries. See also Entries for 23 July 1870, 15 February 1873, 25 October 1873, Fain Diaries.

14. Huddlestun and Walker, *From Heretics to Heroes*, 168–69; Robert E. Perdue, *The Negro in Savannah, 1865–1900* (New York: Exposition Press, 1973), 29; General Assembly of the PCUS, *Minutes*, 1865, 370.

15. "Pastoral Address of the Southern Methodist Bishops," *Southern Christian Advocate*, 31 August 1865; Memphis Annual Conference, *Minutes*, 1865, Report of Committee on Missions.

In April 1865, Eliza Fain wrote in her diary, "May some of the poor creatures be faithful to the persons whom they serve who are really the only beings upon this earth who have any right feeling for the poor African." Entry for 22 April 1865, Fain Diaries.

16. Memphis Annual Conference, *Minutes*, 1866, Report of Committee on Religious Interests of the Colored People; Bethel Baptist Association, *Minutes*, 1870, 8–10. The Bethel Association had 2,972 black members in 1865, but by 1870 it retained only 231. See also "What Shall Be Done for the Blacks," *Baptist*, 11 May 1867.

17. Southern Baptist Convention, *Proceedings*, 1866, 86; *Christian Index*, 10 June 1869.

18. *Episcopal Methodist*, 2 August 1865.

19. Western Baptist Association, *Minutes*, 1866, 6–7; 1868, 3–4.

20. Ebenezer Baptist Association, *Minutes*, 1867, 2.

Southern white Baptists in other areas of the South expressed similar feelings. A committee report suggesting that churches and associations be allowed to use their own judgment in admitting black members sparked a heated debate in the 1867 North Carolina Convention. James D. Hufham, editor of the state Baptist paper, led the fight against the report, declaring that he would not sanction any report that allowed the reception of both races "promiscuously, with equal privileges, into our Churches, Associations and Conventions." Black members, he insisted, must be received "on the old footing, without any voice in the discipline of the church or the management of its affairs." After debate, the committee report was amended to recommend that churches aid black members in the organization of their own churches. North Carolina Baptist Convention, *Minutes*, 1867, 25; Rufus B. Spain, *At Ease in Zion: A Social History of Southern Baptists, 1865–1900* (Nashville, TN: Vanderbilt University Press, 1967), 50.

21. Western Baptist Association, *Minutes*, 1866, 6–7.

22. *Christian Index*, 24 February 1866.

23. General Conference of the MECS, *Journal*, 1866, 58–59. See also Kenneth K. Bailey, "The Post–Civil War Racial Separations in Southern Protestantism: Another Look," *Church History* 46 (December 1977): 466–67.

24. William B. Gravely, "The Social, Political and Religious Significance of the Formation of the Colored Methodist Episcopal Church (1870)," *Methodist History* 18 (October 1979): 19; Othal Hawthorne Lakey, *The History of the CME Church* (Memphis, TN: CME Publishing, 1985), 153–63; John Brother Cade, *Holsey—The Incomparable* (New York: Pageant Press, 1964), 21.

25. Thomas D. Campbell, *One Family under God: A Story of Cumberland Presbyterians in Black and White* (Memphis, TN: Board of Christian Education of the Cumberland Presbyterian Church, 1982), 38; Ben M. Barrus, Milton L. Baughn, and Thomas H. Campbell, *A People Called Cumberland Presbyterians* (Memphis, TN: Frontier Press, 1972), 168.

26. Thompson, *Presbyterians in the South*, 2:309; General Assembly of the PCUS, *Minutes*, 1874, 588–96; H. Shelton Smith, *In His Image, But . . . : Racism in Southern Religion, 1780–1910* (Durham, NC: Duke University Press, 1972), 241.

27. Western Baptist Association, *Minutes*, 1866, 6; General Assembly of the Cumberland Presbyterian Church, *Minutes*, 1869, 23–24 (first General Assembly quotation); Campbell, *One Family under God*, 40; Barrus, Baughn, and Campbell, *A People Called Cumberland Presbyterians*, 165–67 (remaining General Assembly quotations).

The Cumberland Presbyterian General Assembly of 1868 urged the presbyteries to provide ministers for the freedpeople. However, it stated, "the leadings of Providence may hereafter show more plainly whether they should be constituted a separate ecclesiastical body." Barrus, Baughn, and Campbell, *A People Called Cumberland Presbyterians*, 166.

Baptist leader Basil Manly II wrote in the spring of 1866, "The experiment of freeing the blacks is too new, and unfinished, for us to understand the divine procedure. Both the giving and the learning of the lesson require time and patience. We have the promise that God will strengthen our heart. Let us *wait on the Lord*, therefore." Basil Manly II to Miss Jane Smith, 6 March 1866, Manly Collection of Manuscripts, Southern Baptist Historical Library and Archives, Nashville, TN.

28. Lakey, *The History of the CME Church*, 174–79; General Conference of the MECS, *Journal*, 1870, 167.

The editor of the *Christian Advocate* in Nashville revealed the necessity for a separate denomination for those blacks who had remained in the MECS but denied any moral responsibility for the change:

> We served the colored people when they were slaves . . . and we are willing to labor for them still . . . but our "occupation is gone"—we cannot serve them now, as we served them. This is not our fault—if there be any sin in this it lieth not at our door. The next best thing that we can do for them, is that which, with one voice they desire of us—develop them into a perfect organization, with Quarterly, District, Annual, and General Conferences; local preachers, traveling preachers, deacons, elders, and bishops.

Because black Christians would no longer accept a subordinate status, "as we served them," they had to be set apart in their own denomination. *Christian Advocate*, 25 June 1870.

29. *Christian Advocate*, 7 January 1871; Isaac Lane, *Autobiography of Bishop Isaac Lane, LL. D., With a Short History of the C. M. E. Church in America and Methodism* (Nashville, TN: Publishing House of the Methodist Episcopal Church, South, 1916), 18–26, 57–63; Gravely, "The Social, Political and Religious Significance," 22–25; Lakey, *The History of the CME Church*, 195–223; Cade, *Holsey—The Incomparable*, 24–25.

30. Campbell, *One Family under God*, 38–39; Barrus, Baughn, and Campbell, *A People Called Cumberland Presbyterians*, 168; B. W. McDonnold, *History of the Cumberland Presbyterian Church*, 4th ed. (Nashville, TN: Board of Publication of Cumberland Presbyterian Church, 1899), 437.

Estimates of twenty thousand black members in the Cumberland Presbyterian Church before the war are probably exaggerations, but most black Cumberland Presbyterians left the denomination before the formation of the Colored Cumberland Presbyterian Church. Barrus, Baughn, and Campbell, *A People Called Cumberland Presbyterians*, 168.

31. Thompson, *Presbyterians in the South*, 2:323, 325; Murray, *Presbyterians and the Negro*, 150–51.

32. PCUSA (Old School), *First Annual Report of the Committee for Freedmen*, 1866, 10; *Christian Recorder*, 13 March 1869; "School Burned," *Christian Recorder*, 27 March 1869.

33. See, for example, the *Christian Index*, 17 June 1869, in which northern teachers are denounced as "abolitionist emissaries" who "engender strife and disaffection," "encourage the negro in insolent assumption," and "fan the flames of open hostility between the races."

34. *Christian Recorder*, 24 November 1866. The overall black population in Georgia increased by 17 percent between 1860 and 1870. United States, Census Office, *The Statistics of the Population of the United States: Compiled from the Original Returns of the Ninth Census (June 1, 1870), under the Direction of the Secretary of the Interior* (Washington, DC: Government Printing Office, 1872), 21–22.

35. William E. Montgomery, *Under Their Own Vine and Fig Tree: The African-American Church in the South, 1865–1900* (Baton Rouge: Louisiana State University Press, 1993), 101.

Baptist minister Thomas O. Fuller wrote in 1917: "It is generally thought that a large number of men entered the ministry as a mark of appreciation for what the Lord had done for them in breaking the chains of slavery." Thomas O. Fuller, *History of the Negro Baptists of Tennessee* (Memphis, TN: Haskins Printing, 1936), 47–48.

36. In Vicksburg, Mississippi, "some of the leaders of the white [Methodist] congregation promised to help the blacks build a church and permitted them to use the basement of their church until the new building was completed." However, AME minister Hiram Revels reported, "so far as my knowledge extends, our people, from a painful recollection of their past and a happy realization of their present ecclesiastical relations, determined to decline the offer." *Christian Recorder*, 5 August, 7 October 1865.

The AME minister Wesley J. Gaines took charge of the Atlanta, Georgia, congregation in 1867, and they worshiped "in an old church given to our people before the war." However, "as we had no deeds to the property, we bought a lot of ground on Wheat St." In March 1868, they laid the foundation of a large church building. By May 1869, the congregation was meeting in the building but still needed $1,500 to complete it. Gaines issued a call for assistance through the AME Church's newspaper, the *Christian Recorder*. *Christian Recorder*, 8 May 1869.

37. "Letter from Georgia," *Christian Recorder*, 14 September 1867. Also in 1867 the black Ebenezer Baptist Association reported that a majority of its churches were "in a destitute condition for want of shelter and of Ministers to organize them, and to aid in gathering their scattered members together." Ebenezer Baptist Association, *Minutes*, 1867, 11.

38. From 1865 to 1871, the Freedmen's Bureau spent $5,262,500 for educational purposes in the South. U. S. Department of the Interior, Bureau of Education, *Negro Education: A Study*

of the Private and Higher Schools for Colored People in the United States, 2 vols. (Washington, DC: Government Printing Office, 1917; reprint, New York: Negro Universities Press, 1969), 289.

For a discussion of the Freedmen's Bureau, the primary vehicle for government assistance to the freedpeople, see William S. McFeely, *Yankee Stepfather: General O. O. Howard and the Freedmen* (New Haven: Yale University Press, 1968).

39. Huddlestun and Walker, *From Heretics to Heroes*, 168–69; Entry for 25 October 1873, Fain Diaries. For other examples of southern whites' providing organizational assistance to the freedpeople, see Bethel Baptist Association, *Minutes*, 1869, 6; Central Baptist Association, *Minutes*, 1866, 8–9.

For examples of southern whites ordaining black ministers, see Fuller, *History of the Negro Baptists of Tennessee*, 58, and Mechal Sobel, "'They Can Never Both Prosper Together': Black and White Baptists in Antebellum Nashville, Tennessee," *Tennessee Historical Quarterly* 38 (Fall 1979): 303–4.

In some cases, whites served as secretaries for black denominational meetings. When no member of a meeting could write and no other person was available, some Baptist associations "chose some good brother as the 'memorandum' of the meeting and it was the duty of this person to tell what was done at the last meeting, when the next meeting convened." Fuller, *History of the Negro Baptists of Tennessee*, 106–7.

40. Holsey, *Autobiography*, 20–21; Cade, *Holsey—The Incomparable*, 30–31, 38–39, 50–53; Lakey, *History of the CME Church*, 241–47. In his autobiography, Holsey boasted that the history of the CME Church "cannot be written, nor its records compiled without me as one of the chief actors in its drama and one who has deeply impressed himself upon its character and production." Holsey, *Autobiography*, 29.

41. Gross Alexander, *A History of the Methodist Episcopal Church, South* (New York: Christian Literature, 1894), 92; Georgia Annual Conference (MECS), *Minutes*, 1865, 12–13; J. E. Parker, *A Brief History of the Churches in the New Sunbury Baptist Association* (n.p.: Wayne County Press, 1966), 5.

42. Sobel, "They Can Never Both Prosper Together," 303–7.

43. Spain, *At Ease in Zion*, 53, 60–61; Georgia Baptist Convention, *Minutes*, 1872, 17; 1873, 19 (quotation); 1874, 27; 1875, 26; 1876, 21 (quotation); 1877, 20; *Christian Index*, 11 April 1878 (Love quotations). See also Harold Lynn McManus, "The American Baptist Home Mission Society and Freedmen Education in the South, With Special Reference to Georgia: 1862–1897" (Ph.D. diss., Yale University, 1953), 291–300; Willard Range, *The Rise and Progress of Negro Colleges in Georgia, 1865–1949* (Athens: University of Georgia Press, 1951), 24–27; Wagner, *Profiles of Black Georgia Baptists*, 130–32.

Between 1871 and 1881, 371 students attended the school; 142 trained as teachers, and 229 studied for the ministry. Atlanta Baptist Seminary became Morehouse College in 1913. Charles Edgeworth Jones, *Education in Georgia, Contributions to American Educational History*, ed. Herbert B. Adams (Washington, DC: Government Printing Office, 1889), 148.

Some northern black missionaries similarly condemned what they considered to be the "excesses" and "superstitions" of the ex-slaves. Washington, *Frustrated Fellowship*, 109–12.

44. Lakey, *The History of the CME Church*, 446–51; George Esmond Clary Jr., "The Founding of Paine College —A Unique Venture in Inter-Racial Cooperation in the New South (1882–1903)" (Ed.D. diss., University of Georgia, 1965); Eskew, "Black Elitism and the Failure of Paternalism in Postbellum Georgia," 648–53; Anna L. Cooke, *Lane College: Its Heritage and Outreach, 1882–1982* (Jackson, TN: Lane College, 1987), 9, 14–15.

James Albert Bray, a black Georgian, replaced Saunders as the president of Lane in 1903; Paine did not have a black president until 1971.

Clary compared the support of the MECS for antebellum plantation missions and for postbellum black education. In the first two decades of its existence (1845–1865), the MECS spent over $1.7 million on plantation missions; in the two decades from 1882 to 1903, it expended only $160,000 on Paine and Lane Institutes. Clary, "The Founding of Paine College," 95–96.

45. The work of northern white denominations among both the freedpeople and whites in the South is addressed more extensively in chapter 8.

46. Washington, *Frustrated Fellowship*, 79–131; Montgomery, *Under Their Own Vine and Fig Tree*, 226–27; Paul Harvey, *Redeeming the South: Religious Cultures and Racial Identities among Southern Baptists, 1865–1925* (Chapel Hill: University of North Carolina Press, 1997), 45–74.

47. The African Methodist Episcopal Zion Church first met under that name in New York in June 1821; ordained black superintendents first governed the denomination independently in Philadelphia in June 1822. Various sources use one of these two dates as the appropriate founding date. See Frederick A. Maser and George A. Singleton, "Further Branches of Methodism are Founded," in *The History of American Methodism*, ed. Emory Stevens Bucke, 3 vols. (Nashville, TN: Abingdon Press, 1964), 1:609–14, and Reginald F. Hildebrand, *The Times Were Strange and Stirring: Methodist Preachers and the Crisis of Emancipation* (Durham, NC: Duke University Press, 1995), xxiii, 133.

48. Clarence E. Walker, *A Rock in a Weary Land: The African Methodist Episcopal Church during the Civil War and Reconstruction* (Baton Rouge: Louisiana State University Press, 1982), 50; James W. Hood, *One Hundred Years of the African Methodist Episcopal Zion Church: The Centennial of African Methodism* (New York: AME Zion Book Concern, 1895), 85; David Henry Bradley Sr., *A History of the AME Zion Church, 1796–1872* (Nashville, TN: Parthenon Press, 1956), 158, 163.

49. In December 1865 Henry M. Turner wrote, "colored preachers, from all quarters, are calling upon me for authority to preach." *Christian Recorder*, 30 December 1865.

50. Theophilus G. Steward, *Fifty Years in the Gospel Ministry* (Philadelphia, PA: AME Book Concern, 1921), 72, quoted in Angell, *Bishop Henry McNeal Turner*, 69; Angell, *Bishop Henry McNeal Turner*, 62–80, 108–22; *Christian Recorder*, 7 July 1866; Walker, *A Rock in a Weary Land*, 71–72.

51. Dvorak, *An African-American Exodus*, 138–43. Other denominations participated fully in this competition as well. See, for example, the efforts of Congregationalist Edward Parmelee Smith as an agent of the American Missionary Association. William H. Armstrong, *A Friend to God's Poor: Edward Parmelee Smith* (Athens: University of Georgia Press, 1993), 114–16. For other Congregationalist efforts, see Joe M. Richardson, "The Failure of the American Missionary Association to Expand Congregationalism among Southern Blacks," *Southern Studies* 18 (Spring 1979): 51–73; Joe M. Richardson, *Christian Reconstruction: The American Missionary Association and Southern Blacks, 1861–1890* (Athens: University of Georgia Press, 1986), 143–59; and Thomas F. Armstrong, "The Building of a Black Church: Community in Post Civil War Liberty County, Georgia," *Georgia Historical Quarterly* 66 (Fall 1982): 346–67. For Baptist efforts, see Washington, *Frustrated Fellowship*, 49–105.

52. Montgomery, *Under Their Own Vine and Fig Tree*, 86. The Bethel Methodist Protestant Church, which existed as an independent congregation under Drayton's leadership before joining the AME in 1866, and the Mount Zion AMEZ Church, organized in Augusta in 1866, drew most of their membership from the black laboring classes. Trinity drew much of its membership from the ranks of black artisans, craftspeople, and service workers. For a perceptive analysis of class differences among Augusta's postwar black Methodist congregations, see Glenn T. Eskew, "Paternalism among Augusta's Methodists: Black, White, and Colored" (paper presented at "Race, Religion and Gender in Augusta" Conference, Augusta, GA, 29 February 1996).

53. Christopher Hendrick Owen, "Sanctity, Slavery, and Segregation: Methodists and Society in Nineteenth-Century Georgia" (Ph.D. diss., Emory University, 1991), 413, 416; Walker, *A Rock in a Weary Land*, 96–98.

The alliance of the MECS and the AME did not last beyond 1867. In 1869, the AME newspaper published an indictment against the MECS, charging it with treason against God, Jesus, the church, the government, and liberty. *Christian Recorder*, 13 March 1869.

54. *Southern Christian Advocate*, 6 July, 20 July 1866. The congregation joined the AME Church late in 1866. See Angell, *Bishop Henry McNeal Turner*, 74–75.

55. *Christian Recorder*, 20 January 1866 (Turner on West quotations); Hood, *One Hundred Years of the African Methodist Episcopal Zion Church*, 364–65 (AMEZ in Georgia quotation, 365), Henry M. Turner, "Georgia Correspondence," *Christian Recorder*, 5 October 1867 (Turner on Clinton quotation); Cade, *Holsey—The Incomparable*, 83 (Holsey on West quotation).

General Superintendent of Education John W. Alvord of the Freedmen's Bureau reported in 1870 that the freedpeople in Augusta suffered from "some division among themselves in religious matters." John W. Alvord, *Letters from the South Relating to the Condition of the Freedmen* (Washington, DC: Howard University Press, 1870), 15.

The Trinity Methodist congregation was organized in 1842 as the church for the black members from Augusta's biracial Methodist congregation. In 1850 the congregation purchased the freedom of their first pastor, James Harris. Edward S. "Ned" West (1816–1887) succeeded Harris and served as pastor of Trinity during the Civil War and Reconstruction. He also served as a clerical delegate from Georgia to the organizing conference of the CME Church, which met in Jackson, Tennessee, in December 1870. The brevity of the church's affiliation with the AMEZ Church may have been due to the radicalism of AMEZ minister Tunis Campbell, who was deeply involved in state politics; to Trinity's concern over retaining its church property; or to the AMEZ Church's failure to deliver institutional support. "Whatever the reason," Glenn T. Eskew concludes, "Trinity rejected the AMEZ denomination and accepted the ecclesiastical authority of the MEC,S." Eskew, "Paternalism among Augusta's Methodists," 7–8, 18–21; Journal of the General Conference of the Colored Methodist Episcopal Church in America, 1870–1906, 1–2, Christian Methodist Episcopal Church Archives, Memphis, TN.

56. Andrew W. Caldwell to James F. Chalfant, 27 June 1867, Methodist Episcopal Church, Records of the Tennessee Conference, The Georgia and Alabama Mission District, The Reverend James F. Chalfant, Superintendent, 1865–1867, Incoming Letters to the Rev. James F. Chalfant, 1865–1878, Atlanta University Center Woodruff Library, Archives Department, Atlanta, GA; Henry M. Turner, "From Macon, Ga.," *Christian Recorder*, 7 July 1866. See also Jacqueline Jones, *Soldiers of Light and Love: Northern Teachers and Georgia Blacks, 1865–1873* (Chapel Hill: University of North Carolina Press, 1980), 156.

57. *Christian Recorder*, 19 May, 2 June 1866, 10 August 1867 (quotations). Similar quarrels plagued black congregations in other states. In New Bern, North Carolina, the Reverend James W. Hood of the AMEZ Church convinced a local black Methodist congregation to unite with his church, despite the efforts of a white missionary of the Methodist Episcopal Church and two black AME missionaries to attract the congregation into their denominations. Hood, *One Hundred Years of the African Methodist Episcopal Zion Church*, 290–92.

58. Thomas Crayton, "Letter from Georgia," *Christian Recorder*, 14 September 1867; J. H. Caldwell to Maj. J. R. Lewis, 5 August 1867, J. R. Lewis to J. H. Caldwell, 7 August 1867, United States, Department of War, Bureau of Refugees, Freedmen, and Abandoned Lands, Record Group 105, Records of the Superintendent of Education for the State of Georgia, 1865–1870, National Archives, Washington, DC; Alvord, *Letters from the South*, 24.

Blacks in Savannah contributed $1,000 as early as 1865 for teachers, and by 1867 the freedpeople wholly or partly supported 152 schools and owned thirty-nine of the school buildings there. Range, *The Rise and Progress of Negro Colleges in Georgia*, 14.

59. J. B. Mahone, "Letter from Georgia," *Christian Recorder*, 2 May 1868.

60. Note regarding Session of Presbyterian Church, Darien, Georgia, 26 July 1878, Henry Francis Hoyt Collection, Historical Foundation of the Presbyterian and Reformed Churches, Montreat, NC.

6 Southern Churches Resurgent

1. Georgia Baptist Convention, *Minutes*, 1874, 24. The Constitution of the Noonday Baptist Association of Georgia, formed in 1858, declared that the object of the association was "the promotion of vital piety in its members, the nurture of all the churches, especially new or struggling ones, in its bounds, the fostering of educational enterprises in the denomination, the encouragement of Sunday-schools, the diffusion of religious books, and the collection and distributions to missionary and other objects." George T. Light, *A Brief History of the Noonday Baptist Association (1858–1958)* (South Pittsburg, TN: Hustler Printing, 1958), 6.

2. Western Baptist Association, *Minutes*, 1866, 6; Robert Langdon Neely Collection, Manuscript Historical Sketch of the Synod of Memphis, 1880, 172, Historical Foundation of the Presbyterian and Reformed Churches, Montreat, NC.

3. Memoirs of Thomas Hooke McCallie (1901–12), McCallie Family Papers, McCallie School, Chattanooga, TN.

Although the Presbyterian Church in Chattanooga had 150 members before the war, only ten or fifteen remained in 1865. By 1867 McCallie's labors and the return of refugees had boosted the membership to ninety-four communicants, with 125 pupils in the Sunday school. David Cooper, *Catalyst for Christ, 150 Years: First Presbyterian Church, Chattanooga, Tennessee* (Chattanooga, TN: Chattanooga News-Free Press, 1990), 24.

4. Clement A. Evans, "General Clement A. Evans Asks to Be a Methodist Preacher," *Historical Highlights* 22 (Spring 1992): 34–35.

5. Robert Grier Stephens Jr., ed. and comp., *Intrepid Warrior: Clement Anselm Evans, Confederate General From Georgia: Life, Letters, and Diaries of the War Years* (Dayton, OH: Morningside, 1992), 123, 558–60.

Evans served as a preacher of the MECS in Georgia for twenty-five years. Alfred Mann Pierce, *Lest Faith Forget: The Story of Methodism in Georgia* (Atlanta: Georgia Methodist Information, 1951), 113.

6. "The Condition and Wants of the Church," *Southern Presbyterian*, 25 January 1866; Entry for 26 May 1867, Eliza Rhea Fain Diaries, John N. Fain Collection, McClung Historical Collection, Knox County Public Library System, Knoxville, TN.

J. L. M. Curry wrote from Alabama, "many churches are without pastors. Many preachers are seeking support in secular occupations. Very few young men have the ministry in view. Those who have are unable to educate themselves, and the churches imagine themselves to be too poor to furnish the 'wherewith.'" J. L. M. Curry to Basil Manly II, 26 October 1866, Manly Collection of Manuscripts, Southern Baptist Historical Library and Archives, Nashville, TN.

After returning from Confederate service to Mississippi, Baptist James B. Gambrell found that "there were many difficulties about getting into the ministry, even after it came to be pretty plain to my mind that that was my calling." James B. Gambrell, *Parable and Precept: A Baptist Message* (New York: Fleming H. Revell, 1917), 92–93.

7. "The Condition and Wants of the Church," *Southern Presbyterian*, 25 January 1866; Synod of Nashville, Minutes, January 1866, 268–69, Historical Foundation of the Presbyterian and Reformed Churches, Montreat, NC; Synod of Georgia, *Minutes*, 1868, 9; "Our Necessities," *Christian Index* (Atlanta, GA), 6 January 1866.

Thomas H. McCallie himself had taught a school of from sixty to eighty pupils in Chattanooga from September 1864 to June 1865. He charged $3 per pupil per month. He closed the school in the summer of 1865 because "the times were becoming more settled, the war was over and there was every prospect not only that there would be schools in abundance, but that my ministry would require all my time." Memoirs of Thomas Hooke McCallie.

8. Tennessee Annual Conference, Pastoral Address, 1865, quoted in Hunter Dickinson Farish, *The Circuit Rider Dismounts: A Social History of Southern Methodism, 1865–1900* (Richmond, VA: Dietz Press, 1938), 32; Holston Annual Conference (MECS), *Minutes*, 1873, 8. Other conferences voiced similar complaints. The 1867 Missouri Annual Conference estimated that only 50 percent of the pastors' salaries had been paid. The 1868 South Carolina Annual Conference reported that many preachers had to undertake secular work to supplement their salaries. Missouri Annual Conference (MECS), *Minutes*, 1867, 27; South Carolina Annual Conference (MECS), *Minutes*, 1868, 39.

9. Memoirs of Thomas Hooke McCallie; Thomas C. Johnson, *History of the Southern Presbyterian Church* (New York: Christian Literature, 1894), 373–74.

10. "Revivals in Georgia," *Christian Index*, 9 November 1865.

11. New Sunbury Association, *Minutes*, 1867, 7; Bethel Baptist Association, *Minutes*, 1867, 12.

Charles Manly reported the same conditions in the area around Tuscaloosa, Alabama in the fall of 1866: "I find the people throughout the whole country in quite a depressed condition. . . . there is little interest in religion. . . . The condition of a great many is much worse now than it was at the time of the surrender. But the general decay of godliness is one of the most distressing features of our whole condition." Three weeks later, Manly wrote, "the people have little religion." Charles Manly to Basil Manly Jr., 5, 25 September 1866, Manly Collection of Manuscripts.

12. Georgia Baptist Convention, *Minutes*, 1869, 9–10.

13. Georgia Baptist Convention, *Minutes*, 1871, 8–9; 1874, 28; 1875, 27–28.

14. Comer Hastings, "The Methodist Episcopal Church, South during the Reconstruction Period" (M.A. thesis, Duke University, 1932), 70–71.

15. Middle Cherokee Baptist Association, *Minutes*, 1866, 6–7.

16. Georgia Baptist Convention, *Minutes*, 1869, 9–10.

17. Georgia Annual Conference, Minutes, 30 November, 3 December 1866, Special Collections, Pitts Theology Library, Emory University, Atlanta, GA; John W. Burke, *Autobiography: Chapters from the Life of a Preacher* (Macon, GA: J. W. Burke, 1884), 112.

18. Tennessee Baptist Convention, *Minutes*, 1874, 3–5; W. Fred Kendall, *A History of the Tennessee Baptist Convention* (Brentwood, TN: Executive Board of the Tennessee Baptist Convention, 1974), 144–49.

In 1907 the trustees of Southwestern Baptist University voted to change the name to Union University. Kendall, *A History of the Tennessee Baptist Convention*, 197.

19. Kendall, *A History of the Tennessee Baptist Convention*, 155–56.

20. "The General Assembly of 1865," *Southern Presbyterian Review* 17 (July 1866): 77–78.

21. Charles T. Thrift Jr., "Rebuilding the Southern Church," in *The History of American Methodism*, ed. Emory Stevens Bucke, 3 vols. (Nashville, TN: Abingdon Press, 1964), 2:275–76; Farish, *The Circuit Rider Dismounts*, 64–65. In 1882 an accommodationist faction attempted again to change the name of the denomination, this time to the "Methodist Episcopal Church in America." The annual conferences emphatically rejected the proposal by a vote of 3,415 to 91, again demonstrating their intense sectional loyalty. Kenneth K. Bailey, "The Post–Civil War Racial Separations in Southern Protestantism: Another Look," *Church History* 46 (December 1977): 466.

22. Gross Alexander, *A History of the Methodist Episcopal Church, South* (New York: Christian Literature, 1894), 87.

23. Hastings, "The Methodist Episcopal Church, South during the Reconstruction Period," 31.

24. Christopher Hendrick Owen, "Sanctity, Slavery, and Segregation: Methodists and Society in Nineteenth-Century Georgia" (Ph.D. diss., Emory University, 1991), 439, 441; Hastings, "The Methodist Episcopal Church, South during the Reconstruction Period," 32.

25. Georgia Baptist Convention, *Minutes*, 1869, 13. See also *Baptist*, 18 May 1867.

26. Stephen V. Ash, *Middle Tennessee Society Transformed, 1860–1870: War and Peace in the Upper South* (Baton Rouge: Louisiana State University Press, 1988), 177–78, 244–46.

27. Although Presbyterians were also divided in eastern Tennessee, southern Presbyterians did not suffer the dramatic loss in membership that hindered southern Methodists. Southern Presbyterian membership in the eastern Tennessee presbyteries of Knoxville and Holston grew by 235 percent from 1,007 members in 1860 to 3,370 members in 1877. The larger southern Presbyterian memberships in the central presbyteries of the state grew by 84 percent and in the western presbyteries by 28 percent during the same period. General Assembly of the PCUSA (Old School), *Minutes*, 1860; General Assembly of the PCUS, *Minutes*, 1877.

28. Robert Langdon Neely, Manuscript Historical Sketch of the Synod of Memphis, 1880, Robert Langdon Neely Collection.

29. "To Our Readers," *Southern Presbyterian*, 4 January 1866.

30. Entries for 29 June 1865, 19 December 1869, Fain Diaries. See also entries for 16 July 1865, 13 September 1868, 14 February 1869, Fain Diaries.

The offices of the *Christian Observer* did not share in the general destruction of Richmond, and the paper was reestablished there in June 1865. In 1869, the newspaper moved to Louisville, Kentucky, where it continued to serve southern Presbyterians in the Upper South. Arnold Shankman, "Converse, *The Christian Observer*, and Civil War Censorship," *Journal of Presbyterian History* 52 (1974): 240–41.

31. *American Annual Cyclopaedia and Register of Important Events* 5, 1865 (New York: Appleton, 1870), 553; Bishop James O. Andrew to Bishop Holland N. McTyeire, 7 June 1866, John J. Tigert IV Collection, Papers of Holland Nimmons McTyeire, Incoming Correspondence, Special Collections, Vanderbilt University Library, Nashville, TN.

32. *Southern Christian Advocate*, 29 June 1865.

33. Bainbridge District Conference, Minutes, 1867–1878, April 1870 meeting, South Georgia Conference Archives, Epworth-by-the-Sea, GA.

34. North Georgia Annual Conference (MECS), *Minutes*, 1868, 16; 1871, 33.

35. John Abernathy Smith, *Cross and Flame: Two Centuries of United Methodism in Middle Tennessee* (Nashville, TN: Commission on Archives and History of the Tennessee Conference, 1984), 163–64; James Penn Pilkington, *The Methodist Publishing House, A History, Volume I: Beginnings to 1870* (Nashville, TN: Abingdon Press, 1968), 468–70.

The Southern Methodist Publishing House also published the *Banner of Peace* newspaper for the Cumberland Presbyterian Church and the *Christian Index* for the CME Church.

36. *Christian Index*, 6 January 1866; Houston Baptist Association, *Minutes*, 1865, 4.

37. "Our Aim," *Christian Index*, 9 November 1865.

38. "Editor's Salutatory," *Christian Index*, 6 January 1866; Rufus B. Spain, *At Ease in Zion: A Social History of Southern Baptists, 1865–1900* (Nashville, TN: Vanderbilt University Press, 1967), 25.

39. *Baptist*, 1 February 1867.

Landmarkism arose over the question of whether pedobaptist organizations were true churches, entitled to recognition as such. Graves and his many followers insisted that they were not legitimate churches. Landmarkism was also distinguished by its insistence upon a continuous existence of a minority of true (Baptist) churches from the time of Christ and by the practice of closed communion.

In 1889, the *Baptist* of Memphis and the *Baptist Reflector* of Chattanooga merged into the *Baptist and Reflector*, published in Nashville.

40. Samuel Henderson, "To the Patrons and Friends of the South-Western Baptist," *Christian Index*, 6 January 1866.

41. Ben M. Barrus, Milton L. Baughn, and Thomas H. Campbell, *A People Called Cumberland Presbyterians* (Memphis, TN: Frontier Press, 1972), 246.

42. "Shall We Succeed?" *East Tennessee Baptist*, 11 February 1870; "Faults and Failings," *East Tennessee Baptist*, 1 April 1870.

43. *Christian Advocate*, 21 June 1866; Pilkington, *Methodist Publishing House, A History*, 478; Smith, *Cross and Flame*, 207; Walter Newton Vernon Jr., *The United Methodist Publishing House, A History, Volume II: 1870 to 1988* (Nashville, TN: Abingdon Press, 1989), 23.

44. Vernon, *United Methodist Publishing House, A History*, 27–36; O. P. Fitzgerald, *John B. McFerrin: A Biography* (Nashville, TN: Publishing House of the Methodist Episcopal Church, South, 1888), 358–67.

45. Edward H. Myers, *The Disruption of the Methodist Episcopal Church, 1844–1846* (Nashville, TN: Publishing House of the Methodist Episcopal Church, South, 1875), 13–14.

46. A. W. Miller, "Southern Views and Principles Not 'Extinguished' by the War," *Southern Presbyterian Review* (January 1870): 61–62.

7 *Educating Confederate Christians*

1. John McCardell, *The Idea of a Southern Nation: Southern Nationalists and Southern Nationalism, 1830–1860* (New York: Norton, 1979), 183, 202–3.

2. Central Baptist Association, *Minutes*, 1859, 6; 1860, 7.

3. Samuel Boykin, "Salutatory," *Child's Index*, September 1862; B. D. Ragsdale, *Story of Georgia Baptists*, 3 vols. (Macon, GA: Mercer University Press, 1935–38), 3:195; Henry Smith Stroupe, *The Religious Press in the South Atlantic States, 1802–1865* (Durham, NC: Duke University Press, 1956; reprint, New York: AMS Press, 1970), 56.

4. "A Sunday-School Paper for the South," *Southern Presbyterian*, 16 March 1861.

5. *Children's Friend*, August 1862, November 1862.

6. Advertisement for the *Child's Index*, *Christian Index*, 5 January 1865.

7. "A Furlough and Discharge," *Children's Friend*, October 1862.

8. "Close of the Volume," *Children's Friend*, July 1863; "Our Second Volume," *Children's Friend*, August 1863.

9. Mrs. M. J. M., "A Little Hero," *Christian Index*, 9 March 1865 (reprinted from the *Child's Index*).

10. Samuel Boykin, "Landing of the Pilgrims," *Child's Index*, September 1864.

11. "Report of Committee on the Need for a Sunday School Board," 1862, Manly Collection of Manuscripts, Southern Baptist Historical Library and Archives, Nashville, TN; "Books for Sunday Schools," *Christian Index*, 5 January 1865.

In June 1863 Manly, as president of the Sunday School Board, sent a letter through Union lines under flag of truce to Baptist pastor Richard Fuller of Baltimore requesting twenty-five thousand New Testaments. Manly wrote, "We wish to push on vigorously the work of Sunday School instruction for the sake of the children, and for the sake of our Lord and Master, Jesus Christ." The American Bible Society donated the requested books, and Federal authorities allowed them to pass through Union lines. Letter from Basil Manly Jr. to Richard Fuller, 15 June 1863, Manly Collection of Manuscripts; W. Harrison Daniel, *Southern Protestantism in the Confederacy* (Bedford, VA: Print Shop, 1989), 106–7.

Various ministers also tried to get political leaders involved in providing support for Sunday schools. The Reverend C. W. Parker of Waynesville, Georgia, asked the Confederate vice-president, Alexander H. Stephens, if he or President Jefferson Davis would "write me or the children through me a few thoughts on the Sunday School." Parker wanted "to use every inducement to get the uprising generation interested in the Sabbath School cause." Rev. C. W. Parker to A. H. Stephens, 15 February 1862, Alexander H. Stephens Papers, Library of Congress, quoted in T. Conn Bryan, "Churches in Georgia during the Civil War," *Georgia Historical Quarterly* 33 (1949): 292.

12. Washington Baptist Association, *Minutes*, 1864, 5; T. E. Smith, *History of the Washington Baptist Association of Georgia* (Milledgeville, GA: Doyle Middlebrooks, 1979), 72; Anne M. Boylan, *Sunday School: The Formation of an American Institution, 1790–1880* (New Haven: Yale University Press, 1988), 114–26.

13. Central Baptist Association, *Minutes*, 1865, 4; West Tennessee Baptist Convention, *Proceedings*, 1865, 10; 1866, 6.

14. Entries for 5 July 1868, 24 December 1869, Eliza Rhea Fain Diaries, John N. Fain Collection, McClung Historical Collection, Knox County Public Library System, Knoxville, TN.

15. *A Chronicle of Christian Stewardship: St. James Methodist Church, 1856–1967* (Augusta, GA: n.p., 1968), 16–17.

16. Constitution of the Sunday School Society of the South Georgia Annual Conference, 1867, South Georgia Conference Archives, Epworth-by-the-Sea, GA; Minutes of December 1868, December 1869, and December 1870, Minutes of the Officers and Board of Managers of the Sunday School Society, 1867–1872, South Georgia Conference Archives, Epworth-by-the-Sea, GA.

17. Ragsdale, *Story of Georgia Baptists*, 3:195; Georgia Baptist Convention, *Minutes*, 1874, 18; Georgia Baptist Sunday School Association, "Address to the Churches," Georgia Baptist Convention, *Minutes*, 1868, 29–30; Tennessee Baptist Convention, *Minutes*, 1881, 18–20; W. Fred Kendall, *A History of the Tennessee Baptist Convention* (Brentwood, TN: Executive Board of the Tennessee Baptist Convention, 1974), 178–79.

In 1878 the Hephzibah Baptist Association in Georgia commended the work of Thomas C. Boykin. He "visited some of our churches last spring, and seemed to impart a new impetus to the work. Churches that before could not keep up a school more than a few weeks at a time have been in successful operation ever since his visit, and have good prospects for the future." W. L. Kilpatrick, *The Hephzibah Baptist Association Centennial, 1794–1894* (Augusta, GA: Richards and Shaver, 1894), 142–43.

18. Harold W. Mann, *Atticus Greene Haygood: Methodist Bishop, Editor, and Educator* (Athens: University of Georgia Press, 1965), 73–79.

19. Southern Baptist Convention, *Proceedings*, 1870, 20–21.

20. "A Sunday School Paper," *Southern Presbyterian*, 18 January 1866; J. W. Burke, "To the Patrons of the *Children's Guide*," *Southern Christian Advocate*, 29 June 1865; T. Otto Nall, "Methodist Publishing in Historical Perspective, 1865–1939," in *The History of American Methodism*, ed. Emory Stevens Bucke, 3 vols. (Nashville, TN: Abingdon Press, 1964), 3:153.

21. Advertisement by Samuel Boykin, Central Baptist Association, *Minutes*, 1865, 16; "The Child's Delight," *Christian Index*, 9 November 1865; "Read This Carefully," *Kind Words*, December 1866; "The Readers of the Delight," *Kind Words: The Child's Delight*, 1 February 1870; Clifton Judson Allen et al., eds., *Encyclopedia of Southern Baptists*, 2 vols. (Nashville, TN: Broadman Press, 1958), s.v. "Samuel Boykin," by Homer L. Grice.

A letter from Georgia in 1866 to *Kind Words* demonstrates the support such publications had: "I like your little paper very much. The color of it is not quite as white as that of some papers, but I do not think any the less of it for that. It has an *honest* look. Everybody knows that the war has broken us; and I like to see a coat that is in keeping with a man's purse. I think, too, the little shady countenance, which tells of our late troubles, has a tale in it of itself, and only makes *Kind Words* sweeter and more interesting." *Kind Words*, April 1866.

22. *Biblical Recorder*, 19 April 1866; "Report of Committee on Sabbath Schools," North Georgia Annual Conference (MECS), *Minutes*, 1869, 26; Minutes of December 1870, Minutes of the Officers and Board of Managers of the Sunday School Society, 1867–1872; "Conducting Sunday-Schools," *Christian Advocate*, 29 January 1870. See Charles Reagan Wilson, *Baptized in Blood: The Religion of the Lost Cause, 1865–1920* (Athens: University of Georgia Press, 1980), 140–41.

The North Georgia Conference committee also complained, "all of our Sunday School music, and most of the hymns are Northern productions. Many of them are sentimental and silly, and some of them are worse."

23. The full text of the poem was as follows:

Glad and Free.

Oh! none in all the world before
    Were e'er as glad as we;
We're free on Carolina's shore,
    We're all at home, and free!

Thou friend and helper of the poor
    Who suffered for our sake,
To open every prison door,
    And every yoke to break —

Look down, O Saviour sweet! and smile,
    And help us sing and pray;
The hands that blessed the little child
    Upon our foreheads lay.

To-day, in all our fields of corn,
    No driver's whip we hear;
The holy day that saw thee born
    Was never half so dear.

The very oaks are greener clad;
    The waters brighter smile;
Oh, never shone a day so glad
    On sweet St. Helen's Isle.

For none in all the world before
    Were ever glad as we;
We're free on Carolina's shore,
    We're all at home, and free!

The Young Reaper 10 (1 April 1866): 26; Charles Manly to Basil Manly Jr., 28 May 1866, Manly Collection of Manuscripts.

24. G. B. T., "She Never Gave Me Aught But Pleasure," *Kind Words*, November 1866; J. Lovechild [John Broadus], "Tommy and His Rules," *Kind Words*, February 1866.

25. Minutes of 24 July 1871, Macon District Conference, Minutes, 1871–1880, South Georgia Conference Archives, Epworth-by-the-Sea, GA; Robert G. Gardner et al., *A History of the Georgia Baptist Association, 1784–1984* (Atlanta: Georgia Baptist Historical Society, 1988), 226–28 (quotation, 228); Georgia Baptist Convention, *Minutes*, 1876, 24; 1877, 24.

26. John Abernathy Smith, *Cross and Flame: Two Centuries of United Methodism in Middle Tennessee* (Nashville, TN: Commission on Archives and History of the Tennessee

Conference, 1984), 211; North Georgia Annual Conference (MECS), *Minutes*, 1871; 1877; South Georgia Annual Conference (MECS), *Minutes*, 1867; 1877, 27.

27. Minutes of 13 December 1872, Minutes of the Officers and Board of Managers of the Sunday School Society, 1867–1872; Minutes of 4 April 1873, 2 April 1874, Americus District Conference, Minutes, 1867–1878, South Georgia Conference Archives, Epworth-by-the-Sea, GA; Minutes of April 1871, April 1873, Bainbridge District Conference, Minutes, 1867–1878, South Georgia Conference Archives, Epworth-by-the-Sea, GA; Georgia Baptist Convention, *Minutes*, 1876; Synod of Georgia, *Minutes*, 1875, 18.

28. "Report of the Board of Trustees of Mercer University," Georgia Baptist Convention, *Minutes*, 1866, 16; "Report on Education," Georgia Baptist Convention, *Minutes*, 1866, 14; "Report on Education," Georgia Baptist Convention, *Minutes*, 1867, 9–10; Christopher Hendrick Owen, "Sanctity, Slavery, and Segregation: Methodists and Society in Nineteenth-Century Georgia" (Ph.D. diss., Emory University, 1991), 390–91.

The 1861 catalog of Mercer University demonstrates the tenor of its teaching. Part of the student's senior year would be devoted to "a special study of the subject of *Slavery* . . . in order that our young men may be qualified to defend the institutions of their country. It is needless to say that the teachings of the Bible on this subject will be thoroughly examined, and considered authoritative." Every student was expected to develop "a practical mastery of the argument on that question, which of all others of earthly interest, is most important to the people of the Confederate States." *Catalogue of the Officers and Students of Mercer University, 1860–1861* (Penfield, GA: Mercer University, 1861), 31–32.

29. Spright Dowell, *A History of Mercer University, 1833–1953* (Macon, GA: Mercer University, 1958), 122, 409; "Report of the Board of Trustees of Mercer University," Georgia Baptist Convention, *Minutes*, 1866, 15 (quotation).

30. Peter Wallenstein, *From Slave South to New South: Public Policy in Nineteenth-Century Georgia* (Chapel Hill: University of North Carolina Press, 1987), 161; Georgia Baptist Convention, *Minutes*, 1867, 15.

In 1868, 89 of Emory's 103 students were supported by the state program, and the college received $4,511.50 for their tuition and expenses. Ralph Eugene Reed Jr., "Fortresses of Faith: Design and Experience at Southern Evangelical Colleges, 1830–1900" (Ph.D. diss., Emory University, 1991), 278.

31. "Report of the Trustees of Mercer University," Georgia Baptist Convention, *Minutes*, 1867, 15; "Report of the Board of Trustees of Mercer University," Georgia Baptist Convention, *Minutes*, 1868, 15; "Report on Mercer University," Georgia Baptist Convention, *Minutes*, 1868, 11–12; Peter Wallenstein, *From Slave South to New South*, 161.

32. "Report of the Board of Trustees of Mercer University," Georgia Baptist Convention, *Minutes*, 1868, 17; "Report on Mercer University," Georgia Baptist Convention, *Minutes*, 1868, 11.

33. "Report of the Board of Trustees of Mercer University," Georgia Baptist Convention, *Minutes*, 1870, 15; Georgia Baptist Association, *Minutes*, 1870, 6; "Report of the Board of Trustees of Mercer University," Georgia Baptist Convention, *Minutes*, 1871, 17 ("easy access" quotation). Several other cities offered inducements to attract Mercer, including Forsyth, Griffin, Atlanta, Newnan, Marietta, and Gainesville.

34. Synod of Georgia, *Minutes*, 1865, 13; 1867, 22; 1868, 13; 1869, 13–14; 1870, 19; 1871, 18; 1872, 15–16.

Oglethorpe University had some $30,000 of its endowment left at the end of the war; by 1872 this fund had dwindled to $2,608. "Oglethorpe University," *Southern Presbyterian*, 18 January 1866; Synod of Georgia, *Minutes*, 1872, 15.

35. Reed, "Fortresses of Faith," 299–300, 377.

In 1861 the Mercer University catalog, reflecting antebellum concerns, praised the institution's location as the "retired and quiet village of Penfield." There students would be "protected by law from the most fruitful sources of temptation; and the moral and religious influences of the place are well calculated to promote good order and diligent habits." The Georgia Baptist Association continued to embrace these concerns when the Georgia Baptist Convention debated the university's relocation in 1870. The association insisted that the "sylvan retreats of the present locality are incomparably more favorable to the good morals of young men than the haunts and purlieus of vice of Macon, or any other city." *Catalogue of the Officers and Students of Mercer University, 1860–1861*, 23; Georgia Baptist Association, *Minutes*, 1870, 5.

Between the Civil War and World War I, eight evangelical colleges moved from villages to cities and towns along the railroads. Besides Mercer and Oglethorpe universities, they were: Randolph-Macon College, 1868; Howard College, 1887; Trinity College, 1892; Centenary College, 1906; Emory College, 1914; and Southern University, 1919. No state-sponsored colleges in the South moved from their antebellum locations during the same period. Reed, "Fortresses of Faith," 300.

36. Georgia Annual Conference (MECS), *Minutes*, 1866, 20; George Gilman Smith, *The Life and Times of George Foster Pierce* (Sparta, GA: Hancock Publishing, 1888), 496, 503; North Georgia Annual Conference (MECS), *Minutes*, 1869, 17.

37. The Southwestern Baptist University became Union University in 1907. The Southwestern Presbyterian University moved to Memphis in 1925 and became Southwestern. In 1945 the name was changed to Southwestern at Memphis. In 1984 Southwestern at Memphis became Rhodes College.

38. "Union of Synodical Colleges," *Southern Presbyterian*, 15 February 1866; Synod of Memphis, *Minutes*, 1866, 195, quoted in Ernest Trice Thompson, *Presbyterians in the South*, 3 vols. (Richmond, VA: John Knox Press, 1963–73), 2:353; Robert L. Neely, Manuscript Historical Sketch of the Synod of Memphis, 1880, Robert Langdon Neely Collection, Historical Foundation of the Presbyterian and Reformed Churches, Montreat, NC.

39. Synod of Nashville, Minutes, October 1868, October 1869, Historical Foundation of the Presbyterian and Reformed Churches, Montreat, NC; Neely, Historical Sketch of the Synod of Memphis, Robert Langdon Neely Collection; Waller Raymond Cooper, *Southwestern at Memphis, 1848–1948* (Richmond, VA: John Knox Press, 1949), 36–46.

40. Thompson, *Presbyterians in the South*, 2:353–56; Cooper, *Southwestern at Memphis*, 47–59.

41. Tennessee Baptist Convention, *Minutes*, 1874, 3–4; Kendall, *A History of the Tennessee Baptist Convention*, 139–40, 146–51; 165–67; Richard Hiram Ward, *A History of Union University* (Jackson, TN: Union University Press, 1975), 30–35.

42. Hunter Dickinson Farish, *The Circuit Rider Dismounts: A Social History of Southern Methodism, 1865–1900* (Richmond, VA: Dietz Press, 1938), 263–75; Edwin Mims, *History of Vanderbilt University* (Nashville, TN: Vanderbilt University Press, 1946), 20–44; Paul K. Conkin, *Gone with the Ivy: A Biography of Vanderbilt University* (Knoxville: University of Tennessee Press, 1985), 7–12, 17–22. After losing a lawsuit over the right to appoint members to Vanderbilt University's board of trust, the General Conference of the MECS in 1914 voted by a narrow margin to sever all relations with the university.

43. Samuel Luttrell Akers, *The First Hundred Years of Wesleyan College, 1836–1936* (Macon, GA: Beehive Press, 1976), 89–92; North Georgia Annual Conference (MECS), *Minutes*, 1868, 13; Bethel Baptist Association, *Minutes*, 1866, 9; 1869, 8; Ragsdale, *Story of Georgia Baptists*, 2:176.

44. Irby D. Engram, "A History of Andrew College" (M.A. thesis, Emory University, 1939); "Report on Education," Georgia Annual Conference (MECS), *Minutes*, 1866, 22; *Almanac of Andrew Female College*, 3 January 1867, Andrew College Records, Andrew Col-

lege, Cuthbert, GA, quoted in Engram, "A History of Andrew College," 37. Sarah V. Clement, *A College Grows . . . MCFI-Lambuth* (Jackson, TN: Lambuth College Alumni Association, 1972), 12–23. See also Wilson, *Baptized in Blood*, 142–45.

Eliza Fain noted in her diary, "there is a great responsibility resting upon the teachers in a female school. They are giving to those minds a training which is to exert on other minds an influence for or against the religion of Jesus. Oh how important to have Christian teachers for our daughters. I have ever felt female education was so important — directed aright." Entry for 2 September 1872, Fain Diaries.

Baptist minister J. L. M. Curry was another Confederate soldier who later served in southern denominational colleges — as president of Howard College from 1865–68 and professor at Richmond College from 1868–81.

45. Minutes of April 1870, Bainbridge District Conference, Minutes, 1867–1878; North Georgia Annual Conference (MECS), *Minutes*, 1869, 17; 1874, 13; West Tennessee Baptist Convention, *Proceedings*, 1866, 11; Georgia Baptist Convention, *Minutes*, 1870, 12.

46. Atticus G. Haygood, *The Church and the Education of the People: An Address Delivered Before the Alumni Association of Emory College* (Nashville, TN: Southern Methodist Publishing House, 1874), 46–47.

8   "A Pure and Loyal Gospel"

1. Oliver Saxon Heckman, "Northern Church Penetration of the South, 1860 to 1880" (Ph.D. diss., Duke University, 1939), 232; *American Annual Cyclopaedia and Register of Important Events* 5 (1865) (New York: Appleton, 1870), 106 (quotation); Robert Andrew Baker, *Relations between Northern and Southern Baptists* (n.p., 1954; reprint, New York: Arno Press, 1980), 101–4, 109.

2. Letter dated 8 November 1866, Freedmen's Aid Society of the Methodist Episcopal Church, *Annual Report*, 1869, 2.

3. U. S. Department of the Interior, Bureau of Education, *Negro Education: A Study of the Private and Higher Schools for Colored People in the United States*, 2 vols. (Washington, DC: Government Printing Office, 1917; reprint, New York: Negro Universities Press, 1969), 281; Freedmen's Aid Society of the Methodist Episcopal Church, *Annual Report*, 1867, 11 (quotation).

4. James H. Moorhead, *American Apocalypse: Yankee Protestants and the Civil War, 1860–1869* (New Haven: Yale University Press, 1978), 204.

5. ABHMS, *Annual Report*, 1873, 34.

6. Baker, *Relations between Northern and Southern Baptists*, 127.

From 1881, when the program was reorganized, until 1894, the ABHMS gave $28,902.38 in gifts and $13,888.05 in loans to nonblack (white and Native American) churches in the South, and $8,271 in gifts and $29,720 in loans to black churches. Baker, *Relations between Northern and Southern Baptists*, 132.

7. Ernest Trice Thompson, *Presbyterians in the South*, 3 vols. (Richmond, VA: John Knox Press, 1963–73), 2:152–53; Memoirs of Thomas Hooke McCallie (1901–12), McCallie Family Papers, McCallie School, Chattanooga, TN; General Assembly of the PCUSA (Old School), *Minutes*, 1866, 71.

8. Ralph E. Morrow, *Northern Methodism and Reconstruction* (East Lansing: Michigan State University Press, 1956), 34–35, 40; John Abernathy Smith, *Cross and Flame: Two Centuries of United Methodism in Middle Tennessee* (Nashville, TN: Commission on Archives and History of the Tennessee Conference, 1984), 160–61, 168; James E. Kirby, "The McKendree Chapel Affair," *Tennessee Historical Quarterly* 25 (1966): 363–68.

9. *American Missionary* 12 (June 1868), 126–27, quoted in Henry Lee Swint, *The Northern Teacher in the South, 1862–1870* (Nashville, TN: Vanderbilt University Press, 1941;

reprint, New York: Octagon Books, 1967), 98–99 (Bainbridge quotations); *Independent*, 16 April 1868 ("disposed to be generous" and "would accept no sympathy" quotations); "Coveting Persecution," *Southern Christian Advocate*, 9 March 1866; J. W. Yarbrough to J. F. Chalfant, 26 February 1866, Methodist Episcopal Church, Records of the Tennessee Conference, The Georgia and Alabama Mission District, The Reverend James F. Chalfant, Superintendent, 1865–1867, Incoming Letters to the Rev. James F. Chalfant, 1865–1878, Atlanta University Center Woodruff Library, Archives Department, Atlanta, GA.

10. United States, Congress, *Report of the Joint Select Committee to Inquire into the Condition of Affairs in the Late Insurrectionary States* (Washington, DC: Government Printing Office, 1872), 6:439; "The Future of the Freedmen," *Southern Presbyterian Review* 19 (1867): 272–73.

11. Richard Nelson Current, *Lincoln's Loyalists: Union Soldiers from the Confederacy* (Boston: Northeastern University Press, 1992), 215.

12. General Assembly of the PCUSA (New School), *Minutes*, 1865, 14–21; 1866, 207–8; Harold M. Parker Jr., *The United Synod of the South: The Southern New School Presbyterian Church* (Westport, CT: Greenwood Press, 1988), 271–77.

13. Memoirs of Thomas Hooke McCallie.

14. Washington County Clerk and Master Court Minutes, 1869–1874, Tennessee State Library and Archives, Nashville, TN; *Deaderick v. Lampson*, 58 Tenn. (11 Heisk) 523–38 (1872); *Christian Observer*, 12 June 1872.

In 1880 the southern portion of the Jonesboro Presbyterian Church bought the interest of the northern group in the joint church property for $1,000. Thereafter, the two churches met in separate facilities. *Historic Sketch and Directory of the Second Presbyterian Church, Jonesboro, Tenn.* (Jonesboro, TN: Herald and Tribune Print, 1895), 4.

15. McMinn County Chancery Court Minutes, 1868–1875, Tennessee State Library and Archives, Nashville, TN; Mars Hill Presbyterian Church Records, 1832–1967, Tennessee State Library and Archives, Nashville, TN; *Bridges v. Wilson*, 58 Tenn. (11 Heisk) 458–71 (1872); Reba B. Boyer and Budd L. Duncan, *A History of the Mars Hill Presbyterian Church* (Athens, TN: Mars Hill Presbyterian Church, 1973), 9–13; Thompson, *Presbyterians in the South*, 2:130–34.

After the southern faction recovered the session minutes, the clerk wrote in the volume, "From page 115 to this point the Book was in the hands, and records the doings of the philistines."

The northern Mars Hill Presbyterian Church continued to meet in Wilson's home. In 1884, the southern congregation invited the northern group to join them in worship, "they having no minister or place of worship at present." By 1886, the remnants of the northern congregation had rejoined the southern church.

16. *Chrisitian Observer*, 31 August 1870; Ralph Waldo Lloyd, *Maryville College: A History of 150 Years, 1819–1969* (Maryville, TN: Maryville College Press, 1969), 10–11; Thompson, *Presbyterians in the South*, 2:126–27.

17. Entry for 20 April 1870, Eliza Rhea Fain Diaries, John N. Fain Collection, McClung Historical Collection, Knox County Public Library System, Knoxville, TN.

18. Isaac Patton Martin, *Methodism in Holston* (Knoxville, TN: Methodist Historical Society, 1945), 74–78.

19. *Knoxville Whig and Rebel Ventilator*, 30 April 1864; R. N. Price, *Holston Methodism: From Its Origin to the Present Time*, 5 vols. (Nashville, TN: Publishing House of the Methodist Episcopal Church, South, 1913), 4:356 (convention quotations); Martin, *Methodism in Holston*, 83–88, 109, 115, 125, 127; W. B. Hesseltine, "Methodism and Reconstruction in East Tennessee," *East Tennessee Historical Society's Publications* 3 (1931): 50–53; E. Merton Coulter, *William G. Brownlow: Fighting Parson of the Southern Highlands* (Chapel Hill:

University of North Carolina Press, 1937; reprint, Knoxville: University of Tennessee Press, 1971), 294–301.

The statistics for the Holston Conference of the MECS presented here differ from those in figure 6-2 because the Holston Conference comprised eleven districts — three in Virginia, six in Tennessee, and two in North Carolina. Figure 6-2 reports only the membership of churches in Tennessee.

20. Martin, *Methodism in Holston*, 94–97.

East Tennessee Wesleyan became Grant Memorial University in 1886. Also in 1886, Chattanooga University opened in Chattanooga, Tennessee. Despite the General Conference ruling that "no student shall be excluded from instruction in any and every school under the supervision because of race, color, or previous condition of servitude," the administration of Chattanooga University refused to admit several black students in 1886. School trustees insisted that black students would be "fatal to the prosperity of the institution" and would "excite prejudice and passion." In 1889 Grant Memorial University and Chattanooga University united under one chancellor and board of trustees with the name U. S. Grant University, but the school retained the two campuses. Freedmen's Aid Society of the Methodist Episcopal Church, *Annual Report*, 1886, 23–29; Walter W. Benjamin, "The Methodist Episcopal Church in the Postwar Era," in *The History of American Methodism*, ed. Emory Stevens Bucke, 3 vols. (Nashville, TN: Abingdon Press, 1964), 2:377–78; Martin, *Methodism in Holston*, 96, 176–77.

21. Price, *Holston Methodism*, 4:455–58, 485–86, 5:5 (quotation), 5:6–22; Martin, *Methodism in Holston*, 110, 135–37; *Reeves et al. v. Walker et al.*, 67 Tenn. (8 Baxt.) 277–84 (1874).

22. Martin, *Methodism in Holston*, 110.

23. General Assembly of the PCUSA (New School), *Minutes*, 1867, 555.

24. Freedmen's Aid Society of the Methodist Episcopal Church, *Annual Report*, 1867, 9–10; Wade Crawford Barclay, *History of Methodist Missions, Part II: The Methodist Episcopal Church, 1845–1939*, 3 vols. (New York: Board of Missions of the Methodist Church, 1957), 3:322; Smith, *Cross and Flame*, 159–60; Jacqueline Jones, *Soldiers of Light and Love: Northern Teachers and Georgia Blacks, 1865–1873* (Chapel Hill: University of North Carolina Press, 1980), 209; Harold Lynn McManus, "The American Baptist Home Mission Society and Freedmen Education in the South, with Special Reference to Georgia: 1862–1897" (Ph.D. diss., Yale University, 1953), 254.

25. Heckman, "Northern Church Penetration of the South," 278.

26. Smith, *Cross and Flame*, 170, 173.

27. John H. Caldwell, *Reminiscences of the Reconstruction of Church and State in Georgia* (Wilmington, DE: J. Miller Thomas, 1895), 7–9; Daniel W. Stowell, "'The Negroes Cannot Navigate Alone': Religious Scalawags and the Biracial Methodist Episcopal Church in Georgia, 1866–1876," in *Georgia in Black and White: Explorations in the Race Relations of a Southern State, 1865–1950*, ed. John C. Inscoe (Athens: University of Georgia Press, 1994), 65–90; Daniel W. Stowell, "The Failure of Religious Reconstruction: The Methodist Episcopal Church in Georgia, 1865–1871" (M.A. thesis, University of Georgia, 1988), 33–61.

Religious scalawags in other states confronted hostility as well. During religious reconstruction, Alabama Methodist John Jackson Brasher endured death threats and carried his pistol when in the pulpit. His son, John Lakin Brasher, later recalled, "My father organized a church which was as welcome in the South as a wet dog in a lady's dressing room." J. Lawrence Brasher, *The Sanctified South: John Lakin Brasher and the Holiness Movement* (Urbana: University of Illinois Press, 1994), 8–16.

28. *Western Christian Advocate*, 26 September 1866 (Griffin quotation); 12 April 1865 (Lewis quotation); William E. Montgomery, *Under Their Own Vine and Fig Tree: The African-*

American Church in the South, 1865–1900 (Baton Rouge: Louisiana State University Press, 1993), 72.

The General Conference of 1872 supported the missionaries' claims of equality by passing what became known as the "*magna charta* of black rights in the Methodist Episcopal Church." This document declared, "There is no word 'white' to discriminate against either race or color known in our legislation; and being of African descent does not prevent membership with white men in Annual Conferences, nor ordination at the same altars, nor appointment to presiding eldership, nor election to the General Conference, nor eligibility to the highest office in the Church." Quoted in Heckman, "Northern Church Penetration of the South," 195.

29. Thomas O. Fuller, *History of the Negro Baptists of Tennessee* (Memphis, TN: Haskins Printing, 1936), 23–24; McManus, "The American Baptist Home Mission Society and Freedmen Education in the South," 128; U. S. Department of the Interior, Bureau of Education, *Negro Education*, 281.

30. McManus, "The American Baptist Home Mission Society and Freedmen Education in the South," 281–82; *Home Evangelist* 1 (December 1865): 48, quoted in McManus, "The American Baptist Home Mission Society and Freedmen Education in the South," 282; *Baptist Home Mission Monthly* 1 (September 1878): 46–47, quoted in McManus, "The American Baptist Home Mission Society and Freedmen Education in the South," 286–87.

31. ABHMS, *Annual Report*, 1878, 19; 1880, 37; Baker, *Relations between Northern and Southern Baptists*, 116–19; Tennessee Baptist Convention, *Minutes*, 1881, 14–15; W. Fred Kendall, *A History of the Tennessee Baptist Convention* (Brentwood, TN: Executive Board of the Tennessee Baptist Convention, 1974), 170–71.

32. McManus, "The American Baptist Home Mission Society and Freedmen Education in the South," 279; Baker, *Relations between Northern and Southern Baptists*, 137 (quotations); Georgia Baptist Convention, *Minutes*, 1878, 18.

The Georgia Missionary Baptist State Convention was organized in 1879.

33. Joanna P. Moore, "*In Christ's Stead*": *Autobiographical Sketches* (Chicago: Women's Baptist Home Mission Society, 1903), 60–61; Mrs. John H. Chapman, "They Needed a Woman's Help" and "Joanna P. Moore: Pioneer Apostle to the Negroes," unpublished manuscripts, 1932, Una Roberts Lawrence Papers, Southern Baptist Historical Library and Archives, Nashville, TN.

34. U. S. Department of the Interior, Bureau of Education, *Negro Education*, 289, 296–97; Willard Range, *The Rise and Progress of Negro Colleges in Georgia, 1865–1949* (Athens: University of Georgia Press, 1951), 14.

35. Many of these colleges have changed their names since their founding. The Nashville Normal and Theological Institute became Roger Williams University in 1883. Late in the nineteenth century, Central Tennessee College was renamed Walden University; fire and financial difficulties forced it to close in 1922. The Atlanta Baptist Seminary, formerly the Augusta Institute, became Morehouse College in 1913. Clark University was renamed Clark College in 1940. The Biddle Memorial Institute became Johnson C. Smith University in 1923.

36. Smith, *Cross and Flame*, 185–89; James P. Brawley, *Two Centuries of Methodist Concern: Bondage, Freedom, and the Education of Black People* (New York: Vantage Press, 1974), 385; James Summerville, *Educating Black Doctors: A History of Meharry Medical College* (University: University of Alabama Press, 1983).

37. Range, *The Rise and Progress of Negro Colleges in Georgia*, 23, 28.

38. Ibid., 24–27 (quotation, 27); Baker, *Relations between Northern and Southern Baptists*, 120; Benjamin Brawley, *History of Morehouse College* (Atlanta, GA: Morehouse College Press, 1917; reprint, College Park, MD: McGrath Publishing, 1970), 15–20; Addie Louise Joyner Butler, *The Distinctive Black College: Talladega, Tuskegee and Morehouse* (Metuchen, NJ: Scarecrow Press, 1977), 102–3.

39. Edward L. Wheeler, *Uplifting the Race: The Black Minister in the New South, 1865–1902* (Lanham, MD: University Press of America, 1986), 113 ("primary object" quotation); *Catalogue of the Officers and Students of the Nashville Normal and Theological Institute, Nashville, Tenn., for the Academic Year 1876–77* (Nashville, TN: Wheeler Brothers, 1877), 4 (pastors' needs quotation), inside back cover (women's education quotation); *Catalogue of the Officers and Students of the Nashville Institute, 1873–1874* (Nashville, TN: Wheeler, Marshall and Bruce, 1874); Eugene TeSelle, "The Nashville Institute and Roger Williams University: Benevolence, Paternalism, and Black Consciousness, 1867–1910," *Tennessee Historical Quarterly* 41 (Winter 1982): 360–79; Fuller, *History of the Negro Baptists of Tennessee*, 24–25; Baker, *Relations between Northern and Southern Baptists*, 120.

40. Range, *The Rise and Progress of Negro Colleges in Georgia*, 31; Smith, *Cross and Flame*, 186.

41. Barclay, *History of Methodist Missions*, 3:323.

42. Paul Clyde Brownlow, "The Northern Protestant Pulpit on Reconstruction, 1865–1877" (Ph.D. diss., Purdue University, 1970), 168–69, 175–77, 180.

43. Baker, *Relations between Northern and Southern Baptists*, 109–10.
The number of missionaries in the South supported by the ABHMS climbed again in the 1880s and 1890s, but the majority continued to be located in the Southwest — in Indian Territory, Texas, and New Mexico. Baker, *Relations between Northern and Southern Baptists*, 111–12.

44. General Assembly of the PCUSA (Old School), *Minutes*, 1867, 446; 1866, 76; PCUSA, *Annual Report of the Committee on Freedmen*, 1872, 77–79; Freedmen's Aid Society of the Methodist Episcopal Church, *Annual Report*, 1875, 54.

45. General Assembly of the PCUSA, *Minutes*, 1871, 510.

46. *Methodist Advocate*, 16 September 1874 (East Tennessee quotation); *Christian Advocate*, 12 April 1872 (Georgia quotation); Morrow, *Northern Methodism and Reconstruction*, 193.

47. Martin, *Methodism in Holston*, 138, 156–57.

48. Edmund J. Hammond, *The Methodist Episcopal Church in Georgia* (n.p., 1935), 124–26 ("Two services" quotation, 124–25); Georgia Annual Conference (MEC), *Minutes*, 1871, 13 (petition quotation); *Methodist Advocate*, 15 September 1869.

49. Georgia Annual Conference (MEC), *Minutes*, 1871, 13; Heckman, "Northern Church Penetration of the South," 195 (1872 General Conference quotation); *Methodist Advocate*, 26 June 1872; Barclay, *History of Methodist Missions*, 3:314.

50. *Methodist Advocate*, 6 November 1872, 12 November 1873, 27 October 1875 (quotation); Hammond, *Methodist Episcopal Church in Georgia*, 139; Frank K. Pool, "The Southern Negro in the Methodist Episcopal Church" (Ph.D. diss., Duke University, 1939), 214–33; William B. Gravely, *Gilbert Haven, Methodist Abolitionist: A Study in Race, Religion, and Reform, 1850–1880* (Nashville, TN: Abingdon Press, 1973), 231; Morrow, *Northern Methodism and Reconstruction*, 196.

51. General Conference of the MEC, *Journal*, 1876, 331. The Georgia Conference initially consisted of the Atlanta, Dalton, and Ogeechee Districts; the Savannah Conference embraced the Rome, Macon, Augusta, and Savannah districts. General Conference of the MEC, *Journal*, 1876, 372, 377.

52. "Division of Georgia Conference," *Methodist Advocate*, 8 November 1876 (quotations); Hammond, *Methodist Episcopal Church in Georgia*, 139. See also Stowell, "The Negroes Cannot Navigate Alone," 81–82.

53. Smith, *Cross and Flame*, 172–73; Barclay, *History of Methodist Missions*, 3:318.

54. Dwight W. Culver, *Negro Segregation in the Methodist Church* (New Haven: Yale University Press, 1953), 59. Of the twenty-five segregated conferences, twelve were white and thirteen were black. The three mixed conferences consisted mainly of whites.

9 *Voting the Bible*

1. Richard J. Carwardine, *Evangelicals and Politics in Antebellum America* (New Haven: Yale University Press, 1993), 321–22.

2. Mitchell Snay, *Gospel of Disunion: Religion and Separatism in the Antebellum South* (New York: Cambridge University Press, 1993), 41, 143–45, 163, 182.

3. On the interaction of politics and religion during the war itself, see James W. Silver, *Confederate Morale and Church Propaganda* (Tuscaloosa, AL: Confederate Publishing, 1957); Richard E. Beringer et al., *Why the South Lost the Civil War* (Athens: University of Georgia Press, 1986); Drew Gilpin Faust, *The Creation of Confederate Nationalism: Ideology and Identity in the Civil War South* (Baton Rouge: Louisiana State University Press, 1988); Victor B. Howard, *Religion and the Radical Republican Movement, 1860–1870* (Lexington: University Press of Kentucky, 1990); Phillip Shaw Paludan, *"A People's Contest": The Union and Civil War, 1861–1865* (New York: Harper and Row, 1988); and David B. Chesebrough, *Clergy Dissent in the Old South, 1830–1865* (Carbondale: Southern Illinois University Press, 1996), 50–85.

4. Thomas Smyth, "National Righteousness," *Southern Presbyterian Review* 12 (April 1859): 25; General Assembly of the PCUS, *Minutes*, 1866, 30; Jack P. Maddex, "From Theocracy to Spirituality: The Southern Presbyterian Reversal on Church and State," *Journal of Presbyterian History* 54 (Winter 1976): 448–50. See also James Oscar Farmer Jr., *The Metaphysical Confederacy: James Henley Thornwell and the Synthesis of Southern Values* (Macon, GA: Mercer University Press, 1986), 256–60; John R. Bodo, *The Protestant Clergy and Public Issues, 1812–1848* (Princeton: Princeton University Press, 1954), 3–60.

5. "Reflections on the Elections," *Christian Index*, 12 November 1874; "The Victory — Rejoice!" *Christian Index*, 19 november 1874; *Religious Herald*, 12 November 1874; Rufus B. Spain, *At Ease in Zion: A Social History of Southern Baptists, 1865–1900* (Nashville, TN: Vanderbilt University Press, 1967), 22–25. For limited commentary on the 1868 elections, see *Christian Index*, 30 July 1868; and *Baptist*, 14 November 1868.

6. Entries for 4 March, 28 April, 16 May 1865, Eliza Rhea Fain Diaries, John N. Fain Collection, McClung Historical Collection, Knox County Public Library System, Knoxville, TN. For Johnson's religious views, see Hans L. Trefousse, *Andrew Johnson: A Biography* (New York: Norton, 1989), 41, 49, 89, 160–61.

7. Memoirs of Thomas Hooke McCallie (1901–12), McCallie Family Papers, McCallie School, Chattanooga, TN. Stevens, the leader of the radical Republicans in the House of Representatives, died in 1868. On his career, see Eric Foner, *Reconstruction: America's Unfinished Revolution, 1863–1877* (New York: Harper and Row, 1988), 228–39; Donald K. Pickens, "The Republican Synthesis and Thaddeus Stevens," *Civil War History* 31 (March 1985): 57–73.

8. *Central Christian Advocate*, 24 October 1866; *Christian Advocate and Journal*, 6 December 1866.

9. *Christian Advocate and Journal*, 30 August 1866; *Zion's Herald*, 22 August 1867, 12 December 1867; General Conference of the MEC, *Journal*, 1868, 152–53; Howard, *Religion and the Radical Republican Movement*, 155–64 (telegram quotation, 163); Ralph E. Morrow, *Northern Methodism and Reconstruction* (East Lansing: Michigan State University Press, 1956), 207–13.

10. *Zion's Herald*, 28 November 1866, 17 October 1867; Joanna P. Moore, *"In Christ's Stead": Autobiographical Sketches* (Chicago: Women's Baptist Home Mission Society, 1903), 138; Howard, *Religion and the Radical Republican Movement*, 128–45, 199–211. On Haven, see William B. Gravely, *Gilbert Haven, Methodist Abolitionist: A Study in Race, Religion, and Reform, 1850–1880* (Nashville, TN: Abingdon Press, 1973).

11. Edmund L. Drago, *Black Politicians and Reconstruction in Georgia: A Splendid Failure* (Baton Rouge: Louisiana State University Press, 1982), 22–23; Foner, *Reconstruction*, 93–94, 112, 282–83; William E. Montgomery, *Under Their Own Vine and Fig Tree: The African-American Church in the South, 1865–1900* (Baton Rouge: Louisiana State University Press, 1993), 179–84.

12. *National Monitor*, 21 May 1870 (Banks quotations), quoted in James Melvin Washington, *Frustrated Fellowship: The Black Baptist Quest for Social Power* (Macon, GA: Mercer University Press, 1986), 118; *American Baptist*, 29 December 1868 ("political outrages" quotation), 26 May 1870 ("make the ballot" and "educate and Christianize" quotations, quoted in Washington, *Frustrated Fellowship*, 116; Daniel Payne, *Address Before the College Aid Society* (1868), 5, quoted in Katharine L. Dvorak, *An African-American Exodus: The Segregation of the Southern Churches* (Brooklyn, NY: Carlson Publishing, 1991), 154. See also Montgomery, *Under Their Own Vine and Fig Tree*, 156–57, 163–79; Clarence E. Walker, *A Rock in a Weary Land: The African Methodist Episcopal Church during the Civil War and Reconstruction* (Baton Rouge: Louisiana State University Press, 1982), 127–39; Reginald F. Hildebrand, *The Times Were Strange and Stirring: Methodist Preachers and the Crisis of Emancipation* (Durham, NC: Duke University Press, 1995), 67.

13. Benjamin T. Tanner, "The Religious Bearings of the XVth Amendment," *Christian Recorder*, 8 January 1870; William E. Walker, "What Do the Colored People Want?" *New National Era and Citizen*, 11 December 1873.

Tanner's assertion that "the negro votes the Bible" was actually his answer to the rhetorical question, "Shall the Bible or the Pope be schoolmaster?" However, he employed the phrase as a double-entendre; blacks voted for the Bible over the pope, but they would also vote according to the principles they found in the Bible.

14. CABMC *Report*, 1872, 17–18, quoted in Washington, *Frustrated Fellowship*, 119.

15. Journal of the General Conference of the CME Church in America, 1870–1906, 15, CME Church Archives, Memphis, TN; Lucius H. Holsey, *Autobiography, Sermons, Addresses, and Essays*, 2d ed. (Atlanta, GA: Franklin Printing and Publishing, 1899), 218; William B. Gravely, "The Social, Political and Religious Significance of the Formation of the Colored Methodist Episcopal Church (1870)," *Methodist History* 18 (October 1979): 17–25; Hildebrand, *The Times Were Strange and Stirring*, 23–24; Othal Hawthorne Lakey, *The History of the CME Church* (Memphis, TN: CME Publishing, 1985), 207–10. The *Christian Advocate* in Nashville reported the phrase as "and they shall, on no account be used for political assemblages or purposes." *Christian Advocate*, 7 January 1871.

George Washington Dupee, an ex-slave preacher in Paducah, Kentucky, took a similar stance among black Baptists. Washington, *Frustrated Fellowship*, 117.

16. John Brother Cade, *Holsey—The Incomparable* (New York: Pageant Press, 1964), 125, 131; Lakey, *History of the CME Church*, 210 (Jamison and Lakey quotations). Little John Scurlock, the CME Church's publishing agent, resigned his position in 1872 to run for political office in Mississippi. Lakey, *History of the CME Church*, 248–49, 296–97.

17. Journal of the General Conference of the CME Church, 68–69 (Holsey and Anderson quotations); *Southern Christian Advocate*, 3 April 1873; Lakey, *History of the CME Church*, 252–53.

18. Elizabeth Studley Nathans, *Losing the Peace: Georgia Republicans and Reconstruction, 1865–1871* (Baton Rouge: Louisiana State University Press, 1968), 3–16; Alan Conway, *The Reconstruction of Georgia* (Minneapolis: University of Minnesota Press, 1966), 20, 40–60. For overviews of Reconstruction in Georgia in addition to Conway's volume, see Edwin C. Wooley, *The Reconstruction of Georgia* (New York: Columbia University Press, 1901; reprint, New York: AMS Press, 1970) and C. Mildred Thompson, *Reconstruction in Georgia: Economic, Social, Political, 1865–1872* (New York: Columbia University Press, 1915).

19. J. H. Caldwell to J. F. Chalfant, 3 April 1866, 1 October 1866, Methodist Episcopal Church, Records of the Tennessee Conference, The Georgia and Alabama Mission District, The Reverend James F. Chalfant, Superintendent, 1865–1867, Incoming Letters to the Rev. James F. Chalfant, 1865–1878, Atlanta University Center Woodruff Library, Archives Department, Atlanta, GA (hereafter Chalfant Correspondence); Morrow, *Northern Methodism and Reconstruction*, 209.

20. C. W. Parker to G. L. Eberhart, 8 April 1867, United States, Department of War, Bureau of Refugees, Freedmen, and Abandoned Lands, Records of the Superintendent of Education for the State of Georgia, 1865–1870, Record Group 105, National Archives, Washington, DC; R. H. Waters to J. F. Chalfant, 20 March 1867, Chalfant Correspondence; John Murphy to J. F. Chalfant, 16 April 1867, Chalfant Correspondence; Roberta F. Cason, "The Loyal League in Georgia," *Georgia Historical Quarterly* 20 (June 1936): 136 (La Grange quotation). See also Daniel W. Stowell, "'The Negroes Cannot Navigate Alone': Religious Scalawags and the Biracial Methodist Episcopal Church in Georgia, 1866–1876," in *Georgia in Black and White: Explorations in the Race Relations of a Southern State, 1865–1950*, ed. John C. Inscoe (Athens: University of Georgia Press, 1994), 78–80, and Daniel W. Stowell, "The Failure of Religious Reconstruction: The Methodist Episcopal Church in Georgia, 1865–1871" (M.A. thesis, University of Georgia, 1988), 109–15. For an examination of the Union League movement in Alabama and Mississippi, see Michael W. Fitzgerald, *The Union League Movement in the Deep South: Politics and Agricultural Change during Reconstruction* (Baton Rouge: Louisiana State University Press, 1989), esp. 31, 58–59.

21. Edwin S. Redkey, ed., *Respect Black: The Writings and Speeches of Henry McNeal Turner* (New York: Arno Press, 1971), 30–31; Russell Duncan, *Freedom's Shore: Tunis Campbell and the Georgia Freedmen* (Athens: University of Georgia Press, 1986), 42–46.

22. Drago, *Black Politicians and Reconstruction in Georgia*, 20, 166–71.

23. J. H. Caldwell to J. F. Chalfant, 8 August 1867 ("uniting Church & state" quotation), 3 September 1867, Chalfant Correspondence; John H. Caldwell, *Reminiscences of the Reconstruction of Church and State in Georgia* (Wilmington, DE: J. Miller Thomas, 1895), 10–11 ("secure . . . liberty" and "called of God" quotations); United States, Congress, *Report of the Joint Select Committee to Inquire into the Condition of Affairs in the Late Insurrectionary States*, 13 vols. 42d Congress, 2d Session, 1870–1871, Georgia Testimony (Washington, DC: Government Printing Office, 1872), 2:1034 (Turner quotation).

Some Methodist religious scalawags in Georgia opposed Caldwell's political involvement, believing that it damaged the prospects of the Methodist Episcopal Church in Georgia. At the 1868 Georgia Annual Conference, a delegate offered a resolution declaring, "when any member of the Conference accepts a nomination to civil office, he should tender the resignation of his charge to his presiding elder or Bishop." The conference discussed but "indefinitely postponed" the resolution, which was obviously aimed at Caldwell, who had recently been elected to the state legislature. Although the resolution failed in 1868, it "soon afterward became the law of the conference and remained so for several years." Georgia Annual Conference (MEC), *Minutes*, 1868, 4, 6; Edmund J. Hammond, *The Methodist Episcopal Church in Georgia* (n.p., 1935), 123.

24. Conway, *The Reconstruction of Georgia*, 148–61; Drago, *Black Politicians and Reconstruction in Georgia*, 30–47; Nathans, *Losing the Peace*, 32–55; Ruth Currie-McDaniel, *Carpetbagger of Conscience: A Biography of John Emory Bryant* (Athens: University of Georgia Press, 1987), 78–88; Stephen Ward Angell, *Bishop Henry McNeal Turner and African-American Religion in the South* (Knoxville: University of Tennessee Press, 1992), 82–85; Russell Duncan, *Entrepreneur for Equality: Governor Rufus Bullock, Commerce, and Race in Post–Civil War Georgia* (Athens: University of Georgia Press, 1994), 49–50.

25. *Athens Southern Watchman*, 9 September 1868, quoted in Angell, *Bishop Henry Mc-*

Neal Turner and African-American Religion in the South, 87–88 (quotations, 88); John Dittmer, "The Education of Henry McNeal Turner," in *Black Leaders of the Nineteenth Century*, ed. Leon F. Litwack and August Meier (Urbana: University of Illinois Press, 1988), 258–59; Conway, *The Reconstruction of Georgia*, 166–67; Drago, *Black Politicians and Reconstruction in Georgia*, 48–50; Nathans, *Losing the Peace*, 120–24. Four mulatto representatives retained their seats, claiming that they had less than one-eighth black blood; in doing so, they earned the scorn of Turner and other black legislators.

On September 8, the Columbus *Weekly Sun* supported the expulsion of "niggers" and mulattoes and expressed the attitude of many whites toward Henry M. Turner: "We are opposed to individual violence and lynch law. But in the peculiar condition of affairs now existing in this State, we should neither be seized with astonishment or regret if Elder Turner should reach the top of a tree without climbing." Quoted in Conway, *The Reconstruction of Georgia*, 167.

On September 12, the Georgia Senate expelled its two remaining black members, Tunis G. Campbell and George Wallace, by a vote of twenty-one to eleven. Black senator Aaron A. Bradley had resigned in the face of charges that he had been convicted of a crime in New York. Conway, *The Reconstruction of Georgia*, 166–67; Duncan, *Entrepreneur for Equality*, 64, 197–98, n. 19.

26. J. H. Caldwell to Wm. Caflin, 1 September 1868, William E. Chandler Papers, Library of Congress, quoted in Drago, *Black Politicians and Reconstruction in Georgia*, 23; Currie-McDaniel, *Carpetbagger of Conscience*, 94–95.

27. Conway, *The Reconstruction of Georgia*, 171–86; Duncan, *Entrepreneur for Equality*, 78–94; Nathans, *Losing the Peace*, 147–66.

28. Conway, *The Reconstruction of Georgia*, 186–89, 198–201; Nathans, *Losing the Peace*, 167–91, 204–5, 219; Duncan, *Entrepreneur for Equality*, 95–97, 135–38. For the retreat of the Grant administration and congressional Republicans from Reconstruction generally, see William Gillette, *Retreat from Reconstruction, 1869–1879* (Baton Rouge: Louisiana State University Press, 1979) and Michael Les Benedict, *A Compromise of Principle: Congressional Republicans and Reconstruction, 1863–1869* (New York: Norton, 1974).

29. Kenneth M. Stampp, *The Era of Reconstruction, 1865–1877* (New York: Knopf, 1965), 186; Mobile *Register*, 13 January 1871, quoted in Michael Perman, *The Road to Redemption: Southern Politics, 1869–1879* (Chapel Hill: University of North Carolina Press, 1984), 78.

30. Georgia Annual Conference (MEC), *Minutes*, 1882, 8–9; Stowell, "The Failure of Religious Reconstruction," 113–15.

31. Trefousse, *Andrew Johnson*, 152–75, 185–88. For overviews of Reconstruction in Tennessee, see James Welch Patton, *Unionism and Reconstruction in Tennessee, 1860–1869* (Chapel Hill: University of North Carolina Press, 1934), 75–241; Thomas B. Alexander, *Political Reconstruction in Tennessee* (Nashville, TN: Vanderbilt University Press, 1950); Stephen V. Ash, *Middle Tennessee Society Transformed, 1860–1870: War and Peace in the Upper South* (Baton Rouge: Louisiana State University Press, 1988), 106–253.

32. E. Merton Coulter, *William G. Brownlow: Fighting Parson of the Southern Highlands* (Chapel Hill: University of North Carolina Press, 1937; reprint, Knoxville: University of Tennessee Press, 1971), 1–52; Steve Humphrey, *"That D——d Brownlow," Being a Saucy and Malicious Description of Fighting Parson William Gannaway Brownlow, Knoxville Editor and Stalwart Unionist* (Boone, NC: Appalachian Consortium Press, 1978), 1–217.

33. For a similar set of attitudes held by a Primitive Baptist, see Stephen V. Ash, ed., "Conscience and Christianity: A Middle Tennessee Unionist Renounces His Church, 1867," *East Tennessee Historical Society's Publications* 54/55 (1982–83): 111–15.

34. *Knoxville Whig*, 18 May 1861, 6 July 1861; William G. Brownlow, *Portrait and Biog-*

raphy of Parson Brownlow, the Tennessee Patriot (Indianapolis, IN: Asher and Company, 1862), 44 ("worst class" and "review of the battles" quotations); William G. Brownlow, *Sketches of the Rise, Progress, and Decline of Secession; with a Narrative of Personal Adventures among the Rebels [Parson Brownlow's Book]* (Philadelphia: George W. Childs, 1862), 108–9, 146; Coulter, *William G. Brownlow*, 134–234; Humphrey, "That D——d Brownlow," 218–77; W. B. Hesseltine, "Methodism and Reconstruction in East Tennessee," *East Tennessee Historical Society's Publications* 3 (1931): 42–46. For Brownlow's opposition to secession, see Daniel W. Crofts, *Reluctant Confederates: Upper South Unionists in the Secession Crisis* (Chapel Hill: University of North Carolina Press, 1989), 22–25.

35. *Knoxville Whig and Rebel Ventilator*, 28 June 1865; Coulter, *William G. Brownlow*, 235–93, 325–30; Patton, *Unionism and Reconstruction in Tennessee*, 124–34; Alexander, *Political Reconstruction in Tennessee*, 113–31. For Brownlow's change in his attitude toward slavery and blacks, see *Knoxville Whig*, 14 November 1866; John Cimprich, *Slavery's End in Tennessee, 1861–1865* (University: University of Alabama Press, 1985), 101–2, 116–17; Humphrey, "That D——d Brownlow," 324–25. By 1867, Brownlow was ready to admit that when he had defended slavery in the 1850s, "I was on the wrong side of the subject!" *Knoxville Whig*, 8 May 1867.

Eliza Fain found Brownlow's course and his newspaper reprehensible. In July 1865, she asked God to "keep my heart for I do feel that there is in it much that is not right. I find there is bitterness." Upon further reflection, she thought that "it may today have arisen within me because I have been reading some Union papers particularly the Knoxville Whig (Brownlow's organ). I think it is so corrupt, so vile, so anything but what high souled Americans should be." Entry for 17 July 1865, Fain Diaries.

36. *Daily Press and Times*, 14 April 1867, quoted in Alrutheus Ambush Taylor, *The Negro in Tennessee, 1865–1880* (Washington, DC: Associated Publishers, 1941), 53–54; Patton, *Unionism and Reconstruction in Tennessee*, 135–43; Ash, *Middle Tennessee Society Transformed*, 218–19.

37. Entry for 1 August 1867, Fain Diaries; Taylor, *The Negro in Tennessee*, 55–57; Patton, *Unionism and Reconstruction in Tennessee*, 139–40, 177; Alexander, *Political Reconstruction in Tennessee*, 141–62.

38. Memoirs of Thomas Hooke McCallie.

39. Synod of Nashville, Minutes, January 1866, 269–70, Historical Foundation of the Presbyterian and Reformed Churches, Montreat, NC.

40. Thomas H. Pearne, *An Address on the Two Churches* (Cincinnati, OH: Methodist Book Concern, 1867), 22–23; *Knoxville Whig*, 30 October 1867, quoted in Hesseltine, "Methodism and Reconstruction in East Tennessee," 59. See also Thomas H. Pearne, *Sixty-One Years of Itinerant Christian Life in Church and State* (Cincinnati, OH: Methodist Book Concern, 1899).

41. *Daily Press and Times*, 22 July 1869; Entry for 9 August 1869, Fain Diaries; Patton, *Unionism and Reconstruction in Tennessee*, 226–41; Alexander, *Political Reconstruction in Tennessee*, 199–225.

42. Taylor, *The Negro in Tennessee*, 73–82, 244–48; Alexander, *Political Reconstruction in Tennessee*, 226–38; Humphrey, "That D——d Brownlow," 376–79.

43. Violence was particularly effective in decreasing the Republican vote in the presidential election of November 1868. See Taylor, *The Negro in Tennessee*, 60–63; Stanley Kenneth Deaton, "Violent Redemption: The Democratic Party and the Ku Klux Klan in Georgia, 1868–1871" (M.A. thesis, University of Georgia, 1988).

44. William Thomas Richardson, *Historic Pulaski: Birthplace of the Ku Klux Klan, Scene of Execution of Sam Davis* (Nashville, TN: Methodist Publishing House, 1913), 22–23,

quoted in Charles Reagan Wilson, *Baptized in Blood: The Religion of the Lost Cause, 1865–1920* (Athens: University of Georgia Press, 1980), 112–13 (tombstone inscription); Lou Falkner Williams, *The Great South Carolina Ku Klux Klan Trials, 1871–1872* (Athens: University of Georgia Press, 1996), 119 (Bond quotations). On white violence, see Allen W. Trelease, *White Terror: The Ku Klux Klan Conspiracy and Southern Reconstruction* (New York: Harper and Row, 1971); George C. Rable, *But There Was No Peace: The Role of Violence in the Politics of Reconstruction* (Athens: University of Georgia Press, 1984); and Michael Perman, "Counter Reconstruction: The Role of Violence in Southern Redemption," in *The Facts of Reconstruction: Essays in Honor of John Hope Franklin*, ed. Eric Anderson and Alfred A. Moss Jr. (Baton Rouge: Louisiana State University Press, 1991), 121–40. For a different interpretation that views violence as decisive in the southern counterrevolution that ended Reconstruction, see John Hope Franklin, *Reconstruction: After the Civil War* (Chicago: University of Chicago Press, 1961). For the interaction of southern evangelicalism and the Klan, see also Wilson, *Baptized in Blood*, 100–01, 110–18.

45. Foner, *Reconstruction*, 575–83.

46. Entries for 22, 30 November 1876, Fain Diaries.

47. *Christian Recorder*, 6 July 1876, 26 April 1877; Angell, *Bishop Henry McNeal Turner and African-American Religion in the South*, 127–33.

48. Morrow, *Northern Methodism and Reconstruction*, 226–28; Montgomery, *Under Their Own Vine and Fig Tree*, 188–89.

10   One Nation under God?

1. Paul H. Buck, *The Road to Reunion, 1865–1900* (Boston: Little, Brown, 1937), 60; C. Vann Woodward, *Reunion and Reaction: The Compromise of 1877 and the End of Reconstruction* (Boston: Little, Brown, 1951); William Gillette, *Retreat from Reconstruction, 1869–1879* (Baton Rouge: Louisiana State University Press, 1979); Nina Silber, *The Romance of Reunion: Northerners and the South, 1865–1900* (Chapel Hill: University of North Carolina Press, 1993).

2. *North Carolina Presbyterian*, 28 December 1864, quoted in Haskell M. Monroe Jr., "The Presbyterian Church in the Confederate States of America" (Ph.D. diss., Rice University, 1961), 321–22.

3. "Pastoral Address of the Southern Methodist Bishops," *Southern Christian Advocate*, 31 August 1865. See also Hunter Dickinson Farish, *The Circuit Rider Dismounts: A Social History of Southern Methodism, 1865–1900* (Richmond, VA: Dietz Press, 1938), 52–61.

4. *Southern Christian Advocate*, 31 August 1865.

5. Nora C. Chaffin, "A Southern Advocate of Methodist Unification in 1865," *North Carolina Historical Review* 18 (January 1941): 38, 42–43.

6. Ibid., 43–45. Southern Methodist bishops declared in August 1865, "the abolition, for military and political considerations, of the institution of domestic slavery in the United States does not affect the moral question that was prominent in our separation in 1844." "Pastoral Address of the Southern Methodist Bishops," *Southern Christian Advocate*, 31 August 1865.

7. Chaffin, "A Southern Advocate of Methodist Unification," 45–47.

Dr. Daniel Whedon, editor of the *Methodist Review*, represents the moderate group in northern Methodism. Early in 1866, he wrote hopefully of the southern bishops' declarations of loyalty to the national government. Several months later, he wrote, "with the efforts I, almost alone, have made with the Church, South, I have found that reasoning appeals, made as a reasonable Christian man, to Southern Methodism, do meet with a cheering response." He warned the northern Methodists against ruining their efforts in the South through "bad temper mistakenly supposed by us to be high moral sternness." *Methodist Review* 48 (January 1866): 124–30; *Christian Advocate*, 9 August 1866.

8. *American Annual Cyclopaedia and Register of Important Events* 5 (1865) (New York: Appleton, 1870), 553.

9. Christopher Hendrick Owen, "Sanctity, Slavery, and Segregation: Methodists and Society in Nineteenth-Century Georgia" (Ph.D. diss., Emory University, 1991), 399; General Conference of the MECS, *Journal*, 1866, 18–19.

Fraternal relations or fraternity indicated a formal recognition of one ecclesiastical organization by another. The practical aspects of the relationship included the exchange of greetings between conferences, conventions, or assemblies; cooperation in revivals and mission work; and the opening of pulpits and churches to the opposite denomination. In many cases, individual instances of local cooperation existed before the denominations recognized the fact officially. Ralph E. Morrow, *Northern Methodism and Reconstruction* (East Lansing: Michigan State University Press, 1956), 93–94.

10. James O. Andrew to Holland N. McTyeire, 7 June 1866, John J. Tigert IV Collection, Papers of Holland Nimmons McTyeire, Incoming Correspondence, Special Collections, Vanderbilt University Library, Nashville, TN.

11. *North Carolina Presbyterian*, quoted in "The Southern Churches," *Presbyter*, 3 May 1865; "The General Assembly of 1865," *Southern Presbyterian Review* (July 1866), 96; "A Pastoral Letter from the General Assembly to the Churches under their Care," *Southern Presbyterian*, 11 January 1866.

The Holston Presbytery in eastern Tennessee resolved in the fall of 1865 that it was "ready and willing to unite with the General Assembly of the Presbyterian Church in the U.S.A. whenever that body was willing to receive it on such terms as are laid down in the Word of God and the time-tried Standards of the Presbyterian Church." Likewise in 1866, the Nashville Presbytery in central Tennessee declared its willingness "to resume our connection with that branch of the church North as soon as the Synod can do so in honor and with good conscience." Ernest Trice Thompson, *Presbyterians in the South*, 3 vols. (Richmond, VA: John Knox Press, 1963–73), 2:128, 153.

12. "The Condition and Wants of the Church," *Southern Presbyterian*, 25 January 1866; "Who Has Prevented Reconstruction?" *Southern Presbyterian*, 8 February 1866; "Is Reunion with the Northern Church Desirable?" *Southern Presbyterian*, 22 February 1866.

13. *American Annual Cyclopaedia and Register of Important Events* 5 (1865), 105–6; Baptist General Association of Virginia, *Minutes*, 1865, 16–17; John Lee Eighmy, *Churches in Cultural Captivity: A History of the Social Attitudes of Southern Baptists*, rev. ed. (Knoxville: University of Tennessee Press, 1987), 33–34; Southern Baptist Convention, *Proceedings*, 1866, 48–51.

14. Ben M. Barrus, Milton L. Baughn, and Thomas H. Campbell, *A People Called Cumberland Presbyterians* (Memphis, TN: Frontier Press, 1972), 149–50.

15. Ibid., 154–59.

16. B. W. McDonnold, *History of the Cumberland Presbyterian Church*, 4th ed. (Nashville, TN: Board of Publication of Cumberland Presbyterian Church, 1899), 383, 404–5.

17. Barrus, Baughn, and Campbell, *A People Called Cumberland Presbyterians*, 161–63; General Assembly of the Cumberland Presbyterian Church, *Minutes*, 1866, 48–49.

18. General Assembly of the Cumberland Presbyterian Church, *Minutes*, 1866, 37; Barrus, Baughn, and Campbell, *A People Called Cumberland Presbyterians*, 187.

19. *Independent*, 10 August 1865.

20. *Central Christian Advocate* and *Northwestern Christian Advocate*, quoted in *Methodist*, 17 June 1865; *Christian Advocate*, 12 October 1865.

21. "Who Has Prevented Reconstruction?" *Southern Presbyterian*, 8 February 1866; *Christian Index*, 9 November 1865.

22. "Invasion" and "distintegration and absorption" are northern Methodist editor Daniel

Curry's prescription for dealing with southern Methodism; see "Reconstruction," *Christian Advocate and Journal*, 25 May 1865; "Our Policy in the South," *Christian Advocate and Journal*, 25 April 1867; *Methodist*, 17 June 1865; *New York Daily Tribune*, 30 November 1867, quoted in Oliver Saxon Heckman, "Northern Church Penetration of the South, 1860 to 1880" (Ph.D. diss., Duke University, 1939), 375 (Summers quotations). See also "Does the Northern Church Desire to Rob Us of Our Church Property?" *Southern Presbyterian*, 22 February 1866.

23. The New School Presbyterian church had divided in 1857. Its southern wing, the United Synod of the South, united with the Presbyterian Church in the Confederate States of America (Old School) in 1864. The northern wing united with the PCUSA (Old School) in 1869.

24. General Assembly of the PCUSA (Old School), *Minutes*, 1865, 554, 560–61; J. Treadwell Davis, *Relations between the Northern and Southern Presbyterian Churches, 1861–1888* (Nashville, TN: Joint University Libraries, 1951), 9–11.

25. Davis, *Relations between the Northern and Southern Presbyterian Churches*, 12–13 (quotation, 13); Ernest Trice Thompson, "Presbyterians North and South—Efforts toward Reunion," *Journal of Presbyterian History* 43 (March 1965): 2.

26. General Assembly of the PCUSA, *Minutes*, 1870, 529–30; Thompson, *Presbyterians in the South*, 2:224–26.

27. Entry for 5 June 1870, Eliza Rhea Fain Diaries, John N. Fain Collection, McClung Historical Collection, Knox County Public Library System, Knoxville, TN.

28. General Assembly of the PCUSA, *Minutes*, 1873, 503; General Assembly of the PCUS, *Minutes*, 1874, 502–6; Thompson, *Presbyterians in the South*, 2:229–31.

29. Thompson, *Presbyterians in the South*, 2:232–33 (quotations); Davis, *Relations between the Northern and Southern Presbyterian Churches*, 16–18.

30. Thompson, *Presbyterians in the South*, 2:245–48; Thompson, "Presbyterians North and South—Efforts toward Reunion," 2–3.

31. General Assembly of the PCUS, *Minutes*, 1883, 57–58; 1887, 222–23.

32. General Assembly of the PCUS, *Minutes*, 1888, 456–63 (northern committee quotation); *Southern Presbyterian*, 18 August 1887 (Dabney et al. quotations); Thompson, *Presbyterians in the South*, 2:256–58.

33. Thompson, *Presbyterians in the South*, 2:258 (quotation); Davis, *Relations between the Northern and Southern Presbyterian Churches*, 33–34.

Among the younger recruits was Dr. Thomas Cary Johnson, professor of church history at Union Theological Seminary, whose history of the southern Presbyterian church, published in 1894, defended its continued separate existence. He lamented that when the southern General Assembly issued its apology in 1882, "she lowered her banner. She merged her witness for the truth—forsaking the nobler course under the whips of some goody-goody scolds." Thomas C. Johnson, *History of the Southern Presbyterian Church* (New York: Christian Literature, 1894), 473.

34. Thompson, *Presbyterians in the South*, 2:260–61. For a discussion of reunion efforts to the 1960s, see Thompson, "Presbyterians North and South," 5–15.

The PCUS and the (United) Presbyterian Church in the United States of America (the result of a 1958 merger between the PCUSA and the United Presbyterian Church) united in 1983.

35. General Conference of the MECS, *Journal*, 1866, 26–27 (quotation); Farish, *The Circuit Rider Dismounts*, 56; William A. Russ Jr., "The Failure to Reunite Methodism after the Civil War," *Susquehanna University Studies* 1 (1936): 9–13.

36. Bishop Thomas A. Morris was also appointed to go, but was unable to because his wife was ill.

37. *Formal Fraternity. Proceedings of the General Conferences of the Methodist Episco-*

pal Church and of the Methodist Episcopal Church, South, In 1872, 1874, and 1876, and of the Joint Commission of the Two Churches on Fraternal Relations, at Cape May, New Jersey, August 16–23, 1876 (New York: Nelson and Phillips, 1876), 8.

38. Holland N. McTyeire, *History of Methodism* (Nashville, TN: Southern Methodist Publishing House, 1884), 680 ("sufficient length" quotation); *Formal Fraternity*, 10–12.

39. General Conference of the MECS, *Journal*, 1870, 230–31.

40. *Formal Fraternity*, 18–19, 35–40 (quotations, 37, 38, 40).

41. General Conference of the MEC, *Journal*, 1876, 418 ("disturbing questions" quotation); *Formal Fraternity*, 18–19, 35–40; Dow Kirkpatrick, "Early Efforts at Reunion," in *The History of American Methodism*, ed. Emory Stevens Bucke, 3 vols. (Nashville, TN: Abingdon Press, 1964), 2.664–71.

Many ministers of the MEC in the South were outraged by the Cape May meeting. One of their number insisted, "we met the enemy and we surrendered." *Zion's Herald*, 12 October 1876, quoted in Morrow, *Northern Methodism and Reconstruction*, 89–90.

42. Morrow, *Northern Methodism and Reconstruction*, 195; *Christian Recorder*, quoted in Owen, "Sanctity, Slavery, and Segregation," 487.

43. *Methodist Advocate*, 15 July 1874.

44. Frederick E. Maser, "The Story of Unification," in Bucke, *The History of American Methodism*, 3:412–38. The 1924–25 vote in the southern annual conferences was 4,528 for unification and 4,108 against.

45. John Abernathy Smith, *Cross and Flame: Two Centuries of United Methodism in Middle Tennessee* (Nashville, TN: Commission on Archives and History of the Tennessee Conference, 1984), 268, 280–81.

46. Dwight W. Culver, *Negro Segregation in the Methodist Church* (New Haven: Yale University Press, 1953), 79–95; Smith, *Cross and Flame*, 281–82.

47. Southern Baptist Convention, *Proceedings*, 1867, 79; 1868, 17–18, 20–21.

48. Robert Andrew Baker, *Relations between Northern and Southern Baptists* (n.p., 1954; reprint, New York: Arno Press, 1980), 97–98; Eighmy, *Churches in Cultural Captivity*, 34 (quotations).

49. Southern Baptist Convention, *Proceedings*, 1870, 36.

50. Joe W. Burton, *Road to Recovery: Southern Baptist Renewal Following the Civil War, As Seen Especially in the Work of I. T. Tichenor* (Nashville, TN: Broadman Press, 1977), 82–94 (quotations); Baker, *Relations between Northern and Southern Baptists*, 128–32, 155; Victor I. Masters, *Baptist Missions in the South*, 3rd ed. (Atlanta, GA: Home Mission Board of the Southern Baptist Convention, 1915), 19.

H. H. Tucker, the editor of the *Christian Index* in Georgia and one of the SBC's fraternal delegates, said in his address to the ABHMS in 1879:

> We of the South hold firmly to our separate organization as Baptists: we do this with singular unanimity, and with great feeling and enthusiasm, and I think that the feeling will grow stronger rather than weaker with the lapse of time. . . . I think that you will see that we are wise in the stand that we have taken and that the cause of Christ, in which we are all mutually and equally interested, will be better promoted by letting things remain as they are, than by an attempt to consolidate our forces. (*Christian Index*, 9 June 1879)

51. Baker, *Relations between Northern and Southern Baptists*, 159–69; Eighmy, *Churches in Cultural Captivity*, 35; Georgia Baptist Convention, *Minutes*, 1878, 18; Harold Lynn McManus, "The American Baptist Home Mission Society and Freedmen Education in the South, With Special Reference to Georgia: 1862–1897" (Ph.D. diss., Yale University, 1953), 279–80, 303; Tennessee Baptist Convention, *Minutes*, 1881, 14–15.

52. Baker, *Relations between Northern and Southern Baptists*, 175–77; McManus, "The American Baptist Home Mission Society and Freedmen Education," 225; Burton, *Road to Recovery*, 102–3.

53. Baker, *Relations between Northern and Southern Baptists*, 178–81; Rufus B. Spain, *At Ease in Zion: A Social History of Southern Baptists, 1865–1900* (Nashville, TN: Vanderbilt University Press, 1967), 61–64.

Conclusion

1. "Church Reconstruction in Rebeldom," *Christian Advocate and Journal* (New York), 9 February 1865.

2. United States, Census Office, *Statistics of the United States, in 1860; Compiled from the Original Returns and Being the Final Exhibit of the Eighth Census, under the Direction of the Secretary of the Interior* (Washington, DC: Government Printing Office, 1866), 368–70; United States, Census Office, *The Statistics of the Population of the United States: Compiled from the Original Returns of the Ninth Census (June 1, 1870), under the Direction of the Secretary of the Interior* (Washington, DC: Government Printing Office, 1872), 533. Property value for all Georgia churches rose by $1,121,564 from 1860 to 1870. In 1860, Baptists, Methodists, and Presbyterians owned 96 percent of all Georgia churches, but only 83 percent of the church property in value. The 1870 census does not give property value by denomination, but if these denominations (still comprising 96 percent of Georgia church organizations) held the same proportion of church property, their holdings would have risen in value by approximately $931,350 between 1860 and 1870.

3. United States, Census Office, *Statistics of the United States, in 1860*, 468–70; United States, Census Office, *The Statistics of the Population of the United States . . . 1870*, 554.

4. An Old Pastor, "Mrs. Eliza R. Fain," undated obituary clipping, 1892, John N. Fain Collection, McClung Historical Collection, Knox County Public Library System, Knoxville, TN; entry for 22 February 1885, Eliza Rhea Fain Diaries, John N. Fain Collection.

5. Glenn T. Eskew, "Black Elitism and the Failure of Paternalism in Postbellum Georgia: The Case of Bishop Lucius Henry Holsey," *Journal of Southern History* 58 (November 1992): 654–66 (quotation, 666).

6. Memoirs of Thomas Hooke McCallie (1901–12), McCallie Family Papers, McCallie School, Chattanooga, TN.

7. John H. Caldwell, *Reminiscences of the Reconstruction of Church and State in Georgia* (Wilmington, DE: J. Miller Thomas, 1895), 2, 17; John A. Munroe, *The University of Delaware: A History* (Newark, DE: University of Delaware, 1986), 155–59.

8. Stephen Ward Angell, *Bishop Henry McNeal Turner and African-American Religion in the South* (Knoxville: University of Tennessee Press, 1992), 123–252 (quotation, 244); John Dittmer, "The Education of Henry McNeal Turner," in *Black Leaders of the Nineteenth Century*, ed. Leon F. Litwack and August Meier (Urbana: University of Illinois Press, 1988), 259–72. For Turner's role in the growth of the AME Church in South Africa, see James T. Campbell, *Songs of Zion: The African Methodist Episcopal Church in the United States and South Africa* (New York: Oxford Unviversity Press, 1995).

9. Joanna P. Moore, *"In Christ's Stead": Autobiographical Sketches* (Chicago: Women's Baptist Home Mission Society, 1903), 191–96; Grace M. Eaton, *A Heroine of the Cross: Sketches of the Life and Work of Miss Joanna P. Moore* (n.p., n.d.), 14–15, 86–88 (quotation, 87); Mrs. John H. Chapman, "They Needed a Woman's Help," 1932, Una Roberts Lawrence Papers, Southern Baptist Historical Library and Archives, Nashville, TN; *Nashville Globe*, 21 April 1916.

When it began in 1885, *Hope* had a circulation of five hundred. By 1892, circulation had increased to five thousand, and in 1902, eleven thousand were distributed. Moore, *"In Christ's Stead,"* 220–21.

10. Roy P. Basler, ed., *The Collected Works of Abraham Lincoln*, 8 vols. (New Brunswick, NJ: Rutgers University Press, 1953), 8:333; William A. Clebsch, *Christian Interpretations of the Civil War* (Philadelphia: Fortress Press, 1969), 15.

AME bishop Daniel A. Payne extended the tragic scope of the Civil War for Christians when he noted in his autobiography, "the most extraordinary thing of all, and that which forms the greatest anomaly, is the circumstance that the South was earnestly invoking God against the North, the North invoking God against the South, and the blacks invoking God against both!" Daniel A. Payne, *Recollections of Seventy Years* (Nashville, TN: Publishing House of the AME Sunday School Union, 1888), 145.

11. Edward L. Ayers, *The Promise of the New South: Life after Reconstruction* (New York: Oxford University Press, 1992), 160.

Bibliography

Manuscript Collections

Atlanta University Center Woodruff Library, Archives Department, Atlanta, GA
    Records of the Tennessee Conference, The Georgia and Alabama Mission District, 1865–1878
Christian Methodist Episcopal Church Archives, Memphis, TN
    General Conference of the Colored Methodist Episcopal Church in America, Journal, 1870–1906
Emory University, Pitts Theology Library, Special Collections, Atlanta, GA
    Georgia Annual Conference, Minutes, 1846–1866
Emory University, Robert W. Woodruff Library, Special Collections, Atlanta, GA
    Morgan Callaway Papers
    Charles James Oliver Collection
Georgia Department of Archives and History, Atlanta, GA
    Eatonton Methodist Church, Quarterly Conference Minutes, 1857–1907
    Monticello Presbyterian Church, Session Book, 1829–1904
Historical Foundation of the Presbyterian and Reformed Churches, Montreat, NC
    Henry Francis Hoyt Collection
    James Adair Lyon, Diary
    Robert Quarterman Mallard Papers, Pastoral Record, 1855–1865
    Thaddeus W. McRae Papers
    Robert Langdon Neely Collection
    Safford Family Papers
    South Carolina Presbytery, Minutes, 1865
    Synod of Memphis, Minutes, 1860–1865
    Synod of Nashville, Minutes, 1860–1877
    Robert Alexander Webb Papers
    George William White Collection
Lambuth College, Luther L. Gobbell Library, Jackson, TN
    Memphis Annual Conference, Minutes, 1865
McCallie School, Chattanooga, TN
    McCallie Family Papers

McClung Historical Collection, Knox County Public Library System, Knoxville, TN
>   John N. Fain Collection
Mercer University Library, Special Collections, Macon, GA
>   Albany Baptist Church Records, 1860–1899
National Archives, Washington, DC
>   United States, Department of War, Bureau of Refugees, Freedmen, and Abandoned
>   Lands, Records of the Superintendent of Education for the State of Georgia,
>   1865–1870, Record Group 105, available on microfilm (M-799)
South Georgia Conference Archives, Epworth-by the-Sea, GA
>   Americus District Conference, Minutes, 1867–1878
>   Bainbridge District Conference, Minutes, 1867–1878
>   Constitution of the Sunday School Society of the South Georgia Annual Conference, 1867
>   Macon District Conference, Minutes, 1871–1880
>   Minutes of the Officers and Board of Managers of the Sunday School Society, 1867–1872
Southern Baptist Historical Library and Archives, Nashville, TN
>   Manly Collection of Manuscripts
>   Una Roberts Lawrence Papers
Tennessee State Library and Archives, Nashville, TN
>   Candays Creek Baptist Church, Minute Book, 1846–1866
>   Sarah Jane Johnston Estes Diary, 1862
>   Nannie Haskins Diary, 1863–1865
>   McMinn County Chancery Court Minutes, 1868–1875
>   Mars Hill Presbyterian Church Records, 1832–1967
>   St. Paul's Presbyterian Church, Record Book, 1858–1875
>   Washington County Clerk and Master Court Minutes, 1869–1874
University of Virginia, Alderman Library, Charlottesville, VA
>   John Esten Cooke Collection
Vanderbilt University Library, Special Collections, Nashville, TN
>   John J. Tigert IV Collection, Papers of Holland Nimmons McTyeire

Newspapers

American Baptist (New York)
The Baptist (Nashville, TN, and Memphis, TN)
Biblical Recorder (Raleigh, NC)
Central Christian Advocate (St. Louis)
Central Presbyterian (Richmond, VA)
Chattanooga Daily Gazette (Chattanooga, TN)
Child's Index (Macon, GA)
Children's Friend (Richmond, VA)
Christian Advocate (Nashville, TN)
Christian Advocate and Journal (New York)
Christian Index (Macon, GA, and Atlanta, GA)
Christian Observer (Richmond, VA)
Christian Recorder (Philadelphia)
Christian Times and Illinois Baptist (Chicago)
Cincinnati Gazette (Cincinnati, OH)
Daily Advertiser (Montgomery, AL)
Daily Press and Times (Nashville, TN)
East Tennessee Baptist (Knoxville, TN)

Episcopal Methodist (Richmond, VA)
Independent (New York)
Kind Words (Greenville, SC, and Memphis, TN)
Knoxville Whig [and Rebel Ventilator] (Knoxville, TN)
Lexington Gazette (Lexington, VA)
The Methodist (New York)
Methodist Advocate (Atlanta, GA)
Methodist Quarterly Review (New York)
Methodist Review (New York)
Mobile Daily Register (Mobile, AL)
Nashville Globe (Nashville, TN)
Nation (New York)
National Freedman (New York)
National Monitor (Brooklyn, NY)
New York Times (New York)
North Carolina Christian Advocate (Raleigh, NC)
North Carolina Presbyterian (Fayetteville, NC)
Presbyter (Cincinnati, OH)
Religious Herald (Richmond, VA)
Southern Christian Advocate (Charleston, SC, Augusta, GA, and Macon, GA)
Southern Presbyterian (Columbia, SC)
Southern Presbyterian Review (Columbia, SC)
Texas Baptist Herald (Abilene, TX)
Tri-Weekly Telegraph (Houston, TX)
Western Christian Advocate (Cincinnati, OH)
The Young Reaper (Philadelphia)
Zion's Herald (Boston)

Denominational Records

Alabama Baptist Convention. *Minutes.* 1865.
American Baptist Home Mission Society. *Annual Report.* 1862–1880.
Atlantic Synod. *Minutes.* 1873.
Baptist General Association of Virginia. *Minutes.* 1865.
Bethel Baptist Association. *Minutes.* 1865–1870.
Central Baptist Association. *Minutes.* 1859–1866.
Coosa River Baptist Association. *Minutes.* 1866.
Detroit Annual Conference. *Minutes.* 1861.
Ebenezer Baptist Association. *Minutes.* 1864–1867.
Freedmen's Aid Society of the Methodist Episcopal Church. *Annual Report.* 1867–1886.
General Assembly of the Cumberland Presbyterian Church. *Minutes.* 1866–1869.
General Assembly of the Presbyterian Church in the Confederate States of America. *Minutes.*
    1861–1864.
General Assembly of the Presbyterian Church in the United States. *Minutes.* 1865–1888.
General Assembly of the Presbyterian Church in the United States of America. *Minutes.*
    1870–1877.
General Assembly of the Presbyterian Church in the United States of America (New School).
    Minutes. 1860–1869.
General Assembly of the Presbyterian Church in the United States of America (Old School).
    Minutes. 1860–1869.

General Conference of the Methodist Episcopal Church. *Journal*. 1864, 1868, 1872, 1876.
General Conference of the Methodist Episcopal Church, South. *Journal*. 1866, 1870, 1874, 1878.
Georgia Annual Conference (AME). *Minutes*. 1869–1874.
Georgia Annual Conference (CME). *Minutes*. 1871.
Georgia Annual Conference (MEC). *Minutes*. 1867–1882.
Georgia Annual Conference (MECS). *Minutes*. 1860–1866.
Georgia Baptist Association. *Minutes*. 1865–1877.
Georgia Baptist Convention. *Minutes*. 1860–1878.
Holston Annual Conference (MEC). *Minutes*. 1865–1877.
Holston Annual Conference (MECS). *Minutes*. 1860–1877.
Houston Baptist Association. *Minutes*. 1865.
Memphis Annual Conference. *Minutes*. 1865–1866.
Middle Cherokee Baptist Association. *Minutes*. 1866.
Minutes of the Annual Conferences of the Methodist Episcopal Church, South, 1845–1877. Nashville, TN: Methodist Publishing House, 1845–78.
Missouri Annual Conference. *Minutes*. 1867.
New Sunbury Association. *Minutes*. 1866–1867.
New York East Conference. *Minutes*. 1864.
North Carolina Baptist Convention. *Minutes*. 1865–1867.
North Georgia Annual Conference (AME). *Minutes*. 1874–1877.
North Georgia Annual Conference (MECS). *Minutes*. 1867–1877.
Presbyterian Church in the United States of America (Old School). *First Annual Report of the Committee for Freedmen*. 1866.
Presbyterian Church in the United States of America. *Annual Report of the Committee on Freedmen*. 1870–1877.
Rappahannock Baptist Association. *Minutes*. 1864.
Report of the Board of Domestic Missions. *Minutes of the General Assembly of the Presbyterian Church in the United States of America*. 1866.
South Carolina Annual Conference (AME). *Minutes*. 1865–1867.
South Carolina Annual Conference (MECS). *Minutes*. 1868.
South Carolina Baptist Convention. *Minutes*. 1871.
South Georgia Annual Conference (AME). *Minutes*. 1874–1877.
South Georgia Annual Conference (MECS). *Minutes*. 1867–1877.
Southern Baptist Convention. *Proceedings*. 1859–1892.
Synod of Atlanta. *Minutes*. 1873.
Synod of Georgia. *Minutes*. 1860–1877.
Synod of Memphis. *Minutes*. 1860–1877.
Tennessee Annual Conference (AME). *Minutes*. 1868–1877.
Tennessee Baptist Convention. *Minutes*. 1874–1881.
Washington Baptist Association. *Minutes*. 1864.
West Tennessee Baptist Convention. *Proceedings*. 1865–1873.
Western Baptist Association. *Minutes*. 1865–1877.

Published Primary Sources

Alvord, John W. *Letters from the South Relating to the Condition of the Freedmen*. Washington, DC: Howard University Press, 1870.
American Annual Cyclopaedia and Register of Important Events. New York: Appleton, 1870.
Ash, Stephen V.; ed. "Conscience and Christianity: A Middle Tennessee Unionist Renounces

His Church, 1867." *East Tennessee Historical Society's Publications* 54/55 (1982–83): 111–15.

Avary, Myrta Lockett, ed. *Recollections of Alexander H. Stephens.* New York: Doubleday, Page, 1910.

Basler, Roy P., ed. *The Collected Works of Abraham Lincoln.* 8 vols. New Brunswick, NJ: Rutgers University Press, 1953.

Beers, Fannie A. *Memories: A Record of Personal Experience and Adventure during Four Years of War.* Philadelphia: J. B. Lippincott, 1889.

Bledsoe, Albert Taylor. *Is Davis a Traitor; or Was Secession a Constitutional Right Previous to the War of 1861?* Baltimore: Innes, 1866.

Bridges v. Wilson, 58 Tenn. (11 Heisk) 458–71 (1872).

Brownlow, William G. *Portrait and Biography of Parson Brownlow, the Tennessee Patriot.* Indianapolis, IN: Asher and Company, 1862.

———. *Sketches of the Rise, Progress, and Decline of Secession; with a Narrative of Personal Adventures among the Rebels [Parson Brownlow's Book].* Philadelphia: George W. Childs, 1862.

Burge, Dolly Sumner Lunt. *A Woman's Wartime Journal: An Account of the Passage over a Georgia Plantation of Sherman's Army on the March to the Sea.* Macon, GA: J. W. Burke, 1927.

Burke, John W. *Autobiography: Chapters from the Life of a Preacher.* Macon, GA: J. W. Burke, 1884.

Burr, Virginia Ingraham, ed. *The Secret Eye: The Journal of Ella Gertrude Clanton Thomas, 1848–1889.* Chapel Hill: University of North Carolina Press, 1990.

Caldwell, John H. *A Fast Day Sermon, Preached in Newnan, Ga., April 8, 1864, On the Occasion of the President's Proclamation.* La Grange, GA: Daily Bulletin Office, 1864.

———. *Reminiscences of the Reconstruction of Church and State in Georgia.* Wilmington, DE: J. Miller Thomas, 1895.

———. *Slavery and Southern Methodism: Two Sermons Preached in the Methodist Church in Newnan, Georgia.* New York: published by the author, 1865.

Caskey, Thomas W. *Caskey's Last Book, Containing an Autobiographical Sketch of His Ministerial Life, with Essays and Sermons.* Nashville, TN: Messenger Publishing, 1896.

Catalogue of the Officers and Students of Mercer University, 1860–1861. Penfield, GA: Mercer University, 1861.

Catalogue of the Officers and Students of the Nashville Institute, 1873–1874. Nashville, TN: Wheeler, Marshall and Bruce, 1874.

Catalogue of the Officers and Students of the Nashville Normal and Theological Institute, Nashville, Tenn., for the Academic Year 1876–77. Nashville, TN: Wheeler Brothers, 1877.

Churches and Institutions of Learning Destroyed by the United States Military Forces During the Civil War, But Not as an Act of Military Necessity, The Materials Having Been Appropriated and Used. Washington, DC: Government Printing Office, 1912.

Crozier, Robert H. *The Confederate Spy: A History of the War of 1861.* Gallatin, TN: R. B. Harmon, 1866.

Cumming, Kate. *Kate: The Journal of a Confederate Nurse.* Edited by Richard Barksdale Harwell. Baton Rouge: Louisiana State University Press, 1959.

Dabney, Robert Lewis. *A Defence of Virginia, and Through Her, of the South.* New York: E. J. Hale and Son, 1867.

———. *The Life and Campaigns of Lieut.-Gen. Thomas J. Jackson.* New York: Blelock, 1866.

———. *True Courage: A Discourse Commemorative of Lieut. General Thomas J. Jackson.* Richmond, VA: Presbyterian Committee of Publication of the Confederate States, 1863.

Deaderick v. Lampson, 58 Tenn. (11 Heisk) 523–38 (1872).

Doctrine and Discipline of the Methodist Episcopal Church, 1864. Cincinnati, OH: Poe and Hitchcock, 1864.

Dowdey, Clifford, ed. *The Wartime Papers of R. E. Lee.* Boston: Little, Brown, 1961.

Dunaway, Thomas S. *A Sermon Delivered by Elder Thomas S. Dunaway, of Lancaster County Virginia, before Coan Baptist Church, in Connection with a Day of National Fasting, Humiliation and Prayer, April, 1864.* Richmond, VA: Enquirer Book and Job Press, 1864.

Evans, Clement A. "General Clement A. Evans Asks to Be a Methodist Preacher." *Historical Highlights* 22 (Spring 1992): 34–35.

Fleharty, Stephen F. *Our Regiment. A History of the 102nd Illinois Infantry Volunteers.* Chicago: Brewster and Hanscom, 1865.

Foote, H. S. "Review of the War of the Rebellion." *Methodist Quarterly Review* 48 (April 1866): 306–7.

Ford, S. H. "Duty of Southern Churches." *Christian Repository and Family Visitor: A Southern Religious and Literary Monthly* 10 (June 1866): 65–69.

Formal Fraternity. Proceedings of the General Conferences of the Methodist Episcopal Church and of the Methodist Episcopal Church, South, In 1872, 1874, and 1876, and of the Joint Commission of the Two Churches on Fraternal Relations, at Cape May, New Jersey, August 16–23, 1876. New York: Nelson and Phillips, 1876.

French, Austa M. *Slavery in South Carolina and the Ex-Slaves; or, The Port Royal Mission.* New York: W. M. French, 1862.

Gaines, Wesley J. *African Methodism in the South, or Twenty Five Years of Freedom.* Atlanta, GA: Franklin Publishing, 1890.

Hall, William A. *The Historic Significance of the Southern Revolution: A Lecture Delivered by Invitation in Petersburg, Va., March 14 and April 29th, 1864, and in Richmond, Va., April 7th and April 21st, 1864.* Petersburg, VA: A. F. Crutchfield, 1864.

Harrison, William Pope, ed. *The Gospel among the Slaves.* Nashville, TN: Publishing House of the Methodist Episcopal Church, South, 1893; reprint, New York: AMS Press, 1973.

Haygood, Atticus G. *The Church and the Education of the People: An Address Delivered Before the Alumni Association of Emory College.* Nashville, TN: Southern Methodist Publishing House, 1874.

Hoge, Peyton Harrison. *Moses Drury Hoge: Life and Letters.* Richmond, VA: Presbyterian Committee of Publication, 1899.

Holsey, Lucius H. *Autobiography, Sermons, Addresses, and Essays.* 2d ed. Atlanta, GA: Franklin Printing and Publishing, 1899.

Hoole, W. Stanley. "The Diary of Dr. Basil Manly, 1858–1867," pt. 2. *Alabama Review* 4 (July 1951): 221–36.

———. "The Diary of Dr. Basil Manly, 1858–1867," pt. 3. *Alabama Review* 4 (October 1951): 270–89.

———. "The Diary of Dr. Basil Manly, 1858–1867," pt. 4. *Alabama Review* 5 (January 1952): 61–74.

———. "The Diary of Dr. Basil Manly, 1858–1867," pt. 5. *Alabama Review* 5 (April 1952): 142–55.

Howard, Oliver O. "The Eleventh Corps at Chancellorsville." In *Battles and Leaders of the Civil War,* 4 vols., edited by Robert Underwood Johnson and Clarence Clough Buel, 3:202. New York: Century, 1884–88.

Hundley, Daniel R. *Prison Echoes of the Late Rebellion.* New York: S. W. Green, 1874.

Hurlburt, J. S. *History of the Rebellion in Bradley County, East Tennessee.* Indianapolis: n.p., 1866; reprint, n.p.: Sink-Moore, 1988.

Jackson, Mary Anna. *Memoirs of Stonewall Jackson.* Louisville, KY: Prentice Press, 1895.

Johnson, Thomas L. *Twenty-Eight Years a Slave.* Bournemouth, England: W. Mate and Sons, 1909.

Jones, John William. *The Davis Memorial; or Our Dead President, Jefferson Davis.* Richmond, VA: B. F. Johnson, 1890.

Lane, Isaac. *Autobiography of Bishop Isaac Lane, LL. D., With a Short History of the C. M. E. Church in America and Methodism.* Nashville, TN: Publishing House of the Methodist Episcopal Church, South, 1916.

Lee, Leroy Madison. *Our Country—Our Dangers—Our Duty. A Discourse in Centenary Church, Lynchburg, Va., on the National Fast Day, August 21, 1863.* Richmond, VA: Soldiers' Tract Association, 1863.

Lee, Luther, and E. Smith. *The Debates of the General Conference of the M. E. Church, May, 1844, to which is added a review of the proceedings of said conferences.* New York: O. Scott for the Wesleyan Methodist Connection of America, 1845.

Lee, Robert E. *Recollections and Letters of General Robert E. Lee.* Garden City, NJ: Garden City Publishing, 1924.

List of War Claims, Confined Entirely to Claims for Use and Occupation or Rent of Church Buildings, College Buildings, and Other Public Buildings, by the Military Forces of the United States During the War, Coupled in Some Cases with a Claim for Damages Done to the Building During the Occupancy With a Statement of Each Case Compiled for Convenience of Members of the Senate Committee on Claims in Connection with an Examination of H. R. 19115. Washington, DC: Government Printing Office, 1912.

List of War Claims Including a Few Exceptional Cases for Churches; Also List of Other Claims to Which Objections Appear, Such as Laches, No Proof of Loyalty, Insufficient Evidence as to Facts, Evidence of Payment and Statutory Bars, With a Statement of Each Case Compiled for the Convenience of Members of the Senate Committee on Claims in Connection With an Examination of H.R. 19115. Washington, DC: Government Printing Office, 1912.

Longstreet, Augustus Baldwin. *Fast-Day Sermon.* Columbia, SC: Townsend and North, 1861.

McGuire, Hunter. "The Death of Stonewall Jackson." In *The Confederate Soldier in the Civil War,* edited by John S. Blay, 158–60. Princeton, NJ: Pageant Books, 1959.

McPherson, Edward. *The Political History of the United States of America during the Great Rebellion.* 2d ed. Washington, DC: Philip and Solomons, 1865.

Matlack, L. C. "The Methodist Episcopal Church in the Southern States." *Methodist Review* (January 1872): 108.

Memorials of Methodism in Macon, Georgia, from 1828 to 1878. Macon, GA: J. W. Burke, 1879.

Miers, Earl Schenck, ed. *When the World Ended: The Diary of Emma LeConte.* Lincoln: University of Nebraska Press, 1987.

Miller, A. W. "Southern Views and Principles Not 'Extinguished' by the War." *Southern Presbyterian Review* (January 1870): 61–88.

Moore, Joanna P. *"In Christ's Stead": Autobiographical Sketches.* Chicago: Women's Baptist Home Mission Society, 1903.

Myers, Edward H. *The Disruption of the Methodist Episcopal Church, 1844–1846.* Nashville, TN: Publishing House of the Methodist Episcopal Church, South, 1875.

Myers, Robert Manson, ed. *The Children of Pride: A True Story of Georgia and the Civil War.* New Haven: Yale University Press, 1972.

O'Brien, Andrew Leary. *The Journal of Andrew Leary O'Brien; Including an Account of the Origin of Andrew College.* Athens: University of Georgia Press, 1946.

Oldfield, J. R., ed. *Civilization and Black Progress: Selected Writings of Alexander Crummell on the South.* Charlottesville: University of Virginia Press, 1995.

Palmer, Benjamin Morgan. *A Discourse Before the General Assembly of South Carolina on December 10, 1863, Appointed by the Legislature as a Day of Fasting, Humiliation and Prayer.* Columbia, SC: Charles P. Pelham, State Printer, 1864.

——. *The South: Her Peril and Her Duty. A Discourse delivered in the First Presbyterian Church, New Orleans, on Thursday, November 29, 1860*. New Orleans, LA: n.p., 1860.

Patton, Alfred S. *The Nation's Loss and Its Lessons*. Utica, NY: Curtiss and White, 1865.

Pearne, Thomas H. *An Address on the Two Churches*. Cincinnati, OH: Methodist Book Concern, 1867.

——. *Sixty-One Years of Itinerant Christian Life in Church and State*. Cincinnati, OH: Methodist Book Concern, 1899.

Pendleton, J. M. *Reminiscences of a Long Life*. Louisville, KY: Press Baptist Book Concern, 1891.

Pierce, George Foster, and Benjamin Morgan Palmer. *Sermons of Bishop Pierce and Rev. B. M. Palmer, D.D. Delivered Before the General Assembly at Milledgeville, Ga., on Fast Day, March 27, 1863*. Milledgeville, GA: Boughton, Nisbet and Barnes, 1863.

Ramsey, James B. *True Eminence Founded on Holiness: A Discourse Occasioned by the Death of Lieut. Gen. T. J. Jackson*. Lynchburg, VA: n.p., 1863.

Redkey, Edwin S., ed., *Respect Black: The Writings and Speeches of Henry McNeal Turner*. New York: Arno Press, 1971.

Reeves et al. v. Walker et al., 67 Tenn. (8 Baxt.) 277–84 (1874).

Renfroe, J. J. D. *The Battle Is God's: A Sermon Preached Before Wilcox's Brigade on Fast Day, the 21st of August, 1863, Near Orange Court-House, Va*. Richmond, VA: MacFarlane and Fergusson, 1863.

Smyth, Thomas. "The Battle of Fort Sumter: Its Mystery and Miracle — God's Mastery and Mercy." *Southern Presbyterian Review* 14 (October 1861): 365–99.

——. "National Righteousness." *Southern Presbyterian Review* 12 (April 1859): 25–36.

——. "The War of the South Vindicated." *Southern Presbyterian Review* 15 (April 1863): 479–514.

Stanton, R. L. *The Church and the Rebellion*. New York: Derby and Miller, 1864; reprint, Freeport, NY: Books for Libraries Press, 1971.

Stephens, Robert Grier, Jr., ed. and comp. *Intrepid Warrior: Clement Anselm Evans, Confederate General from Georgia: Life, Letters, and Diaries of the War Years*. Dayton, OH: Morningside, 1992.

Taylor, George B. *Life and Times of James B. Taylor*. Philadelphia: Bible and Publication Society, 1872.

Tucker, John Randolph. *The Southern Church Justified in Its Support of the South in the Present War*. Richmond, VA: n.p., 1863.

United States. Congress. *Report of the Joint Select Committee to Inquire into the Condition of Affairs in the Late Insurrectionary States*, 13 vols. 42d Congress, 2d Session, 1870–1871. Washington, DC: Government Printing Office, 1872.

United States. Census Office. *The Statistics of the Population of the United States: Compiled from the Original Returns of the Ninth Census (June 1, 1870), under the Direction of the Secretary of the Interior*. Washington, DC: Government Printing Office, 1872.

United States. Census Office. *Statistics of the United States, in 1860; Compiled from the Original Returns and Being the Final Exhibit of the Eighth Census, under the Direction of the Secretary of the Interior*. Washington, DC: Government Printing Office, 1866.

A Virginian [John Esten Cooke]. *The Life of Stonewall Jackson*. Richmond, VA: Ayers and Wade, 1863.

The War of the Rebellion: A Compilation of the Official Records of the Union and Confederate Armies. 128 vols. Washington, DC: Government Printing Office, 1881–1901.

Wiley, Calvin H. *Scriptural Views of National Trials: Or the True Road to Independence and Peace of the Confederate States of America*. Greensboro, NC: Sterling, Campbell and Albright, 1863.

Secondary Sources

Abbott, Richard H. *The Republican Party and the South, 1855–1877.* Chapel Hill: University of North Carolina Press, 1986.

Akers, Samuel Luttrell. *The First Hundred Years of Wesleyan College, 1836–1936.* Macon, GA: Beehive Press, 1976.

Alexander, Gross. *A History of the Methodist Episcopal Church, South.* New York: Christian Literature, 1894.

Alexander, Thomas B. *Political Reconstruction in Tennessee.* Nashville, TN: Vanderbilt University Press, 1950.

Allan, Elizabeth Preston. *The Life and Letters of Margaret Junkin Preston.* New York: Houghton Mifflin, 1903.

Allen, Clifton Judson, et al., eds. *Encyclopedia of Southern Baptists.* 2 vols. Nashville, TN: Broadman Press, 1958.

Anderson, Eric, and Alfred A. Moss Jr. *The Facts of Reconstruction: Essays in Honor of John Hope Franklin.* Baton Rouge: Louisiana State University Press, 1991.

Angell, Stephen Ward. *Bishop Henry McNeal Turner and African-American Religion in the South.* Knoxville: University of Tennessee Press, 1992.

Armstrong, Thomas F. "The Building of a Black Church: Community in Post Civil War Liberty County, Georgia." *Georgia Historical Quarterly* 66 (Fall 1982): 346–67.

Armstrong, William H. *A Friend to God's Poor: Edward Parmelee Smith.* Athens: University of Georgia Press, 1993.

Ash, Stephen V. *Middle Tennessee Society Transformed, 1860–1870: War and Peace in the Upper South.* Baton Rouge: Louisiana State University Press, 1988.

———. *When the Yankees Came: Conflict and Chaos in the Occupied South, 1861–1865.* Chapel Hill: University of North Carolina Press, 1995.

Ayers, Edward L. *The Promise of the New South: Life after Reconstruction.* New York: Oxford University Press, 1992.

Bailey, Fred Arthur. *Class and Tennessee's Confederate Generation.* Chapel Hill: University of North Carolina Press, 1987.

Bailey, Kenneth K. "The Post–Civil War Racial Separations in Southern Protestantism: Another Look." *Church History* 46 (December 1977): 453–73.

Baker, Robert Andrew. *Relations between Northern and Southern Baptists.* N.p., 1954; reprint, New York: Arno Press, 1980.

Barclay, Wade Crawford. *History of Methodist Missions, Part II: The Methodist Episcopal Church, 1845–1939.* 3 vols. New York: Board of Missions of the Methodist Church, 1957.

Barrus, Ben M., Milton L. Baughn, and Thomas H. Campbell. *A People Called Cumberland Presbyterians.* Memphis, TN: Frontier Press, 1972.

Benedict, Michael Les. *A Compromise of Principle: Congressional Republicans and Reconstruction, 1863–1869.* New York: Norton, 1974.

Benjamin, Walter W. "The Methodist Episcopal Church in the Postwar Era." In *The History of American Methodism,* edited by Emory Stevens Bucke, 2:315–80. Nashville, TN: Abingdon Press, 1964.

Beringer, Richard E., et al. *Why the South Lost the Civil War.* Athens: University of Georgia Press, 1986.

Berkeley, Kathleen C. "'Colored Ladies Also Contributed': Black Women's Activities from Benevolence to Social Welfare, 1866–1896." In *The Web of Southern Social Relations: Women, Family, and Education,* edited by Walter J. Fraser Jr., R. Frank Saunders Jr., and Jon L. Wakelyn, 181–203. Athens: University of Georgia Press, 1985.

Blassingame, John W. *Black New Orleans, 1860–1880*. Chicago: University of Chicago Press, 1973.

——. *The Slave Community: Plantation Life in the Antebellum South*. New York: Oxford University Press, 1972.

——, ed. *Slave Testimony: Two Centuries of Letters, Speeches, Interviews, and Autobiographies*. Baton Rouge: Louisiana State University Press, 1977.

Bode, Frederick A. "The Formation of Evangelical Communities in Middle Georgia: Twiggs County, 1820–1861." *Journal of Southern History* 60 (November 1994): 711–48.

Bodo, John R. *The Protestant Clergy and Public Issues, 1812–1848*. Princeton: Princeton University Press, 1954.

Boles, John B. *Black Southerners, 1619–1869*. Lexington: University Press of Kentucky, 1984.

——, ed. *Masters and Slaves in the House of the Lord: Race and Religion in the American South, 1740–1870*. Lexington: University Press of Kentucky, 1988.

——, and Evelyn Thomas Nolen, eds. *Interpreting Southern History: Essays in Honor of Sanford W. Higginbotham*. Baton Rouge: Louisiana State University Press, 1987.

Bone, Winstead Paine. *A History of Cumberland University*. Lebanon, TN: published by the author, 1935.

Boothe, Charles Octavius. *The Cyclopedia of the Colored Baptists of Alabama: Their Leaders and Their Work*. Birmingham: Alabama Publishing, 1895.

Bowden, Haygood S. *History of Savannah Methodism from John Wesley to Silas Johnson*. Macon, GA: J. W. Burke, 1929.

Bowers, Claude. *The Tragic Era*. Cambridge, MA: Riverside Press, 1922.

Boyd, Jesse L. *A Popular History of the Baptists in Mississippi*. Jackson, MS: Baptist Press, 1930.

Boyer, Reba B., and Budd L. Duncan. *A History of the Mars Hill Presbyterian Church*. Athens, TN: Mars Hill Presbyterian Church, 1973.

Boylan, Anne M. *Sunday School: The Formation of an American Institution, 1790–1880*. New Haven: Yale University Press, 1988.

Bradley, David Henry, Sr. *A History of the AME Zion Church, 1796–1872*. Nashville, TN: Parthenon Press, 1956.

Brasher, J. Lawrence. *The Sanctified South: John Lakin Brasher and the Holiness Movement*. Urbana: University of Illinois Press, 1994.

Brawley, Benjamin. *History of Morehouse College*. Atlanta, GA: Morehouse College Press, 1917; reprint, College Park, MD: McGrath Publishing, 1970.

Brawley, James P. *Two Centuries of Methodist Concern: Bondage, Freedom, and the Education of Black People*. New York: Vantage Press, 1974.

Brooks, Steven Edwards. "Out of the Galleries: The Northern Presbyterian Mission in Reconstruction North Carolina." M.A. thesis, University of North Carolina at Chapel Hill, 1974.

Brownlow, Paul Clyde. "The Northern Protestant Pulpit on Reconstruction, 1865–1877." Ph.D. diss., Purdue University, 1970.

Bryan, T. Conn. "Churches in Georgia during the Civil War." *Georgia Historical Quarterly* 33 (1949): 283–302.

Buck, Paul H. *The Road to Reunion, 1865–1900*. Boston: Little, Brown, 1937.

Bucke, Emory Stevens, ed. *The History of American Methodism*. 3 vols. Nashville, TN: Abingdon Press, 1964.

Bullock, Henry M. *A History of Emory University*. Nashville, TN: Parthenon Press, 1936.

Burkhead, L. S. "History of the Difficulties of the Pastorate of the Front Street Methodist Church, Wilmington, N.C., for the Year 1865." *Historical Papers*. Durham, NC: Historical Society of Trinity College, 1909; reprint, New York: AMS Press, 1970.

Burton, Joe W. *Road to Recovery: Southern Baptist Renewal Following the Civil War, As Seen Especially in the Work of I. T. Tichenor*. Nashville, TN: Broadman Press, 1977.

Butchart, Ronald E. *Northern Schools, Southern Blacks, and Reconstruction: Freedmen's Education, 1862–1875*. Westport, CT: Greenwood Press, 1980.

Butler, Addie Louise Joyner. *The Distinctive Black College: Talladega, Tuskegee and Morehouse*. Metuchen, NJ: Scarecrow Press, 1977.

Cade, John Brother. *Holsey—The Incomparable*. New York: Pageant Press, 1964.

Campbell, James T. *Songs of Zion: The African Methodist Episcopal Church in the United States and South Africa*. New York: Oxford University Press, 1995.

Campbell, Thomas D. *One Family under God: A Story of Cumberland Presbyterians in Black and White*. Memphis, TN: Board of Christian Education of the Cumberland Presbyterian Church, 1982.

Carwardine, Richard J. *Evangelicals and Politics in Antebellum America*. New Haven: Yale University Press, 1993.

Cashin, Edward J. *Old Springfield: Race and Religion in Augusta, Georgia*. Augusta, GA: Springfield Village Park Foundation, 1995.

Cason, Roberta F. "The Loyal League in Georgia," *Georgia Historical Quarterly* 20 (June 1936): 125–53.

Chaffin, Nora C. "A Southern Advocate of Methodist Unification in 1865." *North Carolina Historical Review* 18 (January 1941): 38–47.

Chesebrough, David B. *Clergy Dissent in the Old South, 1830–1865*. Carbondale: Southern Illinois University Press, 1996.

——. *God Ordained This War: Sermons on the Sectional Crisis, 1830–1865*. Columbia: University of South Carolina Press, 1991.

——. "A Holy War: The Defense and Support of the Confederacy by Southern Baptists." *American Baptist Quarterly* 6 (March 1987): 17–30.

——. "No Sorrow Like Our Sorrow": Northern Protestant Ministers and the Assassination of Lincoln*. Kent, OH: Kent State University Press, 1994.

A Chronicle of Christian Stewardship: St. James Methodist Church, 1856–1967. Augusta, GA: n.p., 1968.

Cimprich, John. *Slavery's End in Tennessee, 1861–1865*. University: University of Alabama Press, 1985.

Clark, Robert D. *The Life of Matthew Simpson*. New York: Macmillan, 1956.

Clarke, Erskine. *Wrestlin' Jacob: A Portrait of Religion in the Old South*. Atlanta, GA: John Knox Press, 1979.

Clary, George Esmond, Jr. "The Founding of Paine College—A Unique Venture in Inter-Racial Cooperation in the New South (1882–1903)." Ed.D. diss., University of Georgia, 1965.

Clebsch, William A. *Christian Interpretations of the Civil War*. Philadelphia: Fortress Press, 1969.

Clement, Sarah V. *A College Grows . . . MCFI-Lambuth*. Jackson, TN: Lambuth College Alumni Association, 1972.

Clinton, Catherine, and Nina Silber, eds. *Divided Houses: Gender and the Civil War*. New York: Oxford University Press, 1992.

Conkin, Paul K. *Gone with the Ivy: A Biography of Vanderbilt University*. Knoxville: University of Tennessee Press, 1985.

Connelly, Thomas L., and Barbara L. Bellows. *God and General Longstreet: The Lost Cause and the Southern Mind*. Baton Rouge: Louisiana State University Press, 1982.

Conway, Alan. *The Reconstruction of Georgia*. Minneapolis: University of Minnesota Press, 1966.

Cooke, Anna L. *Lane College: Its Heritage and Outreach, 1882–1982.* Jackson, TN: Lane College, 1987.

Cooper, David. *Catalyst for Christ, 150 Years: First Presbyterian Church, Chattanooga, Tennessee.* Chattanooga, TN: Chattanooga News-Free Press, 1990.

Cooper, Waller Raymond. *Southwestern at Memphis, 1848–1948.* Richmond, VA: John Knox Press, 1949.

Cornelius, Janet Duitsman. *"When I Can Read My Title Clear": Literacy, Slavery, and Religion in the Antebellum South.* Columbia: University of South Carolina Press, 1991.

Coulter, E. Merton. *The Civil War and Readjustment in Kentucky.* Chapel Hill: University of North Carolina Press, 1926.

———. *William G. Brownlow: Fighting Parson of the Southern Highlands.* Chapel Hill: University of North Carolina Press, 1937; reprint, Knoxville: University of Tennessee Press, 1971.

Crofts, Daniel W. *Reluctant Confederates: Upper South Unionists in the Secession Crisis.* Chapel Hill: University of North Carolina Press, 1989.

Crowther, Edward R. "Holy Honor: Sacred and Secular in the Old South." *Journal of Southern History* 58 (November 1992): 619–36.

Culver, Dwight W. *Negro Segregation in the Methodist Church.* New Haven: Yale University Press, 1953.

Current, Richard Nelson. *Lincoln's Loyalists: Union Soldiers from the Confederacy.* Boston: Northeastern University Press, 1992.

Currie-McDaniel, Ruth. *Carpetbagger of Conscience: A Biography of John Emory Bryant.* Athens: University of Georgia Press, 1987.

Curry, Daniel. *Life-Story of Rev. Davis Wasgatt Clark.* New York: Nelson and Phillips, 1874.

Daniel, W. Harrison. "A Brief Account of the Methodist Episcopal Church, South in the Confederacy." *Methodist History* 6 (January 1968): 27–41.

———. "The Effects of the Civil War on Southern Protestantism." *Maryland Historical Magazine* 69 (Spring 1974): 44–63.

———. "Protestant Clergy and Union Sentiment in the Confederacy." *Tennessee Historical Quarterly* 23 (September 1964): 284–90.

———. "Protestantism and Patriotism in the Confederacy." *Mississippi Quarterly* 24 (Spring 1971): 117–34.

———. "Southern Presbyterians in the Confederacy." *North Carolina Historical Review* 44 (Summer 1967): 231–55.

———. "Southern Protestantism—1861 and After." *Civil War History* 5 (September 1959): 276–82.

———. *Southern Protestantism in the Confederacy.* Bedford, VA: Print Shop, 1989.

Davis, J. Treadwell. *Relations between the Northern and Southern Presbyterian Churches, 1861–1888.* Nashville, TN: Joint University Libraries, 1951.

Deaton, Stanley Kenneth. "Violent Redemption: The Democratic Party and the Ku Klux Klan in Georgia, 1868–1871." M.A. thesis, University of Georgia, 1988.

Dowell, Spright. *A History of Mercer University, 1833–1953.* Macon, GA: Mercer University, 1958.

Drago, Edmund L. *Black Politicians and Reconstruction in Georgia: A Splendid Failure.* Baton Rouge: Louisiana State University Press, 1982.

DuBois, W. E. B. *Black Reconstruction: An Essay toward a History of the Part Which Black Folk Played in the Attempt to Reconstruct Democracy in America, 1860–1880.* New York: Russell and Russell, 1935.

———. *The Souls of Black Folk.* New York: Penguin Books, 1989.

Duncan, Russell. *Entrepreneur for Equality: Governor Rufus Bullock, Commerce, and Race in Post–Civil War Georgia*. Athens: University of Georgia Press, 1994.

——. *Freedom's Shore: Tunis Campbell and the Georgia Freedmen*. Athens: University of Georgia Press, 1986.

Dunham, Chester Forrestor. *The Attitude of the Northern Clergy toward the South, 1860–1865*. Toledo, OH: Gray, 1942.

Durham, Walter T. *Nashville: The Occupied City, The First Seventeen Months, February 16, 1862, to June 30, 1863*. Nashville: Tennessee Historical Society, 1985.

——. *Reluctant Partners: Nashville and the Union, July 1, 1863, to June 30, 1865*. Nashville: Tennessee Historical Society, 1987.

Dvorak, Katharine L. *An African-American Exodus: The Segregation of the Southern Churches*. Brooklyn, NY: Carlson Publishing, 1991.

Eaton, Grace M. *A Heroine of the Cross: Sketches of the Life and Work of Miss Joanna P. Moore*. N.p., n.d.

Eighmy, John Lee. *Churches in Cultural Captivity: A History of the Social Attitudes of Southern Baptists*. Rev. ed. Knoxville: University of Tennessee Press, 1987.

Engram, Irby D. "A History of Andrew College." M.A. thesis, Emory University, 1939.

Eskew, Glenn T. "Black Elitism and the Failure of Paternalism in Postbellum Georgia: The Case of Bishop Lucius Henry Holsey." *Journal of Southern History* 58 (November 1992): 637–66.

——. "Paternalism among Augusta's Methodists: Black, White, and Colored." Paper presented at "Race, Religion and Gender in Augusta" Conference, Augusta, GA, 29 February 1996.

Eubank, Wayne C. "Benjamin Morgan Palmer's Thanksgiving Sermon, 1860." In *Antislavery and Disunion, 1858–1861: Studies in the Rhetoric of Compromise and Conflict*, edited by J. Jeffery Auer, 291–309. New York: Harper and Row, 1963.

Farish, Hunter Dickinson. *The Circuit Rider Dismounts: A Social History of Southern Methodism, 1865–1900*. Richmond, VA: Dietz Press, 1938.

Farmer, James Oscar, Jr. *The Metaphysical Confederacy: James Henley Thornwell and the Synthesis of Southern Values*. Macon, GA: Mercer University Press, 1986.

Farwell, Byron. *Stonewall: A Biography of General Thomas J. Jackson*. New York: Norton, 1992.

Faust, Drew Gilpin. "Christian Soldiers: The Meaning of Revivalism in the Confederate Army." *Journal of Southern History* 53 (February 1987): 63–90.

——. *The Creation of Confederate Nationalism: Ideology and Identity in the Civil War South*. Baton Rouge: Louisiana State University Press, 1988.

——. *Mothers of Invention: Women of the Slaveholding South in the American Civil War*. Chapel Hill: University of North Carolina Press, 1996.

Fitzgerald, Michael W. *The Union League Movement in the Deep South: Politics and Agricultural Change during Reconstruction*. Baton Rouge: Louisiana State University Press, 1989.

Fitzgerald, O. P. *John B. McFerrin: A Biography*. Nashville, TN: Publishing House of the Methodist Episcopal Church, South, 1888.

Fletcher, Jesse C. "A History of the Foreign Mission Board of the Southern Baptist Convention during the Civil War." *Baptist History and Heritage* 10 (October 1975): 204–19, 232, 255.

Foner, Eric. *Reconstruction: America's Unfinished Revolution, 1863–1877*. New York: Harper and Row, 1988.

Ford, Paul M. "Calvin H. Wiley's View of the Negro." *North Carolina Historical Review* 41 (January 1964): 1–20.

Foster, Gaines M. *Ghosts of the Confederacy: Defeat, the Lost Cause, and the Emergence of the New South*. New York: Oxford University Press, 1987.

———. "Guilt over Slavery: A Historiographical Analysis." *Journal of Southern History* 56 (November 1990): 665–94.

Fox-Genovese, Elizabeth, and Eugene D. Genovese. "The Divine Sanction of the Social Order: Religious Foundations of the Southern Slaveholders' World View." *Journal of the American Academy of Religion* 55 (Summer 1987): 211–33.

Franklin, John Hope. *The Emancipation Proclamation.* Garden City, NY: Doubleday, 1963; reprint, Wheeling, IL: Harlan Davidson, 1995.

———. *From Slavery to Freedom: A History of American Negroes.* 2d ed. New York: Knopf, 1965.

———. *Reconstruction: After the Civil War.* Chicago: University of Chicago Press, 1961.

Frazier, E. Franklin. *The Negro Church in America.* New York: Schocken Books, 1964.

Fuller, Thomas O. *History of the Negro Baptists of Tennessee.* Memphis, TN: Haskins Printing, 1936.

Furgurson, Ernest B. *Chancellorsville, 1863: The Souls of the Brave.* New York: Knopf, 1992.

Gambrell, James B. *Parable and Precept: A Baptist Message.* New York: Fleming H. Revell, 1917.

Gardner, Robert G., et al., *A History of the Georgia Baptist Association, 1784–1984.* Atlanta: Georgia Baptist Historical Society, 1988.

Gaston, Paul M. *The New South Creed: A Study in Southern Mythmaking.* New York: Knopf, 1970.

Gaustad, Edwin S. *Historical Atlas of Religion in America.* New York: Harper and Row, 1962.

Genovese, Eugene D. *Roll, Jordan, Roll: The World the Slaves Made.* New York: Pantheon Books, 1974.

———. "Slavery Ordained of God": The Southern Slaveholders' View of Biblical History and Modern Politics. Gettysburg, PA: Gettysburg College, 1985.

———, and Elizabeth Fox-Genovese. "The Religious Ideals of Southern Slave Society." *Georgia Historical Quarterly* 70 (Spring 1986): 1–16.

Gillette, William. *Retreat from Reconstruction, 1869–1879.* Baton Rouge: Louisiana State University Press, 1979.

Goen, C. C. *Broken Churches, Broken Nation: Denominational Schisms and the Coming of the Civil War.* Macon, GA: Mercer University Press, 1985.

Gravely, William B. *Gilbert Haven, Methodist Abolitionist: A Study in Race, Religion, and Reform, 1850–1880.* Nashville, TN: Abingdon Press, 1973.

———. "The Social, Political and Religious Significance of the Formation of the Colored Methodist Episcopal Church (1870)." *Methodist History* 18 (October 1979): 3 –25.

Hammond, Edmund J. *The Methodist Episcopal Church in Georgia.* N.p., 1935.

Harvey, Paul. *Redeeming the South: Religious Cultures and Racial Identities among Southern Baptists, 1865–1925.* Chapel Hill: University of North Carolina Press, 1997.

Hastings, Comer. "The Methodist Episcopal Church, South during the Reconstruction Period." M.A. thesis, Duke University, 1932.

Heckman, Oliver Saxon. "Northern Church Penetration of the South, 1860 to 1880." Ph.D. diss., Duke University, 1939.

Herskovits, Melville J. *The Myth of the Negro Past.* Boston: Beacon Press, 1958.

Hesseltine, W. B. "Methodism and Reconstruction in East Tennessee." *East Tennessee Historical Society's Publications* 3 (1931): 42–61.

Higginbotham, Evelyn Brooks. *Righteous Discontent: The Women's Movement in the Black Baptist Church, 1880–1920.* Cambridge: Harvard University Press, 1993.

Hildebrand, Reginald F. *The Times Were Strange and Stirring: Methodist Preachers and the Crisis of Emancipation.* Durham, NC: Duke University Press, 1995.

Hill, Samuel S., Jr. *The South and the North in American Religion.* Athens: University of Georgia Press, 1980.

Historic Sketch and Directory of the Second Presbyterian Church, Jonesboro, Tenn. Jonesboro, TN: Herald and Tribune Print, 1895.

Hobson, Fred. *Tell about the South: The Southern Rage to Explain.* Baton Rouge: Louisiana State University Press, 1983.

Hood, James W. *One Hundred Years of the African Methodist Episcopal Zion Church: The Centennial of African Methodism.* New York: AME Zion Book Concern, 1895.

Howard, Victor B. *Religion and the Radical Republican Movement, 1860–1870.* Lexington: University Press of Kentucky, 1990.

Huddlestun, J. R., and Charles O. Walker. *From Heretics to Heroes: A Study of Religious Groups in Georgia with Primary Emphasis on the Baptists.* Jasper, GA: Pickens Tech Press, 1976.

Humphrey, Steve. *"That D——d Brownlow," Being a Saucy and Malicious Description of Fighting Parson William Gannaway Brownlow, Knoxville Editor and Stalwart Unionist.* Boone, NC: Appalachian Consortium Press, 1978.

Irons, George V. "Howard College as a Confederate Military Hospital." *Alabama Review* 9 (January 1956): 22–45.

Jeter, Edith M. "Under the Banner of King Jesus: Foreign Missions and the Civil War." *Baptist History and Heritage* 32 (July/October 1997): 89–99.

Jimerson, Randall C. *The Private Civil War: Popular Thought during the Sectional Conflict.* Baton Rouge: Louisiana State University Press, 1988.

Johnson, Michael P. *Toward a Patriarchal Republic: The Secession of Georgia.* Baton Rouge: Louisiana State University Press, 1977.

Johnson, Thomas C. *History of the Southern Presbyterian Church.* New York: Christian Literature, 1894.

Jones, Charles Edgeworth. *Education in Georgia, Contributions to American Educational History.* Edited by Herbert B. Adams. Washington, DC: Government Printing Office, 1889.

Jones, Donald G. *The Sectional Crisis and Northern Methodism: A Study in Piety, Political Ethics, and Civil Religion.* Metuchen, NJ: Scarecrow Press, 1979.

Jones, Jacqueline. *Soldiers of Light and Love: Northern Teachers and Georgia Blacks, 1865–1873.* Chapel Hill: University of North Carolina Press, 1980.

Jones, James Pickett. *Yankee Blitzkrieg: Wilson's Raid through Alabama and Georgia.* Athens: University of Georgia Press, 1976.

Kendall, W. Fred. *A History of the Tennessee Baptist Convention.* Brentwood, TN: Executive Board of the Tennessee Baptist Convention, 1974.

Kilpatrick, W. L. *The Hephzibah Baptist Association Centennial, 1794–1894.* Augusta, GA: Richards and Shaver, 1894.

Kirby, James E. "The McKendree Chapel Affair." *Tennessee Historical Quarterly* 25 (1966): 360–70.

Kirkland, Thomas J., and Robert M. Kennedy. *Historic Camden.* Columbia, SC: State, 1926.

Kolchin, Peter. *First Freedom: The Responses of Alabama's Blacks to Emancipation and Reconstruction.* Westport, CT: Greenwood Press, 1972.

Krick, Robert K. "The Smoothbore Valley That Doomed the Confederacy." In *Chancellorsville: The Battle and Its Aftermath,* edited by Gary W. Gallagher, 107–42. Chapel Hill: University of North Carolina Press, 1996.

Lakey, Othal Hawthorne. *The History of the CME Church.* Memphis, TN: CME Publishing, 1985.

Lee, Ronald Glenn. "Exploded Graces: Providence and the Confederate Israel in Evangelical Southern Sermons, 1861–1865." M.A. thesis, Rice University, 1990.

Leonard, Elizabeth D. *Yankee Women: Gender Battles in the Civil War.* New York: Norton, 1994.

Levine, Lawrence W. *Black Culture and Black Consciousness: Afro-American Folk Thought from Slavery to Freedom*. New York: Oxford University Press, 1977.

Ley, John C. *Fifty-Two Years in Florida*. Nashville, TN: Publishing House of the Methodist Episcopal Church, South, 1899.

Light, George T. *A Brief History of the Noonday Baptist Association (1858–1958)*. South Pittsburg, TN: Hustler Printing, 1958.

Lindsley, J. Barien. "Outline History of Cumberland University at Lebanon, Tennessee, 1842–1876." *Theological Medium* 12 (October 1876): 437–38.

Litwack, Leon F. *Been in the Storm So Long: The Aftermath of Slavery*. New York: Random House, 1980.

——, and August Meier, eds. *Black Leaders of the Nineteenth Century*. Urbana: University of Illinois Press, 1988.

Lloyd, Ralph Waldo. *Maryville College: A History of 150 Years, 1819–1969*. Maryville, TN: Maryville College Press, 1969.

McCardell, John. *The Idea of a Southern Nation: Southern Nationalists and Southern Nationalism, 1830–1860*. New York: Norton, 1979.

McDonnold, B. W. *History of the Cumberland Presbyterian Church*. 4th ed. Nashville, TN: Board of Publication of Cumberland Presbyterian Church, 1899.

McDowell, John Patrick. *The Social Gospel in the South: The Woman's Home Mission Movement in the Methodist Episcopal Church, South, 1886–1939*. Baton Rouge: Louisiana State University Press, 1982.

McFeely, William S. *Yankee Stepfather: General O. O. Howard and the Freedmen*. New Haven: Yale University Press, 1968.

McKivigan, John R. *The War against Proslavery Religion: Abolitionism and the Northern Churches, 1830–1865*. Ithaca, NY: Cornell University Press, 1984.

McManus, Harold Lynn. "The American Baptist Home Mission Society and Freedmen Education in the South, With Special Reference to Georgia: 1862–1897." Ph.D. diss., Yale University, 1953.

McPherson, James M. *Battle Cry of Freedom: The Civil War Era*. New York: Oxford University Press, 1988.

McTyeire, Holland N. *History of Methodism*. Nashville, TN: Southern Methodist Publishing House, 1884.

Maddex, Jack P. "From Theocracy to Spirituality: The Southern Presbyterian Reversal on Church and State." *Journal of Presbyterian History* 54 (Winter 1976): 438–57.

——. "Proslavery Millenialism: Social Eschatology in Antebellum Southern Calvinism." *American Quarterly* 31 (Spring 1979): 46–62.

Mann, Harold W. *Atticus Greene Haygood: Methodist Bishop, Editor, and Educator*. Athens: University of Georgia Press, 1965.

Martin, Isaac Patton. *Methodism in Holston*. Knoxville, TN: Methodist Historical Society, 1945.

Masters, Victor I. *Baptist Missions in the South*. 3rd ed. Atlanta, GA: Home Mission Board of the Southern Baptist Convention, 1915.

Mathews, Donald G. *Religion in the Old South*. Chicago: University of Chicago Press, 1977.

Mims, Edwin. *History of Vanderbilt University*. Nashville, TN: Vanderbilt University Press, 1946.

Mitchell, Joseph. "Southern Methodist Newspapers during the Civil War." *Methodist History* 11 (January 1973): 20–39.

Mitchell, Reid. *Civil War Soldiers: Their Expectations and Their Experiences*. New York: Viking Penguin, 1988.

—— *The Vacant Chair: The Northern Soldier Leaves Home*. New York: Oxford University Press, 1993.

Monroe, Haskell. "Bishop Palmer's Thanksgiving Day Address." *Louisiana History* 4 (Spring 1963): 105–18.

——. "The Presbyterian Church in the Confederate States of America." Ph.D. diss., Rice University, 1961.

Montgomery, William E. *Under Their Own Vine and Fig Tree: The African-American Church in the South, 1865–1900.* Baton Rouge: Louisiana State University Press, 1993.

Moore, John Jamison. *History of the A. M. E. Zion Church, in America.* York, PA: Teachers' Journal Office, 1884.

Moorhead, James H. *American Apocalypse: Yankee Protestants and the Civil War, 1860–1869.* New Haven: Yale University Press, 1978.

Morris, Robert C. *Reading, 'Riting, and Reconstruction: The Education of Freedmen in the South, 1861–1870.* Chicago: University of Chicago Press, 1981.

Morrow, Ralph E. *Northern Methodism and Reconstruction.* East Lansing: Michigan State University Press, 1956.

Munroe, John A. *The University of Delaware: A History.* Newark, DE: University of Delaware, 1986.

Murray, Andrew E. *Presbyterians and the Negro—A History.* Philadelphia: Presbyterian Historical Society, 1966.

Nall, T. Otto. "Methodist Publishing in Historical Perspective, 1865–1939." In *The History of American Methodism,* edited by Emory Stevens Bucke, 3:129–69. Nashville, TN: Abingdon Press, 1964.

Nathans, Elizabeth Studley. *Losing the Peace: Georgia Republicans and Reconstruction, 1865–1871.* Baton Rouge: Louisiana State University Press, 1968.

Nelson, William H. *A Burning Torch and a Flaming Fire: The Story of Centenary College of Louisiana.* Nashville, TN: Methodist Publishing House, 1931.

Noll, Mark A., ed. *Religion and American Politics: From the Colonial Period to the 1980s.* New York: Oxford University Press, 1990.

Norton, Wesley. "The Role of a Religious Newspaper in Georgia during the Civil War." *Georgia Historical Quarterly* 48 (June 1964): 125–46.

Ogilvie, Charles Finney. "Alabama Baptists during the Civil War and Reconstruction." Th.M. thesis, Southwestern Baptist Theological Seminary, 1956.

Overy, David Henry. "Robert Lewis Dabney: Apostle of the Old South." Ph.D. diss., University of Wisconsin, 1967.

Owen, Christopher Hendrick. "Sanctity, Slavery, and Segregation: Methodists and Society in Nineteenth-Century Georgia." Ph.D. diss., Emory University, 1991.

Ownby, Ted. *Subduing Satan: Religion, Recreation, and Manhood in the Rural South, 1865–1920.* Chapel Hill: University of North Carolina Press, 1990.

Paludan, Phillip Shaw. *"A People's Contest": The Union and Civil War, 1861–1865.* New York: Harper and Row, 1988.

Parish, Peter J. "The Instruments of Providence: Slavery, Civil War and the American Churches." In *The Church and War,* edited by W. J. Sheils, 291–320. Oxford: Basil Blackwell, 1983.

Parker, Harold M., Jr. *The United Synod of the South: The Southern New School Presbyterian Church.* Westport, CT: Greenwood Press, 1988.

Parker, J. E. *A Brief History of the Churches in the New Sunbury Baptist Association.* N.p.: Wayne County Press, 1966.

Partin, Robert. "The Sustaining Faith of an Alabama Soldier." *Civil War History* 6 (December 1960): 425–38.

Patton, James Welch. *Unionism and Reconstruction in Tennessee, 1860–1869.* Chapel Hill: University of North Carolina Press, 1934.

Payne, Daniel A. *A History of the African Methodist Episcopal Church.* Edited by C. S. Smith. Nashville, TN: Publishing House of the AME Sunday School Union, 1891.

———. *Recollections of Seventy Years.* Nashville, TN: Publishing House of the AME Sunday School Union, 1888.

Perdue, Robert E. *The Negro in Savannah, 1865–1900.* New York: Exposition Press, 1973.

Perman, Michael. *Reunion without Compromise: The South and Reconstruction, 1865–1868.* Cambridge: Cambridge University Press, 1973.

———. *The Road to Redemption: Southern Politics, 1869–1879.* Chapel Hill: University of North Carolina Press, 1984.

Phelan, Macum. *A History of Early Methodism in Texas, 1817–1866.* Nashville, TN: Cokesbury Press, 1924.

Pickens, Donald K. "The Republican Synthesis and Thaddeus Stevens." *Civil War History* 31 (March 1985): 57–73.

Pierce, Alfred Mann. *Lest Faith Forget: The Story of Methodism in Georgia.* Atlanta: Georgia Methodist Information, 1951.

Pilkington, James Penn. *The Methodist Publishing House, A History, Volume I: Beginnings to 1870.* Nashville, TN: Abingdon Press, 1968.

Pitts, Charles F. *Chaplains in Gray: The Confederate Chaplains' Story.* Nashville, TN: Broadman Press, 1957.

Pool, Frank K. "The Southern Negro in the Methodist Episcopal Church." Ph.D. diss., Duke University, 1939.

Price, R. N. *Holston Methodism: From Its Origin to the Present Time.* 5 vols. Nashville, TN: Publishing House of the Methodist Episcopal Church, South, 1913.

Rable, George C. *But There Was No Peace: The Role of Violence in the Politics of Reconstruction.* Athens: University of Georgia Press, 1984.

———. *Civil Wars: Women and the Crisis of Southern Nationalism.* Urbana: University of Illinois Press, 1989.

Raboteau, Albert J. *A Fire in the Bones: Reflections on African American Religious History.* Boston: Beacon Press, 1995.

———. *Slave Religion: The "Invisible Institution" in the Antebellum South.* New York: Oxford University Press, 1978.

Ragsdale, B. D. *Story of Georgia Baptists.* 3 vols. Macon, GA: Mercer University Press, 1935–38.

Range, Willard. *The Rise and Progress of Negro Colleges in Georgia, 1865–1949.* Athens: University of Georgia Press, 1951.

Rankin, Charles Hays. "The Rise of Negro Baptist Churches in the South through the Reconstruction Period." Th.M. thesis, New Orleans Baptist Theological Seminary, 1955.

Ransom, Roger L., and Richard Sutch. *One Kind of Freedom: The Economic Consequences of Emancipation.* New York: Cambridge University Press, 1977.

Rawick, George P., ed. *The American Slave: A Composite Autobiography.* 39 vols. Westport, CT: Greenwood Press, 1972–79.

Reed, Ralph Eugene, Jr. "Fortresses of Faith: Design and Experience at Southern Evangelical Colleges, 1830–1900." Ph.D. diss., Emory University, 1991.

Richardson, Harry V. *Dark Salvation: The Story of Methodism as It Developed among Blacks in America.* Garden City, NJ: Anchor Press, 1976.

Richardson, Joe M. *Christian Reconstruction: The American Missionary Association and Southern Blacks, 1861–1890.* Athens: University of Georgia Press, 1986.

———. "The Failure of the American Missionary Association to Expand Congregationalism among Southern Blacks." *Southern Studies* 18 (Spring 1979): 51–73.

Riley, Benjamin F. *History of the Baptists of Alabama.* Birmingham, AL: Roberts and Son, 1895.

Robinson, Armistead L. "Plans Dat Comed from God: Institution Building and the Emergence of Black Leadership in Reconstruction Memphis." In *Toward a New South? Studies in Post–Civil War Southern Communities*, edited by Orville Vernon Burton and Robert C. McMath Jr. Westport, CT: Greenwood Press, 1982.

Romero, Sidney J. "Louisiana Clergy and the Confederate Army." *Louisiana History* 2 (Summer 1961): 277–300.

——. *Religion in the Rebel Ranks*. Lanham, MD: University Press of America, 1983.

Royster, Charles. *The Destructive War: William Tecumseh Sherman, Stonewall Jackson, and the Americans*. New York: Knopf, 1991.

Russ, William A., Jr. "The Failure to Reunite Methodism after the Civil War." *Susquehanna University Studies* 1 (1936): 8–16.

Ryland, Garnett. *The Baptists of Virginia, 1699–1926*. Richmond, VA: Baptist Board of Missions and Education, 1955.

Saum, Lewis O. *The Popular Mood of Pre–Civil War America*. Westport, CT: Greenwood Press, 1980.

Service in Fruition: The Story of the Work for the Betterment of the Colored People of James City and Newbern, North Carolina. Chicago: Woman's American Baptist Home Mission Society, 1916.

Shackleford, Josephus. *History of the Muscle Shoals Baptist Association*. Trinity, AL: published by the author, 1891.

Shankman, Arnold. "Converse, *The Christian Observer*, and Civil War Censorship." *Journal of Presbyterian History* 52 (1974): 227–44.

Shattuck, Gardiner H., Jr. "'Appomattox as a Day of Blessing': Religious Interpretations of Confederate Defeat in the New South Era." *Journal of Confederate History* 7 (1991): 1–18.

——. *A Shield and Hiding Place: The Religious Life of the Civil War Armies*. Macon, GA: Mercer University Press, 1987.

Silber, Nina. *The Romance of Reunion: Northerners and the South, 1865–1900*. Chapel Hill: University of North Carolina Press, 1993.

Silver, James W. *Confederate Morale and Church Propaganda*. Tuscaloosa, AL: Confederate Publishing, 1957.

——. "The Confederate Preacher Goes to War." *North Carolina Historical Review* 33 (October 1956): 499–509.

Singleton, George A. *The Romance of African Methodism: A Study of the African Methodist Episcopal Church*. New York: Exposition Press, 1952.

Smith, George Gilman. *The Life and Times of George Foster Pierce*. Sparta, GA: Hancock Publishing, 1888.

Smith, Gerald J. *Smite Them Hip and Thigh! Georgia Methodist Ministers in the Confederate Military*. Augusta, GA: published by the author, 1993.

Smith, H. Shelton. *In His Image, But . . . : Racism in Southern Religion, 1780–1910*. Durham, NC: Duke University Press, 1972.

Smith, J. W. "A History of the Seventh Street Presbyterian Church of Charlotte, North Carolina." B.D. thesis, Theological Seminary, J. C. Smith University, 1948.

Smith, John Abernathy. *Cross and Flame: Two Centuries of United Methodism in Middle Tennessee*. Nashville, TN: Commission on Archives and History of the Tennessee Conference, 1984.

Smith, T. E. *History of the Washington Baptist Association of Georgia*. Milledgeville, GA: Doyle Middlebrooks, 1979.

Snay, Mitchell. "American Thought and Southern Distinctiveness: The Southern Clergy and the Sanctification of Slavery." *Civil War History* 35 (December 1989): 311–28.

————. *Gospel of Disunion: Religion and Separatism in the Antebellum South*. New York: Cambridge University Press, 1993.

Sobel, Mechal. "'They Can Never Both Prosper Together': Black and White Baptists in Antebellum Nashville, Tennessee." *Tennessee Historical Quarterly* 38 (Fall 1979): 296–307.

————. *The World They Made Together: Black and White Values in Eighteenth-Century Virginia*. Princeton: Princeton University Press, 1987.

————. *Trabelin' On: The Slave Journey to an Afro-Baptist Faith*. Westport, CT: Greenwood Press, 1979.

Spain, Rufus B. *At Ease in Zion: A Social History of Southern Baptists, 1865–1900*. Nashville, TN: Vanderbilt University Press, 1967.

Stacy, James. *A History of the Presbyterian Church in Georgia*. Elberton, GA: Press of the Star, 1912.

Stampp, Kenneth M. *The Era of Reconstruction, 1865–1877*. New York: Knopf, 1965.

Stevenson, George J. *Increase in Excellence: A History of Emory and Henry College*. New York: Appleton-Century-Crofts, 1963.

Stowell, Daniel W. "The Failure of Religious Reconstruction: The Methodist Episcopal Church in Georgia, 1865–1871." M.A. thesis, University of Georgia, 1988.

————. "'The Negroes Cannot Navigate Alone': Religious Scalawags and the Biracial Methodist Episcopal Church in Georgia, 1866–1876." In *Georgia in Black and White: Explorations in the Race Relations of a Southern State, 1865–1950*, edited by John C. Inscoe, 65–90. Athens: University of Georgia Press, 1994.

————. "Stonewall Jackson and the Providence of God." In *Religion and the American Civil War*, edited by Randall Miller, Harry S. Stout, and Charles Reagan Wilson. New York: Oxford University Press, forthcoming.

————. "'We Have Sinned, and God Has Smitten Us!' John H. Caldwell and the Religious Meaning of Confederate Defeat." *Georgia Historical Quarterly* 78 (Spring 1994): 1–38.

Stroupe, Henry Smith. *The Religious Press in the South Atlantic States, 1802–1865*. Durham, NC: Duke University Press, 1956; reprint, New York: AMS Press, 1970.

Stuckey, Sterling. *Slave Culture: Nationalist Theory and the Foundations of Black America*. New York: Oxford University Press, 1987.

Sullins, David. *Recollections of an Old Man: Seventy Years in Dixie, 1827–1897*. Bristol, TN: King Printing, 1910.

Sulzby, James F., Jr. *Toward a History of Samford University*. 2 vols. Birmingham, AL: Samford University Press, 1986.

Summerville, James. *Educating Black Doctors: A History of Meharry Medical College*. University: University of Alabama Press, 1983.

Sweet, William Warren. *The Methodist Episcopal Church and the Civil War*. Cincinnati, OH: Methodist Book Concern Press, 1912.

Swint, Henry Lee. *The Northern Teacher in the South, 1862–1870*. Nashville, TN: Vanderbilt University Press, 1941; reprint, New York: Octagon Books, 1967.

Talmage, Franklin C. *The Story of the Synod of Georgia*. N.p., 1961.

Tankersley, Allen. *College Life at Old Oglethorpe*. Athens: University of Georgia Press, 1951.

Taylor, Alrutheus Ambush. *The Negro in Tennessee, 1865–1880*. Washington, DC: Associated Publishers, 1941.

————. *The Negro in the Reconstruction of Virginia*. Washington, DC: Association for the Study of Negro Life and History, 1926.

Taylor, Charles E. *The Story of Yates the Missionary, As Told in His Letters and Reminiscences*. Nashville, TN: Sunday School Board, 1898.

TeSelle, Eugene. "The Nashville Institute and Roger Williams University: Benevolence, Paternalism, and Black Consciousness, 1867–1910." *Tennessee Historical Quarterly* 41 (Winter 1982): 360–79.

Thomas, Emory M. *The Confederate Nation, 1861–1865*. New York: Harper and Row, 1979.

Thompson, C. Mildred. *Reconstruction in Georgia: Economic, Social, Political, 1865–1872*. New York: Columbia University Press, 1915.

Thompson, Ernest Trice. *Presbyterians in the South*. 3 vols. Richmond, VA: John Knox Press, 1963–73.

———. "Presbyterians North and South —Efforts toward Reunion." *Journal of Presbyterian History* 43 (March 1965): 1–15.

Thrift, Charles T., Jr. "Rebuilding the Southern Church." In *The History of American Methodism*, edited by Emory Stevens Bucke, 2:257–314. Nashville, TN: Abingdon Press, 1964.

Tigert, J. J., IV. *Bishop Holland Nimmons McTyeire: Ecclesiastical and Educational Architect*. Nashville, TN: Vanderbilt University Press, 1955.

Tindall, George B. *South Carolina Negroes, 1870–1900*. Baton Rouge: Louisiana State University Press, 1966.

Toomey, Glenn A. *Jubilee Three: History of the Sweetwater Baptist Association and its Affiliated Churches, 1830–1980*. Madisonville, TN: n.p., 1980.

Trefousse, Hans L. *Andrew Johnson: A Biography*. New York: Norton, 1989.

Trelease, Allen W. *White Terror: The Ku Klux Klan Conspiracy and Southern Reconstruction*. New York: Harper and Row, 1971.

Turner, Thomas Reed. *Beware the People Weeping: Public Opinion and the Assassination of Abraham Lincoln*. Baton Rouge: Louisiana State University Press, 1982.

Tuveson, Ernest Lee. *Redeemer Nation: The Idea of America's Millenial Role*. Chicago: University of Chicago Press, 1968.

Urwin, Gregory J. W. "'The Lord Has Not Forsaken Me and I Won't Forsake Him': Religion in Frederick Steele's Union Army, 1863–1864." *Arkansas Historical Quarterly* 52 (Autumn 1993), 318–40.

U. S. Department of the Interior. Bureau of Education. *Negro Education: A Study of the Private and Higher Schools for Colored People in the United States*. 2 vols. Washington, DC: Government Printing Office, 1917; reprint, New York: Negro Universities Press, 1969.

Vander Velde, Lewis G. *The Presbyterian Churches and the Federal Union, 1861–1869*. Cambridge: Harvard University Press, 1932.

Vernon, Walter Newton, Jr. *The United Methodist Publishing House, A History, Volume II: 1870 to 1988*. Nashville, TN: Abingdon Press, 1989.

Waddel, John N. *Memorials of Academic Life*. Richmond, VA: Presbyterian Committee of Publication, 1891.

Wade, John D. *Augustus Baldwin Longstreet: A Study of the Development of Culture in the South*. New York: Macmillan, 1924; reprint, Athens: University of Georgia Press, 1969.

Wagner, Clarence M. *Profiles of Black Georgia Baptists*. Gainesville, GA: privately published, 1980.

Walker, Clarence E. *A Rock in a Weary Land: The African Methodist Episcopal Church during the Civil War and Reconstruction*. Baton Rouge: Louisiana State University Press, 1982.

Wallenstein, Peter. *From Slave South to New South: Public Policy in Nineteenth-Century Georgia*. Chapel Hill: University of North Carolina Press, 1987.

Ward, Richard Hiram. *A History of Union University*. Jackson, TN: Union University Press, 1975.

Washington, James Melvin. *Frustrated Fellowship: The Black Baptist Quest for Social Power*. Macon, GA: Mercer University Press, 1986.

Weaver, Richard M. *The Southern Tradition at Bay: A History of Postbellum Thought*. Edited by George Core and M. E. Bradford. New Rochelle, NY: Arlington House, 1968.

Wheeler, Edward L. *Uplifting the Race: The Black Minister in the New South, 1865–1902.* Lanham, MD: University Press of America, 1986.

Whites, LeeAnn. *The Civil War as a Crisis in Gender: Augusta, Georgia, 1860–1890.* Athens: University of Georgia Press, 1995.

Wight, Willard E. "The Churches and the Confederate Cause." *Civil War History* 6 (December 1960): 361–73.

———. "Churches in the Confederacy." Ph.D. diss., Emory University, 1957.

———, ed. "Pay the Preacher! Two Letters from Louisiana, 1864." *Louisiana History* 1 (Summer 1960): 251–59.

Wiley, Bell Irvin. "The Movement to Humanize the Institution of Slavery during the Confederacy." *Emory University Quarterly* 5 (December 1949): 207–20.

———. *Southern Negroes, 1861–1865.* New Haven: Yale University Press, 1938.

Williams, Lou Falkner. *The Great South Carolina Ku Klux Klan Trials, 1871–1872.* Athens: University of Georgia Press, 1996.

Williamson, Joel. *After Slavery: The Negro in South Carolina during Reconstruction, 1861–1877.* Chapel Hill: University of North Carolina Press, 1965.

Wilson, Charles Reagan. *Baptized in Blood: The Religion of the Lost Cause, 1865–1920.* Athens: University of Georgia Press, 1980.

———. "Robert Lewis Dabney: Religion and the Southern Holocaust." *Virginia Magazine of History and Biography* 89 (January 1981). 79–89.

Wilson, Harold. "Basil Manly, Apologist for Slavocracy." *Alabama Review* 15 (January 1962): 38–53.

Wood, Forrest G. *The Arrogance of Faith: Christianity and Race in America from the Colonial Era to the Twentieth Century.* New York: Knopf, 1990.

Woodson, Carter G. *The History of the Negro Church.* 2d ed. Washington, DC: Associated Publishers, 1945.

Woodward, C. Vann. *Reunion and Reaction: The Compromise of 1877 and the End of Reconstruction.* Boston: Little, Brown, 1951.

Wooley, Edwin C. *The Reconstruction of Georgia.* New York: Columbia University Press, 1901; reprint, New York: AMS Press, 1970.

Wooster, Ralph A. "An Analysis of the Membership of Secession Conventions in the Lower South." *Journal of Southern History* 24 (August 1958): 360–68.

Wooten, Fred T., Jr. "Religious Activities in Civil War Memphis." *Tennessee Historical Quarterly* 3 (June 1944): 131–49; (September 1944): 248–72.

Yetman, Norman R., ed. *Life under the "Peculiar Institution": Selections from the Slave Narrative Collection.* New York: Holt, Rinehart and Winston, 1970.

Index

Abbey, Richard, 110, 151
Addison, O. M., 31
African Americans. *See* freedpeople
African Methodist Episcopal (AME) Church, 91,
    138, 174, 185–86
  alliance with MECS of, 95–96, 221 n. 53
  appeal to freedpeople of, 94–95, 182, 209 n. 1
  establishing and receiving churches in the
    South by, 71, 74–75, 77–78, 84, 95–97
  membership statistics of, 29, 94, 96
  missionaries in the South of, 29, 69, 71, 77–78,
    90, 95–98, 150, 179, 209 n. 1, 221 n. 57
  opposition to, 89
  organizing of, 94
  and politics, 95, 150, 153–54, 160
African Methodist Episcopal Zion (AMEZ)
    Church, 91, 138, 221 n. 55
  appeal to freedpeople of, 94–95, 182, 209 n. 1
  establishing and receiving churches in the
    South by, 71–72, 78, 84, 95, 97, 221 n. 57
  membership statistics of, 94, 96
  missionaries in the South of, 29, 71–72, 78, 95,
    97, 150, 179, 209 n. 1, 221 n. 57
  organizing of, 94, 220 n. 47
  and politics, 153–54
Afro-American Presbyterian Synod, 89
Alabama Baptist Convention, 34, 46
Albany Baptist Church (Albany, GA), 75
Alexander, Samuel C., 74
Allen, Young J., 20
Alvord, John W., 98, 221 n. 55
American Baptist Free Mission Society, 197 n. 41
American Baptist Home Mission Society
    (ABHMS), 182, 209 n. 3

attitude toward the Confederacy of, 50, 57,
    209 n. 1
attitude toward the SBC of, 57, 132, 139, 166,
    175–77, 243 n. 50
and church property in the South, 30, 132,
    197 n. 41, 230 n. 6, 234 n. 43
and freedpeople's education, 58, 78, 139, 141,
    175, 177
missionaries in the South of, 27–29, 52, 56, 58,
    94, 131–32, 137–42, 176–77
American Baptist Publication Society, 119–20, 131,
    209 n. 3
American Bible Society, 225 n. 11
American Missionary Association, 76, 220 n. 51
American Presbyterian, 109
American Sunday School Union, 115
Americus Baptist Institute (Americus, GA), 83
Ames, Edward R., 30, 163–64
Anderson, Isaac H., 151
Andrew, James O., 24, 44, 110, 163, 165
Andrew Chapel (Nashville, TN), 137
Andrew Chapel (Savannah, GA), 71, 84
Andrew Female College (Cuthbert, GA), 9, 21,
    22
Antioch Baptist Church (Savannah, GA), 73, 85
Arkansas Annual Conference (MECS), 17
Ashby, Nathan, 76
Associate Reformed Presbyterian Church, 30
Athens Female College (Athens, TN), 136
Atlanta Baptist Seminary (Atlanta, GA), 93,
    141–42, 219 n. 43, 233 n. 35
Atlantic Presbytery, 85, 137
Augusta Institute (Augusta, GA), 93, 140–41
Austin Presbytery, 62